Communications
in Computer and Information Science 1621

More information about this series at https://link.springer.com/bookseries/7899

Antonio Vallecillo · Joost Visser ·
Ricardo Pérez-Castillo (Eds.)

Quality of Information and Communications Technology

15th International Conference, QUATIC 2022
Talavera de la Reina, Spain, September 12–14, 2022
Proceedings

 Springer

Editors
Antonio Vallecillo ⓘ
University of Malaga
Málaga, Spain

Joost Visser ⓘ
Leiden University
Leiden, The Netherlands

Ricardo Pérez-Castillo ⓘ
University of Castila-La Mancha
Ciudad Real, Spain

ISSN 1865-0929 ISSN 1865-0937 (electronic)
Communications in Computer and Information Science
ISBN 978-3-031-14178-2 ISBN 978-3-031-14179-9 (eBook)
https://doi.org/10.1007/978-3-031-14179-9

This Springer imprint is published by the registered company Springer Nature Switzerland AG
The registered company address is: Gewerbestrasse 11, 6330 Cham, Switzerland

Preface

The International Conference on the Quality of Information and Communications Technology (QUATIC) serves as a forum for disseminating advanced methods, techniques, and tools for supporting quality approaches to ICT engineering and management. Practitioners and researchers meet at the conference to exchange ideas and approaches on how to adopt a quality culture in ICT process and product improvement and to provide practical studies in varying contexts.

QUATIC 2022 was held during September 12–14, 2022, in Talavera de la Reina, Spain, with Antonio Vallecillo (University of Málaga) and Joost Visser (University of Leiden) as Program Chairs. The Organizing Chair of this 15th edition of QUATIC was Ricardo Pérez-Castillo (University of Castilla-La Mancha) and it was locally organized by the University of Castilla-La Mancha. Fortunately, it was the first edition conducted in a face-to-face manner after the effects of the COVID-19 pandemic.

This volume collates the papers selected by the members of the Program Committee to be presented at the conference and published in the conference proceedings. QUATIC 2022 attracted a good number of submissions from different areas spanning several thematic tracks, proposed in the call for papers, in various cutting-edge technologies of specialized focus. The following ten thematic tracks (together with their track chairs) were considered in QUATIC 2022:

- ICT Verification and Validation (Domenico Amalfitano, University of Naples, Italy)
- Safety, Security, and Privacy (Valentina Casola, University of Naples Federico II, Italy)
- ICT Process Improvement, Organisation, and Governance (Karol Frühauf, INFOGEM AG, Switzerland)
- Quality Aspects in Modeling and Low Code Environments (Alfonso Pierantonio, Università degli Studi dell'Aquila, Italy)
- Quality Aspects in Software Product Management and Requirements Engineering (Emilio Insfran, Valencia Polytechnic University, Spain)
- Quality Aspects in Machine Learning, AI and Data Analytics (Michael Felderer, University of Innsbruck, Austria)
- Quality Aspects in Digital Twins and Cyber-physical Systems (Aitor Arrieta, Mondragon University, Spain)
- Quality Aspects in Quantum Computing (Rui Abreu, University of Porto and INESC-ID, Portugal)
- Software Quality Education and Training in Academia and Industry (Kathia Oliveira, Université Polytechnique Hauts-de-France, France)
- Quality Aspects in Software Evolution (Péter Hegedűs, University of Szeged, Hungary)

Due to the exigent review process, some of the tracks had no papers accepted, while others with few accepted papers were merged into another related session. As a result, the following five sessions were finally organized within the scientific program of QUATIC 2022, which correspond with the proceedings' sections:

- Smart and Advanced Systems
- Verification and Validation
- Skills and Education
- Industrial Experiences and Applications
- Safety, Security and Privacy

The Program Committee of QUATIC 2022 was formed by 164 international academic and industrial domain experts, from organizations in 31 different countries on five continents. Based on a rigorous peer-review process by the Program Committee members along with external experts as reviewers, the best quality papers were identified for presentation and publication.

The review was carried out using a double-blind process, with a minimum of three reviews per submission. Submitted papers came from more than 32 countries and accepted papers originated from 14 countries. Out of the submission pool of 54 papers, 18 (33.3%) were accepted as full papers for inclusion in the proceedings, and three (5.5%) as short papers. Thus, the total acceptance ratio was 38.9%.

Apart from these papers, three 'Journal-first' papers were included in the QUATIC 2022 program. These papers correspond to articles published in 2021 or 2022 in top-notch journals that did not have any prior publication as workshop or conference papers. These three papers were the following:

- Amna, A. R., & Poels, G. (2022). Ambiguity in user stories: A systematic literature review. Information and Software Technology, 145, 106824. https://doi.org/10.1016/j.infsof.2022.106824
- Garcia-Alonso, J., Rojo, J., Valencia, D., Moguel, E., Berrocal, J., & Murillo, J. M. (2022). Quantum Software as a Service Through a Quantum API Gateway. IEEE Internet Computing, 26(1), 34–41. https://doi.org/10.1109/MIC.2021.3132688
- Gualo, F., Rodriguez, M., Verdugo, J., Caballero, I., & Piattini, M. (2021). Data quality certification using ISO/IEC 25012: Industrial experiences. Journal of Systems and Software, 176, 110938. https://doi.org/10.1016/j.jss.2021.110938

QUATIC 2022 featured three invited talks presented by outstanding keynote speakers.

The first keynote speaker was Mauricio Aniche. Mauricio leads the Tech Academy of Adyen, a Dutch payment company that allows businesses to accept e-commerce, mobile, and point-of-sale payments. Mauricio is also an assistant professor of software engineering at Delft University of Technology in the Netherlands, where he conducts research on improving developers' productivity in testing and maintenance. His talk in QUATIC 2022 was entitled "Software Engineering Theory in Practice: The Good, The Bad, and The Ugly". In the talk, he described many examples from industry and academia where both worlds are perfectly aligned, and where they are not.

The second keynote speaker was Sergio Segura, who is an associate professor at the University of Seville, Spain, and a senior member of the Applied Software Engineering

(ISA) research group. He is also a co-founder and a member of the direction board of the Unit of Excellence Smart Computer Systems Research and Engineering (SCORE), where he leads the university's research line on software and services engineering. His talk entitled "Quality assessment of untestable programs: the metamorphic way" aimed to guide researchers and practitioners through the area of metamorphic testing, including an introduction to the technique, its evolution, successful applications, and open problems.

Last but not least, Nicole Novielli, who is an assistant professor at the University of Bari, Italy, delivered the third keynote speech. Her research interests lie at the intersection of software engineering and affective computing, with a specific focus on emotion mining from software repositories, natural language processing of developers' communication traces, and biometric recognition of developers' emotions. Her talk was entitled "Recognizing Developers' Emotions: Advances and Open Challenges", which provided an overview of recent research findings of sentiment analysis in software engineering (SE), addressed the open challenges, and provided empirically-based guidelines for safe (re)use of SE-specific tools in order to obtain meaningful results.

As proceedings editors, we wish to thank all the people and organizations that directly or indirectly supported this event. Thanks to the thematic track chairs and all other members of the Program Committee for their many contributions and reviews that guarantee the overall quality of the QUATIC 2022 conference.

Thanks to our colleagues from the University of Castilla-La Mancha for all the organizational details required for hosting the conference. Thanks to our colleagues that participate at different levels in the organization of the conference. Thanks to the Steering Committee members for trusting us to organize the conference, and for their guidance and support throughout this process.

Also, a special thanks to all the organizations involved in this conference, including supporters at the University of Castilla-La Mancha (Facultad de Ciencias Sociales de Talavera de la Reina, Instituto de Tecnologías y Sistemas de Información, Departamento de Tecnologías y Sistemas de Información, and Alarcos Research Group), as well as our sponsors (AQC Lab, aQuantum, DQTeam, Cátedras Telefónica, and Aula SMACT by avanttic) and promoters (IPQ and CS03).

Finally, special thanks to all the authors and participants at the conference. Without their efforts, there would be no conference or proceedings. Thank you for contributing to the critical mass of researchers that keep this conference alive for what we expect to be many years to come.

September 2022   Antonio Vallecillo
                                                                    Joost Visser
                                                          Ricardo Pérez-Castillo

Organization

Program Committee Chairs

Antonio Vallecillo	University of Málaga, Spain
Joost Visser	Leiden University, The Netherlands

Thematic Track Chairs

ICT Verification and Validation

Domenico Amalfitano	University of Naples, Italy

Safety, Security, and Privacy

Valentina Casola	University of Naples Federico II, Italy

ICT Process Improvement, Organisation, and Governance

Karol Frühauf	INFOGEM AG, Switzerland

Modeling and Low Code Environments

Alfonso Pierantonio	Università degli Studi dell'Aquila, Italy

Software Product Management and Requirements Engineering

Emilio Insfran	Valencia Polytechnic University, Spain

Machine Learning, Artificial Intelligence and Data Analytics

Michael Felderer	University of Innsbruck, Austria

Digital Twins and Cyber-physical Systems

Aitor Arrieta	Mondragon University, Spain

Quality Aspects in Quantum Computing

Rui Abreu	University of Porto and INESC-ID, Portugal

Software Quality Education and Training in Academia and Industry

Kathia Oliveira   Université Polytechnique Hauts-de-France,
                                   France

Software Evolution

Péter Hegedűs   University of Szeged, Hungary

Program Committee

Ákos Horváth	IncQuery, Hungary
Alessandra Bagnato	Softeam, France
Alessandra De Benedictis	University of Napoles Federico II, Italy
Alessio Gambi	University of Passau, Germany
Alessio Merlo	University of Genoa, Italy
Alexander Chatzigeorgiou	University of Macedonia, Greece
Alin Stefanescu	University of Bucharest, Romania
Amleto Di Salle	Università degli Studi dell'Aquila, Italy
Ana Cavalli	Telecom SudParis, France
Ana Paiva	University of Porto, Portugal
Ana Regina Rocha	Federal University of Rio de Janeiro, Brazil
Andreas Nehfort	Nehfort IT-Consulting, Austria
Andreas Ulrich	Siemens AG, Germany
Andrew Meneely	Rochester Institute of Technology, USA
Andriy Miranskyy	Ryerson University, Canada
Antonia Bertolino	ISTI-CNR, Italy
Antonio Cicchetti	Mälardalen University, Sweden
Barbara Plank	IT University of Copenhagen, Denmark
Bartosz Walter	Poznan University of Technology, Poland
Benoit Combemale	University of Rennes 1 and Inria, France
Bin Lin	Università della Svizzera italiana, Switzerland
Breno Miranda	Federal University of Pernambuco, Brazil
Bruno Lima	University of Porto, Portugal
Carmelo R. Cartiere	NEXTSENSE SRL, Italy
Christian Esposito	University of Salerno, Italy
Christophe Kolski	Université Polytechnique Hauts-de-France, France
Claudia Werner	Federal University of Rio de Janeiro, Brazil
Csaba Nagy	Università della Svizzera italiana, Switzerland
Daniel Fernández Lanvin	University of Oviedo, Spain
David White	University of Sheffield, UK
Dragos Truscan	Åbo Akademi University, Finland
Eduard Paul Enoiu	Mälardalen University, Sweden

Eduardo Figueiredo	Federal University of Minas Gerais, Brazil
Elena Navarro	Universidad de Castilla-La Mancha, Spain
Emily Oh Navarro	University of California, Irvine, USA
Erkuden Rios	Tecnalia Research & Innovation, Spain
Esther Guerra	Universidad Autónoma de Madrid, Spain
Eva Navarro-Lopez	University of Wolverhampton, UK
Fabio Palomba	University of Salerno, Italy
Farnaz Fotrousi	University of Hamburg, Germany
Felipe Ebert	Eindhoven University of Technology, The Netherlands
Ferdinand Gramsamer	INFOGEM AG, Switzerland
Foutse Khomh	Polytechnique Montréal, Canada
Francesca Lonetti	ISTI-CNR, Italy
Frank Leymann	University of Stuttgart, Germany
Frank Phillipson	TNO, The Netherlands
Gabriel García-Mireles	Universidad de Sonora, Mexico
Gemma Catolino	Tilburg University, The Netherlands
Gerhard Fessler	Fessler Sprenger und Partner GmbH, Switzerland
Goeran Wendin	Chalmers University of Technology, Sweden
Gopi Krishnan Rajbahadur	Queen's University, Canada
Gordana Rakic	University of Novi Sad, Serbia
Guido Peterssen	aQuantum, Spain
Guillermo Hernandez	aQuantum, Spain
Gunel Jahangirova	Universitá della Svizzera italiana, Switzerland
Hans-Bernd Kittlaus	InnoTivum Consulting, Germany
Harald Foidl	University of Innsbruck, Austria
Hausi A. Muller	University of Victoria, Canada
Hieke Keuning	Utrecht University, The Netherlands
Ignacio G-Rodríguez de Guzmán	University of Castilla–La Mancha, Spain
Isabel Brito	Instituto Politécnico de Beja, Portugal
Jaejoon Lee	University of East Anglia, UK
Jaelson Castro	Universidade Federal de Pernambuco, Brazil
Javier Troya	University of Malaga, Spain
Jean Carlo R. Hauck	Universidade Federal de Santa Catarina, Brazil
Jianjun Zhao	Kyushu University, Japan
Jingyue Li	Norwegian University of Science and Technology, Norway
Joachim Denil	University of Antwerp, Belgium
João Araújo	Universidade Nova de Lisboa, Portugal
Joao Fernandes	University of Porto, Portugal
João Paulo Fernandes	Universidade do Porto, Portugal
João-Pascoal Faria	Universidade do Porto, Portugal

Johannes Noppen	BT Group, UK
Johnny Marques	Instituto Tecnológico de Aeronáutica, Brazil
Jordi Tura	Max-Planck-Institut für Quantenoptik, Germany
Jose A. Cruz-Lemus	Universidad de Castilla-La Mancha, Spain
Jose Campos	University of Lisbon, Portugal
José de la Vara	University of Castilla-La Mancha, Spain
José Luis Hevia	aQuantum, Spain
Jose Oliveira	University of Minho, Portugal
Juan Manuel Murillo	Universidad de Extremadura, Spain
Juan Pablo Carvallo	Universidad del Azuay, Ecuador
Juncal Alonso	Tecnalia Research & Innovation, Spain
Jürgen Grossmann	Fraunhofer FOKUS, Germany
Juri Di Rocco	Università degli Studi dell'Aquila, Italy
Kevin Moran	College of William & Mary, USA
Konstantinos Barmpis	University of York, UK
Krzysztof Wnuk	Blekinge Tekniska Högskola, Sweden
Leandro Minku	University of Birmingham, UK
Lei Zhang	Ryerson University, Canada
Leire Orue Echevarria	Tecnalia Research & Innovation, Spain
Lerina Aversano	Università degli Studi del Sannio, Italy
Lidia López	Universitat Politècnica de Catalunya, Spain
Loek Cleophas	Eindhoven University of Technology, The Netherlands
Loli Burgueno	Open University of Catalonia, Spain
Luigia Petre	Åbo Akademi University, Finland
Luis Olsina	National University of La Pampa, Argentina
Luís Soares Barbosa	University of Minho, Portugal
Lydie du Bousquet	LIG, France
M. J. Escalona	University of Seville, Spain
Macario Polo	Universidad de Castilla-La Mancha, Spain
Man Zhang	Kristiania University College, Norway
Manuel Wimmer	Johannes Kepler University Linz, Austria
Marcela Ruiz	Zurich University of Applied Sciences, Switzerland
Marcos Kalinowski	Pontifical Catholic University of Rio de Janeiro, Brazil
Maria Lencastre	Escola Politécnica de Pernambuco, Brazil
Mario Piattini	aQuantum, Spain
Markus Borg	RISE SICS AB, Sweden
Martin Gonzalez-Rodriguez	University of Oviedo, Spain
Massimiliano Rak	University of Campania Luigi Vanvitelli, Italy
Massimo Tisi	IMT Atlantique, France

Matteo Camilli	Free University of Bozen-Bolzano, Italy
Maya Daneva	University of Twente, The Netherlands
Michael Felderer	University of Innsbruck, Austria
Miguel Ehécatl Morales Trujillo	University of Canterbury, New Zealand
Moisés Rodríguez	AQCLab and Universidad de Castilla-La Mancha, Spain
Nelly Condori-Fernández	Universidade da Coruña, Spain
Niklas Lavesson	Blekinge Institute of Technology, Sweden
Paolo Arcaini	National Institute of Informatics, Japan
Pedro Molina	Metadev, Spain
Pekka Aho	Open Universiteit, The Netherlands
Pierre-Emmanuel Arduin	Paris-Dauphine University, France
Rafael Capilla	Rey Juan Carlos University, Spain
Rafael Duque	University of Cantabria, Spain
Ralf Kneuper	IU International University, Germany
Ricardo Pérez-Castillo	University of Castilla-La Mancha, Spain
Richard Paige	McMaster University, Canada
Roberto Nardone	Mediterranean University of Reggio Calabria, Italy
Rolf-Helge Pfeiffer	IT University of Copenhagen, Denmark
Ronnie E. de Souza Santos	Recife Center for Advanced Studies and Systems (CESAR), Brazil
Rudolf Ramler	Software Competence Center Hagenberg, Austria
Rui Maranhao Abreu	University of Porto and INESC-ID, Portugal
Salvatore Barone	University of Napoles Federico II, Italy
Samira Cherfi	Conservatoire National des Arts et Métiers, France
Santiago Matalonga	University of the West of Scotland, UK
Sebastian Feldt	Delft University of Technology, The Netherlands
Sebastiano Panichella	Zurich University of Applied Science, Switzerland
Shaohan Hu	IBM, USA
Shaukat Ali	Simula Research Laboratory, Norway
Sheila Reinehr	Pontifical Catholic University of Parana, Brazil
Shingo Takada	Keio University, Japan
Silverio Martínez-Fernández	Universitat Politècnica de Catalunya-Barcelona Tech, Spain
Silvia Abrahao	Universitat Politecnica de Valencia, Spain
Sotirios Liaskos	York University, Canada
Stefan Wagner	University of Stuttgart, Germany
Steffen Herbold	Clausthal University, Germany
Steve Counsell	Brunel University London, UK

Sybille Caffiau	Université Grenoble Alpes, France
Takashi Ishio	Nara Institute of Science and Technology, Japan
Tao Yue	Nanjing University of Aeronautics and Astronautics, China
Thomas Bach	SAP AG, Germany
Tim Lethbridge	University of Ottawa, Canada
Toacy Oliveira	Federal University of Rio de Janeiro, Brazil
Tommi Mikkonen	University of Helsinki, Finland
Torsten Bandyszak	Paluno - The Ruhr Institute for Software Technology, Germany
Umberto Villano	University of Sannio, Italy
Valentina Lenarduzzi	University of Oulu, Finland
Vera Werneck	Universidade do Estado do Rio de Janeiro, Brazil
Wasif Afzal	Mälardalen Univesity, Sweden
Wille Robert	Johannes Kepler University Linz, Austria
Wissam Mallouli	Montimage, France
Wolfgang Mauerer	OTH Regensburg, Germany
Xiaodi Wu	University of Maryland, USA
Yannis Zorgios	Zapdev, Greece

Additional Reviewers

Alessandra Somma
Daniele Granata
Huu Nghia Nguyen
Joost Mertens
Luong Nguyen
Manh-Dung Nguyen
Vinh-Hoa La

Organizing Committee

Organizing Chair

| Ricardo Pérez-Castillo | University of Castilla-La Mancha, Spain |

Proceedings Chair

| Jose Antonio Cruz Lemus | University of Castilla-La-Mancha, Spain |

Web Chair

| Américo Rio | ISCTE-IUL and Universidade Nova de Lisboa, Portugal |

Publicity Chair

Paula Muñoz   University of Málaga, Spain

Volunteer Chair

Luis Jiménez-Navajas   University of Castilla-La Mancha, Spain

Contributing Organizations

Supporters

Sponsors

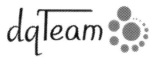

Promoters

Contents

Smart and Advanced Systems

Quality Characteristics of a Software Platform for Human-AI Teaming in Smart Manufacturing

Philipp Haindl[1]([✉])[ID], Thomas Hoch[1][ID], Javier Dominguez[2][ID],
Julen Aperribai[2], Nazim Kemal Ure[3][ID], and Mehmet Tunçel[3][ID]

[1] Software Competence Center Hagenberg, Hagenberg, Austria
{philipp.haindl,thomas.hoch}@scch.at
[2] IDEKO Research Center, Elgoibar, Spain
{jdominguez,japerribai}@ideko.es
[3] Istanbul Technical University, Istanbul, Turkey
{ure,tuncelm}@itu.edu.tr

Abstract. As AI-enabled software systems become more prevalent in smart manufacturing, their role shifts from a reactive to a proactive one that provides context-specific support to machine operators. In the context of an international research project, we develop an AI-based software platform that shall facilitate the collaboration between human operators and manufacturing machines.

We conducted 14 structured interviews with stakeholders of the prospective software platform in order to determine the individual relevance of selected quality characteristics for human-AI teaming in smart manufacturing. These characteristics include the ISO 25010:2011 standard for software quality and AI-specific quality characteristics such as trustworthiness, explicability, and auditability. The interviewees rated trustworthiness, functional suitability, reliability, and security as the most important quality characteristics for this context, and portability, compatibility, and maintainability as the least important. Also, we observed agreement regarding the relevance of the quality characteristics among interviewees having the same role. On the other hand, the relevance of each quality characteristics varied depending on the concrete use case of the prospective software platform.

The interviewees also were asked about the key success factors related to human-AI teaming in smart manufacturing. They identified improving the production cycle, increasing operator efficiency, reducing scrap, and reducing ergonomic risks as key success criteria. In this paper, we also discuss metrics for measuring the fulfillment of these quality characteristics, which we intend to operationalize and monitor during operation of the prospective software platform.

Keywords: Quality characteristics · Human-AI teaming · Smart manufacturing · Trustworthiness · Explicability · Auditability

A. Vallecillo et al. (Eds.): QUATIC 2022, CCIS 1621, pp. 3–17, 2022.
https://doi.org/10.1007/978-3-031-14179-9_1

1   Introduction

The applications of AI in smart manufacturing are numerous, ranging from improving maintenance times for machinery to detecting defects in the machine or the product to preventing injury to workers. In general, collaborative processes in smart manufacturing are characterized by alternating phases of reactive and proactive elements, with each actor supporting the other alternately. AI-enabled smart manufacturing systems are capable of self-sensing, self-adapting, self-organizing, and self-decision [19,21], enabling them to respond to physical changes in the production environment in a variety of ways. AI-guided interactions in the manufacturing process might include stopping machines, adapting production tasks, or suggesting a change in production parameters. Achieving effective teaming between machine operators and AI-enabled manufacturing systems, however, requires mutual trust based primarily on self-sensing and self-adaptation of each actor. In the frame of the EU-funded Teaming.AI project[1], we develop a software platform that allows for human-AI teaming in smart manufacturing. While we already presented a reference architecture in [9], in this work we elaborate on the individual relevance of different quality characteristics towards such a software platform. For this purpose we conducted 14 structured interviews with different stakeholders of the prospective platform in which they rated the individual relevance of 11 different quality characteristics. A further objective of our study was the identification of key success factors and metrics that serve to evaluate the fulfillment of these quality characteristics during development and operation of the platform.

The remainder of the paper is structured as follows: Subsequently, we sketch the research context of the project in Sect. 2, before we elaborate on the current state of research in this field in Sect. 3. Afterwards, in Sect. 4 we describe our research questions and the used methodology in this study. Following to that, in Sect. 5 we present the results of this study and discuss our findings in Sect. 6. Subsequently, in Sect. 7 we describe possible threats to the validity of our study and conclude our paper in Sect. 8.

2   Research Context

The research consortium of our project consists of six research and development centers and universities, three specialized SMEs for software development of AI-based software systems, two industry partners in the automotive industry for plastic injection of car components, and one industry partner for wind power plant assembly. One key contribution of this research project is the develoment of an AI-based software platform for human-AI teaming in smart manufacturing. In the following, we describe the use cases (UC) of the three industry partners that shall be supported by this software platform.

---

[1] https://www.teamingai-project.eu.

2.1   UC1: Quality Inspection

Our first industry partner manufactures injection molded components for the automotive industry. The main objective of this use case is to support the machine operator during visual quality inspection. The software platform shall classify products as OK or not-OK (NOK) with the latter being double-checked by the machine operator. Therefore, it interacts with the machine operator during quality inspection and fault analysis and provides context-specific information for adjusting parameters in order to mitigate product defects.

2.2   UC2: Parameter Optimization

The second industry partner also produces plastic parts for the automotive industry and its use case focuses primarily on optimizing injection parameters. To this end, the software platform should predict possible process deviations and identify likely root failure causes. Thereby, it can provide explanations for its findings (e.g. likelihoods), and the machine operator can provide feedback to the software platform. As opposed to the previous use case, in this instance visual quality inspection is performed by the machine operator. Moreover, in this use case, the software platform shall monitor the interaction between the machine operator and the injection machine as well as analyze its sensor data and parameters in order to detect process deviations prematurely.

2.3   UC3: Large-Scale Parts Assembly

The third industrial partner specializes in high-precision manufacturing of large-scale parts used in wind turbines, as an example. In this time-consuming production process, automated and manual tasks are incorporated. Both of these production tasks are characterized by high variability in their execution times, making task management challenging. The software platform should identify manual tasks associated with milling operations of large-scale parts and collect information about the estimated time for each of these tasks. With its tracking system, the software platform can determine the location of the machine operator. By combining this information with context information, such as machine data, the software platform acts as a mediator between the milling machine and the operator. Therefore, it should (a) improve communication between the operator and the machine, (b) allow rescheduling of similar assembly tasks, for example, combining automatic milling tasks with manual tasks, and (c) perform an ergonomic risk assessment of two simultaneous tasks as regards static loads.

2.4   Stakeholder Roles

In the following we describe the different stakeholder roles with their exemplary activities, which were identified during requirements engineering.

- **Data Protection Officer (DPO):** Ensures that a company respects the laws protecting individuals' personal data (e.g., the GDPR, by controlling the processing of data and auditing the system.
- **Software Scientist (SS):** Queries runtime data of the software components of the software platform, e.g., logging information, for evaluating and optimizing the behaviour of the system.
- **Data Scientist (DS):** Applies statistical methods onto data processed by the software platform, e.g., parameter tuning of ML components.
- **Machine Operator (MO):** Visually inspects the produced parts, clamping and adjusting the workpieces or performing manual tasks on the machine, e.g., obtaining measurements and making parameter adjustments.
- **Production Line Manager (PLM):** Monitors and optimizes the processes for producing and assembling the product or its parts on the shopfloor.

3   Related Work

We separate the current state of research related to our study into three streams. The first stream focuses on quality requirements of ML-based software systems. Based on a qualitative interview study with ten requirements engineers, Habibullah and Horkoff [8] explored the engineers' experiences and perceptions of quality requirements for ML-based software systems. The study shows that most engineers in industrial settings have difficulties formulating quality requirements for ML-based software systems. This often leads to quality requirements neither being organized, prioritized, nor effectively monitored during the development of such systems. Vogelsang and Borg [26] interviewed four data scientists using semi-structured questionnaires to examine how they elicit and specify functional and quality requirements of ML-based software systems. The authors stress that it is vital to understand ML-related performance measures to state good functional requirements for such systems. Also, systems must be designed from the beginning in such a manner that additional requirements towards explainability, trustworthiness, or even specific legal requirements can later be implemented with moderate effort. Horkoff [11] examined requirements engineering (RE) practices for eliciting quality requirements towards ML-based software systems. The author states that researchers and users of ML-based software systems lack an effective methodology to express and specify quality requirements for ML-based software systems, including targets and trade-offs, e.g., based on domain-specific best practices. Khan et al. [15] reviewed current RE methodologies for eliciting and documenting quality requirements for ML-based IIoT systems. To this end, the authors compared SysML, GORE-MLOps [12], and Pinto's RE methodology [20] for autonomous systems. The paper stresses the lack of a generic RE methodology for elicitating quality requirements of ML-based software systems.

The second stream of related works examines quality characteristics of ML-based software systems. Siebert et al. [23] presented a categorization of quality characteristics complemented by an operational software quality model for ML-based software systems. The definition and relevance of the quality characteristics is based on a literature-based review, complemented by workshops with industrial partners. The quality model allows to objectively assess the adherence to quality requirements throughout the development of ML-based software systems. An important prerequisite for the operationalization of the quality characteristics relates to their decomposition using metrics which can be measured throughout the engineering cycle of such systems. Lenarduzzi et al. [17] elaborated a method for identification of quality issues in ML-based software systems, gathered from experience reports of their research group and self-ethnography. According to the authors, root failure causes for the most frequent quality issues can be attributed to six groups, ranging from lack of developer skills, deficiencies in development and test processes, model version incompatibilities, and communication problems. They argue that training software developers is the most efficient way to mitigate quality issues in ML-based systems.

Finally, the third stream of related works focuses on quality assurance and quality models for ML-based software systems. Fujii et al. [5] conducted a survey to evaluate the usefulness of quality guidelines for ML-based software systems. These quality guidelines address the handling of quality characteristics, test architecture, and test viewpoints for different domains. The authors criticize that the analyzed guidelines do not address the integration of explainability tools in the engineering activities of ML-based software systems. The authors assume that in practice this often leads to disregarding the quality assurance of explainability requirements or conducting it incompletely. Kuwajima et al. [16] studied quality models for safety-critical ML-based software systems. Therefore they analyzed the gaps between the ISO 25010:2011 (SQuaRE) standard [13] for software quality and quality characteristics relevant for ML-based software systems. Their results show that the quality requirements towards machine learning models are often vaguely specified, which in turn negatively affects their interpretability and robustness. Felderer and Ramler [4] analyzed terminology and challenges for quality assurance of AI-based software systems along the perspectives of artifact type, process, and quality characteristics. In total, they identified eight key challenges for this context, e.g., understandability and interpretability of AI models, accuracy and correctness measures, or the handling of quality requirements in AI-based software systems.

4   Research Questions and Methodology

Our study started with the definition of candidate scenarios [24, 25] that encompass the context and the anticipated functionality from the stakeholders' perspectives when interacting with the prospective software platform. These scenarios were originally defined by our research group and were therefore only described at a high level of abstraction. Based on these candidate scenarios we designed an interview-based case study to (a) refine these scenarios into more fine-grained functional requirements, (b) assess the completeness of the scenarios to fully cover the required functionality of the software platform, (c) assess each of 11 quality characteristics in terms of its importance to the overall platform from the stakeholders' perspective, and (d) elicit the key success criteria

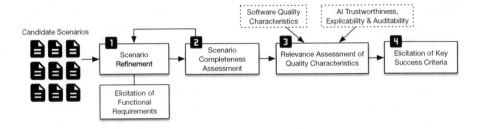

Fig. 1. Structure and process of the interview-based case study.

related to the software platform. Figure 1 shows the structure and process of the case study. In total, we conducted 14 interviews with stakeholders from the 3 industry partners and from the 3 specialized SMEs for software development of AI-based systems. The numbers of interviewees per stakeholder role distributed as follows: DPO (2), SS (2), DS (3), MO (4), PLM (3). As in this paper our research concentrates on the individual relevance of quality characteristics and success criteria of the software platform, we only describe the results of steps 3 and 4 of the case study in more detail. To this end, we formulated the following three research questions:

- **RQ1:** How do the stakeholders of the software platform assess the relevance of the ISO 25010:2011 (SQuaRE) [13] characteristics for software quality, AI trustworthiness, explicability, and auditability?
- **RQ2:** What are the key success factors of the stakeholders for human-AI teaming in smart manufacturing?
- **RQ3:** What are potential metrics to evaluate these key success factors?

Based on the guidelines by Runeson and Höst [22], we designed a questionnaire[2] for interviewing the stakeholders in step 3 and 4 of the case study regarding the relevance of quality characteristics and their success criteria towards the software platform. These interviews followed the refinement of the scenarios into functional requirements (step 1) and the completeness assessment of the scenarios (step 2). We also conducted a pilot interview as suggested by Yin [28] with a highly experienced stakeholder and used his feedback to improve the questionnaire. Specifically, we refined definitions of quality characteristics in order to ensure a uniform level of understanding among the stakeholders.

At the beginning of the interviews we explained the research context of our study - human-AI teaming in smart manufacturing - to the interviewees. Each interviewee had a thorough understanding of the research context since they have been participating in the project for over one year. Interviewees holding roles such as production line manager, data protection officer, and machine operator came from our industry partners. Likewise, interviewees holding roles such as software and data scientists came from the three specialized SMEs for software development of AI-based systems (cf. Section 2).

---

[2] https://bit.ly/3lV3aFw.

The questionnaire comprised two closed and one open questions. In the first closed question, we asked the interviewees to select the role (cf. Sect. 2.4) that they most frequently perform. In order to not overlook any important stakeholder role, we deliberately asked them whether their most frequently performed role is on the presented list. The second closed question of the questionnaire examined the individual relevance of 11 quality characteristics, i.e., 8 quality characteristics of the ISO 25010:2011 (SQuaRE) [13] standard for software quality and 3 AI-specific quality characteristics such as trustworthiness, explicability, and auditability. For easier reading, this question was divided into 11 sub-questions. To ensure common understanding of the quality characteristics, we presented the interviewees with a uniform definition of them. For the relevance assessment we adapted the *Quality Attribute Workshop* format [1] and asked the interviewees to assign, in total, 100 points to the different quality characteristics according to their subjective relevance for human-AI teaming in smart manufacturing. In the final open question, we asked them to describe the key success factors in this context for their typical role.

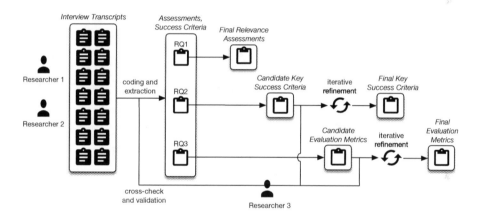

Fig. 2. Overview of research process and activities to answer the research questions.

Figure 2 shows the research process that structures the activities and specifies the outcome of each process step. The interviews were conducted by two researchers and the transcripts analyzed according to a predefined coding scheme. This scheme defined the coding and extraction of quantitative and qualitative data for each research question. The quantitative data related to RQ1 (relevance assessments of the quality characteristics) did not require further analysis. In the first step of analyzing the qualitative data from RQ2 and RQ3, two researchers highlighted the individual statements in the interview transcripts. After that, they iteratively refined the candidate key success criteria and evaluation metrics until they arrived at a consolidated set of criteria and metrics. A third researcher continuously checked and validated this refinement process. We repeated this process until we reached an agreement among all researchers.

5 Results

In the following we present the results of our research questions, as defined in Sect. 4.

5.1 RQ1

The results of this research question include the relevance ratings of the 11 quality characteristics by the interviewees. In Fig. 3, we show the rating results for each use case as well as the average rating for each quality characteristic. As shown in the illustration, the interviewees considered trustworthiness, functional suitability, and reliability as the most important quality characteristics for human-AI teaming.

Figure 4 analyzes if the relevance assessments of the quality characteristics are also influenced by the stakeholder role (cf. Sect. 2.4) of the interviewee. As we

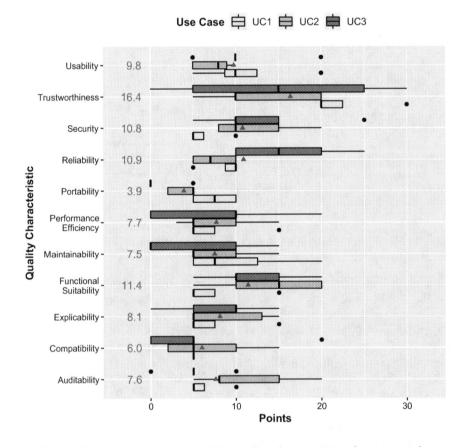

Fig. 3. Relevance assessments of the quality characteristics (per use case).

can see, each quality characteristic has a different relevance to each stakeholder role. In the following, we present the two quality characteristics rated most relevant for each stakeholder role, with the average rating in brackets. **Software Scientist (SS)**: Performance Efficiency (17.5) and Maintainability (15); **Data Scientist: (SS)**: Reliability (15) and Trustworthiness (11.7); **Data Protection Officer (DPO)**: Trustworthiness (30) and Security (25); **Machine Operator (MO)**: Trustworthiness (25) and Usability (10); **Production Line Manager (PLM)**: Functional Suitability/Trustworthiness (ex aequo 18.3) and Reliability (10.7). In order to assess the dispersion of the relevance assessments, we finally calculated the standard deviation per quality characteristic: **Trustworthiness** (9.29), **Maintainability** (6.12), **Security** (6.04), **Functional Suitability** (6.02), **Performance Efficiency** (5.89), **Reliability** (5.71), **Compatibility** (5.57), **Auditability** (5.00), **Explicability** (4.86), **Usability** (4.84), **Portability** (3.39). In this context, the standard deviation can serve as a basic indicator of consensus or disagreement among the interviewees about the relevance of a quality characteristic.

5.2   RQ2 and RQ3

Following, we summarize key success criteria for human-AI teaming in smart manufacturing and metrics for evaluating them for each stakeholder role.

Data Protection Officer (DPO): The interviewees mentioned (a) Traceability of data processing, (b) Ensuring operator anonymity, and c) Ensuring operator and machine data confidentiality as key success criteria. We consider these identified success criteria to be functional requirements and did not formulate metrics for them.

Table 1. Key success criteria and metrics for data scientists.

UC	Key success criteria	Metrics
1–3	Extensibility of data sources	–
1–3	Customizability of dashboards	–
1–3	Interoperability with explainable AI frameworks	–
3	Reliable production scene recognition	Scene recognition accuracy
3	Reliable operator posture recognition	Operator posture recognition accuracy

Software Scientist (SS): The condensed two key success criteria for this role cover a) Monitoring of realtime and historical production data, and b) Customizability of dashboards. Similary to the previous role, we regard these success criteria as functional requirements and abstained from formulating metrics.

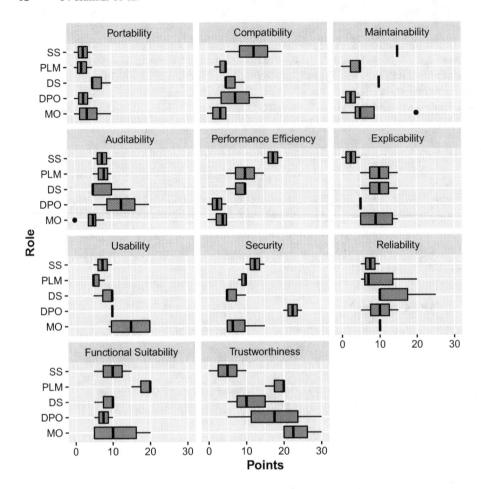

Fig. 4. Relevance assessments of the quality characteristics (per stakeholder role).

Data Scientist (DS): In Table 1 we enlist the condensed key success criteria from the perspective of data scientists. Similarly to the previous roles, not for all identified criteria meaningful metrics can be defined.

Machine Operator: For this role, we identified eight key success criteria and seven metrics for their evaluation. As shown in Table 2, the criteria and metrics tend to focus on time spans for failure detection and notification, as well as idle (waiting) times for either the machine or operator.

We use the frequency of particular unfavorable postures taken by the operator within the manufacturing process to assess the ergonomic risk. In this context, the notion of *unfavorable postures* is taken from workplace safety methods (e.g., WISHA Caution Zone Checklist [27], RULA [18], REBA [10], OWAS [14]). This includes, for example, awkward postures, heavy hand forces, repetitive motions,

Table 2. Key success criteria and metrics for machine operators.

UC	Key success criteria	Metrics
1	Reduction of scrap rate	Scrap rate
1	Shortening of production cycle time	Production cycle time
1	Reliable prediction of faulty parts	Faulty part prediction accuracy
1	Facilitating root cause analysis	–
2	Realtime detection of product quality deviations	Time between product part analysis and prediction result
2	Realtime notification of production failures	Time between detection and notification of production failures
3	Prevention of ergonomic risk	Freq. of unfavorable operator postures
3	Improvement of operator efficiency	Operator idle time

Table 3. Key success criteria and metrics for production line managers.

UC	Key success criteria	Metrics
1	Reduction of scrap rate	Scrap rate
1	Shortening of production cycle time	Production cycle time
1	Reliable prediction of faulty parts	Faulty part prediction accuracy
1–3	Improvement of OEE	OEE
2	Realtime failure prediction	Time between product part analysis and failure notification
2	Shortening of machine downtimes	Machine downtime
2	Shortening of machine idle times	Machine idle time
3	Prevention of ergonomic risk	Frequency of unfavorable operator postures
3	Improvement of OLE	OLE
3	Increasing operator satisfaction	Operator satisfaction score

repeated impacts on the limbs, heavy or frequent lifting, and moderate to high hand-arm vibrations.

Production Line Manager (PLM): As depicted in Table 3, the majority of success criteria for this role focus on maximizing efficiency and effectiveness in the production process.

In this regard, *Overall Equipment Effectiveness (OEE)* is used to determine how well machines are utilized in comparison to their potential. Similarly, *Overall*

Labor Effectiveness (OLE) quantifies the utilization, performance, and quality of the human workforce in the manufacturing process. In order to measure the satisfaction of the machine operator, we define the *Operator Satisfaction Score* similarly to the *System Usability Score (SUS)* [2,3]. It measures operator satisfaction with specific aspects of the manufacturing process using Likert scales. This shall facilitate detecting changes in operator satisfaction as a result to changes in the production process.

6   Discussion

From the perspective of the use cases, the quality characteristics related to the SQuaRE standard [13], portability, compatibility, and maintainability were rated as least relevant. Out of the three AI-specific quality characteristics, the interviewees rated auditability as the least important. Also it can be noted that the relevance of each quality characteristic is assessed differently for each use case. The use cases for parameter optimization (UC2) and large-scale parts assembly (UC3) directly affect the manufacturing process, whereas the use case for quality inspection (UC1) only supports the machine operator during quality inspection. The assessment results confirm this slightly different objective of the use cases, with functional suitability and security ranking less important for UC1 than for UC2 and UC3. However, we cannot identify a generic pattern that describes the connection between the use cases and their impact on the relevance assessments of each quality characteristic.

The qualitative analysis of the interview responses revealed that some of the key success criteria are more closely related to functional requirements than to quality (non-functional) requirements. Broy and Glinz [6,7] already pointed out that there is often a lack of clarity in practice regarding the difference between functional and quality requirements. Unlike functional requirements, however, quality requirements can also be assessed by evaluating the extent to which they have been met. Therefore, we only defined metrics for key success criteria that are implicitly linked to quality requirements.

7   Threats to Validity

Different interpretations of the quality characteristics by the interviewees undermine the *construct validity* of this study, which is primarily due to the fact that they have different roles and experiences. We tried to mitigate this threat by showing each interviewee a uniform definition of the quality characteristics that did not require any specialized knowledge. In addition, each interviewee was asked to raise any questions prior to the interview so that we could clarify any ambiguities. We also considered the role of each interviewee within the company when summarizing the interview answers, so we could determine from what perspective and with what intent each statement was delivered.

Because our research project focuses on the applicability of AI in smart manufacturing, the greatest threat to *internal validity* can be observed among interviewees, who tend to emphasize exclusively the AI-related quality characteristics. In our opinion, however, this threat is negligible, since as soon as we noticed this trend, we made the interviewee aware that overemphasizing one quality characteristic may result in underestimating the significance of others. In addition, only 100 points were available to distribute among the quality characteristics to reflect their relative importance.

As a final point, we recognize that the small sample size of interviewees in total might undermine the *external validity* of our study. To mitigate this threat, we conducted interviews with different companies and with interviewees who hold different roles. Despite this, we see a threat to the generalizability of the results to other industries due to the functional and quality requirements their products must meet.

8   Conclusion and Future Work

This paper presented the results of an interview-based case study to examine the relevance of 11 quality characteristics for human-AI teaming in smart manufacturing. The quality characteristics comprised the 11 characteristics of the ISO 25010:2011 standard for software quality (SQuaRE) and 3 AI-specific quality characteristics such as trustworthiness, explicability, and auditability. In the frame of an international research project, we develop an AI-based software platform that shall facilitate the cooperation between machine operators and manufacturing systems. For the presented case study, we conducted 14 interviews with stakeholders working in automotive industry, wind power plant assembly, and software development for AI-based software systems to assess the individual relevance of the 11 quality characteristics. Therefore, they were asked to distribute 100 points across the quality characteristics according to their relevance.

The interviewees rated trustworthiness, functional suitability, reliability, and security as the most important quality characteristics, and portability, compatibility, and maintainability as the least important. Furthermore, the results indicate consensus regarding the relevance of the quality characteristics among interviewees with the same role. However, we also recognized that the relevance of the quality characteristics varies according to the concrete use case for the prospective software platform. Accordingly, we identified the improved production cycle efficiency, lower faulty parts and scrap, and reduced ergonomic risks as the key success criteria for human-AI teaming in smart manufacturing. The time span for detecting deviations (product or process quality), *Overall Equipment Effectiveness (OEE)*, *Overall Labor Effectiveness (OLE)*, the accuracy of fault prediction and scene recognition, and the accuracy of operator posture recognition are the most relevant metrics for evaluating these criteria.

Future research should focus on operationalizing these quality characteristics so that they can be continuously monitored during operation of AI-based smart manufacturing systems. In addition, an empirical study on the relevance of these quality characteristics is recommended after the interviewees have acquired experience with the prospective software platform.

Acknowledgements. This project has received funding from the European Union's Horizon 2020 Research and Innovation Programme under grant agreement number 957402.

References

1. Barbacci, M.R., Ellison, R.J., Lattanze, A., Stafford, J.A., Weinstock, C.B., Wood, W.: Quality Attribute Workshops (QAWs), 3rd edn (2003)
2. Brooke, JDCUVK.: SUS: A 'Quick and Dirty' Usability Scale. In: Usability Evaluation In Industry. CRC Press, Boca Raton (1996)
3. Brooke, J.: SUS: a retrospective. J. Usability Stud. **8**(2), 29–40 (2013)
4. Felderer, M., Ramler, R.: Quality assurance for AI-based systems: overview and challenges (Introduction to Interactive Session). In: Winkler, D., Biffl, S., Mendez, D., Wimmer, M., Bergsmann, J. (eds.) SWQD 2021. LNBIP, vol. 404, pp. 33–42. Springer, Cham (2021). https://doi.org/10.1007/978-3-030-65854-0_3
5. Fujii, G., et al.: Guidelines for quality assurance of machine learning-based artificial intelligence. Int. J. Software Eng. Knowl. Eng. **30**, 1589–1606 (2020)
6. Glinz, M.: On non-functional requirements. In: 15th IEEE International Requirements Engineering Conference (RE 2007), pp. 21–26 (2007)
7. Glinz, M.: Rethinking the notion of non-functional requirements. In: Proceedings of the Third World Congress for Software Quality (3WCSQ 2005), vol. 2, pp. 55–64. Munich, Germany (2005)
8. Habibullah, K.M., Horkoff, J.: Non-functional requirements for machine learning: understanding current use and challenges in industry. In: 2021 IEEE 29th International Requirements Engineering Conference (RE), pp. 13–23 (2021)
9. Haindl, P., Buchgeher, G., Khan, M., Moser, B.: Towards a reference software architecture for human-AI teaming in smart manufacturing. In: 2022 IEEE/ACM 44th International Conference on Software Engineering: New Ideas and Emerging Results (ICSE-NIER), pp. 96–100 (2022). https://doi.org/10.1109/ICSE-NIER55298.2022.9793509
10. Hignett, S., McAtamney, L.: Rapid entire body assessment (REBA). Appl. Ergon. **31**(2), 201–205 (2000)
11. Horkoff, J.: Non-functional requirements for machine learning: challenges and new directions. In: 2019 IEEE 27th International Requirements Engineering Conference (RE), pp. 386–391 (2019)
12. Ishikawa, F., Matsuno, Y.: Evidence-driven requirements engineering for uncertainty of machine learning-based systems. In: 2020 IEEE 28th International Requirements Engineering Conference (RE), pp. 346–351 (2020)
13. ISO/IEC 25010: ISO/IEC 25010:2011, Systems and Software Engineering - Systems and Software Quality Requirements and Evaluation (SQuaRE) - System and Software Quality Models (2011)
14. Karhu, O., Kansi, P., Kuorinka, I.: Correcting working postures in industry: a practical method for analysis. Appl. Ergon. **8**(4), 199–201 (1977)
15. Khan, A., Siddiqui, I.F., Shaikh, M., Anwar, S., Shaikh, M.: Handling non-fuctional requirements in IoT-based machine learning systems. In: 2022 Joint International Conference on Digital Arts, Media and Technology with ECTI Northern Section Conference on Electrical, Electronics, Computer and Telecommunications Engineering), pp. 477–479 (2022)

16. Kuwajima, H., Yasuoka, H., Nakae, T.: Engineering problems in machine learning systems. Mach. Learn. **109**(5), 1103–1126 (2020). https://doi.org/10.1007/s10994-020-05872-w
17. Lenarduzzi, V., Lomio, F., Moreschini, S., Taibi, D., Tamburri, D.A.: Software quality for AI: where we are now? In: Winkler, D., Biffl, S., Mendez, D., Wimmer, M., Bergsmann, J. (eds.) SWQD 2021. LNBIP, vol. 404, pp. 43–53. Springer, Cham (2021). https://doi.org/10.1007/978-3-030-65854-0_4
18. McAtamney, L., Nigel Corlett, E.: RULA: a survey method for the investigation of work-related upper limb disorders. Appl. Ergon. **24**(2), 91–99 (1993)
19. Phuyal, S., Bista, D., Bista, R.: Challenges, Opportunities and future directions of smart manufacturing: a state of art review. Sustain. Futures **2**, 100023 (2020)
20. Pinto, A.: Requirement specification, analysis and verification for autonomous systems. In: 2021 58th ACM/IEEE Design Automation Conference (DAC), pp. 1315–1318 (2021)
21. Qu, Y.J., Ming, X.G., Liu, Z.W., Zhang, X.Y., Hou, Z.T.: Smart manufacturing systems: state of the art and future trends. Int. J. Adv. Manuf. Technol. **103**(9), 3751–3768 (2019)
22. Runeson, P., Höst, M.: Guidelines for conducting and reporting case study research in software engineering. Empirical Soft. Eng. **14**(2), 131–164 (2009)
23. Siebert, J., et al.: Towards guidelines for assessing qualities of machine learning Systems. In: Shepperd, M., Brito e Abreu, F., Rodrigues da Silva, A., Pérez-Castillo, R. (eds.) QUATIC 2020. CCIS, vol. 1266, pp. 17–31. Springer, Cham (2020). https://doi.org/10.1007/978-3-030-58793-2_2
24. Sutcliffe, A.: Scenario-based requirements engineering. In: Proceedings. 11th IEEE International Requirements Engineering Conference, vol. 2003, pp. 320–329 (2003)
25. Sutcliffe, A., Maiden, N., Minocha, S., Manuel, D.: Supporting scenario-based requirements engineering. IEEE Trans. Software Eng. **24**(12), 1072–1088 (1998)
26. Vogelsang, A., Borg, M.: Requirements engineering for machine learning: perspectives from data scientists. In: 2019 IEEE 27th International Requirements Engineering Conference Workshops (REW), pp. 245–251 (2019)
27. Washington state department of labour industries: hazard zone checklist (2022). https://lni.wa.gov/safety-health/_docs/HazardZoneChecklist.pdf. Accessed 31 May 2022
28. Yin, R.: Case Study Research and Applications: Design and Methods. SAGE Publications Inc, Los Angeles, 6th edn. (2017)

Architectural Decisions in AI-Based Systems: An Ontological View

Xavier Franch[(⊠)] [iD], Silverio Martínez-Fernández[iD], Claudia P. Ayala[iD], and Cristina Gómez[iD]

Universitat Politècnica de Catalunya, Barcelona, Spain
{xavier.franch,silverio.martinez,claudia.ayala,
cristina.gomez}@upc.edu

Abstract. Architecting AI-based systems entails making some decisions that are particular to this type of systems. Therefore, it becomes necessary to gather all necessary knowledge to inform such decisions, and to articulate this knowledge in a form that facilitates knowledge transfer among different AI projects. In this exploratory paper, we first present the main results of a literature survey in the area, and then we propose a preliminary ontology for architectural decision making, which we exemplify using a subset of the papers selected in the literature review. In the discussion, we remark on the variety of decision types and system contexts, highlighting the need to further investigate the current state of research and practice in this area. Besides, we summarize our plans to move along this research area by widening the literature review and incorporating more AI-related concepts to this first version of the ontology.

Keywords: AI-based systems · Software architecture · Architectural decisions · Ontologies · Quality attributes · Architectural Views · UML class diagrams

1 Introduction

The conception, development and deployment of software systems that embed artificial intelligence (AI), what we call *AI-based systems*, has become commonplace in the last decade. This is mostly due to the increased computer processing power, availability of larger datasets, and constant formulation of better AI algorithms which has advanced the AI field to unprecedented levels of adoption [2]. Classical software engineering disciplines have been used to produce AI-based systems, from requirements engineering to testing, remarkably including software design principles, methods and techniques to deliver software architectures for AI-based systems [17].

Given that an AI-based system is nothing else than a particular type of software system, it can be thought that the whole discipline of software design and software architectures apply. However, the literature has reported significant challenges that are particular to architecting AI-based systems, related to design principles, design quality and software structure [17]. As a response to these challenges, a number of research approaches have formulated design strategies to cope with specific quality attributes

A. Vallecillo et al. (Eds.): QUATIC 2022, CCIS 1621, pp. 18–27, 2022.
https://doi.org/10.1007/978-3-031-14179-9_2

and concrete AI infrastructure proposals [23]. However, these research approaches take a pragmatic perspective, focusing more on resolving the problem at hand rather than considering the particular problem as an instance of a more generic situation. This fact hinders knowledge transfer from one experience to another and makes it difficult to decide whether a solution formulated in one paper applies to a new problem.

In order to overcome this challenge, in this exploratory paper we present our ongoing research towards the formulation of a unifying conceptual framework aimed at defining the concepts that characterise the process of architectural decision-making [22]. Through a literature review upon a set of 41 papers in the field of software design and software architectures in AI-based systems, we extract the main concepts relevant to architectural decisions for this type of systems, and propose a preliminary ontology that captures the knowledge that is relevant to that process. We finalise the paper with a research agenda for this line of investigation.

2 Background

2.1 Architecting AI-Based Systems

Software design and architecture of AI-based systems, like other software development activities, differs on AI-based systems with respect to traditional software systems. As a result, there has recently been emerging research on software architecture for AI-based systems, as well as dedicated events (e.g., CAIN@ICSE, SAML@ECSA).

Two of the most studied topics have been design strategies to cope with specific quality attributes (e.g., classical attributes such as safety and reliability [11], or emerging attributes such as energy efficiency [7]), and AI infrastructure proposals (e.g., for sharing models as microservices) [17]. Serban et al. argue that traditional software architecture challenges (e.g., component coupling) also play an important role when using AI components; along with new AI specific challenges (e.g., the need for continuous retraining) [20]. They establish a link between architectural solutions and software quality attributes, to provide twenty architectural tactics used to satisfy individual quality requirements of systems with ML components. Furthermore, Yokoyama et al. have studied architectural patterns for AI systems [25].

2.2 Architectural Decisions

Architectural decision-making is a well-established research area in the field of software architecture. In a recent semi-systematic literature review, Bhat et al. report over 250 publications on the area, with a clear increase from the year 2005 [3]. Research proposals can be arranged according to several dimensions, mainly: 1) what are the drivers that influence architectural decisions (e.g., quality attributes [1]), 2) in which type of system architectural decisions apply (e.g., microservice APIs [26]).

In our paper, we are interested in the study of architectural decisions on AI-based systems. Studies in this area are scarce. A notable exception is the work by Warnett et al., which provides initial industrial evidence of architectural decisions faced by practitioners when designing an ML pipeline [24]. While the information provided in this paper is really valuable, it is focused in one particular AI context (ML pipelines) and does not articulate the gathered knowledge into a comprehensive framework, which is our final aim in this exploratory paper.

3 Research Questions and Method

The purpose of this paper is to present the main ideas, current research and future agenda for our research on AI-based system architectural decision making. To this aim, we formulate the following research questions:

RQ1. *What are the concepts that influence architectural decisions in AI-based systems?*

RQ2. *How can we specify a conceptual framework for these concepts and decisions?*

With RQ1, we want to elicit and characterise the concepts that need to be considered when designing AI-based systems. We expect these factors to be related to classical quality attributes such as time efficiency or accuracy [11], but also to emergent concerns, e.g. related to green AI [19].

To answer this research question, we use the result of a recent systematic mapping study on software engineering practices for AI-based systems [17], which includes software design as one of the SWEBOK knowledge areas. In addition, we consider the contributions presented in two recent venues, namely the 1st International Workshop on Software Architecture and Machine Learning[1] (SAML) and the March 2022 special issue on AI and software engineering published in IEEE Computer[2]. We analysed the resulting 41 papers (34 papers from [17] related to software design, and 5 papers from the SAML workshop and 2 architecture-related papers in the IEEE Computer issue) and extracted relevant information that we use to respond to RQ1. In more detail: *(i)* we split the 41 papers among the four authors at approximately equal share; *(ii)* every author read and extracted data of the papers assigned to them; *(iii)* we met at weekly basis and commented the result of the work in that week, consolidating the analysis and converging into a shared understanding; *(iv)* as we advanced, we synthesised the result in a data extraction form represented with a spreadsheet. It is worth noting that some of these 41 papers do not present concrete proposals because they are empirical studies reporting current research or practice; therefore, we were not able to extract information related to RQ1 from them.

For answering RQ2, we synthesised the knowledge gained from this extracted information using an ontology to present the concepts and their relationships. Ontologies are a widely used artefact used for knowledge representation and management [13], which is the primary goal of our work. In the area of architectural decisions, ontologies are widely used to represent architectural knowledge [10, 18]. Therefore, it seems a natural

---

[1] https://saml2021.disim.univaq.it/.

[2] https://www.computer.org/csdl/magazine/co/2022/03.

choice for our goal. In this exploratory paper, we represent ontologies in a lightweight form, using UML class diagrams [14] and a glossary of terms. We define the terms relying on standards and former papers as much as possible, although in some cases we have opted by providing our own definitions, better aligned to the pursued objective of the paper.

4   An Ontology for AI-Based Systems Architectural Decision-Making

Table 1 compiles the main concepts emerging from our analysis, and Fig. 1 presents a class diagram relating these concepts. Central to the ontology is the basic concept of *Architectural Decision*, which we adopt from De Boer *et al.* [4]. Important to this definition is the understanding that an architectural decision may call for the need of *subsequent* architectural decisions. Architectural decisions can be classified into one *Decision Type* and may be constrained in their applicability to one or more *Contexts*. We do not impose a closed enumeration of neither decision types nor contexts; instead we foresee that these types will naturally emerge as the knowledge on AI-based systems architecture grows.

Table 1. Concepts of the ontology.

Concept	Definition	Source
Architectural Decision	Decision that is assumed to influence the architectural design of an AI-based system and can be enforced upon this architectural design, possibly leading to new concerns that result in a need for taking subsequent decisions	[4]
Decision Type	A type in which an architectural decision may be classified	From authors
Context	Any information related to an AI-based system that can be used to characterise the applicability of an architectural decision	Adapted and simplified from [9]
Quality Attribute	Measurable physical or abstract property of an AI-based system that bears on its ability to satisfy stated and implied needs	Adapted from [11]

(*continued*)

Table 1. (*continued*)

Concept	Definition	Source
Impact	The degree in which an architectural decision relates to a quality attribute	From authors
Architectural Element	Any type of element that can appear in an architecture, either an abstract concept (e.g., an architectural style) or some binary object (e.g., a software component or a data file)	From authors
AI-related Architectural Element	A class of Architectural Element that embeds or represents AI knowledge, e.g. an ML model, an implemented AI algorithm or a dataset	From authors
Architectural View	Representation of the whole system from the perspective of a related set of concerns	From [12]

Architectural decisions are taken according to their *impact* on a number of *Quality Attributes* that are considered relevant for the AI-based system under development. To measure the impact of an architectural decision, we use the qualitative scale proposed in the iStar language [8] with four scales ranging from strong positive influence ("make") to strong negative influence ("break"). On the other hand, an architectural decision affects a number of *Architectural Elements* (at least one), which can eventually be *AI-based Architectural Elements*, typically embedding some ML model or offering some AI algorithm (maybe in the form of a library) or even a dataset. Components are related to a particular *Architectural View*, since architectural decisions may be made at different levels of abstraction. Types of architectural elements and views are left open, subject to further investigation.

The ontology recognizes the hierarchical nature of architectural decisions, architectural elements and quality attributes by means of recursive many-to-many associations in the class diagram.

Table 2 exemplifies the conceptual framework on a subset of the 41 selected papers, by giving values to the concepts represented in the class diagram. We describe in more detail three particular cases below.

Example 1. Kumar et al. [16] propose an AI-system to decide the best location of chargers for electric vehicles based on spatiotemporal data from citizens' vehicles. Of course, this raises privacy concerns. The paper wants to exploit the fact that vehicles currently have enough computational power to train AI models.

What We Learnt. Kumar et al. start the architectural decision-making process by applying the design principle (a decision type) of distributing the AI model among the vehicles,

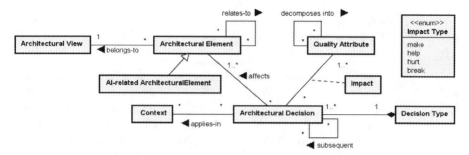

Fig. 1. Class diagram relating all concepts of the ontology

using the cars for privacy-sensitive calculations. This decision implies other subsequent decisions, for instance the need of incorporating technologies over a Blockchain infrastructure to keep track of updates in data through a logging software component (supporting accountability then). As it stands out from the study, the solution given works for a particular context, namely highly distributed systems, from which the smart city design (in relation to smart vehicles) is an exemplification in the paper.

Example 2. Yokohama [25] addresses the problem of ensuring stability of the system when errors occur, in the context of AI-based systems organised according to a three-layered architecture.

What We Learnt. The solution is based on a simple design principle, namely keeping separated AI-components from non-AI-components. Compared to the previous case, the solution is close to the design level and assumes one particular way to structure the overall architecture of the system (three layers). This also makes it possible to get a domain-independent solution. Later in the paper, they elaborate their design principle into a concrete architecture pattern, an AI-aware 3-layer architecture pattern.

Table 2. Ontology in some of the selected papers for our study.

Ref	Architectural decision	Decision type	Context	Quality attribute	Impact	Architectural element	Architectural layer
[16]	Distribute model	Design principle	Highly distributed systems	Privacy, Resilience	Supports	Vehicle	Physical
	Log updates	New technology		Accountability		Blockchain	Component
	Manage access			Scalability			
[25]	Keep AI and non-AI components separated	Design principle	N/A	Stability	Supports	Three layers	Logical
	3-layer AI-aware pattern	Architectural pattern				Subsystem	
[5]	Component replacement	Architectural tactic	Self-adaptation	Modularity	Supports	ML component	Component
	Retrain			Maintainability			Logical

Example 3. Casimiro et al. developed a preliminary framework aimed to self-adapt systems that rely on AI components [5].

What We Learnt. They offer five adaptation tactics for AI-based systems. We discuss two of them. First, the "component replacement" tactic, consisting of replacing an under-performing component by one that better matches the current environment (dealing with concept drift). While this is fast and inexpensive, it may not be available in all scenarios. Second, the "retrain" tactic, which uses new data for retraining and updating the machine learning model's hyper-parameters. This is a generic and robust method, but effective only once a relatively large number of instances of the new data are available, computationally intensive, and with a significant increase of the accuracy and latency of the retrain process.

5   Discussion and Research Agenda

The work reported in this paper is answering two research questions. With respect to RQ1, this preliminary literature review has uncovered a number of remarkable facts:

- The types of architectural decisions are diverse and at different levels of abstraction and detail. In Table 2, we have provided some examples, but there are more, e.g. design pattern or architectural style. Eliciting and categorising these types is utterly important for our research goal.
- Similarly, knowledge about the different contexts and architectural levels in which architectural decisions are made need to be further elicited and consolidated. Concerning the context, we expect research papers to include a proper reflection on the limitations of applicability of their findings, through an appropriate statement of external validity threats.
- While the relevance of quality attributes as decisional drives has become evident in our literature study, papers usually focus on one particular attribute supported by their approach, but they only occasionally discuss negative impact on other attributes. Quality trade-off analysis is well-known to be crucial in architectural decision-making [6], therefore we can expect research in this direction once the area becomes more mature.
- The papers that have surveyed focus on the static view of architecture decisions but they do not include much information about dynamic (process, using Kruchten's 4 + 1 model [15]) view. We also expect this aspect to be targeted in future works because it is of uttermost importance when deciding the most appropriate architecture for the system at hand.

On its turn, some points related to the ontology are worth to mention:

- At a first glance, the ontology seems to incorporate very little AI-related aspects. In fact, looking at the class diagram currently used for this preliminary proposal, only a subclass reflects our focus on AI-based systems. The reason is that, currently, AI-related concepts emerge in the instance level of the class diagram, as we can see in Table 2.

- Given the need to consolidate the current knowledge, as stated above in relation to RQ1, we have chosen not to predefine the values of the different classes e.g. using enumerate values (as we have done with the Impact type, which is the only exception to this rule since it is not really related to the AI domain but to the architectural decision domain only).

From this discussion, we highlight a few points that characterise our research agenda:

- Widen our literature review. The systematic mapping that we have used as baseline includes papers only until March 2020. Given the ever-growing plethora of research contributions in the AI field, we can expect a good number of papers that we have not considered yet.
- Complement the literature review with more practice-oriented knowledge sources, in the form of grey literature and interviews with practitioners.
- Consolidate the architectural knowledge from the literature review. As commented above, we would like to complete a catalogue of decision types, contexts, quality attributes and architectural views which gather all the knowledge related to architecting AI-based systems.
- Refine the ontology to include more specific and low-level AI concepts. This means reflecting in the ontology the consolidation mentioned in the point above. So, for example, we could specialise the concept of AI-related Architectural Element including e.g. Data Ingestion or ML model as subtypes.

6   Conclusions

This exploratory paper presents a summary of concepts related to architectural decisions in AI-based systems, and articulates them in the form of an ontology. This proposed, preliminary ontology can help to improve knowledge transfer among projects by harmonising concepts and actions used in diverse experiences, thus supporting *(i)* better understanding of the effects and implications of design decisions in different contexts; *(ii)* consolidation of architectural knowledge in specific domains and the subsequent definition of useful architectural and design patterns for AI-based systems. We plan to apply to our research agenda to further deepen our understanding and conceptualization of the AI-based systems architectural decision-making area.

Acknowledgment. This paper has been funded by the Spanish Ministerio de Ciencia e Innovación under project/funding scheme PID2020-117191RB-I00/AEI/https://doi.org/10.13039/501100011033.

References

1. Ameller, D., Galster, M., Avgeriou, P., Franch, X.: A survey on quality attributes in service-based systems. Softw. Qual. J. **24**(2), 271–299 (2016)
2. Anthes, G.: Artificial intelligence poised to ride a new wave. Commun. ACM **60**(7), 19–21 (2017)

3. Bhat, M., Shumaiev, K., Hohenstein, U., Biesdorf, A., Matthes, F.: The evolution of archi-tectural decision making as a key focus area of software architecture research: a semi-systematic literature study. In: Proceedings of the IEEE International Conference on Software Architecture (ICSA), pp. 69–80 (2020)

4. de Boer, R.C., Farenhorst, R., Lago, P., van Vliet, H., Clerc, V., Jansen, A.: Architectural knowledge: getting to the core. In: Overhage, S., Szyperski, C.A., Reussner, R., Stafford, J.A. (eds.) QoSA. LNCS, vol. 4880, pp. 197–214. Springer, Heidelberg (2007). https://doi.org/10.1007/978-3-540-77619-2_12

5. Casimiro, M., et al.: Self-adaptation for machine learning based systems. In: Proceedings of the 1st International Workshop on Software Architecture and Machine Learning (SAML) (2021). Paper 6

6. Clements, P., Kazman, R., Klein, M.: Evaluating Software Architectures: Methods and Case Studies. Addison-Wesley (2001)

7. Creus, R., Martínez-Fernández, S., Franch, X.: Which design decisions in AI-enabled mobile applications contribute to greener AI? CoRR abs/2109.15284 (2021)

8. Franch, X., López, L., Cares, C., Colomer, D.: The $i*$ framework for goal-oriented modeling. In: Karagiannis, D., Mayr, H., Mylopoulos, J. (eds.) Domain-Specific Conceptual Modeling, pp. 485–506. Springer, Cham (2016). https://doi.org/10.1007/978-3-319-39417-6_22

9. Dey, A.K., Abowd, G.D.: Towards a better understanding of context and context-awareness. In: Proceedings of the ACM Workshop on the What, Who, Where, When and How of Context-Awareness (2000)

10. Di Noia, T., et al.: A fuzzy ontology-based approach for tool-supported decision making in architectural design. Knowl. Inf. Syst. **58**, 83–112 (2019)

11. ISO/IEC 25010:2011: Systems and software engineering—Systems and software Quality Requirements and Evaluation (SQuaRE)—System and software quality models (2011)

12. ISO/IEC 42010: Systems and Software engineering - Recommended Practice for Architec-tural Description of Software-intensive Systems (2007)

13. Jurisica, I., Mylopoulos, J., Yu, E.: Ontologies for knowledge management: an information systems perspective. Knowl. Inf. Syst. **6**(4), 380–401 (2004). https://doi.org/10.1007/s10115-003-0135-4

14. Kogut, P., et al.: UML for ontology development. Knowl. Eng. Rev. **17**(1), 61–64 (2002)

15. Kruchten, P.B.: The 4 + 1 view model of architecture. IEEE Softw. **12**(6), 42–50 (1995)

16. Kumar, A., Braud, T., Tarkoma, S., Hui, P.: Trustworthy AI in the age of pervasive computing and big data. In: IEEE International Conference on Pervasive Computing and Communications Workshops (PerCom Workshops), pp. 1–6 (2020)

17. Martínez-Fernández, S., et al.: Software engineering for AI-based systems: a survey. ACM Trans. Softw. Methodol. **31**(2), 1–59 (2022)

18. Pahl, C., Giesecke, S., Hasselbring, W.: Ontology-based modelling of architectural styles. Inf. Softw. Technol. **51**, 1739–1749 (2009)

19. Schwartz, R., Dodge, J., Smith, N.A., Etzioni, O.: Green AI. Commun. ACM **63**(12), 54–63 (2020)

20. Serban, V., Visser, J.: Adapting software architectures to machine learning challenges. In: Proceedings of the 29th IEEE International Conference on Software Analysis, Evolution and Reengineering (SANER) (2022)

21. Szyperski, C., Gruntz, D., Murer, S.: Component Software: Beyond Object-Oriented Programming. Pearson Education (2002)

22. Tyree, J., Akerman, A.: Architecture decisions: demystifying architecture. IEEE Softw. **22**(2), 19–27 (2005)

23. Wan, Z., Xia, X., Lo, D., Murphy, G.C.: How does machine learning change software development practices? IEEE Trans. Softw. Eng. **47**(9), 1857–1871 (2019)

24. Warnett, S.J., Zdun, U.: Architectural design decisions for the machine learning workflow. IEEE Comput. **55**(3), 40–51 (2022)
25. Yokoyama, H.: Machine learning system architectural pattern for improving operational stability. In: Proceedings of the IEEE International Conference on Software Architecture – Companion Volume (ICSA-C), pp. 267–274 (2019)
26. Zdun, U., Stocker, M., Zimmermann, O., Pautasso, C., Lübke, D.: Guiding architectural decision making on quality aspects in microservice APIs. In: Pahl, C., Vukovic, M., Yin, J., Yu, Q. (eds.) Proceedings of the International Conference on Service-Oriented Computing (ICSOC), pp. 73–88. Springer, Cham (2018). https://doi.org/10.1007/978-3-030-03596-9_5

Verification and Validation

An Empirical Study to Quantify the SetUp and Maintenance Benefits of Adopting WebDriverManager

Maurizio Leotta[1]($\boxtimes$) , Boni García[2] , and Filippo Ricca[1]

[1] Dipartimento di Informatica, Bioingegneria, Robotica e Ingegneria dei Sistemi (DIBRIS),
Università di Genova, Genova, Italy
{maurizio.leotta,filippo.ricca}@unige.it
[2] University Carlos III of Madrid, Madrid, Spain
boni.garcia@uc3m.es

Abstract. Test automation brings several benefits but also presents significant problems that often force developers/testers to carry out tiring and costly manual tasks. Among these tiring tasks while using Selenium WebDriver for testing Web applications, driver management (i.e., version discovery, download, setup and maintenance) ranks in a top position.

Recently, an open source Java library, named *WebDriverManager*, that carries out automatically the driver management process for Selenium WebDriver has been proposed to alleviate the burden of the developers. This library appears to be very promising but until now no one has experimentally evaluated its effectiveness.

In this paper, we present an empirical study aimed at understanding whether the use of *WebDriverManager* allows to reduce both initial and long-term setup efforts of a multibrowser test suite.

The results are in favor of *WebDriverManager* as it allows an average saving of more than 33% of the time for an initial setup which translated annually corresponds to many hours of bare manual driver management to which must be added the hours for understanding that the outdated driver is the cause of the problems reported by the test suite. Having almost weekly, as we estimated, outdated drivers brings also to a reduction in the perceived reliability of E2E test suites. The adoption of *WebDriverManager* can help to drastically reduce all these problems.

Keywords: E2E testing · Selenium WebDriver · Empirical study

1 Introduction

Selenium[1] is an open source umbrella project devoted to web browser automation. Although it can be used for automating different tasks in the browser, Selenium is mainly used to carry out automated end-to-end (E2E) tests for web applications [7].

---

[1] https://www.selenium.dev/.

A. Vallecillo et al. (Eds.): QUATIC 2022, CCIS 1621, pp. 31–45, 2022.
https://doi.org/10.1007/978-3-031-14179-9_3

A recent survey about software testing identified Selenium as the most valuable testing framework nowadays, followed by JUnit and Cucumber [4].

Selenium WebDriver, the main component of Selenium, automates browsers by providing an Application Programming Interface (API) in different programming languages and uses the native capabilities of each browser to support the automation. For this reason, the execution of a Selenium WebDriver test suite requires an intermediate component, constituted by a binary file, called *driver* that is specific for a certain browser's version (e.g., Firefox 99.0). Thus, in order to run and keep a test suite updated over time, it is necessary to download the driver corresponding to the browser version and keep the versions browser-driver aligned during the natural evolution of the browsers, indeed modern browsers automatically upgrade to the next stable version. This alignment task is usually executed manually by developers and is even more tiring (and costly) if the developed test suite is multi-browser.

In 2015, an open source Java library, named WebDriverManager[2], able to carry out automatically this driver management process for Selenium WebDriver test suites has been released. Since then, it has become a well-known helper utility for Selenium WebDriver developers using Java as language bindings [11].

Since this library appears to be very promising for reducing driver management times, we decided to design an empirical study to evaluate the benefits deriving from its usage (differently from us, García et al. [11] assessed, by means of a survey, the extent to which WebDriverManager is adopted and used, and evaluated the WebDriverManager API following Clarke's usability dimensions). More in detail, by means of a controlled experiment conducted with 25 MSc students in Computer Science, we measured the time the participants took to setup a test suite with and without WebDriverManager. Subsequently, using (1) the data deriving from this first part of the experiment and (2) the number of driver versions actually released for each browser, we tried to estimate the cumulative yearly effort required adopting and non-adopting WebDriverManager.

This paper is organized as follows: Sect. 2 presents the object of our experimental study, that is WebDriverManager. Section 3 reports definition, design and settings of our controlled experiment. Section 4 reports the results of the experiment. Finally, Sect. 5 summarizes related works and Sect. 6 concludes the paper.

2   WebDriverManager

The Selenium ecosystem is composed of three main core components, namely:

– Selenium WebDriver, which is a library for handling browsers via programming;
– Selenium Grid, which is a infrastructure that allows controlling remote browsers installed in different nodes with Selenium WebDriver.
– Selenium IDE (Integrated Development Environment), which is a browser extension that allows recording and replay of user interactions against web browsers.

Selenium WebDriver is considered the core component of Selenium. For this reason, it is a common practice to use "Selenium" to refer to the library for web browser automation. This paper uses "Selenium WebDriver" to refer to the library and "Selenium" for the umbrella project or the ecosystem to avoid misleading.

---

[2] https://bonigarcia.dev/webdrivermanager/.

2.1 Selenium WebDriver

Selenium WebDriver automates browsers by providing a cross-browser API in different programming languages. The languages officially supported by the Selenium project are five: Java, JavaScript, Python, C#, and Ruby. A very recent survey identified Java as the preferred language binding for Selenium WebDriver, followed by Python and JavaScript [8].

Selenium WebDriver uses the native capabilities of each browser to support the automation. For this reason, a test script using the Selenium WebDriver API in order to function correctly requires an intermediate component called *driver* in the Selenium jargon. Each browser vendor provides a specific driver. For example, the driver to control Chrome with Selenium WebDriver is called chromedriver[3], geckodriver[4] for Firefox, or msedgedriver[5] for Edge.

In practice, a driver is a server-side component that receives incoming messages from Selenium WebDriver test scripts using a standard protocol called W3C WebDriver [22]. This protocol is based on JSON messages over HTTP. The driver translates each W3C WebDriver message to a native command that the browser can understand—such as the DevTools protocol in Chromium-based browsers (such as Chrome and Edge) or Marionette in Firefox. Therefore, the Selenium WebDriver architecture has three layers composed by the test scripts using the Selenium WebDriver API, the driver, and the browser.

2.2 Driver Management

A driver is a binary file that must be known by the test script using the Selenium WebDriver API. To implement a Selenium WebDriver test script, a practitioner must first resolve the proper driver required by Selenium WebDriver (e.g., chromedriver for Chrome, geckodriver for Firefox, etc.). This process is known as *driver management*, and it is composed of three main steps [11]:

1. *Download.* The first step is obtaining the proper driver to control a given browser. The driver is a platform-dependent binary file (e.g., geckodriver for Windows). Moreover, the driver version needs to be compatible with the underlying browser version. For that reason, the user needs to find out the browser version and download the correct driver version from its online repository (typically, checking the driver documentation to select the appropriate version).
2. *Setup.* Once the driver is downloaded and available, it needs to be appropriately configured in the Selenium WebDriver test scripts. For example, the driver's absolute path needs to be exported using a given system property before creating a WebDriver object. The following snippet shows an example for Chrome in Linux using Java:

```
System.setProperty("webdriver.chrome.driver", "/opt/chromedriver");
WebDriver driver = new ChromeDriver();
```

---

[3] https://chromedriver.chromium.org/.

[4] https://github.com/mozilla/geckodriver.

[5] https://developer.microsoft.com/en-us/microsoft-edge/tools/webdriver/.

3. *Maintenance*. Modern web browsers (such as Chrome, Firefox, or Edge) are sometimes called *evergreen browsers*. This term reflects a common feature of these
browsers that automatically and silently upgrade to the next stable version. Due to
this upgrade, the previously downloaded driver will need to be updated eventually
since the driver-browser compatibility is not satisfied in the long run.

Nowadays, the driver management process is mainly carried out manually [8]. This
manual activity has different inconveniences, such as:

– *Development effort*. Developers need to invest some time in discovering the browser
  version and driver, download it, and make it available for test scripts.
– *Lack of test portability*. As explained above, the absolute driver path is required in
  a Selenium WebDriver Java test script. As a result, the resulting test script cannot
  be executed on a different machine, for example, in a Continuous Integration (CI)
  server.
– *Maintenance effort*. To avoid a "mismatch problem" between the browser and the
  driver, the user needs to keep track of the driver version. Otherwise, the execution of
  then Selenium WebDriver test will fail in the long run. For example, with Chrome,
  the message that is shown as a consequence of this error is the following: "this
  version of chromedriver only supports chrome version N" (being N is the latest
  version of Chrome supported by a particular version of chromedriver). As reported
  periodically in StackOverflow[6], this is a recurrent problem for Selenium WebDriver
  users.

2.3 Automated Driver Management

To overcome the problems related to manual driver management and listed above, the
automation of this process through a helper utility named WebDriverManager[7] has been
proposed. WebDriverManager is an open source Java library that carries out the driver
management process (i.e., download, setup, and maintenance) for Selenium WebDriver
in a completely automated manner.

WebDriverManager is based on a resolution algorithm that automatically manages
the drivers required by each browser [11]. This algorithm implements the following
steps:

1. *Browser version discovery*. WebDriverManager uses an internal component called
   commands database to execute this step. This database contains a list of shell commands (in different operating systems) that allow discovering the browser versions
   (e.g., `google chrome --version` in Linux).
2. *Driver version discovery*. To that aim, WebDriverManager uses another component
   called *versions database*. This database stores the knowledge to keep the compatibility between the versions of browsers and drivers. Both commands and versions
   database are automatically updated from an online repository. In this way, Web-
   DriverManager always uses the latest knowledge database.

---

[6] https://stackoverflow.com/search?q=this+version+of+chromedriver+only+supports+Chrome+versic
[7] https://bonigarcia.dev/webdrivermanager/.

3. *Driver download.* WebDriverManager downloads the resolved driver, connecting to the proper repository (e.g., chromedriver, geckodriver, msedgedriver, etc.). WebDriverManager stores the downloaded drivers in the local filesystem into a folder called *driver cache.* This driver cache allows reusing the drivers. In addition, WebDriverManager uses a local properties file called *resolution cache.* Inspired by the Domain Name System (DNS), this cache stores the relationship between the resolved driver versions following a time-to-live (TTL) approach [21]. In subsequent invocations, the driver is considered fresh during the TTL (1 day by default). When the TTL expires, the resolution algorithm is executed again. This mechanism prevents the usage of outdated driver versions when the browser automatically gets upgraded.
4. *Driver path export.* Finally, WebDriverManager exports the downloaded driver path using the proper Java system property (e.g., `webdriver.chrome.driver` for chromedriver).

WebDriverManager provides a fluent API based on a set of singletons (called managers) to execute the above mentioned resolution algorithm. These singletons are accessible through the `WebDriverManager` Java class. For instance, it is possible to invoke the method `chromedriver()` to manage the driver required by Chrome, i.e., chromedriver, as follows:

```
WebDriverManager.chromedriver().setup();
WebDriver driver = new ChromeDriver();
```

WebDriverManager promises the following benefits for its users:

1. *Development effort reduction.* The drivers are downloaded automatically and transparently, thanks to the automatic browser and driver discovery. In addition, and thanks to the driver and resolution cache, the resolution algorithm does not affect the overall test performance since the driver management is executed locally during the TTL duration.
2. *Portability.* The resulting Selenium WebDriver test scripts that use WebDriverManager can be executed in different machines without any code change or extra configuration.
3. *Maintainability.* Since the resolution algorithm is executed at runtime, the driver version is checked each time the test script runs. In this way, the driver maintenance is also done automatically and transparently.

3 Experiment Definition, Design and Settings

Based on the Goal Question Metric (GQM) template [2], the main goal of our experiment can be defined as follows: *"Analyze the use of WebDriverManager with the purpose of understanding if there is an impact w.r.t. the management efforts of test suites (in particular due to download, setup, and maintenance of the drivers) from the point of view of SQA Managers and Testers in the context of Junior Testers executing tasks of test suites management."*

Thus, our research questions are:

RQ1. Initial Setup Effort. Does the effort required to setup a test suite project vary when using *WebDriverManager* (or vice-versa) instead of *Plain WebDriver* (i.e., the traditional `setProperty` mechanism to setup the drivers)?

RQ2. Annual Maintenance Effort. How the cumulative yearly effort varies in the time, adopting *WebDriverManager* instead of *Plain WebDriver*, by considering several different releases of the application under test?

To quantitatively investigate the first research question, we measured the time the participants took to setup the test suites using both *Plain WebDriver* and *WebDriverManager*. It is important to note that this initial setup effort is part of the total development effort of a testsuite. For the second research question instead, we evaluated how many time a change in the test suites setup is required during a year (on average) to compute the total time required. In both cases, the time is a proxy for measuring the effort. With these two RQs we can understand the overall effort required for the entire test suites management, i.e., both the test suites first setup and the subsequent maintenance required when the browsers evolve.

The *perspective* is of *SQA Managers* and *Testers* interested in selecting the better option to manage the libraries controlling the web browsers programmatically with the final goal of improving testers productivity. The *context* of the experiment consists of two sample test suites (i.e., the *objects*) both to be implemented with both *Plain WebDriver* and *WebDriverManager* and of *participants*, 25 Computer Science master students.

We conceived and designed the experiment following the guidelines by Wohlin *et al.* [23]. Table 1 summarizes the main elements of the experiment. For replication purposes, the experimental package has been made available: http://sepl.dibris.unige.it/WebDriverManager.php.

Table 1. Overview of the experiment

Goal	Analyse the use of *Plain WebDriver* and *WebDriverManager* during test suites management to understand if there is a difference in terms of required efforts
Quality focus	Effort in test suite management
Context	Objects: two test suites
	Participants: 25 MSc students in Computer Science
Null hypothesis	No effect on effort (measured as time required to complete the tasks)
Treatments	*Plain WebDriver* and *WebDriverManager*
Dependent variable	Time required to complete the tasks

In the following, we present in detail: treatments, objects, participants, design of the experiment, hypotheses, variables and other aspects of the experiment.

Treatment. Our experiment has two treatments: "WD" (*Plain WebDriver*) or "WDM" (*WebDriverManager*). Thus, the tasks require adopting, in the former (latter) case, the *Plain WebDriver* (*WebDriverManager*) libraries.

Objects. The objects of the study are two sample test suites requiring to develop a simple "Hello World" multibrowser test case. In particular, the test case has to be executed on different browsers: Firefox, Chrome, and Edge (for participants working on Linux system, the latter was replaced[8] by Opera). We provided the participants with two similar Eclipse projects containing the code of the "Hello World" test case but with some parts left blank: one project to be completed using *WebDriverManager* and the other to be completed with *Plain WebDriver*, i.e. using the setProperty mechanism (see the previous section). In this way, the entire effort of the participants was focused on the test suite setup and management and not on test case development, since the goal of our experiment.

Participants. The experiment was conducted in a research laboratory under controlled conditions (i.e., online). Participants were 25 students from the Advanced Software Engineering course, in their first year of the MSc degree in Computer Science at the University of Genova (Italy). They had strong skills in the Eclipse IDE usage, matured through the course of the previous year with significant project activity. Automated testing was explained during the Advanced Software Engineering course (i.e., the course in which the experiment was conducted), where detailed explanations on both *Plain WebDriver* and *WebDriverManager* were provided. Students participated into our experiment on a voluntary base, after two mandatory labs about software engineering, including one about unit test automation using both *Plain WebDriver* and *WebDriverManager*. Thus, before the experiment, all the participants have been trained on *Plain WebDriver* and *WebDriverManager* with a one-hour presentation including various kind of test suite management tasks (similar to the ones required in the experiment).

Experiment Design. The experiment adopts a counterbalanced design planned to fit two Lab sessions (see Table 2). Each participant worked in Lab 1 on a treatment and in Lab 2 on the other treatment.

Table 2. Experimental design (WD = *Plain WebDriver*, WDM = *WebDriverManager*)

	Group A	Group B
Lab 1	WD	WDM
Lab 2	WDM	WD

Dependent Variables and Hypothesis Formulation. Our experiment has only one dependent variable, on which treatments are compared measuring the effort construct for which we defined the relative metric (as done, e.g., in [20]). The time required for the test suite management was used as a proxy to measure effort. For each participant and lab, the *Time* variable was recorded by noting down on the experimental sheet. Since

---

[8] Note that the setup of different drivers has approximately the same effort, so adopting different browsers/Drivers do not impact the results of our study.

we could not find any previous empirical evidence that points out a clear advantage of one approach vs. the other, we formulated H_0 as non-directional hypothesis:

H_0. *The use of a test suite management approach w.r.t. the other does not reduce the total effort*

The objective of a statistical analysis is to reject the null hypotheses above, so accepting the corresponding alternative one H_1 (stating instead that an effect exist).

Material, Procedure and Execution.

To answer RQ1, we performed a controlled experiment. Initially, to assess the experimental material and to get an estimate of the time needed to accomplish the tasks, a pilot experiment with a PhD student in Computer Science at University of Genova was performed. The student finished both tasks in 24 min overall and gave us some information on how improving the experimental material, in particular concerning the description of the procedure to follow. Given the times of the student and the time constraint of the labs, we set the total time of the entire experiment to about one hour.

The experiment took place in a laboratory room and was carried on using Eclipse. The participants participated in two laboratory sessions (Lab 1 and Lab 2), with a short ten-minutes break between them. Finally, they were asked to compile a post-experiment questionnaire. It included questions about: availability of sufficient time to complete the tasks, documentation clarity, exercise usefulness, willingness to adopt *WebDriverManager* and *Plain WebDriver* in some future real-world projects, competencies required.

For each group (see Table 2), each lab session required to setup a test suite using *Plain WebDriver* and *WebDriverManager*, respectively. For each Lab session, we provided to the participants a detailed procedure to follow in order to complete the setup of the test suite: the procedure to setup a multi-browser test suite for *Plain WebDriver* and *WebDriverManager* are different but have an initial part in common that is devoted to the standard configuration of the Eclipse project containing the test suite and low level WebDriver setup (also required when using *WebDriverManager*). For this reason, we asked to the participants to record three times for each test suite: (a) the starting time; (b) the ending time for the common part (Part 1); (c) the final time of the complete test suite setup (Part 2). The time spent between (a) and (b) is expected to be almost equal (Part 1), for each participant, for both the treatments (i.e., *Plain WebDriver* and *WebDriverManager*), while the difference, if any, should appear in the time spent between (b) and (c), (Part 2)

To answer RQ2, we decided to note down the number of releases in last three years (April 2019, March 2022) of the various drivers related to the browsers used in the experiment (Chrome[9], Firefox[10], Edge[11], and Opera[12], for the students using Linux). Then, we computed the average number of annual releases for each driver. We combined the additional Time efforts derived from RQ1 with the number of releases in order to compute a minimum effort estimate. Indeed, they do not include several other efforts that cannot be measured with the data of this study but can be by far higher, overall. It is important to highlight that in general it is considered a good practice to maintain the

---

[9] https://chromedriver.chromium.org/.

[10] https://github.com/mozilla/geckodriver.

[11] https://developer.microsoft.com/en-us/microsoft-edge/tools/webdriver/.

[12] https://github.com/operasoftware/operachromiumdriver/.

drivers always updated. However, in case the test suite does not use advanced Selenium WebDriver commands, often even a slightly outdated driver can work fine providing only minor warnings during execution. In this study, to adhere to quality standards, we computed the efforts of maintaining the drivers always updated to the latest version, as it can be required in the case of complex industrial case studies requiring to reach the maximum reliability.

Analysis Procedure. Because of the sample size we adopted non-parametric tests to check the null hypothesis. This choice follows the suggestions given by [16, Chapter 37]. In particular, after computing descriptive statistics, we applied the following analysis procedure: since participants setup two test suites with the two possible treatments (i.e., *Plain WebDriver* and *WebDriverManager*), we used a paired Wilcoxon test to compare the effects of the two treatments on each participant. In the performed statistical tests, we decided, as it is customary, to accept a probability of 5% of committing Type-I-error [23], i.e., rejecting the null hypothesis when it is actually true ($\alpha = 0.05$). While the statistical tests allow checking the presence of significant differences, they do not provide any information about the magnitude of such a difference. Therefore, we used the non-parametric Cliff's delta (d) effect size [12]. The effect size is considered small for $0.148 \leq |d| < 0.33$, medium for $0.33 \leq |d| < 0.474$ and large for $|d| \geq 0.474$.

4   Results

To answer **RQ1**, let us start with a short description of the results from the experiment, analyzing the effect of the main factor on the dependent variable. Table 3 summarizes the essential descriptive statistics (i.e., median, mean, and standard deviation) of *Time*.

Table 3. *Time*: descriptive statistics per treatment. Overall results and detail for part 1 and part 2 measured in minutes.

Exp.	Plain WebDriver			WebDriverManager		
	Mean	Median	SD	Mean	Median	SD
Part 1	3.400	2	3.697	3.800	3	2.784
Part 2	17.520	16	8.106	10.280	9	5.120
Total	21.120	19	9.144	14.080	12	8.495

Figure 1 (left) summarizes the distribution of the *Time* required to complete the Part 1 of the experiment by means of boxplots. Observations are grouped by treatment (*Plain WebDriver* and *WebDriverManager*). The y-axis represents the time measured in minutes. The boxplots clearly show, as expected, that the participants spent a similar time to complete Part 1. By applying a Wilcoxon test (paired analysis), we found that for Part 1, the difference in terms of time is not statistically significant, as p-value=0.7739.

Figure 1 (center) summarizes the distribution of the *Time* required to complete the Part 2 of the experiment by means of boxplots. The boxplots clearly show that the

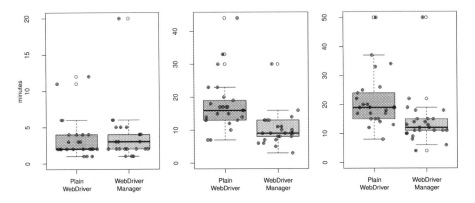

Fig. 1. Boxplots of time for completing Part 1 (left) and Part 2 (center) of the experiment. Boxplots on the right show total time (Part 1 + Part 2). For optimizing the readability each boxplots pair has been shown with optimal Y-scale values.

participants spent a different time to complete Part 2 depending on the treatment. By applying a Wilcoxon test (paired analysis), we found that for Part 2, the difference in terms of time is statistically significant, as p-value=0.000392. The effect size is large d=-0.7008.

Figure 1 (right) summarizes the distribution of the *Time* required to complete the setup of the test suites by means of boxplots. As for Part 2, also in this case boxplots clearly show that the participants spent a different time to setup the entire test suites depending on the treatment. By applying a Wilcoxon test (paired analysis), we found that overall, the difference in terms of correctness is still statistically significant, as p-value=0.0004862. The effect size is large d=-0.6288. Therefore, we can reject the null hypothesis H_0 and accept H_1.

> **RQ1 Summary**: The adoption of *WebDriverManager* instead of *Plain WebDriver* significantly reduces (of about −33%) the time required to setup a multi-browser test suite.

RQ2: Table 4 summarizes the statistics of the analyzed drivers, in particular it reports the number of releases available on the official repositories in the three-years interval we decided to analyze, the identifier of the first and last version considered, and the average number of releases for each year.

While analyzing the results for RQ1, we discovered that the time required to setup a multi-browser test suite (i.e., including three drivers) using *WebDriverManager* is, on average, of about 7 min (21.120-14.080, see Table 3) lower compared with the time needed when using only *Plain WebDriver* (i.e., manual driver management). Thus, the additional time effort due to the manual management of each of the three drivers can be estimated in about 2 min and 20 s per driver. This value appears reasonable since represents the time required to (a) visit the official software repository for the driver of a specific browser, (b) download the driver executable file, and (c) place it in the correct directory as reported in the test suite settings.

Table 4. *Drivers*: Details of the drivers considered in the 3 years interval (April 2019–March 2022) to answer RQ2. For each driver, we reported the number of releases available on the official repositories, the identifier of the first and last version considered and the average number of releases for each year.

Releases	Chrome driver	Firefox driver	Edge driver	Opera driver
04/19->03/22	58	7	1128	25
First version	75.0.3770.8	0.25.0	75.0.139.20	2.45
Last version	100.0.4896.60	0.30.0	101.0.1210.0	99.0.4844.51
Avg. Annual	19.33	2.33	376.00	8.33

Table 5. *Drivers*: Annual effort of maintaining the drivers updated to the latest releases available on the repositories.

Effort (Time)	Chrome driver	Firefox driver	Edge driver	Opera driver
Annual estimate	45.10 m	5.43 m	877.33 m	19.44 m

The estimated annual efforts (Time) of maintaining the drivers updated to the latest releases available on the repositories is reported in Table 5. These estimates include only the bare time required to update the drivers; however, they do not include the major efforts of having a multitude of "false alarms". Such "false alarms" are due to the test suites reporting problems or errors during their runs usually scheduled overnight not caused by real regression of the application under test but only by outdated drivers. A false alarm can require to perform a non-negligible troubleshooting to pin-point the root cause of the problem (i.e., the outdated driver) and differentiate it from the real regressions in the application under test. Moreover, having a large number of "false alarms" could drastically reduce the confidence of the test managers in the usage of E2E test suites.

By looking Table 4, it is evident that the update frequency of the various drivers is by far different when considering the various browsers: by 2.33 times a year for Firefox to 376 for Edge. Even excluding Edge, for the three remaining drivers we can observe about 30 novel driver releases per year. This translates in about a "false alarm" every about 12 days. Although it may seem little, we have experienced in industrial collaborations that this frequency of false alarms is considered a big problem by our industrial partners [18].

RQ2 Summary: The times required for maintaining updated the drivers in a test suite for an entire year span from a few minutes (5.43) to several hours (14.61h) depending on the browser (and thus driver) used for such test suite. However, the time for updating the outdated driver is only a small fraction of the total effort that includes: (a) understanding that the outdated driver is the cause of the problems reported during the execution of the test suite and (b) the reduction in the perceived reliability of E2E test suites. The adoption of *WebDriverManager* can help to drastically reduce all these efforts.

4.1   Post-Experiment Questionnaire

The post-experiment questionnaire is summarized in Table 6, together with the medians of the answers given by the students. The possible choices for each answer, on a 5-point Likert scale, were: Strongly Agree (1), Agree (2), Unsure (3), Disagree (4), Strongly Disagree (5).

Table 6. Post-experiment questionnaire, medians and avg. of the answers

ID	Question	Median	Avg.
PQ1	*WebDriverManager* simplifies driver management and thus speeds up code production	Strongly agree	1.28
PQ2	*WebDriverManager* is also useful during the maintenance phase when browsers are updated automatically	Agree	1.56
PQ3	*WebDriverManager* is simple to use	Strongly agree	1.36
PQ4	*WebDriverManager* is useful	Strongly agree	1.16
PQ5	Finding the right driver to use, consulting the documentation, isn't always easy	Agree	2.24
PQ6	When developing the Selenium WebDriver test suites in the future, I will definitely use *WebDriverManager*	Strongly agree	1.52
PQ7	I found the exercise useful	Strongly agree	1.24
PQ8	I had enough knowledge to answer the questions (i.e., training was sufficient)	Agree	1.80

Students perceived the adoption of *WebDriverManager* as a positive factor supporting both the initial test suites setup (PQ1 median strongly agree) and the subsequent maintenance (PQ2 median agree). They found also *WebDriverManager* simple to use (PQ3 median strongly agree) and useful (PQ4 median strongly agree). They consider the necessary setup operations (for example, how to find the driver) difficult (PQ5 median agree). Finally, they would choose *WebDriverManager* in the future to develop and maintain Selenium test suites (PQ6 median strongly agree).

As experimenters, we are also comforted by the medians relative to PQ7 and PQ8 as the students considered the exercise carried out during the experiment useful and considered the training phase to be sufficient.

4.2   Threats to Validity

This section discusses the threats to validity that could affect our results: *internal, conclusion* and *external* validity threats [23].

Internal validity threats concern factors that may affect a dependent variable (in our case, *Time*). Since the students had to participate in two labs (*WebDriverManager* and *Plain WebDriver*), a learning/fatigue effect may intervene. However, the students were previously trained and the chosen experimental design, with a break between the two labs, should limit this effect. Moreover, the tasks are not really demanding and long (1 h in total), so we believe that fatigue is not an issue.

Threats to *conclusion validity* can be due to the sample size of the experiment (in our case, 25 MSc students) that may limit the capability of statistical tests to reveal any effect, and the object size, that could be insufficient to significantly reveal any effect. However, the Wilcoxon test provided sharp results and the difference between the two treatments is relevant.

Threats to *external validity* can be related to the use of students as experimental participants. We cannot expect students to perform as well as professionals, but we expect to be able to observe similar trends as in other studies [3, 14, 15]. Clearly, further experiments with different test suites and/or more experienced developers (e.g., software practitioners) are needed to confirm or contrast the obtained results.

5   Related Work

The driver management process related to Selenium WebDriver is a novel technique first reported in the Selenium ecosystem survey by García et al. [8]. That article presented the results of a descriptive study conducted in 2019 by 72 participants from 24 countries. That study revealed how practitioners use Selenium concerning its main features, test development, System Under Test (SUT), test infrastructure, testing frameworks, community, or personal experience. Regarding driver management, that survey revealed that 38.89% of the respondents declared to manage driver managers manually, while 34.72% of the respondents declared to carry out this process automatically. The remaining users (26.39%) claimed not to know how drivers are managed in their test codebase. This outcome indicates that around a third of the Selenium users have already adopted automated driver management but remain manual (or unknown) by most users.

In this line, another work by García et al. [11] presents a complete methodology to carry out the driver management process in three stages: download, setup, and maintenance. The reference implementation of that methodology is WebDriverManager. This paper evaluated the usability of the WebDriverManager API following Clarke's dimensions [5]. Nevertheless, the benefits of WebDriverManager for Selenium WebDriver users related to development effort reduction or improved maintainability remain unexplored in that paper.

Finally, again García et al. [10] presents Selenium-Jupiter, a JUnit 5 extension for Selenium WebDriver. Jupiter is the name given to the programming model provided by JUnit 5 [6]. Selenium-Jupiter aims to ease the development of Selenium WebDriver tests thanks to an automated driver management process and the seamless integration with Docker. Selenium-Jupiter delegates the automation of the driver management to WebDriverManager. Then, and thanks to the use of Docker, Selenium-Jupiter allows advanced features for cross-browser testing, load testing, or troubleshooting (e.g., session recordings). That paper presented an end-to-end performance testing example case about video conferencing systems based on WebRTC [9]. That paper suggests that development and maintenance costs promise to be lower using an automated driver management process. Nevertheless, it does not provide any experimental validation of these benefits, declared as future research in that paper.

In addition to the empirical work related to the driver mechanism already mentioned in the context of Selenium WebDriver test cases, there are several other articles in the literature dealing with the comparison of testing tools for Web [17] and Mobile applications [1] and codeless testing frameworks [13, 19].

6   Conclusions and Future Work

In this paper, we have described a controlled experiment aimed at quantifying the benefits of adopting *WebDriverManager*, an open source Java library that carries out automatically the driver management process in the context of Selenium WebDriver test suites. *WebDriverManager* has been proposed to alleviate the burden of the developers in maintaining the drivers updated w.r.t. the actual browsers installed on the testing machine.

Results of the experiment with 25 MSc students show that the adoption of *WebDriverManager* (instead of *Plain WebDriver*) significantly reduces the time required to setup/update a multi-browser test suite (p-value < 0.01). Even if the actual saving for updating a single outdated version of a driver can be quantified in a just few minutes, our analyses show that in a multi-browser test suite this maintenance intervention is required quite often. Moreover, the time for updating the outdated driver is only a fraction of the total efforts that usually include other efforts difficult to quantify: (a) understanding that the outdated driver is the cause of the problems reported by the failing test suite and, (b) the reduction in the perceived reliability of E2E test suites. The adoption of *WebDriverManager* can help to reduce all these efforts.

As a future work, we plan to further extend our experiment with replication including participants having different skills such as professional Testers and PhD students in Software Engineering. Moreover, we are organizing with the help of a industrial partner a long term case study to evaluate the actual benefits of *WebDriverManager* on the field.

Acknowledgement. This work was partially supported in part by the Ministerio de Ciencia e Innovación-Agencia Estatal de Investigación (10.13039/501100011033) through the H2O Learn project under Grant PID2020-112584RB-C31, and in part by the Madrid Regional Government through the e-Madrid-CM Project under Grant S2018/TCS-4307.

References

1. Ardito, L., Coppola, R., Morisio, M., Torchiano, M.: Espresso vs. eyeautomate: an experiment for the comparison of two generations of android gui testing. In: Proceedings of the Evaluation and Assessment on Software Engineering, EASE 2019, pp. 13–22. Association for Computing Machinery, New York (2019). https://doi.org/10.1145/3319008.3319022
2. Basili, V.R., Caldiera, G., Rombach, H.D.: The goal question metric approach. In: Encyclopedia of Software Engineering, Wiley, Hoboken (1994)
3. Cerioli, M., Lagorio, G., Leotta, M., Ricca, F.: Fight silent horror unit test methods by consulting a TestWizard. J. Softw. Evol. Proc. (JSEP) e2396 (2022). https://doi.org/10.1002/smr.2396
4. Cerioli, M., Leotta, M., Ricca, F.: What 5 million job advertisements tell us about testing: a preliminary empirical investigation. In: Proceedings of the 35th Annual ACM Symposium on Applied Computing, pp. 1586–1594 (2020)
5. Clarke, S.: Measuring API usability. Dr. Dobb's J. Windows/.NET Suppl. **9**(5), S6–S9 (2004)
6. Garcia, B.: Mastering Software Testing with JUnit 5: Comprehensive Guide to Develop high Quality Java Applications. Packt Publishing Ltd, Birmingham (2017)
7. García, B.: Hands-On Selenium WebDriver with Java. O'Reilly Media, Sebastopol (2022)
8. García, B., Gallego, M., Gortázar, F., Munoz-Organero, M.: A survey of the selenium ecosystem. Electronics **9**(7), 1067 (2020)
9. Garcia, B., Gortazar, F., Lopez-Fernandez, L., Gallego, M., Paris, M.: WebRTC testing: challenges and practical solutions. IEEE Commun. Stand. Mag. **1**(2), 36–42 (2017)
10. García, B., Kloos, C.D., Alario-Hoyos, C., Munoz-Organero, M.: Selenium-jupiter: a JUnit 5 extension for selenium WebDriver. J. Syst. Softw. **189**, 111298 (2022)

11. García, B., Munoz-Organero, M., Alario-Hoyos, C., Kloos, C.D.: Automated driver management for selenium WebDriver. Empir. Softw. Eng. **26**(5), 1–51 (2021). https://doi.org/10.1007/s10664-021-09975-3

12. Grissom, R.J., Kim, J.J.: Effect sizes for Research: A Broad Practical Approach. 2nd edn. Lawrence Earlbaum Associates, Mahwah (2005)

13. Kirinuki, H., Matsumoto, S., Higo, Y., Kusumoto, S.: NLP-assisted web element identification toward script-free testing. In: 2021 IEEE International Conference on Software Maintenance and Evolution (ICSME), pp. 639–643 (2021). https://doi.org/10.1109/ICSME52107.2021.00072

14. Leotta, M., Biagiola, M., Ricca, F., Ceccato, M., Tonella, P.: A family of experiments to assess the impact of page object pattern in web test suite development. In: Proceedings of 13th IEEE International Conference on Software Testing, Verification and Validation (ICST 2020), pp. 263–273. IEEE (2020). https://doi.org/10.1109/ICST46399.2020.00035

15. Leotta, M., Cerioli, M., Olianas, D., Ricca, F.: Two experiments for evaluating the impact of Hamcrest and AssertJ on assertion development. Software Qual. J. **28**(3), 1113–1145 (2020). https://doi.org/10.1007/s11219-020-09507-0

16. Motulsky, H.: Intuitive Biostatistics: a Non-Mathematical Guide to Statistical Thinking. Oxford University Press, Oxford (2010)

17. Naidu, T.J., Basri, N.A., Nagenthram, S.: SAHI vs. selenium: a comparative analysis. In: 2014 International Conference on Contemporary Computing and Informatics (IC3I), pp. 967–970 (2014). https://doi.org/10.1109/IC3I.2014.7019594

18. Olianas, D., Leotta, M., Ricca, F., Villa, L.: Reducing flakiness in end-to-end test suites: an experience report. In: Paiva, A.C.R., Cavalli, A.R., Ventura Martins, P., Pérez-Castillo, R. (eds.) QUATIC 2021. CCIS, vol. 1439, pp. 3–17. Springer, Cham (2021). https://doi.org/10.1007/978-3-030-85347-1_1

19. Phuc Nguyen, D., Maag, S.: Codeless web testing using selenium and machine learning. In: ICSOFT 2020: 15th International Conference on Software Technologies, pp. 51–60. 15th International Conference on Software and Data Technologies (ICSOFT), ScitePress, France, July 2020. https://doi.org/10.5220/0009885400510060

20. Ricca, F., Torchiano, M., Leotta, M., Tiso, A., Guerrini, G., Reggio, G.: On the impact of state-based model-driven development on maintainability: a family of experiments using UniMod. Empir. Softw. Eng. **23**(3), 1743–1790 (2017). https://doi.org/10.1007/s10664-017-9563-8

21. Sazoglu, F.B., Cambazoglu, B.B., Ozcan, R., Altingovde, I.S., Ulusoy, Ö.: Strategies for setting time-to-live values in result caches. In: Proceedings of the 22nd ACM International Conference on Information & Knowledge Management, pp. 1881–1884 (2013)

22. Stewart, S., Burns, D.: WebDriver, W3C Working Draft. https://www.w3.org/TR/webdriver/ (2022). Accessed 1 Apr 2022

23. Wohlin, C., Runeson, P., Höst, M., Ohlsson, M., Regnell, B., Wesslén, A.: Experimentation in Software Engineering - An Introduction. Kluwer Academic Publishers, Dordrecht (2000)

Assessing Black-box Test Case Generation Techniques for Microservices

Luca Giamattei[✉][iD], Antonio Guerriero[iD], Roberto Pietrantuono[iD], and Stefano Russo[iD]

DIETI, Università Degli Studi di Napoli Federico II, Napoli, Italy
{luca.giamattei,antonio.guerriero,
roberto.pietrantuono,stefano.russo}@unina.it

Abstract. Testing of microservices architectures (MSA) – today a popular software architectural style - demands for automation in its several tasks, like tests generation, prioritization and execution. Automated black-box generation of test cases for MSA currently borrows techniques and tools from the testing of RESTful Web Services.

This paper: *i)* proposes the UTEST stateless pairwise combinatorial technique (and its automation tool) for test cases generation for functional and robustness microservices testing, and *ii)* experimentally compares - with three open-source MSA used as subjects - four state-of-the-art black-box tools conceived for Web Services, adopting evolutionary-, dependencies- and mutation-based generation techniques, and the proposed UTEST combinatorial tool.

The comparison shows little differences in coverage values; UTEST pairwise testing achieves better average failure rate with a considerably lower number of tests. Web Services tools do not perform for MSA as well as a tester might expect, highlighting the need for MSA-specific techniques.

Keywords: Microservices · Black-box testing · Robustness testing

1 Introduction

Microservice Architectures (MSA) are a service-oriented software architectural style where services are loosely coupled, run in their own processes, and interact via lightweight mechanisms [1]. These characteristics favours services' development by different teams and possibly in various programming languages, and their independent deployment. MSA are often engineered with agile practices, enabling rapid and frequent software releases (even many per day).

Testing automation is essential to fully benefit from the MSA architectural paradigm and related practices. Techniques for black-box (or specification-based) automated generation of test cases for microservices are mainly borrowed from testing of RESTful web services, enabled by documentation of their interfaces [2]. The most notable open format for specifying web services and MSA Application

A. Vallecillo et al. (Eds.): QUATIC 2022, CCIS 1621, pp. 46–60, 2022.
https://doi.org/10.1007/978-3-031-14179-9_4

Programming Interfaces (API) is OpenAPI/Swagger [3].[1] Specifications include service Uniform Resource Identifier (URI), HTTP method, type and name of every parameter, and HTTP body. OpenAPI allows to automatically retrieve the interface of a microservice of interest from its IP address and port number.

Testing RESTful services may be challenging, due to dependencies of tests from the state of internal resources (e.g., a database) or from external services [2]. Thus, many test generation techniques are stateful [4–6]. They aim at maximizing coverage values, like those defined by Martin-Lopez *et al.* [7].

With respect to generic RESTful web services, microservices are expected to have finer granularity and to be self-contained (being designed with a single business responsibility), polyglot and independent. An MSA typically includes many RESTful services, whose complex dependencies are challenging to cover by stateful techniques when microservices are tested independently.

This paper provides an empirical comparison of five techniques for test case generation for microservices. Four of them are state-of-the-art techniques for RESTful web services, claimed to be applicable to microservices, namely: Evo-Master [2], RestTestGen [4], RESTler [5] and bBOXRT [8]. The fifth technique (uTEST) is a pairwise combinatorial strategy that we propose here with its support tool, which automatically retrieves OpenAPI specifications of microservices to test, generates test cases, executes them and gathers results.

The experimental comparison uses as subjects three well-known open-source MSA (Train Ticket, SockShop, FTGO), with reference to two scenarios:

i) generation of a suite of tests with only *valid* inputs, i.e., adhering to the service API specification; this is a typical functional testing scenario;
ii) generation of a test suite with both *valid* and *invalid* inputs (thus including tests violating the specification); this may serve to test the service for robustness against unexpected inputs, or for coverage of return codes.

The results of experiments show that tools reach comparable values for eight coverage metrics (five input and three output coverage metrics), but exhibit different average failure rate and test generation/execution cost. The proposed combinatorial approach shows to be more cost-effective as it generates a lower number of test cases - thus exhibiting the best average failure rate.

The rest of the paper is so organized: Sect. 2 discusses related work. Section 3 describes uTEST. Sections 4 and 5 present experiments and results, respectively. Section 6 discusses threats to validity. Section 7 contains final remarks.

2   Related Work

Automated black-box generation of test cases specifically for microservices is a research topic not much investigated so far, yet techniques/tools for Web Services may by applied to microservices as well.

A state-of-the-art tool for automated testing of RESTful web services is Evo-Master [2]; initially conceived for white-box testing, it has been extended for

---

[1] https://www.openapis.org.

black-box testing. This is performed by random testing, adding heuristics to maximize the HTTP response code coverage. During the evolutionary search, EvoMaster runs tests as HTTP service requests and evaluates the fitness of every generation (in the evolutionary meaning) of test cases. The test suite is produced in several formats (e.g., for JUnit).

RestTestGen is a stateful test generator proposed by Corradini et al. [4], that infers operation dependencies, first statically from OpenAPI specifications, and then dynamically, using feedback from executed tests. Input values are generated from a dictionary, from documentation examples, randomly, or re-using past observed values. It generates nominal as well as invalid test cases; these are obtained by mutating successful test cases (those that returned 2xx or 4xx HTTP codes), e.g. by removing values of mandatory parameters.

RESTler has been proposed by Atlidakis et al. at Microsoft Research [5], as a tool for stateful input generation via fuzzing, aiming to find security vulnerabilities. It generates sequences of requests based on data dependencies among operations. These are detected by first statically inferring producer-consumer relations from the OpenAPI specification, and then - like RestTestGen - dynamically analyzing responses of executed tests. Input values are selected from a user-configurable dictionary, or from previously observed values.

bBOXRT is a tool for robustness testing of REST services proposed by Laranjeiro et al. [8]. The authors designed a method for injecting faults in requests, attempting to trigger erroneous behaviors. The tool generates and executes valid requests with random values compliant with the OpenAPI specification, and then mutates inputs observing the system behaviour under a faulty workload. bBOXRT supports a large number of mutations of input parameters values.

Martin-Lopez et al. [6] propose a black-box technique/tool RESTest for RESTful APIs, based on dependencies among parameters, expressed in an Inter-parameter Dependency Language (IDL). Results may benefit from available additional information on dependencies, that however testers need to write in IDL; this is time-consuming and requires a deep knowledge of the system under test.

Three further OpenAPI-based techniques are proposed by Ed-douibi et al. [9], Karlsson et al. [10], and Banias et al. [11]. The first generates (JUnit) tests inferring both valid and invalid parameter values. The second (QuickREST) includes property-based stateless and stateful generators, that are compared in response codes coverage and fault finding ability. The third performs combinatorial generation, adding human intervention to augment the quality of the generation.

An important empirical comparison of black-box techniques for RESTful services, based on the coverage metrics of Martin-Lopez et al. [7], has been presented by Corradini et al. [12]. They analyzed existing tools and selected a number of them for comparison based on "robustness", meant as the ability to run on different case studies. The compared tools include RestTestGen [4], RESTler [5] and bBOXRT [8], but not EvoMaster, whose black-box version was not available yet, and RESTest, that did not pass the robustness filtering.

With respect to the analyzed literature, our contribution is twofold: *i)* we propose the UTEST automated stateless combinatorial test generation technique for microservices; *ii)* we analyze experimentally the performance of the main existing tools for Web Services when used for testing MSA, and compare UTEST to them. Table 1 summarizes compared tools.[2]

Table 1. Compared tools/techniques

Tool	Test specification	Test case generation
EvoMaster [2]	State-based	Evolutionary
RestTestGen [4]	State-based	Data/Operation dependencies random dictionary mutation
RESTler [5]	State-based	Data/Operation dependencies dictionary
bBOXRT [8]	Classes from API specification	Random mutation
UTEST	Classes from API specification combinatorial	Random

3   The UTEST combinatorial testing strategy

3.1   Background

Combinatorial design is a consolidated strategy for automatic test generation [13], extensively studied in the literature [14]. It aims to detect multi-factor faults with the use of combinatorial methods, that demonstrated good fault detection ability [15]. The definition of an Input Space Model, to identify factors (and their values) that might affect the output, is crucial in this strategy. Exhaustive enumeration of all combinations of factor's values can be impractical, as these rapidly explode in number [16]. A solution is to generate a so-called *t-way* test suite, composed of (a subset of all) combinations of t factors.

3.2   Combinatorial Test Case Generation Strategy

We adopt a *pairwise* strategy to generate a *2-way* test suite covering combinations of pairs of input classes. Tests are derived from the specification of the microservice; factors are the parameters of HTTP requests, and their values are generated in compliance to the specification. For any pair of classes c_i, c_j of parameters p_i, p_j, a test case is generated with values $v_i \in c_i$ and $v_j \in c_j$, respectively.

The generation of a *test suite* is composed of three main steps:

---

[2] Our comparison does not include the techniques in references [6,9,10], and [11], whose tools are probably still at proof-of-concept stage. For instance, like Corradini *et al.* [12] we did not manage to run RESTest on our case studies. However, differently from [12], our comparison includes Evomaster, besides RestTestGen, Restler, bBOXRT.

1. Input space partitioning. The OpenAPI specification of all microservices in the MSA is parsed to extract an Input Space Model consisting of HTTP methods, URIs and body templates, HTTP status codes and parameters' details (type, bounds, default value, etc.); equivalence classes for all parameters are then categorized into valid and invalid.
2. Test cases specification. Based on equivalence classes, test cases specifications are produced according to a pairwise combinatorial strategy.
3. Test cases generation. Actual test cases are generated, randomly choosing values from equivalence classes based on the test cases specifications.

Listing 1. A sample microservice OpenAPI specification

```
host:        exampleHost:8080
paths:       '/carts/{customerId}/items':
             post:
             parameters:
                 - name: customerId
                 in: path
                 required: true
                 type: string
                 example: 579f21ae98684924944651bf
                 - name: body
                 in: body
                 required: true
                 schema: '$ref': '#/definitions/CartItem'
             responses:
                 '201': description: 'Created'
                 '400': description: 'Bad Request'
definitions: CartItem:
                 type: object
                 properties:
                   itemId:
                         type: Integer
                   discount:
                         type: boolean
                 required:
                 - itemId
```

Listing 1 shows a snippet of the OpenAPI specification of a microservice with three parameters - one *in path* (`customerId`, required) and two *in body* (`itemId`, required, and `discount`, optional). It returns 201 or 400 HTTP status codes.

At step 1, the domain of values of each parameter is partitioned into *equivalence classes*. We define them like Bertolino *et al.* [17], based on the parameter type and, when specified, value bounds, example value, default value, and obligatoriness. Then, we categorize classes into *valid* or *invalid*: valid classes (invalid classes) contain for input parameters only values compliant to (violating) the microservice specification. An example of input space partitioning for the microservice of Listing 1 is shown in Table 2.

At step 2, *test case specifications* are derived. Table 3 shows an example for the microservice of Listing 1, derived from the partitioning of Table 2. The URI and body templates include for each parameter the equivalence classes, from which a value shall be chosen for a test case. For instance, a test case generated from the specification in Table 3 shall have for p_1 (*customerId*) a value chosen from class $c_{1,2}$ (the *example* value in Listing 1); for p_2 (*itemId*) a value from class $c_{2,2}$ (negative value in range), and for p_3 (*discount*) the value *true* or *false*.

Table 2. Input space partitioning for the microservice of Listing 1

Parameter	Name	Type	Equivalence classes	Category
p_1 *(required, in path)*	*customerId*	*string*	$c_{1,1}$: string in range	*valid*
			$c_{1,2}$: specified example value(s)	*valid*
			$c_{1,3}$: empty string	*invalid*
			$c_{1,4}$: no string	*invalid*
p_2 *(required, in body)*	*itemId*	*integer*	$c_{2,1}$: positive value in range	*valid*
			$c_{2,2}$: negative value in range	*valid*
			$c_{2,3}$: alphanumeric string	*invalid*
			$c_{2,4}$: no value	*invalid*
p_3 *(optional, in body)*	*discount*	*boolean*	$c_{3,1}$: {true,false}	*valid*
			$c_{3,2}$: no value	*valid*
			$c_{3,3}$: empty string	*invalid*
			$c_{3,4}$: alphanumeric string	*invalid*

Table 3. A test case specification for the microservice of Listing 1

URI template	http://examplehost:8080/carts/ $\{c_{1,2}\}$/items
HTTP method	POST
body template	{ "*itemId*":$\{c_{2,2}\}$, "*discount*":$\{c_{3,1}\}$}
HTTP status code	201, 400

A *test suite* shall entail test cases combining values from input classes according to a pairwise strategy. To this aim, uTEST uses a recursive algorithm. Two *valid* equivalence classes per parameter are selected to generate a nominal test suite (when available, examples and default values are preferred as valid classes). Then, for each method of each path uTEST builds a binary tree, whose leaves represent all combinations of classes. The tree for the example of Listing 1 is shown in Fig. 1, having selected the (only) two valid classes for each parameter in Table 2; leaves represent all combinations of pairs of selected classes. Test case specifications like the one in Table 3 shall be generated only for the subset of four combinations in the red boxes in Fig. 1 (output combinations), which includes all possible pairs of classes selected for the three parameters; the example of Table 3 corresponds to the combination in the green box. For functional and robustness testing, one *valid* and one *invalid* class are selected per parameter.

At step 3, actual test cases are finally generated, by randomly picking values from equivalence classes defined in the produced test cases specifications. This is done statically: no test is generated depending on the result of the execution of some previous tests. We call *valid test cases* those containing for all parameters values belonging to valid equivalence classes. We call *invalid test cases* those where the value of at least one parameter belongs to an invalid class.

3.3 The uTEST tool

The proposed pairwise strategy is prototyped in the uTEST tool, whose architecture is in Fig. 2. It is designed as a microservice deployable in a Docker container along with the MSA under test; it retrieves the API of microservices in

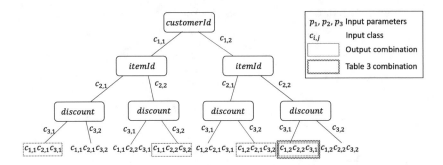

Fig. 1. Generation of valid test cases specifications for microservice of Listing 1

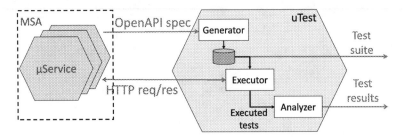

Fig. 2. uTEST architecture

the MSA, including those not directly accessible by the user perspective (e.g., hidden behind a gateway or so-called edge microservices). uTEST includes a *Generator* of the test suite, a tests' *Executor*, and an *Analyzer*, for the computation of coverage metrics.

The generator is fed with a specification (currently, in OpenAPI version 2.0) of the entry points of the microservice under test. uTEST automatically retrieves the specifications of application's microservices, exposed through an OpenAPI interface. Otherwise, it is possible to feed specifications to uTEST manually. uTEST pairwise generation produces test cases specifications for all combinations of two selected equivalence classes of any pair of input parameters. The generated test suite is stored inside the Docker container and can be executed (or exported) by the tester.

Tests are run by the *Executor* which sends HTTP requests to microservices. It is possible to execute requests also in case of authentication, credentials or tokens must be specified in the configuration file. This component provides, as output, all the request-response pairs. The responses are automatically evaluated based on the HTTP response code. We consider failures the *5xx* codes, as they point out the inability of the service to perform the request, due to an error condition, an unhandled exception, or in general an unexpected behaviour.

The *Analyzer* takes a set of request-response couples as input from the *Executor*, and provides a set of basic statistics as output. It provides the results of the test process as output to console and/or to file.

Table 4. Experimental subjects

MSA	Microservices	URIs	Methods	Lines of code
TrainTicket	34	1,152	1,442	20,015
SockShop	5	24	29	5,287
FTGO	7	16	16	14,976

Further details on the implementation and on usage can be found in the GitHub repository[3].

4   Experimental Comparison

4.1   Subjects

For the experimentation, we consider as subjects three open-source MSA, publicly available on GitHub. They are:

- TrainTicket[4]: a benchmark MSA (a booking system for train tickets) [18];
- SockShop[5]: the user-facing part of an online shop that sells socks;
- FTGO[6]: the Richardson's book sample MSA [19].

Table 4 lists their characteristics.

4.2   Experiments

To investigate the ability of the tools in generating effective test cases, we consider the following two scenarios:

- Scenario 1 (functional testing): *valid test cases*;
- Scenario 2 (functional and robustness testing) *valid* and *invalid test cases*.

Scenario 1 is meant to test the MSA behavior with inputs complying to the API. Here we compare EvoMaster and uTest; additionally, we consider as baseline the generation of a single test per method with randomly chosen valid input values (in the example in Fig. 1, this corresponds to the leaf at extreme left).

Scenario 2 mixes both valid and invalid inputs; the latter emulate a robustness testing scenario, where input specifications are intentionally violated for instance to verify return of proper status codes, or to check how the MSA reacts to unexpected inputs. For this scenario we compare RestTestGen, bBOXRT, RESTler and uTest (EvoMaster does not generate invalid inputs). The *baseline* in this Scenario is the generation of two tests per method, one with all parameter values chosen from valid classes and one with all values from invalid classes (this is a sort of *1-way* testing).

The compared tools were configured, when possible, with the values that were shown in the literature to yield the best performance, otherwise with default values. We ran tests 10 times for each microservice of the three subjects.

---

[3] https://github.com/uDEVOPS2020/uTest.
[4] https://github.com/FudanSELab/train-ticket.
[5] https://github.com/microservices-demo/microservices-demo.
[6] https://github.com/microservices-patterns/ftgo-application.

Table 5. Coverage metrics (as defined in ref. [12])

Coverage metric	Description
Path	Ratio of the number of tested paths to the total number of paths documented in the OpenAPI specification. 100% path coverage if its tests send at least one request directed to each path of the API
Operation	Ratio of the number of tested operations to the total number of operations described in the OpenAPI specification. 100% operation coverage if there exists at least one request directed to each path for all documented HTTP methods.
Parameter	Ratio of the number of input parameters used by test cases to the total number of parameters documented in the OpenAPI specification. 100% parameter coverage if all input parameters of all operations are included in requests at least once.
Parameter value	Ratio of the number of the exercised parameter values to the total number of values that parameters can assume according to the OpenAPI specification. Applicable only to domain-limited parameters (es. boolean, enum)
Request content-type	Ratio of the number of tested content-types to the total number of accepted content-types as per the OpenAPI specification. 100% request content-type coverage if there exists at least a test request for each accepted content-type.
Status code class	A test suite reaches 100% status code class coverage when it is able to trigger both correct and erroneous status codes. If it triggers only status codes belonging to the same class (either correct or erroneous), coverage equals 50%. 2XX class represents a correct execution and 4XX and 5XX classes represent an erroneous execution.
Status code	Ratio of the number of obtained status codes to the total number of status codes documented in the OpenAPI specification, for each operation. 100% status code coverage if, for each operation, all status codes are tested.
Response content-type	Ratio of the number of obtained content-types to the total number of response content-types as per the OpenAPI specification. 100% response content-type coverage if there exists at least one test response whose body matches each documented content-type, for each operation

4.3 Metrics

We adopt the coverage metrics defined by Martin-Lopez *et al.* [7], used also in ref. [12]. The definitions are provided in Table 5. The first five metrics concern the goodness of the generation with respect to the input specification (input metrics), while the last three are computed on response codes (output metrics). Coverage metrics are computed with the tools `Burp Suite` [20] and `Restats` [21]. `Burp Suite` logs each request-response pair; we export logs and compute metrics with `Restats`. This is the same process adopted in ref. [12].

In addition with respect to [12], we compare tools in terms of cost, namely the *average number of executed tests*, and *average failure rate* (average number of failures exposed by executed tests over all microservices).

5 Results

5.1 Scenario 1: Tests with Valid Input

We compare the effectiveness of uTest and EvoMaster, when testing MSA microservices as independent services, with inputs complying to their API.

Figure 3 shows boxplots for the eight metrics. Values are averaged over repetitions for all microservices of all subjects. (For all metrics, the standard deviation over repetitions is less than 1.2% of the mean.) The results point out comparable values of uTest and EvoMaster with respect to the *baseline*, outperforming it only in *parameter value* coverage. uTest achieves slightly better results for all metrics, except for *response content-type*.

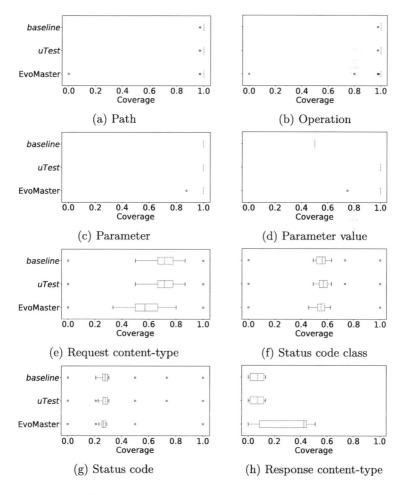

Fig. 3. Scenario 1 (valid test cases): coverage

Figure 4a shows the average failure rate. uTEST achieves a slightly better rate than EvoMaster. As for cost, Fig. 4b shows that the average number of tests executed by EvoMaster is one order of magnitude greater than the other two. Among these, uTEST generates a test suite approximately three times bigger than the baseline, but detecting almost six times more failures.

(a) Average failure rate   (b) Average executed test

Fig. 4. Scenario 1 (valid test cases): average failure rate and executed tests

5.2 Scenario 2: Tests with Valid and Invalid Input

We evaluate coverage, average failure rate, and cost of test suites containing both *valid* and *invalid test cases* genereted by RestTestGen, bBOXRT, RESTler, uTEST, and compare them to the baseline.

Figure 5 shows boxplots of the average coverage. The tools reveal comparable performance, except for *parameter value coverage* (Fig. 3d): in this case, RestTestGen and bBOXRT show full coverage, whereas RESTler, uTEST and *baseline* test boolean values with either true or false, and coverage equals 0.5.

As for failure rate, Fig. 6a shows that uTEST and *baseline* achieve higher values. As for cost, Fig. 6b shows that the average number of tests needed by bBOXRT, RestTestGen and RESTler is an order of magnitude higher than uTEST and the baseline. Similarly to Scenario 1, the pairwise strategy generates a test suite approximately three times bigger than the baseline, but detecting almost five times more failures. In addition, the higher average failure rate and the comparable values of coverage metrics of the combinatorial approach with respect to the other tools are confirmed. The results achieved by the baseline are particularly interesting, as it generates only a single test case for each method in API (greater cost/benefit ratio compared to stateful approaches).

Failures reported by tests execution need to be investigated by debuggers. Microservices in an MSA may originate more complex invocation paths than single RESTful services, making the analysis of failure causes challenging. As for most distributed systems, observability is key to debug and troubleshooting MSA [22,23]. Solutions exist to monitor systems at the microservice level [24], or to mock dependencies in the MSA under test [2].

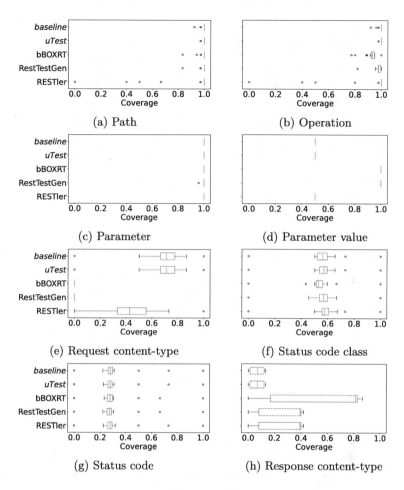

(a) Path

(b) Operation

(c) Parameter

(d) Parameter value

(e) Request content-type

(f) Status code class

(g) Status code

(h) Response content-type

Fig. 5. Scenario 2 (valid and invalid test cases): coverage

6   Threats to Validity

Concerning internal validity, despite our best efforts, the presence of defects in the uTEST prototype cannot be ruled out and might skew the results. The prototype is made anonymously available for reproducibility and repeatability.

External validity is threatened by the case studies adopted. While the three MSA used for experiments are the most used ones in the literature, they are open-source projects far from realistic MSA. However, finding real-world MSA for scientific experiments is a recognized problem [25].

An additional remark in respect to output coverage for the case studies is in order. Stateful tools generate tests trying to cover operation and/or parameter dependencies. When more dependencies are covered, higher HTTP *status code coverage* values can be achieved, because of *2xx* codes that may not been covered

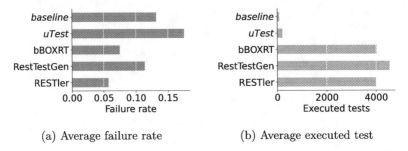

(a) Average failure rate   (b) Average executed test

Fig. 6. Scenario 2 (valid and invalid test cases): average failure rate and tests

otherwise. In our experiments, output coverage values are close to the minimum (e.g., 50% *status code class*, meaning that on average all tests generated per method were able to return only codes of $2xx$ or $4-5xx$ classes). This points out the difficulties of tools in finding realistic *valid* values and/or operation sequences to cover all successful responses – the majority of codes returned belong to the 4xx class. For an MSA, dependencies are challenging to cover with a black-box approach that tests microservices independently. We noted that most tools reach the maximum execution time configured, generating plenty of worthless tests. A contributing cause might be the poor specifications for the case studies, which might affect the trustworthiness of results.

7   Conclusions

We presented an experimental comparison of techniques/tools, borrowed from black-box RESTful Web Services testing, for automatic test case generation for microservices in an MSA, and compared them to a newly proposed own combinatorial strategy. This is a more comprehensive comparison of black-box tools than past studies, as it includes the state-of-the-art tool EvoMaster, and for the first time it includes a stateless pairwise technique.

The experiments show that specification-based techniques can support MSA testers both in functional testing (e.g., for system and acceptance testing) and in robustness testing (e.g., testing fault tolerance means, error handling), indeed alleviating the burden of manually writing tests. Although results may be threatened by actual representativeness of the three case studies, the proposed combinatorial approach demonstrated to achieve coverage comparable to stateful techniques, while requiring an order of magnitude lower number of test cases. However, uTEST like existing tools reach low values of output coverage.

It might be argued that applying specification-based test generation techniques (often, conceived for RESTful Web Services) to the many individual microservices of an MSA may be insufficient to cover complex interaction patterns among them. Microservices have probably better not be tested independently, but considering the entire architecture they are part of. In future work, we will investigate grey-box strategies to test microservice architectures.

Acknowledgements. This project has received funding from the European Union's Horizon 2020 research and innovation programme under the Marie Skłodowska-Curie grant agreement No. 871342.

References

1. Lewis, J., Fowler, M.: Microservices - a definition of this new architectural term. http://martinfowler.com/articles/microservices.html (2014)
2. Arcuri, A.: Automated black- and white-box testing of RESTful APIs with Evo-Master. IEEE Softw. **38**(3), 72–78 (2021)
3. Ma, S., Fan, C., Chuang, Y., Lee, W., Lee, S., Hsueh, N.: Using service dependency graph to analyze and test microservices. In 2018 IEEE 42nd Annual Computer Software and Applications Conference (COMPSAC), vol. 02, pp. 81–86 (2018)
4. Corradini, D., Zampieri, A., Pasqua, M., Viglianisi, E., Dallago, M., Ceccato, M.: Automated black-box testing of nominal and error scenarios in RESTful APIs. Softw. Test. Verification Reliab. **32**, e1808 (2022)
5. Atlidakis, V., Godefroid, P., Polishchuk, M.: RESTler: Stateful rest API fuzzing. In: IEEE/ACM 41st International Conference on Software Engineering (ICSE), pp. 748–758. IEEE (2019)
6. Martin-Lopez, A., Segura, S., Ruiz-Cortés, A.: RESTest: black-box constraint-based testing of RESTful web APIs. In: Kafeza, E., Benatallah, B., Martinelli, F., Hacid, H., Bouguettaya, A., Motahari, H. (eds.) ICSOC 2020. LNCS, vol. 12571, pp. 459–475. Springer, Cham (2020). https://doi.org/10.1007/978-3-030-65310-1_33
7. Martin-Lopez, A., Segura, S., Ruiz-Cortés, A.: Test coverage criteria for RESTful web APIs. In: Proceedings of the 10th ACM SIGSOFT International Workshop on Automating TEST Case Design, Selection, and Evaluation (A-TEST), pp. 15–21. ACM (2019)
8. Laranjeiro, N., Agnelo, J., Bernardino, J.: A black box tool for robustness testing of rest services. IEEE Access **9**, 24738–24754 (2021)
9. Ed-douibi, H., Izquierdo, J.L.C., Cabot, J.: Automatic generation of test cases for REST APIs: a specification-based approach. In: IEEE 22nd International Enterprise Distributed Object Computing Conference (EDOC), pp. 181–190. IEEE (2018)
10. Karlsson, S., Čaušević, A., Sundmark. D.: QuickREST: property-based test generation of OpenAPI-described RESTful APIs. In: 2020 IEEE 13th International Conference on Software Testing, Validation and Verification (ICST), pp. 131–141. IEEE (2020)
11. Bania, O., Florea, D., Gyalai, R., Curiac, D.: Automated specification-based testing of REST APIs. Sensors **21**(16), 5375 (2021)
12. Corradini, D., Zampieri, A., Pasqua, M., Ceccato, M.: Empirical comparison of black-box test case generation tools for RESTful APIs. In: 2021 IEEE 21st International Working Conference on Source Code Analysis and Manipulation (SCAM), pp. 226–236. IEEE (2021)
13. Cohen, D.M., Dalal, S.R., Parelius, J., Patton, G.C.: The combinatorial design approach to automatic test generation. IEEE Software **13**(5), 83–88 (1996)
14. Nie, C., Leung, H.: A survey of combinatorial testing. ACM Comput. Surv. **43**(2), 1–29 (2011)

15. Hu, L., Wong, W.E., Kuhn, D.R., Kacker, R.N.: How does combinatorial testing perform in the real world: an empirical study. Empirical Software Eng. **25**(4), 2661–2693 (2020). https://doi.org/10.1007/s10664-019-09799-2
16. Pezzè, M., Young, M.: Software Testing and Analysis - Process, Principles and Techniques. Wiley, Hoboken (2007)
17. Bertolino, A., De Angelis, G., Guerriero, A., Miranda, B., Pietrantuono, R.. Russo, S.: DevOpRET: continuous reliability testing in DevOps. J. Softw. Evol. Process. e2298 (2020). smr.2298
18. Zhou, X., Peng, X., Xie, T., Sun, J., Ji, C., Li, W., Ding, D.: Fault analysis and debugging of microservice systems: industrial survey, benchmark system, and empirical study. IEEE Trans. Softw. Eng. **47**(2), 243–260 (2021)
19. Richardson, C.: Microservices Patterns. Manning Publications, Shelter Island (2018)
20. Portswigger: burp suite. https://portswigger.net/burp
21. Corradini, D., Zampieri, A.. Pasqua, M., Ceccato, M.: Restats: a test coverage tool for RESTful APIs. CoRR, abs/2108.08209 (2021)
22. Indrasiri, K., Siriwardena, P.: Microservices for the Enterprise: Designing, Developing, and Deploying, 1st edn. Apress, USA (2018)
23. Waseem, M., Liang, P., Shahin, M., Di Salle, A., Márquez, G.: Design, monitoring, and testing of microservices systems: the practitioners' perspective. J. Syst. Softw. **182**, 111061 (2021)
24. Cinque, M., Della Corte, R., Pecchia, A.: Microservices monitoring with event logs and black box execution tracing. IEEE Trans. Serv. Comput. **15**(1), 294–307 (2022)
25. Zhou, X., et al.: Poster: benchmarking microservice systems for software engineering research. In: 2018 IEEE/ACM 40th International Conference on Software Engineering: Companion (ICSE-Companion), pp. 323–324. IEEE (2018)

ReSuMo: Regression Mutation Testing for Solidity Smart Contracts

Morena Barboni[✉] , Francesco Casoni , Andrea Morichetta ,
and Andrea Polini

University of Camerino, Camerino, Italy
{morena.barboni,francesco.casoni,
andrea.morichetta,andrea.polini}@unicam.it

Abstract. Mutation testing is a powerful test adequacy assessment technique that can guarantee the deployment of more reliable Smart Contract code. Developers add new features, fix bugs, and refactor modern distributed applications at a quick pace, thus they must perform continuous re-testing to ensure that the project evolution does not break existing functionalities. However, regularly re-running the entire test suite can be time intensive, especially when mutation testing is involved. This paper presents ReSuMo, the first regression mutation testing approach and tool for Solidity Smart Contracts. ReSuMo uses a static, file-level technique to select a subset of Smart Contracts to mutate and a subset of test files to re-run during a regression mutation testing campaign. ReSuMo incrementally updates the mutation testing results considering the outcomes of the old program version; in this way, it can speed up mutation testing on evolving projects without compromising the mutation score.

Keywords: Mutation testing · Regression testing · Smart contract

1 Introduction

Nowadays, a growing number of industries are using blockchain platforms to perform trustless computations using Smart Contracts. Applications ranging from financial services to supply chains are being developed on the Ethereum blockchain (e.g. [6,7]). The most peculiar feature of a Smart Contract is that its code is immutable; once deployed to the distributed ledger it cannot be updated, even if it contains severe programming defects. As the use of Smart Contracts expands across application domains, the demand for robust testing methodologies has skyrocketed. In our previous work, we proposed SuMo [3], a mutation testing tool for Solidity Smart Contracts; SuMo allows developers to improve their test suites by injecting a wide variety of traditional and Solidity-specific flaws in the Smart Contract code. Despite being a powerful adequacy assessment technique, mutation testing is extremely costly and time-intensive. Developers create new features, fix bugs, and refactor modern distributed applications at a quick pace, thus they must frequently perform re-testing to verify that the

A. Vallecillo et al. (Eds.): QUATIC 2022, CCIS 1621, pp. 61–76, 2022.
https://doi.org/10.1007/978-3-031-14179-9_5

project evolution does not break existing functionalities. However, re-running the whole test suites on a regular basis, especially when mutation testing is used, can be exceedingly time-consuming. Here, we tackle this problem by enhancing SuMo with a regression testing mechanism that aims to reduce time and computational effort during mutation testing campaigns. We call the updated version of the tool ReSuMo, a mutation of REgression SOlidity MUtator. The rest of this paper is organized as follows: in Sect. 2 we provide background knowledge about the topics discussed in this paper. Section 3 describes the proposed regression mutation testing approach, while the design and the workflow of ReSuMo are presented in Sect. 4. In Sect. 5 we describe the experimental setup and we discuss the results of our study. Section 6 reports related work, while 7 summarizes our findings and identifies areas for further research.

2   Background

Ethereum Smart Contracts. Ethereum is a blockchain platform that enables the deployment and execution of Smart Contracts. These are programs that automatically enforce the agreements specified within their code, without the need for a central authority. Most Smart Contracts are written in Solidity, an object-oriented programming language with dedicated features for blockchain development. The most peculiar characteristic of a Smart Contract is its immutability: the code and the resulting transactions cannot be altered once published to the blockchain, even if programming flaws are discovered after deployment. Thus, inadequate pre-release testing campaigns could lead to permanent losses of financial assets or the disclosure of sensitive data.

Mutation Testing. Mutation testing was established as one of the most powerful test adequacy assessment techniques [17]. It purposefully injects minor changes into the code under test to generate faulty versions of the original program, called **mutants**. Then, it tests each mutant to see if the provided test suite can detect the artificial faults. Testing the mutants helps the developer to assess the fault-detection capabilities of the test suite, but also to design new or improved test cases [2]. The core element of mutation testing is a set of replacement rules, called **mutation operators**, which systematically inject mutations into the code under test. Mutation testing performs the adequacy assessment considering the output of the test cases with respect to each mutant; if at least one test case fails the mutant is considered to be *killed*, otherwise it is said to be *live*. The ratio of killed mutants over all *valid* mutants generated, called the **Mutation Score (MS)**, measures the adequacy of the test suite. The set of valid mutants does not include mutants that do not compile (i.e., *stillborn*) and mutants that caused infinite loops during testing (*timed-out*). Moreover, dedicated techniques like the Trivial Compiler Equivalence [16] must be employed to limit the number of *equivalent* or *redundant* mutants included in the calculation of the mutation score. Equivalent mutants contain syntactic modifications, but they behave like the original program, while redundant mutants behave like other mutants, skewing the mutation score.

Regression Testing. Regression testing is an essential step in almost all commercial software development processes. This type of testing improves confidence in the correctness of existing and unchanged code after the developers incorporate corrective and progressive changes into the system under test. Every Regression Test Selection (RTS) technique aims to reduce the test suite of a given program by selecting a minimal test set that traverses the code impacted by the changes. The key requirement for an RTS technique to be adopted is that the end-to-end testing time, on average, is shorter than the time to execute the entire test suite.

SuMo (SOlidity MUtator). SuMo [3] is a mutation testing approach and tool for Solidity Smart Contracts. It includes a set of 44 mutation operators capable of simulating both traditional and Solidity-specific faults. SuMo permits to automatically run a mutation testing process on a Solidity-based project, so as to evaluate the fault-detection capabilities of the implemented test suite. SuMo is open-source and can be found on Github[1].

3   The ReSuMo Approach

In this section, we present ReSuMo, a **Regression Mutation Testing (RMT)** approach for Solidity Smart Contracts. ReSuMo applies a static file-level regression technique to speed up mutation testing on evolving projects without compromising the reliability of the mutation score. To this end, it only performs the adequacy assessment on those tests that traverse smart contracts affected by some changes. The innovation ReSuMo embodies is to reduce the mutants to be generated and tested, yet it is built following the guidelines and best practices that mature Regression Test Selection (RTS) tools drawn to date [9,12]. The concept behind contract selection is as follows: if a contract was not influenced by the latest code changes, it will certainly generate the same mutants as the previous revision. Thus, we can safely re-use the test results for such mutants to calculate the mutation score of the current revision. The RMT technique of ReSuMo includes four phases:

1. Computation of **changed files**;
2. Computation of **files dependencies**;
3. Selection of **contracts to be mutated**;
4. Selection of **regression tests**.

ReSuMo must compute 1) **program revisions differences** and 2) **test dependencies** to achieve regression testing and mutant selection. Starting from these artifacts, our tool can compute: 3) a set of **affected contracts** to be mutated and tested and 4) a set of **modification traversing tests** to include in the regression suite. In the following, we discuss in detail the RMT technique of ReSuMo. We start by explaining the chosen granularity of computation (section 3.1). Then, we describe how ReSuMo computes program changes (Sect. 3.2) and file dependencies (Sect. 3.3), and how it uses such information to identify contracts to be mutated (Sect. 3.4) and regression tests (Sect. 3.5).

---

[1] SuMo repository: https://github.com/MorenaBarboni/SuMo-SOlidity-MUtator.

3.1 Granularity of Computation

The granularity of computation is the nature of the atomic parts in which a program can be divided: *basic blocks*, *methods*, or *files*. The selected granularity heavily affects the RTS process in terms of results, safety, and performance. A **basic block-level** RTS technique only selects those tests that exercise the modified statements of a program. In **method-level**, a small modification to the code causes the entire function to be marked as changed; Any test exercising the function would be included in the regression suite even if it does not reach the changed part. In both cases, the regression test suite would be very accurate and minimized. However, computation at the basic blocks and method levels is extremely costly due to the explosion of statements (or methods) to be analyzed and traced. For instance, the ReMT [18] technique can substantially reduce mutation testing cost, but no tools to date support it due to its fine-grained computation level. Thanks to the STARTS [13] and the Ekstazi [8] works we know that, compared to file-level, a finer-grained analysis incurs large overheads and too often in severe mutation testing precision issues. ReSuMo implements a **file-level** static RTS technique, meaning that entire files (contracts or tests) are treated as the atomic parts of the SUT. File-level computation is more conservative than the other techniques because one small modification causes an entire contract file to be mutated and tested. However, computing programs differences does not require syntax trees comparisons with graph traversal procedures. Most importantly, selecting more contract and test files can often be safer, which is a priority in the case of business-critical programs like Smart Contracts.

3.2 Computing File Changes

To enable the selection of contract and test files, ReSuMo must detect differences among program revisions. Since the implemented approach works at file-level, this can be done with a simple checksum, making the computation of revisions differences almost instantaneous. As soon as ReSuMo begins the mutation testing process, it saves a hash for each contract and test file. If a file has an execution history, the newly computed hash is compared to the previous one to determine whether the file was modified since the latest revision. Otherwise, the file is automatically marked as changed and hence saved for further computations. Note that we do not consider changed files that included trivial modifications, like comments or whitespaces.

3.3 Computing File Dependencies

ReSuMo computes dependencies between contracts and test files via **static program analysis**, eliminating the need to re-run test suites. Dynamic RTS approaches are widely studied and used, but they are also intrinsically unsafe. Indeed, the results can be imprecise if a program includes non-deterministic paths. Time costs are also a big concern; computing dependencies at run-time can be time-intensive for large projects with many contracts and test files. More-over, a static technique is unlikely to miss some dependency due to code changes because the computation is performed on the new code revision. Since mutations can easily divert the regular control flow of a contract, using a more conservative RTS static technique can be beneficial.

Since the chosen RTS technique is static, ReSuMo builds a **dependency graph** to store each file as a node, and each dependency as an oriented arc connecting two nodes. To clarify how the proposed strategy works, we show in Fig. 1 the dependency graph generated by ReSuMo for a rather simple Solidity project. Here, the white circles represent Solidity Smart Contracts, the grey squares represent the test files, and the grey circles are used to denote Solidity test contracts. First, ReSuMo adds one node to the dependency graph for each test and for each contract file. Then, it parses and visits each file in search of Import Directives: statements let a file import another file.

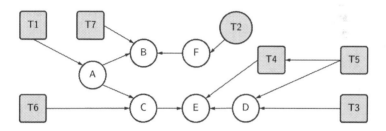

Fig. 1. Example of dependency graph generated by ReSuMo

For instance, let's consider the JavaScript test file T5 shown in Listing 1.1; the `artifact.require` import directive (line 1) lets T5 use contract D, while the `require` statement (line 2) imports another test file T4. ReSuMo uses such statements to quickly establish dependencies among files (both JavaScript tests and Solidity contracts are supported, including Solidity test contracts).

Listing 1.1. A test file T5.js that depends on a contract D.sol and on a test file T4.js

```
1   var D = artifacts.require (''D'');
2   require (''./ T4'');
3
4   contract (''D'', function (accounts) {
5       it(''should do something ...  '', async function () {
6           d = new D(some_address);
7           ...
8       })
9   })
```

3.4 Identifying Contracts to Be Mutated

Selecting the contract files to be mutated can concretely reduce time and resources consumption, but it must be performed carefully to avoid safeness problems. Let's consider a project composed of a set of Smart Contracts C, and a set of test files T. A developer commits some changes, and the project goes from revision R_1 to revision R_2. We define C' as the set of changed contracts, and T' as the set of changed test files. We can identify the following scenarios depending on the nature of the revision:

1. **Changed Contracts**: $c_1, \ldots, c_n \in C$ changed since R_1 ($T' = \emptyset$);
2. **Changed Test Files**: $t_1, \ldots, t_n \in T$ changed since R_1 ($C' = \emptyset$);
3. **Changed Contracts and Test Files**: ($C' \neq \emptyset$) and ($T' \neq \emptyset$);

The starting point of the contract selection technique is the set of changed files $C' \cup T'$. A recent work on Commit-Aware Mutation Testing [15] shows how mutating only the evolved code parts fails to consider the possible interactions between the unmodified and changed code. Thus, we also consider the unchanged contract files that might be impacted by the commit. In the following we briefly discuss how we choose the contracts to be mutated for each scenario: 1) changed C, 2) changed T and 3) changed CT.

Changed C. Any contract $c \in C'$ will certainly generate some different mutants. Thus, we mutate and (re)test c, its **dependencies** (i.e., contracts used by c) and its **dependants** (i.e., contracts that use c or inherit from it). Indeed, dependencies and dependants might be affected by the evolution of c, leading to a different behavior given some inputs.

Changed T. If $C' = \emptyset$, each contract of revision R_2 will generate the same mutants of revision R_1. However, each test file $t \in T'$ might produce different results on the same set of mutants. Thus, each contract $c \in C$ used by an evolved test file is mutated and (re)tested.

Changed CT. If both some contract(s) **and** some test file(s) changed since R_1, we combine the previous strategies selecting: 1) any $c \in C'$, together with its dependencies and dependants 2) any $c \in C$ used by any $t \in T'$.

3.5 Identifying Regression Tests

When a project hits a new revision, running the test suite against the mutants could produce a different mutation score. The core idea of regression mutation testing is excluding those tests that produce redundant results when paired with (executed against) mutants. Indeed, such results can be copied from the kill matrix generated for the previous revision. To select regression tests we answer the following question: *"Which tests can produce different results when executed against the mutated contracts?"*. Thus, we only select those test files that execute a changed contract $c \in C'$, or its dependants, since they can affect the mutation score. Those tests that execute a dependency of a changed contract c - but do not test c itself - are discarded. Indeed, they would test the same mutants of the previous revision.

3.6 Mutation Score Calculation

The mutation score calculated after a regression mutation testing only accounts for some mutants a project can produce. In order to state the adequacy of the entire test suite on the whole SUT, we update the results of a RMT campaign using the test results stored from the previous run. To this aim, ReSuMo memorizes the test outcomes of each mutant during a testing campaign (more details about this aspect are reported in Sect. 4). This allows us to obtain the same mutation score produced by a complete mutation campaign, without actually rerunning the whole process.

4   The ReSuMo Tool

In this section, we present ReSuMo, a regression mutation testing tool for Solidity Smart Contracts. ReSuMo advances the functionalities of SuMo through 1) a regression testing mechanism for evolving projects, and 2) the possibility of using Trivial Compiler Equivalence (TCE) for automatically discarding equivalent and redundant mutants. ReSuMo is open-source and can be found on Github[2]. The implementation and functioning of SuMo were already covered in our previous work [3], thus we will explain how the original SuMo design (Sect. 4.1) and workflow (Sect. 4.2) change based on the integration of the novel Regression Mutation Testing (RMT) approach.

4.1   Design

ReSuMo has been implemented to permit running regression mutation testing on a Solidity project in a NodeJS environment. The architecture of ReSuMo maintains the main high-level modules of SuMo: 1) *Mutation Runner*, 2) *Mutation Generator*, and 3) *Reporter*. However, it includes a novel logical module, called *Regression*, which permits to perform contract and test files selection during mutation testing on new project revisions. Moreover, ReSuMo includes automatic instrumenting functionalities that permit to extend the test configuration file (i.e., *truffle-config.js*) of the project under test with additional fields. This serves two main purposes: 1) adding compiler optimization options to permit the correct functioning of the TCE, and 2) expanding the reporting functionalities of the underlying testing framework with the `mochawesome`[3] reporter. The latter is required to obtain the outcome of each test file with respect to each mutant and incrementally calculate the mutation score among revisions.

ReSuMo still relies on the testing environment set up by the original project developers, which must include: 1) a testing framework and 2) an Ethereum blockchain simulator where the contracts can be deployed and tested. In particular, ReSuMo was designed to work with *Truffle* and *Ganache*, as they are popular among Smart Contract developers. Even so, it is possible to disable Ganache and to make ReSuMo interact with different testing frameworks (e.g., *Hardhat*) with some manual configurations.

---

[2]   ReSuMo repository: https://github.com/MorenaBarboni/ReSuMo.
[3]   Mochawesome: https://www.npmjs.com/package/mochawesome.

4.2   Workflow

Fig. 2 shows the regression mutation testing process of ReSuMo. In the following we summarize the high-level steps of mutation testing when regression is enabled:

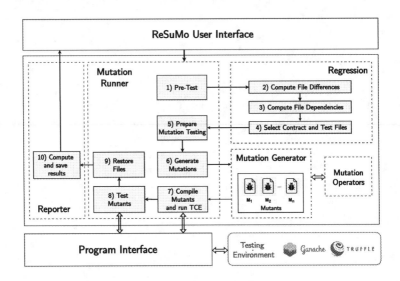

Fig. 2. Regression mutation testing process of ReSuMo

1. **Pre-Test**: ReSuMo performs some setup operations and checks whether the user configuration is valid. Then it verifies whether the provided test suite passes on the original project. If not, the process is interrupted.
2. **File differences computation**: The *regression* module checks if some contract or test files have changed since the last revision by comparing their checksum. The checksum of the current revision is saved for the next mutation campaign.
3. **File dependencies computation**: The *regression* module calculates and saves the dependencies among contracts and test files. Then, it creates the dependency graph required for the selection of contract and test files
4. **File selection**: The *regression* module applies its selection strategy to select a list of contracts to be mutated, and a list of regression tests to be run.
5. **Mutation testing preparation**: ReSuMo performs several steps preparatory to the mutation testing run. First, it sets up the mutation process considering the user configuration file (i.e., the files to be ignored) and the files computed by the *regression* module; in particular, it removes from the test folder any test file that must not be re-run. This step is necessary because the Truffle interface does not yet support the execution of individual tests. Then, ReSuMo compiles the original Smart Contracts and stores their bytecode; this will be later used for applying the Trivial Compiler Equivalence (TCE).

Lastly, it instruments the test configuration file (e.g., *truffle-config.js*) of the project under test to enable compiler optimizations and the `mochawesome` test reporter.

6. **Mutations generation**: ReSuMo visits the AST (Abstract Syntax Tree) of the Smart Contracts to be mutated, and produces mutations according to the rules specified by each user-enabled mutation operator.

Once the mutations are available, ReSuMo applies each mutation to the relative contract, and repeats the following steps for each generated mutant:

7. **Compilation and TCE**: ReSuMo spawns a Ganache instance and compiles the mutant with the underlying testing infrastructure. If the mutant does not compile it is marked as *stillborn* and discarded, otherwise the Trivial Compiler Equivalence (TCE) is run on its bytecode. ReSuMo compares the bytecode of the mutant with the bytecode of its original contract, and with the bytecode of previously generated mutations, to detect if it is *equivalent* or *redundant*.

8. **Testing:** If the mutant is neither *equivalent* nor *redundant*, it must be tested. To this end, ReSuMo starts a new Ganache instance and runs the regression tests on the mutated contract. Once the tests have run, ReSuMo updates the state of the mutant (*live*, *killed* or *timed-out*), restores the mutated contract so that the next mutation can be applied, and closes the Ganache instance. The latter step is necessary to guarantee a clean room testing environment for each mutant. ReSuMo also saves the test results to file through the `mochawesome` reporter so as to enable the calculation of the mutation score on the next regression run.

When all the mutants have been tested, ReSuMo performs two final steps:

9. **File restore:** At the end of the Mutation Testing run, ReSuMo restores all the files that were removed or modified during step 5;

10. **Results computation:** ReSuMo integrates the regression test results with the ones achieved during the previous run, then it calculates the mutation score and saves relevant information to file.

5   Validation

To evaluate ReSuMo we performed regression mutation testing on an open-source Solidity project. In Sect. 5.1 we describe the selected project and the experimental setup, while the results of the experiment are discussed in Sect. 5.2.

5.1   Experiment Set-up

In order to choose a suitable project for the regression mutation testing campaign, we defined three selection criteria. First, the application must have a rather high mutation testing time cost. Indeed, regression testing is performed on evolving systems when the testing effort can be significant. Since ReSuMo computes dependencies and version changes at file level granularity, the application under test must also be complex in structure; if a change occurs in a project with few contract and test files, ReSuMo will likely re-run the entire test suite against all mutants, defeating the purpose of Regression Mutation Testing. Lastly, there must be some commits that alter contract or test files, so that we can simulate the evolution of the application in a real development setting.

Considering these criteria, our choice fell on **Safe Contracts**[4], a smart contract wallet with multi-signature functionalities for the management of blockchain assets. Specifically, we selected three sequential commits that alter the contract or the test files of the project under test: $Commit_1$[5], $Commit_2$[6] and $Commit_3$[7]. Based on these commits, we can identify four corresponding project revisions, R_1, ..., R_4, such that: $R_1 \xrightarrow{Commit_1} R_2 \xrightarrow{Commit_2} R_3 \xrightarrow{Commit_3} R_4$. Safe-Contract features 20 smart contracts and 21 test files with high coverage adequacy; throughout the revisions, the test suite achieved on average 95.5% statement coverage, and 98.5% branch coverage. Note that the metrics refer to a subset of contract and test files: we excluded libraries, interfaces, migrations, and unused contracts from the evaluation. The complete list of contract and test files considered for the experiment is shown in Table 1.

To assess the effectiveness of our approach in terms of mutation score and time costs, we used ReSuMo to mutate and test each project revision.First, we executed four complete mutation testing runs, one for each project revision, and then we repeated the experiment with Regression Mutation Testing (RMT) enabled. On each run, we used the default set of mutation operators implemented by SuMo, with the Trivial Compiler Equivalence (TCE) enabled.

5.2   Results

Table 2 shows the effects of the ReSuMo selection strategy when traversing the selected revisions of the project under test. Here, we provide the revision ID (Col. 1), the number of contract files (Col. 2) and test files (Col. 3) that changed since the previous revision, and the number of contracts to be mutated (Col. 4) and regression tests (Col. 5) selected by ReSuMo (considering the files reported in Table 1). Table 3 shows the results of the mutation testing process performed on the selected revisions. For each revision, the table reports the results for both types of run (Col. 1), which are Complete (marked as C) and Regression (marked as R). The results include the total number of generated mutants (Col. 2), stillborn mutants (Col. 3), timed-out mutants (Col. 4), equivalent mutants discarded by the TCE (Col. 5), and tested mutants (Col. 6). Col. 7 shows the Mutation Score (%) reached by the test suite. Lastly, the table provides the time (in minutes) required for completing the considered run (Col. 8), and the time savings achieved by Regression Mutation Testing (Col. 9). In the following we discuss the results with respect to each revision.

---

[4] https://github.com/gnosis/safe-contracts.

[5] https://github.com/gnosis/safe-contracts/commit/b34157d1bea6e9027cc1ea5ea7d135b4f04a4213.

[6] https://github.com/gnosis/safe-contracts/commit/9b305a0f80da7f1107d1181f52c844f089557d05.

[7] https://github.com/gnosis/safe-contracts/commit/53122d14af0a3f6aa30c5fcd3861573d44c9d7b9.

Table 1. Considered smart contracts and test files of the safe-contracts project

Contract files	Test files
SimulateTxAccessor.sol	SimulateTxAccessor.spec.ts
Executor.sol	GnosisSafe.Estimation.spec.ts
FallbackManager.sol	GnosisSafe.Execution.spec.ts
GuardManager.sol	GnosisSafe.FallbackManager.spec.ts
ModuleManager.sol	GnosisSafe.GuardManager.spec.ts
OwnerManager.sol	GnosisSafe.Incoming.spec.ts
Enum.sol	GnosisSafe.Messages.spec.ts
EtherPaymentFallback.sol	GnosisSafe.ModuleManager.spec.ts
SecuredTokenTransfer.sol	GnosisSafe.OwnerManager.spec.ts
SelfAuthorized.sol	GnosisSafe.Setup.spec.ts
SignatureDecoder.sol	GnosisSafe.Signatures.spec.ts
Singleton.sol	GnosisSafe.StorageAccessible.spec.ts
StorageAccessible.sol	Proxy.spec.ts
CompatibilityFallbackHandler.sol	ProxyFactory.spec.ts
DefaultCallbackHandler.sol	DelegateCallTransactionGuard.spec.ts
HandlerContext.sol	CompatibilityFallbackHandler.spec.ts
GnosisSafeProxy.sol	DefaultCallbackHandler.spec.ts
GnosisSafeProxyFactory.sol	HandlerContext.spec.ts
IProxyCreationCallback.sol	GnosisSafe.0xExploit.spec.ts
GnosisSafe.sol	GnosisSafe.ERC1155.spec.ts
	GnosisSafe.ReservedAddresses.spec.ts

Revision R_1. As can be seen from Table 3, the complete mutation testing run on the initial project revision generated 773 valid mutants over 20 Smart Contracts. The provided test suite required almost 7 h to test all the mutants and achieved a mutation score of 73,6%.

Revision R_2. After applying $Commit_1$ to Safe-Contracts, we re-run the mutation testing process on R_2, with and without RMT enabled. This revision features three modified Smart Contracts: CompatibilityFallbackHandler.sol, OwnerManager.sol, and SecuredTokenTransfer.sol. As can be seen from the data of the complete run (Table 2), the commit caused the generation of the same amount of mutants with respect to R_1, and the testing process was completed in 6,7 h. When we enabled RMT, ReSuMo selected 16 Smart Contracts and 20 regression tests for mutation and re-testing. The tool generated 685 valid mutants and completed the testing process in around 6 h. Although ReSuMo selected many files due to the dense dependency structure of the changed contracts, the regression run saved $\sim 10\%$ of the time required by the complete run.

Table 2. Output of ReSuMo for different program revisions

Rev.	Changed contracts	Changed test files	Mutated contracts	Regression tests
R_1	–	–	20	21
R_2	3	0	16	20
R_3	1	0	3	1
R_4	1	1	18	20

Table 3. Experimental results

Run	Total mutants	Stillborn mutants	Timed-out mutants	Equivalent mutants	Tested mutants	MS	Time (m)	Time saved
R_1 (C)	943	139	2	29	773	73,6	407	–
R_2 (C)	943	139	2	29	773	73,6	402	9,7%
R_2 (R)	826	113	2	26	685	73,6	363	
R_3 (C)	941	140	2	29	770	74	403	98,3%
R_3 (R)	32	7	0	0	25	74	7	
R_4 (C)	947	143	2	29	773	74,1	423	5,7%
R_4 (R)	893	127	2	29	735	74,1	399	

Revision R_3. Revision R_3 differs from R_2 by a single Smart Contract, SimulateTxAccessor.sol. The changes introduced by $Commit_2$ triggered the mutation of three contracts and the execution of a single test file. Although ReSuMo saved about 40 min when re-testing R_2, the benefits of the RMT strategy are clear for R_3. The process generated 25 valid mutants, which were tested in only 7 min; enabling RMT allowed us to reduce the testing time by 98,3%. In this case, the overall mutation score slightly increased, indicating a better adequacy of the tests with respect to the changes applied by $Commit_2$.

Revision R_4. R_4 features a modified contract and a modified test file. The changes affected GnosisSafe.sol, the main contract of the project, which is densely interconnected to other contracts and test files. The evolution of this contract, combined with the changes applied to the GnosisSafe.Signatures.spec test file, caused the selection of 18 contracts and the re-run of 20 test files. As can be seen from Table 3, R_4 (C) took 20 minutes longer than R_3 (C), despite the latter only producing 3 valid mutants less. This is due to the introduction of the new test methods within the GnosisSafe.Signatures.spec file. In this case, enabling RMT generated 54 less mutants with respect to the complete run, reducing the time needed for completing mutation testing by $\sim 5,7\%$.

Overall, the time and effort that can be saved using ReSuMo strictly depend on two factors: 1) the organization and the granularity of the commits and 2) the structure of the project under test. In other words, if a developer does not let the modifications pile up, but instead uses ReSuMo to frequently re-run mutation testing, the time required for assessing the quality of the test suite can be significantly reduced. Moreover, since the implemented approach works at file-level, ReSuMo performs better if the commit changes are not scattered over many files. Lastly, the approach seems to be extremely effective when the changed files are loosely coupled. This is the case for commit C_2, where the affected file, `SimulateTxAccessor.sol`, has two contract dependencies and one test dependant, and the regression mutation testing can be completed in a few minutes. However, if a commit affects a central contract (e.g., `GnosisSafe.sol`) that has many connections in the dependency graph, the conservative strategy implemented by ReSuMo can end up selecting many contracts and test files for mutation and re-testing. In such scenarios, a file-level RMT approach can still help to decrease time, but the overall effort for performing mutation testing can still be rather high, as is the case for revision R_2.

6   Related Work

To date, there are no works that propose a regression mutation testing approach for Ethereum Smart Contracts; the studies closer to our proposal concern 1) approaches for mutating Smart Contracts and 2) techniques that combine regression and mutation testing on traditional software systems.

Regression Mutation Testing. Zhang et al. [18] first introduced Regression Mutation Testing (ReMT), a technique that speeds up mutant execution on evolving systems by progressively calculating the mutation score. ReMT explores the control flow graphs of two program versions to discover edges that may result in different test behaviors. ReMT can identify mutant-test pairs whose execution results can be safely reused, reducing mutation testing costs on evolving systems.

Cachia et al. [4] advocate the usage of incremental mutation testing, a variant of mutation testing that limits the scope of mutant generation to areas of code that changed since the last project version. They showed that this approach can considerably decrease the number of generated mutants and the time required to run the tests against them.

Recently, Ma et al. [15] introduced commit-aware mutation testing, an assessment metric capable of evaluating the extent to which some committed modifications affect program behavior. They conduct experiments on both C and Java projects and showed that traditional mutant selection is non-optimal, as it has fewer chances of revealing commit-introducing faults.

Mutation Testing for Ethereum Smart Contracts. In the latest years, several mutation testing approaches and tools for Ethereum Smart Contracts were proposed, but none of them implements a mechanism for regression testing.

Wu et al. [14] proposed *MuSC*, the first mutation testing framework for assessing the quality of Smart Contract test suites. The authors introduced a compact set of JavaScript-oriented and Solidity-specific mutation operators to inject faults in the Smart Contract code.

Andesta et al. [1] studied known faults in Ethereum Smart Contracts to design a novel set of mutation operators, which was then included in the *Universal Mutator* tool. The proposed classes of operators can recreate the bugs found in 10 of 15 famous Smart Contracts that caused severe financial losses.

The *Deviant* tool proposed by Chapman et al. [5] includes a broad set of mutation operators that work at four levels: inter-module, intra-module, intra-function, and intra-statement. The authors evaluated the approach on three real-world projects and showed that Deviant can help developers to deliver higher quality Solidity applications.

Honig et al. [11] propose a prototype implementation, called *Vertigo*, that targets Smart Contracts written in Solidity. Vertigo also relies on the functionalities exposed by the Truffle interface to enable testing; however, it discourages the use the of Ganache simulator, as some Truffle tests might not use its clean environment feature, leading to unreliable test results. ReSuMo overcomes this problem by re-spawning a clean Ganache instance for each mutant, so as to guarantee isolation between multiple test re-runs.

Lastly, Hartel & Schumi [10] implemented mutation operators derived from the Mothra set, in addition to four Solidity-specific mutation operators, and implemented them in their *ContractMut* tool. The authors also introduced a novel killing condition based on deviations in the gas consumption to improve the effectiveness of the mutation approach.

7   Conclusions and Future Work

This work presented ReSuMo, the first Regression Mutation Testing (RMT) approach for Solidity Smart Contracts. ReSuMo extends the SuMo [3] tool with a regression testing and mutant selection technique to speed up mutation testing on evolving projects without compromising the precision of testing results. ReSuMo applies a static, file-level technique for selecting contracts to mutate and tests to execute during the mutation process, and is responsible for integrating the mutation results with previous data produced by the mutation of unchanged files. In this way, the time and resources consumption of mutation testing can be amortized during the software development life cycle. As a result, ReSuMo permits a faster calculation of the Mutation Score, encouraging the continuous improvement of the test suite during the development of the Smart Contracts.

We evaluated the effectiveness of ReSuMo by running it on a real-world Ethereum application shipped with a high-coverage test suite. The analyzed scenario considers the evolution of the project over three commits pushed on Github by the original developers. Our results show that ReSuMo can help developers to write higher quality test suites and deliver more reliable Solidity applications using mutation testing, without paying the full time costs of this powerful technique. Indeed, ReSuMo can significantly reduce mutation testing time; for one commit, we observed that enabling the proposed RMT technique decreased the testing time from over 6 h to only 7 min. Our results suggest that the time savings strictly depend on the organization and granularity of the commits, but also on the structure of the project under test. If a commit changes a densely interconnected file, or if the modifications are scattered over many contracts and tests, ReSuMo can select many files for mutation and re-testing, while projects with a loosely-coupled structure can benefit the most from the regression.

Future work should apply ReSuMo on more distributed applications, so as to gain additional insights on the benefits of the RMT approach. To further improve the effectiveness of ReSuMo, especially for small and tightly-coupled Smart Contract projects, future work should also focus on analyzing more fine-grained (e.g., method-level) regression mutation testing approaches. Then, it would be possible for the tester to specify a chosen level of computation granularity, so as to adapt the regression testing process to their needs.

References

1. Andesta, E., Faghih, F., Fooladgar, M.: Testing smart contracts gets smarter. CoRR abs/1912.04780 (2019)
2. Andrews, J., Briand, L., Labiche, Y., Namin, A.: Using mutation analysis for assessing and comparing testing coverage criteria. IEEE Transactions on Software Engineering $32(8)$, 608–624 (2006)
3. Barboni, M., Morichetta, A., Polini, A.: Sumo: A mutation testing strategy for solidity smart contracts. In: 2nd IEEE/ACM International Conference on Automation of Software Test, AST@ICSE 2021. pp. 50–59. IEEE (2021)
4. Cachia, M.A., Micallef, M., Colombo, C.: Towards incremental mutation testing. Electronic Notes in Theoretical Computer Science 294, 2–11 (2013)
5. Chapman, P., Xu, D., Deng, L., Xiong, Y.: Deviant: A mutation testing tool for solidity smart contracts. In: IEEE International Conference on Blockchain, Blockchain 2019. pp. 319–324. IEEE (2019)
6. Corradini, F., Marcelletti, A., Morichetta, A., Polini, A., Re, B., Tiezzi, F.: Engineering trustable choreography-based systems using blockchain. In: 35th ACM/SIGAPP Symposium on Applied Computing. pp. 1470–1479. ACM (2020)
7. Corradini, F., Marcelletti, A., Morichetta, A., Polini, A., Re, B., Scala, E., Tiezzi, F.: Model-driven engineering for multi-party business processes on multiple blockchains. Blockchain: Research and Applications 2(3), 100018 (2021)
8. Gligoric, M., Eloussi, L., Marinov, D.: Ekstazi: Lightweight test selection. In: 37th IEEE/ACM International Conference on Software Engineering, ICSE 2015. vol. 2, pp. 713–716. IEEE Computer Society (2015)
9. Gligoric, M., Eloussi, L., Marinov, D.: Practical regression test selection with dynamic file dependencies. In: Young, M., Xie, T. (eds.) Proceedings of the 2015 International Symposium on Software Testing and Analysis, ISSTA 2015. pp. 211–222. ACM (2015)
10. Hartel, Pieter, Schumi, Richard: Mutation testing of smart contracts at scale. In: Ahrendt, Wolfgang, Wehrheim, Heike (eds.) TAP 2020. LNCS, vol. 12165, pp. 23–42. Springer, Cham (2020). https://doi.org/10.1007/978-3-030-50995-8_2
11. Honig, J.J., Everts, M.H., Huisman, M.: Practical Mutation Testing for Smart Contracts. In: Pérez-Solà, C., Navarro-Arribas, G., Biryukov, A., Garcia-Alfaro, J. (eds.) DPM/CBT -2019. LNCS, vol. 11737, pp. 289–303. Springer, Cham (2019). https://doi.org/10.1007/978-3-030-31500-9_19
12. Legunsen, O., Hariri, F., Shi, A., Lu, Y., Zhang, L., Marinov, D.: An extensive study of static regression test selection in modern software evolution. In: Proceedings of the 24th ACM SIGSOFT International Symposium on Foundations of Software Engineering, FSE 2016. pp. 583–594. ACM (2016)

13. Legunsen, O., Shi, A., Marinov, D.: STARTS: static regression test selection. In: Proceedings of the 32nd IEEE/ACM International Conference on Automated Software Engineering, ASE 2017. pp. 949–954. IEEE Computer Society (2017)
14. Li, Z., Wu, H., Xu, J., Wang, X., Zhang, L., Chen, Z.: Musc: A tool for mutation testing of ethereum smart contract. In: 34th IEEE/ACM International Conference on Automated Software Engineering, ASE 2019. pp. 1198–1201. IEEE (2019)
15. Ma, W., Laurent, T., Ojdanic, M., Chekam, T.T., Ventresque, A., Papadakis, M.: Commit-aware mutation testing. In: IEEE International Conference on Software Maintenance and Evolution, ICSME 2020. pp. 394–405. IEEE (2020)
16. Papadakis, M., Jia, Y., Harman, M., Le Traon, Y.: Trivial compiler equivalence: A large scale empirical study of a simple, fast and effective equivalent mutant detection technique. In: 2015 IEEE/ACM 37th IEEE International Conference on Software Engineering. vol. 1, pp. 936–946. IEEE (2015)
17. Papadakis, M., Kintis, M., Zhang, J., Jia, Y., Traon, Y.L., Harman, M.: Mutation testing advances: An analysis and survey. In: Advances in Computers, pp. 275–378. Elsevier (2019)
18. Zhang, L., Marinov, D., Zhang, L., Khurshid, S.: Regression mutation testing. In: International Symposium on Software Testing and Analysis, ISSTA 2012. pp. 331–341. ACM (2012)

Is NLP-based Test Automation Cheaper Than Programmable and Capture&Replay?

Maurizio Leotta[1](✉) ⓘ, Filippo Ricca[1] ⓘ, Simone Stoppa[1],
and Alessandro Marchetto[2] ⓘ

[1] Dipartimento di Informatica, Bioingegneria, Robotica e Ingegneria dei Sistemi (DIBRIS),
Università di Genova, Genova, Italy
{maurizio.leotta,filippo.ricca}@unige.it,
4251721@studenti.unige.it
[2] University of Trento, Trento, Italy
alessandro.marchetto@unitn.it

Abstract. Nowadays, there is a growing interest in the use of Natural-Language Processing (NLP) for supporting software test automation. This paper investigates the adoption of NLP in web testing. To this aim, a case study has been conducted to compare the cost of the adoption of a NLP testing approach, with respect to more consolidated approaches, i.e., programmable testing and capture and replay testing, in two testing tasks: test cases development and test case evolution/maintenance. Even if preliminary, results show that NLP testing is quite competitive with respect to the more consolidated approaches since the cumulative testing effort of a NLP testing approach, computed considering both development and evolution efforts, is almost always lower than the one of programmable testing and capture&replay testing.

Keywords: Test automation · Web testing · NLP · Artificial intelligence

1 Introduction

End-to-End testing frameworks for web applications, such as e.g., Selenium WebDriver and Selenium IDE are nowadays consolidated solutions because they have proven their value in practice by reducing the cost of manual testing and improving the quality of released applications [6]. For this reason, they are used in combination with continuous integration to carry out continuous testing in DevOps processes [4].

However, the cost of test cases development, the cost of maintaining test cases, and the need for experienced developers to develop test suites are limiting their adoption and thus the benefits to the applications under test [9].

Recently, new tools and frameworks called code-less and based on Artificial intelligence (AI) [17]—and more specifically on Natural Language Processing (NLP)—have appeared on the market with the aim of reducing development and maintenance costs. The novelty of NLP-based test automation tools/frameworks is that the test cases are written in natural language and therefore even software testers with limited programming skills can produce executable test cases.

A. Vallecillo et al. (Eds.): QUATIC 2022, CCIS 1621, pp. 77–92, 2022.
https://doi.org/10.1007/978-3-031-14179-9_6

Many vendors have understood the enormous potential of AI in the context of testing and thus have proposed several different NLP-based test automation frameworks/tools (e.g., TestSigma[1], TestRigor[2] and TestProject[3]) capable of interpreting and executing test cases written in natural language. However, the benefits of this new category of approaches, in terms of costs reduction, have not yet been demonstrated in the field and thus, these are currently only promises.

The goal of our research is precisely to test NLP-based test automation tools/frameworks by means of a case study and comparing them on different aspects—e.g., test suite development and maintenance time—with more mature and consolidated solutions: i.e., with tools/frameworks belonging to programmable and capture&replay approaches.

Even if, at the moment, we are still a long way off, the contribution of this work is to start laying the foundations towards an *empirical knowledge base* that is able to guide project managers in choosing the most suitable category of testing frameworks/tools for their purposes. At the moment, thanks to this case study, we have found that this new generation of testing frameworks is very promising.

This paper is organized as follows: Sect. 2 sketches related works while Sect. 3 describes the three compared testing approaches used to implement E2E test suites (i.e., programmable, capture&replay, and NLP). Section 4 describes the main aspects of the empirical study we carried out to compare the approaches, while Sect. 5 reports the results of the study. Finally, Sect. 6 concludes the paper.

2   Related Work

In the literature, there is a growing interest in the adoption of techniques based on Natural Language Processing (NLP) for supporting the software testing automation.

Garousi et al. [7] survey the state-of-the-art. Most existing works investigate approaches to conduct and automate NLP-based analysis (i.e., morphologic, syntactic, and semantic NLP approaches) for assisting software testing in: (i) clustering related test cases, e.g., [12, 18]; (ii) generating test cases and defining input values from requirement specifications, written in natural language (NL), e.g., [16, 19]; and (iii) identifying test oracles aiming at verifying exceptional software behaviors, e.g., [14]. Some approaches adopt an intermediate representation, e.g., behavioral models represented as state machines, between the natural language specifications and the generated test cases and test artifacts (e.g., [1,5]). Gupta et al. [8] pointed-out relevant issues related to the adoption of NLP in software testing: (i) requirement specifications are often constrained to a specific structure that limits their expressiveness; (ii) intermediate behavioral models are often large and complex since they need to be precise and comprehensive; (iii) manual rectification of models is often required; and (iv) additional intervention is often needed to obtain executable test cases.

The development of executable test cases is, in fact, a complex task when NLP techniques are adopted. For instance, in the programmable testing approach, executable

---

[1] https://testsigma.com/.

[2] https://testrigor.com/.

[3] https://testproject.io/.

test cases are developed according to the API/interfaces of the application under test. In model-based testing, (quasi-executable) test cases are developed from an abstract representation of the application under test (e.g., a UML model), thus transformation approaches are required to obtain executable test cases. Similarly, when NLP-based approaches are used to support testing, adequate transformation approaches are required to transform abstract test cases into executable test cases.

Requirement specifications are often written in natural language. Gherkin[4] is a structured quasi-natural language that lets testers specify test cases by using a natural language structured around a set of predefined keywords. Colombo et al. [3] convert Gherkin specifications into models used within a web testing tool. In the work of Cauchi et al. [2], Gherkin is adopted for improving the communication gap, about safety-critical system properties, between developers and non-technical experts. Fitnesse is another structured quasi-natural language adopted for specifying NL-based acceptance test cases. Both Marchetto et al. [15] and Longo et al. [13] evaluate the adoption of Fitnesse. While Marchetto et al. [15] compare Fitnesse with programmable acceptance test cases, Longo et al. [13] compares the adoption of Fitnesse and Gherkin for writing acceptance test cases.

Differently from the literature, this work conducts a preliminary evaluation about the adoption of NLP for test case development and evolution. To the best of our knowledge, in fact, there is a lack in the literature of objective and comparative evaluations of the proposed NLP methods with respect to more traditional approaches, e.g., programming and capture&replay procedures, and others, in test case development and evolution [9–11]. We start filling the gap by reporting a cases study conducted in the Web testing domain.

3 Background

Gherkin is a test specification language that aims at providing a unique language for specifying test cases. The Gherkin language is a structured language composed of a set of keywords including the following ones:

- Feature: provide a high-level description of the test
- Example/Scenario: show an example of the test
- Given: represent the initial context of the test
- When: describe an action occurred
- And: another action occurred
- Then: describe the result

The code in Listing 1.1 shows a small example in which Gherkin is used to specify a test case for an online e-commerce application. The test aims at verifying the correct price of a product when it is added to the shopping cart.

Several testing approaches can be adopted for the functional testing of web applications. The choice among them could depend on different aspects including, e.g., the

---

[4] https://cucumber.io/docs/gherkin.

technology used in the implementation of the application, the available tools (e.g., Selenium WebDriver and Selenium IDE[5]), and the expertise of the involved testers [9]. In this work, we consider three testing approaches: programmable testing (PT), capture&replay testing (CRT), and NLP-based testing (NLT).

Programmable web testing (PT) is based on the manual implementation of test scripts (test cases) using ad-hoc programming languages, e.g., Java, PHP. A test case is a script composed of a set of instructions and programming commands written by developers and executed to exercise the application functionality. Often, testers can use libraries that expose APIs for interacting with web applications and providing the use of commands, e.g., click a button, fill fields and submit a form. Then, the test script is completed by developers with input values and assertions to check the obtained execution results.

Listing 1.1. Example of test case specified with Gherkin

```
1. // Gherkin TC 1: TestVerifyPriceOfaSingleProduct
2. Feature: Add a product to cart and verify the price
3. Scenario: A Customer wants to add a product to the cart
4. Given the user views the homepage
5. When the user adds an item to the cart
6. And clicks to cart
7. Then the page shows the cost for the product on the cart
```

Figure 1 shows a fragment of a programmable test script written adopting the design pattern Page Object[6] that implements the Gherkin code 1.1 in Listing 1.1. @BeforeEach and @AfterEach are constructs defining commands to be executed before and after the execution of the test case body. In the body, methods provided by the Page Objects, such as addFirstProductToCart that contribute to the logic of the test cases, i.e., add a product to the shopping cart in our example, are provided. Assertions (assertEquals condition) are used to verify the price of the product added to the cart. Selenium WebDriver is an example of tool supporting programmable web testing. The advantage of programmable testing is its flexibility and the reusability of the test cases. In fact, working with programming languages allows developers to directly handle in the scripts conditional statements, loops, logging, exceptions, as well as to create parametric (i.e., data-driven) test cases. The drawbacks, however, are that: (i) developers need to be skilled; (ii) to be effective, test development has to be subject to the programming guidelines and best practices typically used for software development; and (iii) a remarkable initial effort is required to develop test cases.

Capture&replay web testing (CRT) is usually used for regression testing. This testing approach is based on a first manual execution in which the tester manually exercises a web application by using a tool that records the whole execution session, thus all user events and interactions with the application elements, as well as all key pressed, mouse movements, link clicks, scripts' execution, are recorded. Test cases are scripts that are automatically composed by the tool and that can be used to replay the recorded testing sessions. Test cases are hence executed by re-executing the whole recorded sessions that

---

[5] https://www.selenium.dev.
[6] https://martinfowler.com/bliki/PageObject.html.

Fig. 1. Example of PT test script

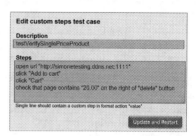

Fig. 2. Example of CRT test script

Fig. 3. Example of NLP test script

can be also enriched with assertions for checking the result of the re-execution. Testers can also customize each re-execution by slightly changing input values and assertions, that can also be parametric to make the test scripts more flexible. Figure 2 shows a fragment of a test script recorded with a capture&replay tool that implements the Gherkin code in Listing 1.1, as example. We see that the starting web page to test is defined at the beginning of the test, then a set of `click` operations have been performed by the tester to add a product to the shopping cart, then the text content of a page element is checked with an assertion (`verify text`). Selenium IDE is an example of tool supporting capture&replay web testing. The advantage of capture&replay tools is that they are relatively simple to use. Hence, even testers without programming skills are able to build complex and complete test suites. The drawbacks, however, are that the resulting test scripts (1) have a lot of duplicated code, (2) are difficult to read in case of complex scenarios, and (3) contain hard-coded values (e.g., data inputs and page references and objects) that make the test scripts strongly coupled with the web application under test and as a consequence difficult to modify, e.g., for test maintenance and evolution purpose.

NLP-based testing uses NLP techniques to let testers write test scripts by using the natural language. NLP, in fact, is the part of artificial intelligence that allows machines to interpret natural language. The use of NLP techniques for testing purposes is still at the infancy and its effectiveness has to be empirically investigated. Figure 3 shows a fragment of a test script that implements the Gherkin code in Listing 1.1, as example. We can see that the test script is written as a sequence of simple natural language sentences in which verbs such as `open`, `click`, `check`, and their synonyms, are used to describe the actions to be executed on the application under test. TestSigma, TestRigor, and TestProject are three examples of commercial tools supporting natural language web testing. The advantage of NLP testing is that it can help in reducing the effort required to human testers for producing test cases. Furthermore, specific programming skills are not required as for the programmable approach. NLP can be used to write test cases in natural language, to transform such descriptions in executable test cases and to run them. The drawbacks, however, are that an adequate transformation approach based on NLP techniques is required to transform test cases written in natural language into executable test cases able to exercise the application under test.

4   Case Study Design

This section details planning and design of the case study we conducted to compare three web testing approaches: programmable testing (PT), capture&replay testing (CRT), and NLP-based testing (NLT). In terms of tools supporting these three testing approaches, we selected Selenium WebDriver (PT) and Selenium IDE (CRT) because they are well known and used. As representative of the NLT available tools, we selected a commercial tool, according to a preliminary analysis we conducted[7]. The rest of this section presents the design of the case study.

4.1   Study Design

The goal of this study is to compare three web testing approaches, *PT*, *CRT* and *NLT* with the purpose of assessing both short-term and long-term (i.e., across multiple releases) effort required in two main testing scenarios: (1) test case development and (2) test case evolution. In fact, we are mainly interested in comparing the effort required for the implementation of the initial test suites from scratch, and the effort required for the evolution of the test suites across subsequent releases of the applications. The results of the study can be useful for (i) practitioners (developers and managers), interested in understanding the usual costs and the possible returns of their investment associated with the adoption of the different web testing approaches; and (ii) researchers, interested in collecting empirical evidence about the usage of the different testing approaches.

The context of the study is defined as follows. The involved human subjects are: one of the authors, who defined the test specifications, and a junior professional web developer, who developed the test cases with the three approaches. The objects of the study are three open-source web applications.

4.2   Software Objects

To perform our experiment, we took into account three web applications (experimental objects) named: ExpressCart, Shopizer and OIM. These applications have been selected since they are: (1) medium-size applications; (2) quite representative of usual web applications in terms of functionality they provide and technology they use, i.e., programming languages, databases, libraries and frameworks; and (3) there are at least two

---

[7] Being a commercial tool, we think it is better not to disclose its identity. In all cases, the other NLP tools considered were also very similar to the one chosen.

major releases available (minor releases have not been considered since small changes between the applications releases lead to a large reuse of test cases, thus limiting the amount of empirical data for our study). This last point is relevant for the estimation of the test case evolution effort, i.e., the effort required to evolve and reuse the test cases for more than one software release. For each application, hence, we consider two subsequent major releases extracted from the application code repository that expose both *logical* and *structural* changes. While a logical change is a change in a system functionality that foresees the modification of the process underlying the specific functionality, a structural change is instead a change on the application structure that implies only some changes to the elements, e.g., of the application GUI layout/structure.

ExpressCart[8] is an e-commerce application that implements functionalities such as: shopping carts, payment methods, and administrative functions. The application is very rich and dynamic: it is mainly written in Javascript, by using frameworks such as Node.js and Express.js. Shopizer[9] is another e-commerce application, mainly written in Java, that implements functionalities such as: catalog management, shopping carts, marketing components, smart pricing management, ordering, payment and shipping management. OIM[10] is an inventory management that implements transactions management, raw material management, batch, supplier, items, categories, and storage management. The application has been mainly developed in PHP by using AppGini[11], a web-database framework for applications building.

4.3 Research Questions and Metrics

The research questions of our study are the following ones:

- **RQ1: Developing Time**. What is the initial development effort required for creating test suites by adopting NLT with respect to more traditional approaches such as PT and CRT?
- **RQ2: Reuse**. How much of the test suites generated by adopting NLT can be reused 'as-is' with respect to more traditional approaches such as PT and CRT, when a new release of the application needs to be tested?
- **RQ3: Evolution Time**. What is the effort required for the evolution of test suites generated by adopting NLT with respect to the effort required to evolve test suites developed with traditional approaches such as PT and CRT, when a new release of the application needs to be tested?
- **RQ4: Trend in Releases**. How the cumulative effort (i.e., combining development and evolution effort) required by NLT varies in the time, with respect to the one required for applying traditional approaches such as PT and CRT, by considering several different application releases?

The first research question deals with the development cost in terms of time required to develop test suites from test specifications. We aim at verifying whether the adoption

---

[8] https://expresscart.markmoffat.com/documentation.html (last access: February 2022).

[9] https://shopizer-ecommerce.github.io/documentation/#/starting (last access: February 2022).

[10] https://bigprof.com/appgini/applications/online-inventory-manager (last access: February 2022).

[11] https://appgini.en.softonic.com/.

of NLT is costly in terms of required time, with respect to the time required to apply the more traditional approaches, PT and CRT. This could give practitioners an idea of the initial investment to be made to adopt the testing approaches. To answer *RQ1*, we measured the test suite development effort in terms of time (minutes) needed by a tester to develop the executable test cases. We compared the different efforts and estimated the ratio between NLT and the more traditional approaches.

The second research question deals with the resilience to changes of the developed test suites. We aim at verifying the capability of the testing approaches in developing test suites that can be reused to test new major releases of the application under test. This could give practitioners an idea of the capability of the testing approach to implement reusable test suites, i.e., suites that can be reused (as-is) to test a new software release. To answer *RQ2*, we considered the next major release of each web application under test ($_{v2}$) and counted the number of test cases reusable (as-is) for testing this new release, i.e., for which the execution does not fail in the new application release.

The third research question deals with the *evolution* cost required to evolve test suites by making them working for testing the new major release of the application under test. We aim at verifying whether a testing approach requires additional evolution costs, with respect to others, and we aim at estimating the ratio between the different costs. This could give practitioners an idea of the effort to be provided to make test suites usable for more than one software release. To answer *RQ3*, we considered the next major release of each web application under test and we evolved the initially developed test suites so as to make them usable also for testing this new release. We, hence, measured the test suite evolution effort, in terms of time (minutes) needed by a tester to fix the test cases that cannot be executed directly with the new application release ($_{v2}$).

The last research question is about the return on investment conducted for the adoption of the testing approaches. We aim at verifying how the cumulative testing effort (computed combining development and evolution effort) required to apply the NLT approach varies over the time and the application releases, with respect to the one required to apply the more traditional approaches PT and CRT. This could give practitioners an idea of the overall effort needed. To answer *RQ4*, we computed the cumulative testing effort for each approach as proposed in [9] and estimated the number of application releases after which the cumulative effort trend changes. For instance, let C_0 and N_0 the effort required for the initial development of CRT and NLT test cases, respectively, and let C_1, C_2,... and N_1, N_2 the test case evolution effort associated with the successive application releases. We are seeking the lowest value n such that: $\sum_{n=0}^{n} C_i \geq \sum_{n=0}^{n} N_i$. That value corresponds to the release number after which NLT test cases start to be cumulatively more convenient than CRT ones. Under the assumption that $C_i = C \ \forall i > 0$ and that $N_i = N \ \forall i > 0$ i.e., the same evolution effort is required for the software releases, we can find the following solution to the equation above: $\frac{N_0 - C_0}{C - N}$. Hence, after n releases, the cumulative effort of the initial development and evolution of NLT test cases is lower than the one of CRT test cases. It is worth to notice that a negative value obtained for n means that the cumulative cost of the NLT is always lower than the one of CRT. Similarly we can estimate the value of n for NLT vs PT and CRT vs PT. By estimating n, we could give practitioners an idea about when the investment in the adoption of a given testing approach could become of interest with respect to the other testing approaches, considering both development and evolution effort.

4.4 Procedure

In the study, programmable testing, capture&replay testing, and NLP-based testing have been adopted in two different testing tasks: (i) test case development and (ii) test case evolution. Two sub-sequent application releases of the objects of the study have been considered: ExpressCart$_{v1}$ / ExpressCart$_{v2}$, Shopizer$_{v1}$ / Shopizer$_{v2}$, and OIM$_{v1}$ / OIM$_{v2}$. In detail, the following procedure has been applied.

1. A preliminary training phase has been organized by asking the junior developer to test the PetClinic[12] application with the three different testing approaches, by starting from Gherkin test specifications, thus to practice them and their corresponding tools.
2. Each application and artifact (e.g., code and documentation) has been analyzed by the junior developer and by one of the authors to acquire knowledge about them, their functionalities, and the technology used to implement them.
3. A test suite specification has been defined by one of the authors by describing a set of end-to-end functional test cases for each application object of the study: Express-Cart, Shopizer, and OIM. The main functionalities provided by each applications' version $_{v1}$ considered in the study have been covered at least once (mainly covered only normal cases, and not many corner cases). The test cases have been specified using the Gherkin language.
4. *Test cases development*: PT, CRT and NLT have been used, by the involved developer, for implementing the previously created test cases specifications for ExpressCart$_{v1}$, Shopizer$_{v1}$, and OIM$_{v1}$. In other terms, three executable test suites have been developed for testing the first release of the applications under test by using the three different tools considered in this case study. The three developed test suites are equivalent from the functional point of view, since they test exactly the same functionalities and have been developed by trying to adhere to the defined test specifications.
5. *Test case evolution:*
   - The executable test suites built at the previous point have been executed, by the developer, on the second application releases (i.e., ExpressCart$_{v2}$, Shopizer$_{v2}$, and OIM$_{v2}$) and identified the failing test cases, i.e., those test cases that, due to application changes between the first and the second application release, report a failure or an error.
   - Both structural and logical changes implemented in ExpressCart$_{v2}$, Shopizer$_{v2}$, and OIM$_{v2}$, with respect to the previous release of the same application, have been identified and considered.
   - The failed test cases have been repaired, by the junior developer, so that the full test suites can be executed without problems also in the second release ($_{v2}$) of the applications under test.

---

[12] https://projects.spring.io/spring-petclinic.

During the whole process, the development effort required for the development of the three test suites, as well as the evolution effort required for the evolution of the test suites, have been measured by the junior developer noting down the times. To balance as much as possible the learning effects in the experiment, the order of test suite development and evolution has been alternated. Finally, metrics (i.e., test cases development and evolution time, number of failed test cases, and cumulative effort trend) needed to answer the four research questions, have been analyzed.

4.5   Threats to Validity

Internal validity threats concern factors that may affect a dependent variable that are not considered in the study. The most relevant threat to the internal validity concerns the subjectivity and variability of the test cases implementation task, e.g., selection of the application functionalities to test, definition of test steps and input data. We tried to limit this threat by involving two persons, one for the definition of the test specifications and another one (the junior developer) for the test development, and by applying well-known testing criteria. Another (possible) impacting threat is related to the learning effect during the test case development and evolution tasks. As explained, we tried to consider it in the experiment design by altering the order of test suite development and evolution. *Construct validity* threats concern the relationship between theory and observation. The most relevant threat to the construct validity concerns the use of time (development and evolution time) as measure of the testing effort. Even if we are conscious that it is questionable since several different aspects could impact the testing effort, we consider time as a reasonably proxy for estimating the testing effort since it is a widely adopted practice in the empirical software engineering. Another threat concern the fact that test cases have been specified in Gherkin: such specifications can be considered quite similar to the one used for NLT. On the one side, however, Gherkin test cases are abstract while NLT test cases are concrete test scripts characterized by executable steps, specific input values and assertions to check the output. Moreover, on the other side, this mimics what normally happens in the industry where E2E test cases are often specified in natural language.

Conclusion validity concerns the relationship between the treatment and the outcome. To analyze the data and answer the research questions of interest we chose to use non-parametric tests (i.e., Wilcoxon paired test), due to the size of the sample and because we could not safely assume normal distributions. Moreover, we applied corrections (specifically, Holm correction) to the statistical tests due to multiple re-executions.

External validity threats are related to the generalization of the results. The most relevant threat to external validity concerns the involvement of only one junior developer. Concerning this point, the involved developer has some industrial experience in the Web domain and testing with Selenium WebDriver and thus is a good representative of junior web developers, in general. Moreover, it is important to underline that the case study is challenging and time-consuming and therefore finding candidates to re-execute it is not easy. Another threat could be related to the applications adopted in the study. The applications are medium-size, realistic and representative of their domain, and based on modern technologies and languages. Other potentially impacting threats are related to the developed test suites and the used tools. Test suites have been developed as much as possible by following a systematic approach and by constructing, at least, one test case for each functionality provided by the applications. In terms of adopted tools, we used third-party frameworks/tools, well-known and available on the Internet, thus avoiding any bias of the authors.

5   Analysis of Results

5.1   RQ1: Developing Time

Table 1 reports general information about the developed test suites in terms of number and characteristics (e.g., lines of code) of test cases developed. To compare the CRT and PT code, we exported the native Selenese code (column "Sel")—the language used by Selenium IDE—in Java using the export feature provided by Selenium IDE. In two cases, as expected, the Java test code (excluded the page objects - POs) is shorten than the CRT one, while in the case of Shopizer, this does not happen since several manual waits has been added by the junior developer in the PT code (on the contrary, CRT manages automatically such cases). Moreover, it is interesting to note that the number of NLT test case lines are always less than the number of Selenese lines: this is reasonable since Selenium records every interaction with the web application (e.g., click on a "name" field + type "John": i.e., 2 lines) while NLT provides a higher level view (e.g., write "John" in the "name" field: i.e., 1 line). The last column of the table shows the average number of steps for the NLT test cases.

Table 1. Test suites code details

Application	#Test cases	Code								
		PT				CRT		NLT	
		Test LOCs	PO LOCs	Total LOCs	#PO	Sel lines	Java LOCs	Lines	AVG lines
ExpressCart	40	842	932	1774	18	635	934	361	9.0
Shopizer	28	506	483	989	7	273	417	150	5.3
OIM	32	462	1065	1527	18	552	765	351	10.9

Table 2 reports the total test suite and average test case development effort (expressed in minutes) and the statistical difference observed (if any) between the distributions of the test development effort, to compare PT and CRT with NLT, computed using the Wilcoxon paired test with Holm correction. The last two columns report the effort ratio measured between PT and CRT with NLT. For instance, a value higher than 1 in the ratio between PT and NLT means that the PT test suite required more development effort (time) than the corresponding NLT test suite.

That Table shows that the development effort for PT is always higher than for NLT (p-value < 0.01), while there is also a trend, statistically relevant for two out of three applications, for which the development effort for NLT is higher than the one of CRT. This is confirmed by the ratio (last columns of Table 2), indeed PT required more effort than NLT (PT/NLT ratio value is higher than 1) and CRT required less effort than NLT (CRF/NLT ratio is lower than 1). The observed result shows that PT requires more

Table 2. Test suite development time (minutes)

Application	Total			Average			p-value		Ratio	
	Time (min)			Time (min)			PT-NLT	CRT-NLT	PT/NLT	CRT/NLT
	PT	CRT	NLT	PT	CRT	NLT				
ExpressCart	315.7	45.8	156.6	9.6	1.4	4.7	<0.01	<0.01	2.02	0.29
Shopizer	225.1	47.7	75.4	8.0	1.7	2.7	<0.01	<0.01	2.98	0.63
OIM	310.4	86.4	93.2	10.0	2.8	3.0	<0.01	0.07	3.33	0.93

development time than NLT, since the former requires to develop the testing code (e.g., in Java) and the latter requires only to describe the test scenarios using a step-by-step natural language description (e.g., derived from the Gherkin descriptions). At the same time, the result of our case study shows also that CRT allows to produce test cases faster than NLT. In fact, the NLT approach requires, unlike CRT, the analysis of the description of test scenarios (written in Gherkin), their conversion in step-by-step actions/steps that exercise the application under test, and the definition of the needed input values. By analyzing the developed NLT test cases, we noticed that the junior developer tried to describe the test actions/steps by using a simple natural language, avoiding complex linguistic constructs; this was done to simplify the task and to avoid problems of understanding by the NLT tool.

RQ1. Summarizing, with respect to the research question RQ1, we can observe that: (i) the programmable test suites (PT) required the largest initial development effort; and (ii) there is a trend for which natural language test suites (NLT) require more effort compared to that required for capture&replay (CRT) suites.

5.2   RQ2: Reuse

Table 3 reports some information about the fixed/repaired test cases, i.e., those test cases developed for testing the application release $v1$ and that failed in exercising the application release $v2$, thus requiring some effort to be fixed. In particular, Table 3 reports, for each testing approach, the number of fixed test cases (column "Fixed") and also the statistical difference (if any) between PT and CRT with NLT distributions, computed by using the Wilcoxon paired test with the Holm correction.

Table 3. Test suites evolution: changes

Application	PT	CRT	NLT	p-value	
	#Test fixed	#Test fixed	#Test fixed	PT-NLT	CRT-NLT
ExpressCart	19	23	19	0.33	1
Shopizer	17	16	17	1	1
OIM	26	28	15	0.01	0.03
Total	62	67	51	–	–
Average	20.7	22.7	17	–	–

About the fixed test cases, we mainly observe trends that are not statistically relevant in most of the cases, apart for OIM. While for OIM, we observed that tests to be repaired differ significantly between PT/CRT and NL, for the other two applications no relevant difference has been observed. In general, we can observe that a large amount of test cases needs to be fixed (in the range between 48% and 90%). CRT has the largest number of test cases to be fixed, on average 73%, and variability for application under test 17% with respect to PT (respectively 67% and 14%) and NLT (respectively 56% and 6%).

As we have already said, the changes between the two selected versions of the web applications $v1$ and $v2$ considered in the experimentation were of two types: structural and logical. The number of structural changes were the following: ExpressCart 14, Shopizer 9 and OIM 9. While the logical changes were: ExpressCart 6, Shopizer 8 and OIM 14. It is possible to note that the number of changes is well distributed both between applications and types.

As expected, PT and CRT show overall a similar levels of reusability (see Table 3) since they are based on the same DOM-based interaction paradigm. More interesting is the result of NLT that appears to be able, on average more often than the other approaches, to compensate for the change and thus finding a working solution in the novel version of the app. This is due to the fact that the NLT actions are more abstract (e.g., Enter "John" into "name" field) than the one required in the PT and CRT approaches (e.g., driver.findElement(By.xpath("//*[@id='username']")).sendKeys("John"); where the web element is localized using a XPath expression) that suffer more from changes to the DOM.

RQ2. Summarizing, with respect to the research question RQ2, we can observe that: (i) the capture&replay suites (CRT) show the lowest reusability, while (ii) the natural language suites (NLT) show the highest test case reusability.

5.3   RQ3: Evolution Time

Table 4 reports (i) general information about the evolution test suites effort in terms of time (expressed in minutes) required to fix the failed test cases and (ii) the statistical difference observed between the distributions of the test evolution time to compare PT and CRT with NLT, which is computed using the Wilcoxon paired test with the Holm correction. The Table also reports the evolution effort ratio measured between PT and CRT with NLT. For instance, a value higher than 1 in the ratio between PT and NLT means that the PT test suite required more evolution time than the corresponding NLT test suite.

Table 4. Test suite evolution time (expressed in minutes)

Application	Total Time (min)			Average Time (min)			p-value		Ratio	
	PT	CRT	NLT	PT	CRT	NLT	PT-NLT	CRT-NLT	PT/NLT	CRT/NLT
ExpressCart	88.1	95.6	44.7	2.7	2.9	1.3	**0.01**	**0.04**	1.97	2.14
Shopizer	62.0	30.1	42.5	2.2	1.1	1.5	**0.03**	0.66	1.46	0.71
OIM	62.6	60.9	38.5	2.1	2.0	1.2	0.08	0.06	1.63	1.58

From Table 4 it is apparent that: (i) PT required a higher evolution effort of NLT in all the applications; and (ii) CRT required a higher evolution effort than NLT in two out of three applications. Indeed, the penultimate column of Table 4 shows that PT has a ratio greater than 1 with respect to NLT. While CRT shows, with respect to NLT (last column), a ratio greater than 1 in two out of three applications. The fact that NLT requires less time to evolve the failed test cases with respect to PT is reasonable since in such a case no programming activities are required and to complete the maintenance task it is enough to edit the test description text. On the other hand, NLT is also faster than CRT for two applications out of three: also in this case edit the test description text seems to be simpler than directly editing the Selenese code, or re-recording the entire scenario. In the case of Shopizer, we can observe that the evolution time of NLT is higher of about 12 min with respect to CRT. This is explainable why the novel version of the application introduced a banner for the user-management of the cookies not straightforward to be managed using the NLT tool. The banner requested, in NLT, a few attempts before finding the correct interaction solution while in the case of CRT a simple recording of the interaction with the approve button was sufficient to solve the problem.

RQ3. Summarizing, concerning the research question RQ3, we can observe that: (i) the programmable test suites (PT) required a higher evolution effort compared to NLT; and (ii) the evolution effort required by the capture&replay suites (CRT) shows a high variability (but in two cases out of three is higher than the one required for NLT).

5.4   RQ4: Cumulative Effort

Table 5 reports the estimated application release n in which we foresee a significant change of the cumulative testing effort trend. Concerning the adoption of NLT, Table 5 shows that the cumulative testing effort of NLT is almost always lower than the one of PT and CRT, apart the case of Shopizer for CRT. The three negative values for n in column PT-NLT confirm what reported in the previous tables: NLT cost less during the initial development and also the cost of each evolution step is lower. Thus, the straight lines representing the cumulative costs never intersect for any positive value of n. Moreover, the two positive values of n in column CRT-NLT means that NLT have an initial higher cost w.r.t. CRT but just after a few releases the cumulative costs of NLT are lower since it requires lower maintenance costs. The only exception is the case of Shopizer, where both the development and evolution costs are lower for CRT, meaning that CRT shows a lower cumulative cost for any positive value of n. Also in this case the explanation could be attributable to the introduction of the banner (see the answer to RQ3).

RQ4. Summarizing, with respect to the research question RQ4, we can observe that overall the natural language suites (NLT) required the lowest cumulative testing effort with respect to the other approaches (i.e., PT and CRT) with only one exception (Shopizer that costs less when adopting CRT).

Table 5. Evolution cost: an approach that costs less starting from a release $n < 0$ means that it costs less for both the initial development and the evolution costs.

Application	Application releases: n	
	PT-NLT	CRT-NLT
ExpressCart	NLT costs less for $n > -3.6$	NLT costs less for $n > +2.2$
Shopizer	NLT costs less for $n > -7.7$	CRT costs less for $n > -2.2$
OIM	NLT costs less for $n > -9.0$	NLT costs less for $n > +0.3$

6   Conclusions

This paper reports a study conducted to compare NL-based web testing (NLT) and two more traditional testing approaches, i.e., programmable testing (PT) and capture&replay testing (CRT). The comparison is based on: the effort required for developing test suites; the resilience to changes and the effort required to evolve test suites; and the overall effort needed to apply each testing approach over multiple application releases.

Results show that: (i) NLT requires less development effort than PT but more effort than CRT; (ii) NLT shows the highest test case reusability, as well as (iii) the lowest evolution effort in most of the cases, with respect to traditional approaches; and (iv) NLT tends to require the lowest cumulative testing effort over the time, with respect to other approaches (we observed only an exception in one of the considered web application using CRT).

For the future, we are planning to: (i) conduct a larger study by extending the set of the considered web applications and involving others developers, currently we have involved only one participant, aiming at consolidating the obtained results; (ii) consider different tools than Selenium IDE/WebDriver and the one for NLT to support the obtained results, and (iii) conduct a study to estimate the expressiveness of the natural language used to develop test cases with the NLT approach and to exploit the potentiality of the engine underlying the NLT approach (i.e., the engine used to transform natural language based test cases into executable test cases).

References

1. Carvalho, G., Falcão, D., Barros, F., Sampaio, A., Mota, A., Motta, L., Blackburnc, M.: Nat2testscr: Test case generation from natural language requirements based on scr specifications. Sci. Comput. Program. **95**, 275–297 (2014). https://doi.org/10.1016/j.scico.2014.06.007
2. Cauchi, A., Colombo, C., Francalanza, A., Micallef, M., Pace, G.: Using gherkin to extract tests and monitors for safer medical device interaction design. In: 8th Symposium on Engineering Interactive Computing Systems (SIGCHI), ACM, June 2016. https://doi.org/10.1145/2933242.2935868
3. Colombo, C., Micallef, M., Scerri, M.: Verifying web applications: from business level specifications to automated model-based testing. Electron. Proc. Theor. Comput. Sci. **141**, 14–28 (2014). https://doi.org/10.4204/eptcs.141.2
4. Ebert, C., Gallardo, G., Hernantes, J., Serrano, N.: DevOps. IEEE Softw. **33**(3), 94–100 (2016). https://doi.org/10.1109/ms.2016.68

5. Fischbach, J., Vogelsang, A., Spies, D., Wehrle, A., Junker, M., Freudenstein, D.: SPEC-MATE: automated creation of test cases from acceptance criteria. In: 13th International Conference on Software Testing, Validation and Verification (ICST), IEEE, October 2020. https://doi.org/10.1109/icst46399.2020.00040

6. García, B., Gallego, M., Gortázar, F., Organero, M.: A survey of the selenium ecosystem. Electronics **9**, 1067 (2020). https://doi.org/10.3390/electronics9071067

7. Garousi, V., Bauer, S., Felderer, M.: NLP-assisted software testing: a systematic mapping of the literature. Inf. Softw. Technol. **126**, 106321 (2020). https://doi.org/10.1016/j.infsof.2020.106321

8. Gupta, A., Mahapatra, R.P.: A circumstantial methodological analysis of recent studies on NLP-driven test automation approaches. In: Udgata, S.K., Sethi, S., Srirama, S.N. (eds.) Intelligent Systems. LNNS, vol. 185, pp. 155–167. Springer, Singapore (2021). https://doi.org/10.1007/978-981-33-6081-5_14

9. Leotta, M., Clerissi, D., Ricca, F., Tonella, P.: Capture-replay vs. Programmable web testing: an empirical assessment during test case evolution. In: Proceedings of 20th Working Conference on Reverse Engineering (WCRE 2013), pp. 272–281. IEEE (2013). https://doi.org/10.1109/WCRE.2013.6671302

10. Leotta, M., Clerissi, D., Ricca, F., Tonella, P.: Visual vs. DOM-based web locators: an empirical study. In: Casteleyn, S., Rossi, G., Winckler, M. (eds.) ICWE 2014. LNCS, vol. 8541, pp. 322–340. Springer, Cham (2014). https://doi.org/10.1007/978-3-319-08245-5_19

11. Leotta, M., Clerissi, D., Ricca, F., Tonella, P.: Approaches and tools for automated end-to-end web testing. Adv. Comput. **101**, 193–237 (2016). https://doi.org/10.1016/bs.adcom.2015.11.007

12. Li, L., et al.: Clustering test steps in natural language toward automating test automation. In: 28th ACM Joint Meeting on European Software Engineering Conference and Symposium on the Foundations of Software Engineering, ACM, November 2020. https://doi.org/10.1145/3368089.3417067

13. Longo, D.H., Vilain, P., da Silva, L.P.: Measuring test data uniformity in acceptance tests for the FitNesse and gherkin notations. J. Comput. Sci. **17**(2), 135–155 (2021). https://doi.org/10.3844/jcssp.2021.135.155

14. Malik, M., Sindhu, M., Abbasi, R.: Test oracle using semantic analysis from natural language requirements. In: 22nd International Conference on Enterprise Information Systems. SCITEPRESS (2020). https://doi.org/10.5220/0009471903450352

15. Marchetto, A., Ricca, F., Torchiano, M.: Comparing "traditional" and web specific fit tables in maintenance tasks: a preliminary empirical study. In: 12th European Conference on Software Maintenance and Reengineering. IEEE, April 2008. https://doi.org/10.1109/csmr.2008.4493327

16. Pribisalic, M.: Automatic generation of test cases from use-case specification using natural language processing. In: 33rd Bled eConference - Enabling Technology for a Sustainable Society, pp. 725–734 (2020). https://doi.org/10.18690/978-961-286-362-3.52

17. Ricca, F., Marchetto, A., Stocco, A.: Ai-based test automation: a grey literature analysis. In: IEEE International Conference on Software Testing, Verification and Validation Workshops (ICSTW), pp. 263–270 (2021). https://doi.org/10.1109/ICSTW52544.2021.00051

18. Tahvili, S., Hatvani, L., Ramentol, E., Pimentel, R., Afzal, W., Herrera, F.: A novel methodology to classify test cases using natural language processing and imbalanced learning. Eng. Appl. Artif. Intell. **95**, 103878 (2020). https://doi.org/10.1016/j.engappai.2020.103878

19. Wang, C., Pastore, F., Goknil, A., Briand, L.C.: Automatic generation of acceptance test cases from use case specifications: an NLP-based approach. IEEE Trans. Softw. Eng. **48**(2), 585–616 (2022). https://doi.org/10.1109/tse.2020.2998503

Effective Spectrum Based Fault Localization Using Contextual Based Importance Weight

Qusay Idrees Sarhan[1,2]([✉]) [iD] and Árpád Beszédes[1] [iD]

[1] Department of Software Engineering, University of Szeged, Szeged, Hungary
[2] Department of Computer Science, University of Duhok, Duhok, Iraq
{sarhan,beszedes}@inf.u-szeged.hu

Abstract. In Spectrum-Based Fault Localization (SBFL), a suspicion score for each program element (e.g., statement, method, or class) is calculated by using a risk evaluation formula based on tests coverage and their results. The elements are then ranked from most suspicious to least suspicious based on their scores. The elements with the highest scores are thought to be the most faulty. The final ranking list of program elements helps testers during the debugging process when seeking the source of a fault in the program under test. In this paper, we present an approach that gives more importance to program elements that are executed by more failed test cases and appear in different contexts of method calls (both as callees and as callers) in these tests compared to other elements. In essence, we are emphasizing the failing test cases factor because there are comparably much less failing tests than passing ones. We multiply each element's suspicion score obtained by a SBFL formula by this importance weight, which is the ratio of covering failing tests over all failing tests combined with the so-called method calls frequency. The proposed approach can be applied to SBFL formulas without modifying their structures. The experimental results of our study show that our approach achieved a better performance in terms of average ranking compared to the underlying SBFL formulas and comparable approaches. It also improved the Top-N categories and increased the number of cases in which the faulty method became the top-ranked element.

Keywords: Debugging · Fault localization · Spectrum-based fault localization · Importance weight · Method calls

The research was supported by the Ministry of Innovation and Technology NRDI Office within the framework of the Artificial Intelligence National Laboratory Program (RRF-2.3.1-21-2022-00004) and the project no. TKP2021-NVA-09 which was implemented with the support provided by the Ministry of Innovation and Technology of Hungary from the National Research, Development and Innovation Fund, financed under the TKP2021-NVA funding scheme.

1 Introduction

Many aspects of our daily lives are automated by software. They are, however, far from being faultless. Software bugs can result in dangerous situations, including death. As a result, various software fault localization techniques, such as spectrum-based fault localization (SBFL) [14], have been proposed over the last few decades. SBFL calculates the likelihood of each program element of being faulty based on program spectra collected from executing test cases and their results. SBFL, on the other hand, is not yet widely used in the industry due to a number of challenges and issues [11].

One of such issues is that program elements are ranked from most to least suspicious in order of their suspicion scores. Testers check each element starting at the top of the ranking list to determine whether it is faulty or not. Thus, the faulty element should be placed near the top of the ranking list to aid testers in discovering it early in the evaluation process and with least effort. Many times, SBFL formulas place the faulty elements far from the ranking list top.

In this paper, we are addressing this issue by presenting an approach that gives more importance to program elements that are executed by more failed test cases and appear in different contexts of method calls (both as callees and as callers) in these tests compared to other elements. The intuition is the following. A typical SBFL matrix is unbalanced in the sense that there are much more passing tests than failing ones, and many SBFL formulas treat passing and failing tests similarly. Also, program elements might behave differently when appearing in different calling contexts. We propose to emphasize the factor of the failing tests in the formulas, which is achieved by introducing a multiplication factor to any SBFL formula. This factor is called *the importance weight*, and is given as the ratio of executed failing tests for a program element with respect to all failing tests combined with the so-called method calls frequency. In other words, a program element will be more suspicious if it is affected by a larger portion of the failing tests and appears in a variety of calling contexts during such test cases. The proposed approach can be applied to any SBFL formula without modifying it.

The experimental results of our study show that our approach achieved a better performance in terms of average ranking and Top-N categories compared to well-known underlying SBFL formulas and Vancsics et al.'s approach in [12].

The following are the main contributions of the paper:

1. A new approach that successfully improves the performance of SBFL in many cases is proposed.
2. The analysis of the impact of the new approach on the overall SBFL effectiveness is discussed.

We defined the following Research Questions (RQs) for this paper:

- **RQ1:** What level of average ranks improvements can we achieve using the proposed enhancing approach?

 – **RQ2:** What is the impact of the proposed approach on SBFL effectiveness across the Top-N categories?

The rest of the paper is structured as follows: Sect. 2 introduces SBFL's work and its key concepts in a nutshell. Section 3 provides a summary of the most relevant works. Section 4 introduces our approach of enhancing SBFL formulas. Section 5 provides an overview on the used subject programs, data collection, and the evaluation baselines. Section 6 presents the experimental results of this study compared to the existing approaches and provides some analysis about the effectiveness of our proposed approach. Section 7 reports the potential threats to validity. Finally, we present our conclusions and potential future works in Sect. 8.

2   Background of SBFL

This section explains SBFL and how it can be used to find software faults by ranking program elements according to their likelihood of being faulty.

2.1   SBFL Process

Many techniques have been proposed in the literature to automate the process of software fault localization [14]. However, SBFL is the most dominant because of its straightforward but potent nature, i.e. it only uses test coverage and results to calculate the suspiciousness of each program element of being faulty.

The execution of test cases on program elements is recorded to extract the spectra (i.e., tests coverage and test results) for the program under test. Program spectra information is a two-dimensional matrix that demonstrate the relationship between test cases and program elements. Its columns depict the test cases, while its rows depict the program elements. If a test case covers an element in the matrix, it is assigned a value of 1; otherwise, it is assigned a value of 0. The test results are also stored in the matrix, where 0 means the test case is passed and 1 when it is failed. For each program element e, the following four basic statistical numbers are frequently calculated from the program spectra: (a) ef: number of failed tests executing e; (b) ep: number of passed tests executing e; (c) nf: number of failed tests not executing e; (d) np: number of passed tests not executing e.

Then, these four basic statistics can be used by a SBFL formula to output a ranked list of program elements. Whichever element is at the top of the list is the most likely to be buggy. As a result, SBFL can assist testers in locating the faulty element in the target program's code.

2.2   Code Example

To demonstrate SBFL's work, consider a Java program, adopted from [12], which consists of four main methods (a, b, f, and g), and its four test cases ($t1$, $t2$, $t3$, and $t4$) as shown in Fig. 1. It can be noted that there is a fault in method g (the correct statement is _x+=i) and only $t1$ and $t4$ execute that faulty method.

```
public class Example{                        public class ExampleTest {
  private int _x = 0;                          @Test public void t1() {
  private int _s = 0;                            Example tester = new Example();
  public int x() {return _x;}                    tester.a(-1);
                                                 tester.a(1);
  public void a(int i){                          tester.b(1);
    _s = 0;                                      // failed -> 8
    if (i==0) return;                            assertEquals(9, tester.x());
    if (i<0)                                   }
      for (int y=0;y<=4;y++)
        f(i);                                  @Test public void t2() {
    else                                         Example tester = new Example();
      g(i);                                       tester.a(1);
  }                                               tester.b(1);
                                                 // failed -> 3
  public void b(int i){                          assertEquals(4, tester.x());
    _s = 1;                                     }
    if (i==0) return;
    if (i<0)                                   @Test public void t3() {
      a(Math.abs(i));                            Example tester = new Example();
    else                                          tester.a(1);
      for (int y=0;y<=1;y++)                       tester.b(0);
        g(i);                                     assertEquals(1, tester.x());
  }                                             }

  private void f(int i){                       @Test public void t4() {
    _x -= i;                                     Example tester = new Example();
  }                                               tester.a(-1);
                                                  tester.a(1);
  private void g(int i){                          tester.b(-1);
    //should be _x += i;                          assertEquals(7, tester.x());
    _x += (i+_s);                               }
  }                                           }
}
```

A - Program Code   B - Test Cases

Fig. 1. Running example – program code and test cases

2.3 Program Spectra and Basic Statistics

Assume the tests were run on the program and the program spectra (i.e., information on how the four program methods were executed in passed and failed test cases) were captured. This data is presented in Table 1.

A 1 in the cell corresponding to the method a and the test case $t1$ indicates that $t1$ has covered the method a, while a 0 indicates that the method a has not been covered. A 1 in the "Results" row indicates that the relevant test case failed, and a 0 indicates that it passed. The $t2$ test case, for example, calls the methods a, b, and g, but it fails because the output of this calls sequence should be 3, not 4.

Table 1's last four columns represent the four basic statistics (i.e., ef, ep, nf, and np) that are calculated from the program spectra. For example, the value of ef of the method a is 2 because it has been executed by two failed tests $t1$ and $t2$.

2.4 SBFL Formulas

A SBFL formula is a mathematical expression that often uses these four basic statistics to compute the suspicion score of each program element of being faulty.

Table 1. Program spectra and four basic statistics

	t1	t2	t3	t4	ef	ep	nf	np
a	1	1	1	1	2	2	0	0
b	1	1	1	1	2	2	0	0
f	1	0	0	1	1	1	1	1
g	1	1	1	1	2	2	0	0
Results	1	1	0	0				

We apply various popular formulas [9] for the experimental evaluation in this paper, as shown in Table 2.

Table 2. SBFL formulas used in the study

Name	Formula
Jaccard (J)	$\frac{ef}{ef+nf+ep}$
Barinel (B)	$\frac{ef}{ef+ep}$
SorensenDice (S)	$\frac{2*ef}{2*ef+nf+ep}$
DStar (DS)	$\frac{ef*ef}{ep+nf}$
Dice (D)	$\frac{2*ef}{ef+nf+ep}$
Interest (I)	$\frac{ef}{(ef+nf)*(ef+ep)}$
Kulczynski1 (K)	$\frac{ef}{nf+ep}$
Cohen (C)	$\frac{2*(ef*np)-2*(nf*ep)}{(ef+ep)*(ep+np)+(nf+np)*(ef+nf)}$

2.5 Suspiciousness Scores

We can get the suspiciousness score for each method in Table 3 by applying some formulas to the spectra of our Java program example in Table 1. It is worth noticing that for several methods in this example, each SBFL formula returns the same suspiciousness score. To put it another way, SBFL formulas in this circumstance are unable to distinguish the techniques just on the basis of their pure scores. Thus, the buggy method g is hardly distinguishable from the other methods. As a result, in this scenario, the SBFL effectiveness is reduced by the tie problem among program methods [11].

2.6 Suspiciousness Ranking

We use the average rank approach in Eq. 1, where S denotes the tie's starting position and E denotes the tie's size, to analyze SBFL efficiency in general. Here, the program elements with the same suspicion score are ranked using the

Table 3. Program example scores and average ranks

Method	J	Rank	B	Rank	S	Rank
a	0.5	2	0.5	2.5	0.67	2
b	0.5	2	0.5	2.5	0.67	2
f	0.33	4	0.5	2.5	0.5	4
g	0.5	2	0.5	2.5	0.67	2

average rank, such elements are called *tied elements*, by taking the average of their positions after they get sorted, in descending order, based on their scores.

$$\text{MID} = S + \left(\frac{E \text{ - } 1}{2} \right) \tag{1}$$

Table 3 presents the average ranks of the sample program using the SBFL formulas that were chosen. Ranks that are part of a tie are highlighted in gray. It can be noted that based on the ranks, Barinel (B) is unable to distinguish the methods from each other, while the other formulas result in a tie-group of three methods.

As a result, such methods are grouped together in the ranking and cannot be distinguished from one another in terms of which one should be investigated first. Therefore, additional information besides the basic hit-spectra are required to break these ties. For example, with a satiable additional information, the buggy method can be moved to a higher place in the ranking list.

3   Related Works

This section summarizes the most important efforts to improve SBFL by focusing on its formulas.

One strategy to improve SBFL is to create new SBFL formulas that outperform the current ones. The authors of [13] presented a new SBFL formula named "DStar", for example. The proposed formula was compared to a number of commonly used formulas, and it outperformed them all. Using Genetic Programming (GP), SBFL formulas can also be created automatically. The authors in [1] employed GP to create SBFL formulas automatically based on program spectra. The authors were able to come up with a total of 30 formulas. According to their findings, the GP is a good strategy for producing effective SBFL formulas.

Improvements can also be achieved by modifying existing SBFL formulas. The authors in [16] also tweaked three well-known SBFL formulas to account for the possibility that some failed tests yield more information than others. As a result, different weights for improving SBFL performance for failed tests were allocated to the three formulas and then used using multi-coverage spectra.

Combining existing SBFL formulas with one another is a different technique. The authors in [3] developed a method for mixing 40 distinct SBFL formulas to create a new SBFL formula suitable to a certain program. The suggested method pulls information from the program via mutation testing, and then uses different voting systems to merge numerous formulae depending on the acquired information to build a new formula. Experiments reveal that the formula created by their method is superior to a number of current formulas. It is worth noting that researchers attempted to combine multiple formulas in order to build new ones. The new formula is regarded as a hybrid formula since it combines the benefits of multiple previous formulations. As stated in [7,10], the performance of a hybrid formula should be superior to that of existing formulas.

Another way is to supplement existing SBFL formulas with new data. The authors in [12] added new contextual information to the underlying SBFL formulas by using the method calls frequency of the subject programs during the execution of failed tests. In each formula, the frequency ef was substituted for the ef. Their findings showed that incorporating additional data from method calls into the underlying formulas can boost SBFL effectiveness. In addition, the authors in [17] proposed a method for improving SBFL by applying the PageRank algorithm to differentiate tests. Their method takes the original program spectrum information and recomputes it using PageRank, taking into account the contributions of various test cases. The standard SBFL formulas on the recomputed spectrum information can be used to improve fault localization.

SBFL can also be improved by breaking ties. Ties in SBFL are dominant; thus it is unlikely that any of the known SBFL formulas will generate distinct scores for all program elements. The authors in [5] proposed an approach, also based on method calls frequency, to break tied program elements. Their experimental results showed that employing information from method calls frequency in failed tests cases for tie breaking can improve the effectiveness of SBFL.

SBFL's performance was improved in several ways as a result of the aforementioned studies. Our proposed approach improves the SBFL performance by giving more importance to program elements that are executed by more failed test cases and appear in different contexts of method calls (both as callees and as callers) in these tests. The advantages of our proposed approach over others are: (a) It does not modify the existing SBFL formulas. Thus, it can be applied to any SBFL formula to enhance its effectiveness. This is very important as it makes the proposed approach more applicable than other approaches. (b) It solves the issue of unbalanced SBFL matrix in the sense that there are much more passing tests than failing ones, and many SBFL formulas treat passing and failing tests similarly. (c) Finally, it also involves information outside the regular SBFL matrix, namely the calling context information.

4 The Proposed SBFL Enhancing Approach

In this section, we present the concept of our proposed approach to enhance the effectiveness of the underlying SBFL formulas and how it works. Then, we present its effectiveness when applied on our motivational example.

4.1 The Frequency-Based Ef (ϕ)

To obtain the frequency-based ef (ϕ), we first create the *frequency-based* SBFL matrix, which replaces the traditional hit-based one. As a result, instead of $\{0, 1\}$, each element will receive an integer reflecting the number of occurrences of the given element in the unique call stacks while running in various calling contexts. In other words, unique call stacks are data structures that store call stack state information during test case execution and count the number of method occurrences within these structures [12].

Table 4 presents the frequency-based matrix for our Java example. The unique call stacks of $t1$, for example, are (a, f), (a, g), and (b, g), hence the frequency of g for test $t1$ will be 2.

Table 4. Frequency-based matrix

	a	b	f	g	Results
t1	2	1	1	2	Failed
t2	1	1	0	2	Failed
t3	1	1	0	1	Passed
t4	3	1	1	2	Passed
ϕ	3	2	1	4	

ϕ is determined by adding the frequency-based values for the failing test cases in the matrix. The greater the value of ϕ for a method, the more suspicious is. For instance, adding the frequency-based values of the faulty method g (i.e., 2 and 2) in the matrix for the failing test cases (i.e., $t1$ and $t2$) will yield 4 as the value of ϕ for the method g, which is the biggest ϕ value compared to others.

4.2 The Proposed Approach

Using the selected SBFL formulas on the program spectra, we calculate the suspicion scores of program methods. The output are the initial suspicion scores of methods. Then, we multiply each initial score of each method by its importance weight which is computed via Eq. 2.

$$\text{Importance Weight} = \left(\frac{\text{ef} * \phi}{\text{ef} + \text{nf}} \right) \tag{2}$$

The order of methods in the initial ranking list will be rearranged based on the value of each method's importance weight, resulting in a final improved ranking list. From Table 5, it can be seen that the faulty method g will get the rank 1 after applying our proposed approach instead of 2 (in case of J and S) or 2.5 (in case of B) as its weight is greater than others. The rationale behind using the ϕ is that if a method appears in a lot of calls during a failed test, it will be considered more suspicious and will be given a higher rank than other methods. We combine the ϕ with $ef/(ef + nf)$ because the later emphasizes the failing test cases factor because there are comparably much less failing tests than passing ones.

Table 5. Program example scores and average ranks after applying our approach

Method	J**	Rank	B**	Rank	S**	Rank
a	1.5	2	1.5	2	2.0	2
b	1.0	3	1.0	3	1.33	3
f	0.17	4	0.25	4	0.25	4
g	2.0	1	2.0	1	2.67	1

5 Evaluation

5.1 Subject Programs

In this study, we used the faulty programs of version v1.5.0 of Defects4J [6]; where 6 open-source Java programs had 438 actual faults found in their repositories[1]. However, due to instrumentation issues or incorrect test results, 27 defects were eliminated from this analysis. As a result, the final dataset used contained a total of 411 faults. Each program's primary characteristics are presented in Table 6.

Table 6. Subject programs

Project	Number of bugs	Size (KLOC)	Number of tests	Number of methods
Chart	25	96	2.2 k	5.2 k
Closure	168	91	7.9 k	8.4 k
Lang	61	22	2.3 k	2.4 k
Math	104	84	4.4 k	6.4 k
Mockito	27	11	1.3 k	1.4 k
Time	26	28	4.0 k	3.6 k
All	411	332	22.1 k	27.4 k

5.2 Granularity of Data Collection

Method-level granularity was used as a program spectra/coverage type in this work. It provides users with a more understandable level of abstraction [2,18]. However, in terms of the proposed approach, there is no theoretical barrier to investigate other granularity levels as well.

---

[1] https://github.com/rjust/defects4j/tree/v1.5.0.

5.3   Evaluation Baselines

Several well-studied SBFL formulas were utilized as baselines in this paper, as presented in Table 2, to evaluate and compare our proposed approach to. It is worth mentioning that Vancsics et al.'s approach proposed in [12] is comparable to ours; thus, we will compare our results to it too.

6   Experimental Results and Discussion

6.1   Achieved Improvements in the Average Ranks

Table 7 presents the average ranks before (column 2) and after (column 3) using our proposed approach (denoted with **) and Vancsics et al.'s approach in [12] (denoted with *), as well as the difference between them (column 4). If the difference is negative, it indicates that the used approach has the potential to improve.

Table 7. Average ranks comparison

			Diff.	Diff.
$J = 38.51$	$J^* = 23.58$	$J^{**} = 21.83$	$J\text{-}J^* = -14.93$	$J\text{-}J^{**} = -16.68$
$B = 38.5$	$B^* = 23.66$	$B^{**} = 21.7$	$B\text{-}B^* = -14.84$	$B\text{-}B^{**} = -16.8$
$S = 38.51$	$S^* = 23.77$	$S^{**} = 21.96$	$S\text{-}S^* = -14.74$	$S\text{-}S^{**} = -16.55$
$DS = 149.03$	$DS^* = 150.59$	$DS^{**} = 136.67$	$DS\text{-}DS^* = 1.56$	$DS\text{-}DS^* = -12.36$
$D = 38.51$	$D^* = 23.58$	$D^{**} = 21.83$	$D\text{-}D^* = -14.93$	$D\text{-}D^{**} = -16.68$
$I = 38.5$	$I^* = 23.66$	$I^{**} = 21.7$	$I\text{-}I^* = -14.84$	$I\text{-}I^{**} = -16.8$
$K = 153.34$	$K^* = 138.26$	$K^{**} = 136.66$	$K\text{-}K^* = -15.08$	$K\text{-}K^{**} = -16.68$
$C = 38.54$	$C^* = 20.76$	$C^{**} = 17.87$	$C\text{-}C^* = -17.78$	$C\text{-}C^{**} = -20.67$

We can see that our proposed approach achieved improvements with all of the selected SBFL formulas: the average rank reduced by about **17** overall, which corresponds to **8–54%** with respect to the total number of methods in the used dataset. It can be noted that the Cohen formula reduced the average rank more than the others. Considering the formulas that have the lower average ranks after applying our proposed approach, Cohen, Barinel, and Interest are the best ones, respectively.

Vancsics et al.'s approach also achieved improvements in the average ranks of all the selected formulas except in the case of DS** formula, disimprovement was observed. However, the average rank reduced by this approach was about **13** overall. The difference is **4** positions between the two approaches. In other words, our approach outperformed Vancsics et al.'s approach by **4** positions in terms of reducing the average rank.

RQ1: Our proposed approach enhanced all the SBFL formulas compared to Vancsics et al's approach. The improvement of average ranks by our approach in the used benchmark was about **17** positions overall while in Vancsics et al's approach was about **13**. In terms of average ranks, our approach reduced more positions. This indicates that using an importance weight could have a positive impact and enhances the SBFL results. Also, it encourages us to investigate other forms of importance weights in the future and measure their impacts on the effectiveness of SBFL.

It is worth mentioning that only using average ranks as an evaluation metric for SBFL effectiveness has its own set of drawbacks: (a) outlier average ranks could distort the overall information on the performance of any proposed approach. (b) it tells nothing about the distribution of the rank values and their changes before and after applying a proposed approach. Therefore, there is a more important category of evaluation than average ranks: improvements in the *Top-N ranks*, where the advantages are more obvious, as presented below.

6.2 Achieved Improvements in the Top-N Categories

According to [8] and [15], testers believe that examining the first five program elements in an SBFL ranking list is acceptable, with the first ten elements being the highest limit for inspection before the list is dismissed. Thus, the success of SBFL can also be measured by concentrating on these rank positions, which are collectively known as Top-N, as follows: (a) Top-N: When the rank of a faulty program element is less or equal to N. (b) Other: When the rank of a faulty program element is more than the highest N value used in the categorizations (it is 10 in our experiments).

Figure 2 shows the number of bugs in the Top-N categories for each approach. Here, improvement is defined as a decrease in the number of cases in the "Other" category and an increase in any of the Top-N categories.

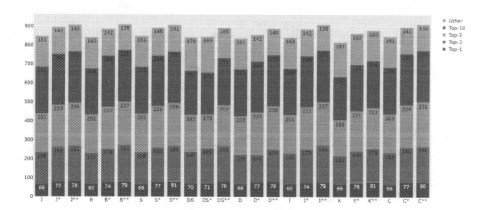

Fig. 2. Top-N categories

It is evident that by relocating many bugs to higher-ranked categories, our proposed approach and Vancsics et al.'s approach improved all Top-N categories. However, our approach placed more bugs (i.e., **19–25** bugs) into one of the Top-N categories from the "Other" category (with rank > 10) compared to Vancsics et al.'s approach (i.e., **16–21** bugs). This is significant since it raises the possibility of finding a bug with our approach while it was not very probable without it. This kind of interesting improvements is also known as *enabling improvements* [4]. Table 8 presents the enabling improvements achieved by each approach.

Table 8. Enabling improvements

	Rank > 10 (%)	Enab. impr. (%)	Enab. impr. (%)
J vs. J* vs. J**	161 (39.2%)	19 (4.6%)	21 (5.1%)
B vs. B* vs. B**	163 (39.7%)	21 (5.1%)	25 (6.0%)
S vs. S* vs. S**	161 (39.2%)	16 (3.9%)	20 (4.9%)
DS vs. DS* vs. DS**	179 (43.6%)	10 (2.4%)	19 (4.6%)
D vs. D* vs. D**	161 (39.2%)	19 (4.6%)	21 (5.1%)
I vs. I* vs. I**	163 (39.7%)	21 (5.1%)	25 (6.0%)
K vs. K* vs. K**	181 (44.0%)	18 (4.4%)	21 (5.1%)
C vs. C* vs. C**	161 (39.2%)	20 (4.9%)	22 (5.4%)

It can be noted that each new formula achieves enabling improvements, the average enabling improvements was about **5%** of the total number of faults in the used dataset by our approach. In these cases the basic SBFL formulas ranked the faulty method in the other category, but our proposed approach managed to bring it forward into the Top-10 (or better) categories. Note that, the formulas B**, I**, and C** are the best in this aspect. Overall, each formula based on our proposed approach was able to achieve enabling improvements in the possible cases. It can be noted that Vancsics et al.'s approach improvements was about **4%** of the total number of faults in the used dataset with the formulas B*, I*, and C* as the best ones. Here, this improvement seems modest considering the fact that only an importance weight was used. Other, more complex weights may yield much more improvement which will be investigated in the future. Higher categories have significant improvements as well, with roughly **8–15** bugs moving to Top-1 by our approach compared to Vancsics et al.'s approach with **1–11** bugs, for example. Here also, our approach outperformed Vancsics et al.'s approach by moving more bugs to the Top-1 category.

RQ2: We were able to raise the number of cases when the faulty method was ranked first by **11–23%**. While Vancsics et al's approach moved less number of bugs to Top-1 category. Another interesting finding is that our approach achieved more enabling improvement compared to Vancsics et al's approach by moving **19-25** bugs from the Other category into one of higher-ranked categories. These cases are now more likely to be discovered and then fixed than before.

7   Threats to Validity

In software engineering, each experimental study has some threats to its validity. In this work, the following actions were considered to avoid or mitigate the threats of validity:

– Selection of evaluation metrics: to be certain that our findings and conclusions are correct, we selected well-known evaluation metrics (i.e., average ranks and Top-N categories) that have been utilized in prior studies too.
– Correctness of implementation: a code review was performed numerous times to guarantee that our experiment implementation was correct. Furthermore, we have executed our proposed strategy multiple times to ensure that it is properly implemented.
– Selection of subject programs: we used Defects4J as a benchmark dataset in our study. Therefore, our findings cannot be generalized to other Java programs. However, we believe that the programs of Defects4J are representative and contain real faults of varied types and complexity. Defects4J is also extensively utilized in other software fault localization research.
– Exclusion of faults: due to technical limits, we had to eliminate 27 faults from the Defects4J dataset (about 6% of the total number of faults). The question is whether or not other researchers working with the same dataset will be able to reproduce our results. Our findings were not influenced in any way by this exclusion and the excluded faults were scattered almost uniformly throughout the dataset, thus we believe that this threat is very low.
– Selection of SBFL formulas: we used a collection of well-known SBFL formulas in our experiment to evaluate the effectiveness of our proposed approach, which represents only a small percentage of the reported formulas in the literature. The results demonstrate that all of them have improved. However, we cannot guarantee that using other different formulas would yield the same results. We used the formulas which are extensively used in other software fault localization research to limit the effect of this issue.

8   Conclusions

This paper presents the use of importance emphasis on the failing tests that execute the program element under consideration in SBFL. We rely on the intuition that if a code element gets executed in more failed test cases and appear in more calling contexts in such tests compared to other elements, it will be more suspicious and gets a higher rank position. This is achieved by multiplying the initial suspicion score, computed by underlying SBFL formulas, of each program method by an importance weight that represents the rate of executing a method in failed test cases combined with the so-called method calls frequency. The following are the primary characteristics of the proposed approach: (a) it can be used to any SBFL formula without changing the structure or notion of the formula. (b) it overcomes the problem of an unbalanced SBFL matrix since there are far more passing tests than failing tests, and many SBFL formulas treat passing and failing tests in the same way. The findings of this study's experiments reveal that relocating many bugs to the top Top-N rankings improved the average ranks for all formulas studied and surpassed previous approaches.

We would like to evaluate the effectiveness of our approach at different levels of granularity in the future, such as at the statement level. Incorporating other SBFL formulas into the study to determine which formulas produce the greatest results and classifying them into groups would be fascinating to investigate further. We would also like to use other expressions of importance weights and see how they affect SBFL efficacy.

References

1. Ajibode, A.A., Shu, T., Ding, Z.: Evolving suspiciousness metrics from hybrid data set for boosting a spectrum based fault localization. IEEE Access **8**, 198451–198467 (2020)
2. Le, B., T.D., Lo, D., Le Goues, C., Grunske, L.: A learning-to-rank based fault localization approach using likely invariants. In: Proceedings of the 25th International Symposium on Software Testing and Analysis, pp. 177–188, ISSTA 2016, Association for Computing Machinery, New York (2016)
3. Bagheri, B., Rezaalipour, M., Vahidi-Asl, M.: An approach to generate effective fault localization methods for programs. In: International Conference on Fundamentals of Software Engineering, pp. 244–259 (2019)
4. Beszédes, A., Horváth, F., Di Penta, M., Gyimóthy, T.: Leveraging contextual information from function call chains to improve fault localization. In: IEEE 27th International Conference on Software Analysis, Evolution and Reengineering (SANER), pp. 468–479 (2020)
5. Idrees Sarhan, Q., Vancsics, B., Beszedes, A.: Method calls frequency-based tie-breaking strategy for software fault localization. In: 2021 IEEE 21st International Working Conference on Source Code Analysis and Manipulation (SCAM), pp. 103–113 (2021). https://doi.org/10.1109/SCAM52516.2021.00021
6. Just, R., Jalali, D., Ernst, M.D.: Defects4J: a database of existing faults to enable controlled testing studies for Java programs. In: International Symposium on Software Testing and Analysis (ISSTA), pp. 437–440. ACM Press (2014)
7. Kim, J., Park, J., Lee, E.: A new hybrid algorithm for software fault localization. In: Proceedings of the 9th International Conference on Ubiquitous Information Management and Communication, pp. 1–8 (2015)
8. Kochhar, P.S., Xia, X., Lo, D., Li, S.: Practitioners' expectations on automated fault localization. In: Proceedings of the 25th International Symposium on Software Testing and Analysis, ISSTA 2016, pp. 165–176. Association for Computing Machinery, New York (2016)

9. Neelofar: spectrum-based fault localization using machine learning (2017). https://findanexpert.unimelb.edu.au/scholarlywork/1475533-spectrum-based-fault-localization-using-machine-learning
10. Park, J., Kim, J., Lee, E.: experimental evaluation of hybrid algorithm in spectrum based fault localization. In: International conference on Software Engineering Research and Practice (SERP) (2014)
11. Sarhan, Q.I., Beszedes, A.: A survey of challenges in spectrum-based software fault localization. IEEE Access **10**, 10618–10639 (2022). https://doi.org/10.1109/ACCESS.2022.3144079
12. Vancsics, B., Horvath, F., Szatmari, A., Beszedes, A.: Call frequency-based fault localization. In: 2021 IEEE International Conference on Software Analysis, Evolution and Reengineering (SANER), pp. 365–376 (2021)
13. Wong, W.E., Debroy, V., Gao, R., Li, Y.: The dstar method for effective software fault localization. IEEE Trans. Reliab. **63**(1), 290–308 (2014)
14. Wong, W.E., Gao, R., Li, Y., Abreu, R., Wotawa, F.: A survey on software fault localization. IEEE Trans. Softw. Eng. **42**(8), 707–740 (2016)
15. Xia, X., Bao, L., Lo, D., Li, S.: "Automated debugging considered harmful" considered harmful: a user study revisiting the usefulness of spectra-based fault localization techniques with professionals using real bugs from large systems. In: 2016 IEEE International Conference on Software Maintenance and Evolution (ICSME), pp. 267–278 (2016)
16. You, Y.S., Huang, C.Y., Peng, K.L., Hsu, C.J.: Evaluation and analysis of spectrum-based fault localization with modified similarity coefficients for software debugging. In: 2013 IEEE 37th Annual Computer Software and Applications Conference, pp. 180–189 (2013)
17. Zhang, M., Li, X., Zhang, L., Khurshid, S.: Boosting spectrum-based fault localization using pagerank. In: Proceedings of the 26th ACM SIGSOFT International Symposium on Software Testing and Analysis, pp. 261–272 (2017)
18. Zou, D., Liang, J., Xiong, Y., Ernst, M.D., Zhang, L.: An empirical study of fault localization families and their combinations. IEEE Trans. Softw. Eng. **47**(2), 332–347 (2021)

Comparing the Effectiveness of Assertions with Differential Testing in the Context of Web Testing

Maurizio Leotta[✉][iD], Davide Paparella, and Filippo Ricca[iD]

Dipartimento di Informatica, Bioingegneria, Robotica e Ingegneria dei Sistemi (DIBRIS),
Università di Genova, Genova, Italy
{maurizio.leotta,filippo.ricca}@unige.it,
3559361@studenti.unige.it

Abstract. Differential testing applied in the Web context compares the current web page under test with a snapshot considered correct taken from a previous version. This technique appears to be promising and an alternative to assertions in catching regressions due to the evolution of the web application under test.

This paper empirically compares Selenium WebDriver test scripts equipped with (1) assertions and (2) differential testing implemented in the Recheck tool. The comparison included costs (both test scripts development time and execution time) and effectiveness (bugs detection capability) considering two different versions of differential testing implemented in Recheck, named implicit and explicit.

Results show that, on average, Recheck (both explicit and implicit) is able to detect more bugs than classic assertions (up to +34% on complex apps). The development time is similar between the two approaches. The execution time is slightly higher than classic assertions for Recheck explicit (+33%), while it is by far higher when Recheck implicit is adopted (3.6 times). In conclusion, the best choice, considering both the effectiveness and the costs, appears to be Recheck explicit.

Keywords: Selenium WebDriver · Recheck · Assertions · End-to-end web testing

1 Introduction

Software testing is a critical phase of the software development process, having the goal of detecting defects as early as possible in the produced code. It can be performed at different levels (e.g., unit, integration, and system) and using different techniques and approaches. But regardless of the technique, level, domain of the application being tested or objective, the concept of *oracle* always plays a fundamental role. Indeed, Software testing implies the execution of a Application Under Test (AUT) using specific input values to assess the outcome. The oracle is used in this last passage for determining whether a test has passed or not. The term "oracle" was introduced in an old paper by William E. Howden [5] and since then many other scientific works (e.g., [1, 13, 16])

ⓒ The Author(s), under exclusive license to Springer Nature Switzerland AG 2022
A. Vallecillo et al. (Eds.): QUATIC 2022, CCIS 1621, pp. 108–124, 2022.
https://doi.org/10.1007/978-3-031-14179-9_8

have investigated, both theoretically and empirically, the nature and properties of this important verification mechanism.

The oracle is also of paramount importance in automated testing. In fact, the structure of a test script in a modern testing framework, as for example JUnit[1] or TestNG[2] is always logically made up of four steps, and the oracle comes into play in step three:

1. *SetUp*: the test script initializes the AUT;
2. *Exercise*: the test script performs actions to get some outcome from the AUT;
3. *Verify*: the test script (i.e., the oracle) decides if the obtained outcome from the AUT is as expected;
4. *Teardown*: the test script returns the AUT to the initial state.

A common approach used very often in modern testing frameworks at the 'verify' step is that of assertions [16]. An assertion is a boolean-valued function that compares if an expected condition is true at a certain point of a test script. The execution of an assertion generates a test verdict, i.e., pass or fail. Although the assertion mechanism is widely used in testing frameworks and there are many libraries providing rich sets of fluent assertions (e.g., AssertJ[3] and Truth[4]) this is not the only way to implement the oracle concept. An alternative mechanism is differential testing [4,9]. It consists of a comparison of outcomes, usually generated by the execution of two different systems' versions; one the old one, considered correct (often called Golden Master), and the other, the new one that is to be tested. In case the comparison leads to (unexpected) differences, then a probable bug has been identified in the new version.

In this paper, we empirically compare these two types of oracles in the Web context, using the state of the art testing framework Selenium WebDriver [3] based on assertions as a baseline and the Recheck tool that implements differential testing. We considered several factors: test script development time, test script execution time, and bugs detection capability.

This paper is organized as follows: Sect. 2 describes the two investigated approaches to implement oracle mechanisms (i.e., classical assertions and differential testing). Section 3 briefly describes the tools and frameworks implementing the two aforementioned approaches. Section 4 describes the main aspects of the empirical study we carried out to compare the approaches, while Sect. 5 reports the results of the study, and Sect. 6 concludes the paper.

2 Differential Testing vs Assertions

The classical way for evaluating tests' results is to employ assertions. A *test assertion* is a boolean expression that asserts if the output of the system under test is correct (i.e., assert expression is *true*) or not (i.e., assert expression is *false*). Usually, a single assertion verifies a chunk of independent information and asserts if the expected information

---

[1] https://junit.org/.
[2] https://testng.org/.
[3] https://assertj.github.io/doc/.
[4] https://truth.dev/.

is the actual output information of the AUT. Some examples of value-based assertions taken by JUnit are the following: *assertTrue, assertFalse, assertNull, assertNotNull, assertEqual, assertNotEqual*. Some, like the equality ones, need two values (*expected* and *actual*), others need only one. To create an assertion, a human tester must have a good knowledge of the AUT, because he/she must know in advance the expected result to be checked.

Differential testing (or *diff testing*) is a testing technique formally introduced by McKeeman as a new method for regression testing of large software systems [4,9]. Differential testing consists of a comparison of outcomes: these are generated by the execution of two different systems' versions, both using the same system under test and the same inputs. One is the *test* version, modified and needing to be tested, the other is the *base* version that is previously verified and guaranteed to produce a correct outcome [4]. The *base* version could be a live version of the software that can be executed whenever the testing procedure is launched; alternatively, it can be just statically stored in case of a fixed expected outcome. In practice, this approach verifies that the behavior of the software remains unchanged. Thus, a difference between the two versions (test and base) highlights a likely bug in the new version. Diff testing is generally closely associated with regression testing due to the natural ability of catching bugs introduced in newer versions of the software. The main peculiarity of diff testing is that no manually created *oracle* is required: the *base* version of the system under test, that is verified to be corrected, is the oracle itself. "A base version is chosen with the assumption that it is bug-free" [4] is an ambitious assumption and maybe either the strong or the weak point of diff testing. On the contrary, the assertions created by test developers play the role of the oracle. Diff testing attempts in part to solve the problem of the generation of the oracle; due to the issue about its generation, differential testing is more applicable to software whose quality is already under control, with few known errors [9]. Indeed, applying diff tests to a software with many bugs in active development and many changes between two versions is harmful to the testing process. When a tester approaches the creation of a new test suite, she/he usually analyzes the "functional requirements", considering them a complete and correct specification, like an "*oracle*". The following step is to "translate" the requirements specification in a test suite that checks and validates them. The assertions can be more or less thorough, but the procedure is always the same: i.e., asserting if the application implements the described functionality correctly. A fundamental difference between diff testing and assertions in the web application context concerns "what is tested". With assertions usually only the functional part of the SUT is verified. On the contrary, differential test also considers other aspects, not only functional ones, such as the style or GUI-related changes, since it compares the entire web pages.

3 Testing Tools and Framework Considered

This section describes the tools and frameworks we used to compare the two approaches: classical assertions vs. differential testing.

3.1   Selenium WebDriver

Selenium WebDriver[5] is a testing framework belonging to the Selenium ecosystem[6] which "drives a browser natively, as a user would" [14]; more specifically, it is an object-oriented API that allows test developers to effectively write test scripts able to drive browsers. This framework is used for automating web-based application testing in order to verify that the AUT performs as expected [17]. The great success of this framework is mainly due to two aspects:

1. it is open-source and thus freely modifiable and usable;
2. test scripts can be written in any programming language (e.g., Java or Python), therefore a test suite can be developed and maintained like every other software project.

We chose Selenium WebDriver in our experiment because it is a mature, open-source, and widely-used state-of-the-art framework for web application testing [3,7]. The assertions were produced using JUnit 5.

3.2   Differential Testing with Recheck

Recheck is a testing framework supporting differential testing in the context of web testing. It is proposed by *Retest*, a start-up company[7] based in Germany founded in 2017 that provides a specific set of tools for test automation. *Recheck* is constituted by four different software products. In our experiment, we used *Recheck-web Maven plug-in*, that integrates with Selenium WebDriver and replaces assertions with differential testing[8].

In practice, Recheck is a library written in Java that is importable in any JVM-based test suite project. It provides methods to apply differential testing on Selenium Web Elements. Given a Selenium Web Element (or also the entire driver) Recheck does the following: (1) generates a snapshot if one doesn't already exist, (2) compares the snapshot previously generated with the current one. Recheck fails the test if: (1) no snapshot is present, so there is nothing to compare with (it happens in the very first run of the test); (2) at least one difference is found between the previously stored snapshot and the current one. **Golden Master** is the name chosen to call the stored snapshots of a web element (or a whole web page). This snapshot is elaborated exclusively from the HTML and CSS code. Recheck creates the Golden Master with its own format (in *xml* language), storing all the information that is needed to represent the page itself. The Golden Master is generated the first time the test script is executed, or more generally, whenever the execution does not find the correspondent Golden Master to compare with. A single test can have one or more Golden Masters associated; every check required in the test has its own Golden Master. This is the *oracle* mechanism of Retest's differential testing.

---

[5] www.selenium.dev/documentation/webdriver/.
[6] www.selenium.dev/.
[7] https://retest.de.
[8] https://github.com/retest/recheck-web.

Recheck provides two differential testing approaches[9] inside Selenium tests:

1. *Explicit check.* By means of the Recheck object, it is possible to explicitly call the Recheck check in the Java test method at any point of the test. With it we can create an instance of Recheck, e.g. via `Recheck re = new RecheckImpl()` and check the complete current webpage via `re.check(driver, "check-name")` or individual web elements via `re.check(webElement, "check-name");`

2. *Implicit check.* Using the Recheck WebDriver that wraps the Selenium WebDriver, Recheck implicitly performs automatic checks inside the test, basically one check after each WebDriver action.

The flowchart in Fig. 1 shows in detail the operation of Recheck with implicit checks inside a Selenium test.

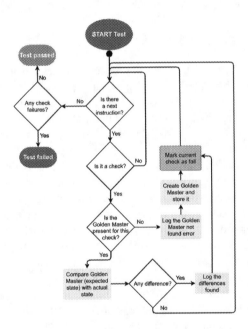

Fig. 1. Flowchart of Recheck driver differential testing

4   Empirical Evaluation

This section describes the definition, design, and settings of the case study we conducted following the guidelines by Wohlin *et al.* [18] and Runeson *et al.* [15] to design experimental studies. We decided to compare the costs and effectiveness of the test scripts based on differential testing and classical assertions. For cost, we mean the time needed

---

[9] https://retest.de/feature-unbreakable-selenium/.

to develop a test suite and the time of execution required with the given test technique; for effectiveness, we mean the ability to detect bugs. However, the comparison is not just between assertions and differential testing since we considered three oracle mechanisms: assertions, Recheck with explicit checks, and Recheck with implicit checks.

The *goal* of the study is to investigate the benefits and costs of adopting different oracle mechanisms in web test scripts. The results of the experiments are interpreted from two *perspectives*: (1) researchers interested in empirically evaluating the effects of adopting different oracle mechanisms in E2E web testing, and (2) quality managers who want to understand what bugs detection improvement (if any), can be achieved by adopting differential testing instead of assertions and at which cost.

The *context* of the study is constituted by a professional software tester executing web test scripts development tasks using the three different treatments, and two open-source web applications. The **professional tester** conducted the experiment under the supervision of the researchers. He is a full-stack developer and software tester having more than five years of experience in the field. He has good knowledge in developing Selenium WebDriver test suites. Moreover, before performing the experiment, he practiced with Recheck by creating several sample test suites for various web applications.

The two web applications included in the study are: **Petclinic** and **Shopizer**. Both applications have common technical properties important for our experiment, such as: being open-source, written in Java programming language, based on *Spring Boot* framework[10], rely on *Apache Maven* as build automation tool, are bootable by Maven command locally, support the *PIT* Maven plug-in (important for applying mutations automatically), support the *Surefire* Maven plug-in (important for collecting testing reports automatically). These common characteristics were fundamental to automate the evaluation of the bug detection capability as we will describe in the next sections.

Petclinic (@spring-projects/spring-petclinic on GitHub[11]) is a sample application of Spring. It is the official application built by the developers of Spring Boot framework to demonstrate how to use it. It allows managing basic data simulating a veterinary clinic.

Shopizer (@shopizer-ecommerce/shopizer on GitHub[12]) is a customizable e-commerce web application. It provides the creation of accounts and several functionalities about e-commerce. The HTML forms are rich and dynamic: there are actions with animations, therefore delayed, and there is a loading overlay in many parts of the app.

4.1 Research Questions

The research questions of the study are the following:

RQ1 (Developer productivity) Which oracle mechanism among those considered is the most advantageous in terms of development effort?

RQ2 (Effectiveness) Which oracle mechanism is the most effective in finding web application bugs?

RQ3 (Efficiency) Which oracle mechanism achieves the fastest execution time?

---

[10] https://stackify.com/what-is-spring-boot/.

[11] https://github.com/spring-projects/spring-petclinic.

[12] https://github.com/shopizer-ecommerce/shopizer.

The metrics used to answer the RQs are: development time of the test suites it took the developer (RQ1), quantity of bugs found (RQ2), and test suites execution time (RQ3). The three test suites developed for each web app contain the same test cases (i.e., steps) but different test oracle mechanisms (i.e., assertions, Recheck with explicit checks, and Recheck with implicit checks).

4.2   Experimental Procedure

We asked the professional tester to develop three test suites for each of the two applications under test; one for the assertions, one for differential testing using the explicit checks of Recheck, and one using the implicit checks of Recheck. This means that there are six test suites in total. We, therefore, have three test suite types: (1) Assertions, (2) Recheck explicit, and (3) Recheck implicit. There are 53 test scripts in each Shopizer test suite type, whereas Petclinic has 31 test scripts. The test suites are realized as 'Java 8' projects using JUnit 5 as unit testing framework. Web element locators have been created using ChroPath[13], a Chrome plugin that automatically generates XPaths inspecting the web element using the browser's developer tools. Selenium WebDriver has been adopted to perform the actions in the web browser for all three test suite types. To develop the three kinds of test suites for each web app, the developer applied the following procedure:

1. Analyze the AUT and select the functionalities to be tested trying to reach a good coverage of the most important features available for a user;
2. Describe the test cases in Gherkin;
3. Develop the test cases in Selenium WebDriver test scripts without any oracle mechanisms;
4. Forking the test suite in three different test suites (one for each treatment) and:
   (a) Add the specific test oracle mechanism to each test script in order to have three distinct test suites (i.e., one with Assertions, one using Recheck implicit, and one using Recheck explicit). Assertions typically check a value on the current page, such as the total value of a cart, while the other test oracle mechanisms checks multiple values as described in Sect. 3.2;
   (b) Validate the application with the test suite; all test scripts must pass.

For Recheck tool, the developer tuned the ignore files (i.e., *ignore-rule*) so that the minimum number of rules is used to pass the tests. A ignore-rule[14] is a filter used to ignore volatile elements, attributes, or sections, using a Git-like syntax. This mechanism is very useful to avoid false positives in the testing phase. For example, the portion of a page showing the current time changes from one snapshot to another, thus without an ignore-rule Recheck would highlight the difference causing the test script to fail without the presence of a real bug.

To answer RQ1, the developer annotated the time needed to implement the test cases in test scripts and the test oracle mechanism for each test suite. The *Darkyen's Time Tracker* IntelliJ IDEA plugin has been adopted to take the effective time spent in

---

[13] https://www.autonomiq.io/deviq-chropath.html.

[14] https://github.com/retest/recheck-web.

development. Note that the developer ran each test script several times and verified that the result is always "passed"; this to be reasonably sure that no flakiness is present.

To answer RQ2 we decided to simulate bugs in web apps using *Mutation Testing* [10]. Mutation testing is a technique that consists in exercising the test suite against slight variations of the original code, simulating the errors a developer could introduce during development and maintenance activities. These variations of the original software system, named *mutants*, are used to identify the weaknesses in the test artefacts by determining the parts of software that are poorly or never tested. For each mutant, the test scripts are executed: if at least one test script fails, the mutant has been detected (killed), and this proves the effectiveness of the test suite in detecting the kind of fault introduced by the mutant. If no test fails, the mutant is not detected (i.e., it survives), and this proves the test suite's weakness in detecting the fault introduced by the mutant. Thus, we decided to measure the bug-detection capability of the three considered test suites (for each app) as the number of mutants detected by each test suite over the total number of mutants generated. In particular, the metric we used to evaluate the overall test suite quality is the percentage of mutants killed out of the total (i.e., the higher, the better).

To answer RQ3, the developer re-executed the three test suites (for each considered web app) against the original AUT 30 times and calculated the average to mediate any fluctuations.

4.3   Additional Details on the Mutations Analysis (RQ2)

To carry out the experiment required to answer RQ2, we implemented a tool based on *PIT*[15], a Maven plugin that creates the code mutations of the application under test working at the bytecode level. PIT currently provides many built-in mutators able to modify the bytecode in many ways; the complete list of mutators, used in this experimental work, can be found in the PIT web site[16]. Our tool can automatically execute each test suite against each mutated version of the current web application and records the number of killed mutants. Our tool is also able to compute the coverage of the test suites against the mutants (i.e., analyze if each mutated line is actually executed or not). It is important to underline that the development of the tool was necessary because the activities described above cannot be carried out simply using PIT.

Number of generated mutants per Web app. PIT generated 107 mutants for the Petclinic application (1932 lines of code, not counting blank lines and comments) and 15025 for Shopizer (86333 lines of code, not counting blank lines and comments).

Coverage of the Mutants. Thanks to our tool, we analyzed the mutation coverage reached by the test suites developed in the context of the empirical evaluation. Basically, we labeled (in the original version of the app) all the lines mutated as covered if they were executed during the test suite execution against the original version of the app. Note that the coverage is the same for all the three versions of each test suite since the Selenium WebDriver actions are the same. The mutation coverage for Petclinic is 98 mutants out of 107 (91.6%). On the contrary, for Shopizer we found that the coverage

---

[15] https://pitest.org/.

[16] https://pitest.org/quickstart/mutators/.

is lower: 1882 mutants covered (12.53%) by the test suites. This low percentage is due to the fact that: (1) Shopizer is very complex and, (2) the developer focused only on the main features.

Execution of the Test Suites against the Mutants. The execution of the three Petclinic test suites against each of the 98 mutants (i.e., the mutants covered by the test suites) took about six hours. On the other hand, for Shopizer, the execution of the test suites against each of the 1882 covered mutants generated would have taken too long (estimated at about 220 h). So we decided to discard a part of the mutants by reducing the set of considered mutants to 491 (in practice, we decided to select up to three mutations for each Java method and therefore we have eliminated about the 74% of the mutations covered by the test suite). Executing 491 mutants still took at least 62 h of computation to run the test suites. So, we decided to use virtual machines in order to parallelize the computation and speed up the evaluation.

5 Results

The following sections report the results for answering each research question.

5.1 RQ1 Development Time

Figure 2 reports in detail data concerning the Petclinic's and Shopizer development times. In addition, to provide a more complete overview, we also provide other information, such as the number of *page objects* (POs), *XPath*s, and "Recheck *ignore-rule*s" created during the development process together with some statistical data. It is important to underline that when assertions are adopted, often new POs and new POs getter methods must be created to retrieve from the current page the values to be checked in the assertions.

Petclinic				Shopizer			
Test Cases [Actions]				**Test Cases [Actions]**			
	Development time	POs created	XPaths created		Development time	POs created	Xpaths created
Total	1h 58m 36s	8	24	Total	5h 26m 44s	14	60
Average	0h 03m 50s		0.77	Average	0h 06m 10s		1.13
Checks [Assertions]				**Checks [Assertions]**			
	Development time	POs created	XPaths created		Development time	POs created	Xpaths created
Total	1h 35m 12s	2	18	Total	3h 33m 10s	1	31
Average	0h 03m 04s		0.58	Average	0h 04m 01s		0.58
Checks [Recheck explicit]				**Checks [Recheck explicit]**			
	Development time	Ignore rules			Development time	Ignore rules	Xpaths created
Total	0h 55m 49s	3		Total	2h 00m 08s	7	3
Average	0h 01m 48s	0.10		Average	0h 02m 16s	0.13	0.06
Checks [Recheck implicit]				**Checks [Recheck implicit]**			
	Development time	Ignore rules			Development time	Ignore rules	Xpaths created
Total	0h 51m 34s	5		Total	4h 02m 42s	13	3
Average	0h 01m 40s	0.16		Average	0h 04m 35s	0.25	0.06

	Time	XPaths		Time	XPaths
Total [Test Cases + Assertions]	3h 33m 48s	42	**Total [Test Cases + Assertions]**	8h 59m 54s	91
Average per Test Case	0h 06m 54s	1.35	Average per Test Case	0h 10m 11s	1.72
Total [Test Cases + Recheck explicit]	2h 54m 25s	24	**Total [Test Cases + Recheck explicit]**	7h 26m 52s	63
Average per Test Case	0h 05m 38s	0.77	Average per Test Case	0h 08m 26s	1.19
Total [Test Cases + Recheck implicit]	2h 50m 10s	24	**Total [Test Cases + Recheck implicit]**	9h 29m 26s	63
Average per Test Case	0h 05m 29s	0.77	Average per Test Case	0h 10m 45s	1.19

Fig. 2. Petclinic and Shopizer test suite development times (Color figure online)

To help to visualize and compare the data, we also report the charts in Figs. 3 and 4. On the left, for each app, we can see in blue the time required to develop the test suite without considering the final oracle mechanism. Then, the time required to add the three kinds of oracle mechanisms (respectively in yellow, green, and light blue) is shown. On the right is instead shown the total time, including both development and oracle mechanisms.

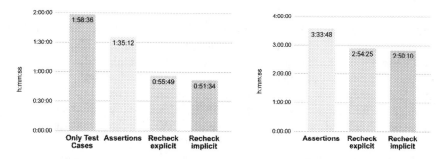

Fig. 3. Petclinic test suite development times. On the left, the times are displayed by separating them by test script and oracle. On the right, considering the total times. (Color figure online)

From the charts, it is possible to observe that: 1) the introduction of the oracle in the test scripts has a very high relative impact in terms of time (this is also because the addition of these checks involved the re-execution of the test scripts) and, 2) there is no winner considering the development time.

Table 1 shows the time difference in percentage terms with respect to the assertions. From these combined data, it is possible to appreciate the fact that the most convenient option seems to be Recheck explicit.

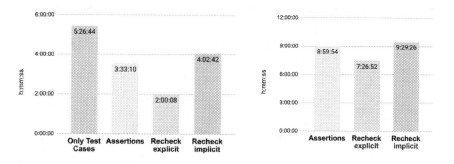

Fig. 4. Shopizer test suite development times. On the left, the times are displayed by separating them by test script and oracle. On the right, considering the total times.

Table 1. Time difference in percentage terms with respect to the assertions

	Recheck explicit	Recheck implicit
Petclinic	−18.31%	−20.19%
Shopizer	−17.40%	5.30%
Average	**−17.86%**	**−7.45%**

Recheck explicit has shown a certain advantage, both against assertions and Recheck implicit: for Petclinic, assertions required about 24% more time to be developed compared to Recheck (both explicit and implicit); for Shopizer, Recheck explicit has been 17% faster to develop than assertions, while Recheck implicit has been 5% slower. The implementation of Recheck implicit becomes increasingly difficult with the complexity of the application under test on the other hand, assertions and Recheck explicit seem to be less affected by the complexity of the application under test.

In conclusion, to answer the RQ1 we can say that our data support the hypothesis that Recheck explicit is more advantageous in terms of Developer productivity.

5.2 RQ2 Effectiveness in Detecting Bugs

Concerning bugs detection, we discovered that of the 98 mutants (i.e., the bugs artificially inserted by mutation) generated for Petclinic the assertions killed 80 of them, Recheck explicit 88, and Recheck implicit 89. In the case of Shopizer, 491 mutants were generated and the assertions killed 190 of them (about 39%), Recheck explicit 249 (about 51%), and Recheck implicit 255 (about 52%).

Figures 5 and 6 shown the charts summarizing the number of mutants killed by the three kinds of test suites divided by application.

Table 2 shows the percentage difference of the number of mutants killed with respect to the assertions. There is a clear advantage from using differential testing (both Recheck implicit and explicit) with respect to the assertions. Recheck implicit is slightly better at killing mutants than Recheck explicit, which is reasonable given the much higher number of differential checks. It is worth noting that for Shopizer, a

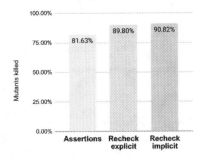

Fig. 5. Mutants killed in Petclinic

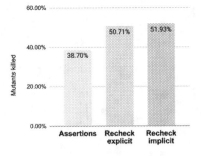

Fig. 6. Mutants killed in Shopizer

Table 2. Percentage difference of number of mutants killed compared to assertions

	Recheck explicit	Recheck implicit
Petclinic	10.00%	11.25%
Shopizer	31.05%	34.21%
Average	**20.53%**	**22.73%**

realistic and complex web app, Recheck's differential testing methods have been able to kill a much higher amount of mutants, about 31–34% more compared to assertions. This can be explained why often a bug in complex code can unpredictably affect the behavior of the app—for instance, causing a small modification of a web page—and being that differential testing checks the entire web page content (and not just a web element as assertions usually do) it has been found to be more effective.

When it comes to RQ2, Recheck implicit is the most effective solution; alongside the other techniques, it performs more checks during the test case actions, which makes it the most effective in finding bugs. However, Recheck explicit is also effective.

5.3   RQ3 Execution Time

In Fig. 7 the full data details and some statistics about the execution time for the test suites are provided, while in Figs. 8 and 9, we provide a graphical representation of the data.

Petclinic				Shopizer			
	Assertion	Recheck Explicit	Recheck Implicit		Assertion	Recheck Explicit	Recheck Implicit
Average	30.07s	39.30s	136.13s	Average	179.96s	243.63s	862.09s
Max	33.69s	41.92s	138.17s	Max	190.97s	246.14s	874.09s
Min	26.23s	37.20s	133.57s	Min	177.59s	240.60s	847.76s
Standard dev.	1.96s	1.14s	1.11s	Standard dev.	3.93s	1.74s	9.37s

Fig. 7. Petclinic and Shopizer test suite execution times

The answer to RQ3 is more straightforward w.r.t. the previous research questions: the execution time is always shorter for the test suites relying on assertions; Recheck uses differential testing, which involves more elaborated calculations requiring more time. Also from Table 3 it is evident that Recheck is slower than the mechanism of assertions in running tests. Recheck explicit takes one-third more of the assertions' execution time. Recheck implicit is remarkably slower, with 3.6 times the assertions' execution time. By looking at Figs. 8 and 9 the difference is graphically remarkable. This can be explained by the numerous checks carried out by Recheck implicit, comparing the current page with a Golden Master at each WebDriver command.

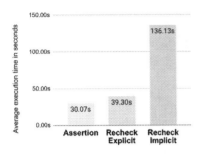

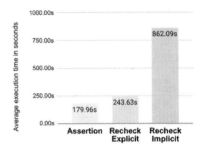

Fig. 8. Petclinic test suite execution times   **Fig. 9.** Shopizer test suite execution times

Table 3. Percentage of execution time difference compared to assertions

	Recheck explicit	Recheck implicit
Petclinic	30.70%	352.71%
Shopizer	35.38%	379.05%
Average	33.04%	365.88%

Table 4. Overall comparison in terms of development and execution time

	Assertions	Recheck explicit	Recheck implicit
Sum of development times (min)	753	620	739
Sum of execution times (s)	210	283	998
Average of mutants killed (%)	60.17%	70.26%	71.38%

5.4 Discussion

Development time is undoubtedly an important factor to consider when developing an industrial automated test suite. From this point of view, Recheck explicit seems to be the best because it requires less development time than the other solutions (mediating on the two applications). This is clearly perceptible in the Shopizer context, which is a real and complex web application. The development time of the Recheck implicit method is similar to that of the Recheck explicit when the application under test is very simple (like in the case of Petclinic, which is a demo application), but with a more realistic AUT, its development time increases more quickly due to the multiple checks performed during the test case actions (possibly requiring, for instance, more ignore-rules to implement). This leads Recheck implicit to be the slowest method to implement.

Execution time is another important factor that influences the costs to choose a testing approach: if a test suite takes a very long time to execute, it could be discarded in several contexts requiring short execution times (as e.g., in software agile development methods requiring daily and rapid releases). To this end, we have carefully analyzed the execution times of the three approaches: the assertions remain the fastest in this respect, but where the explicit Recheck has a reasonable (but acceptable) increase in the execution time, the implicit Recheck is much slower.

Table 4 shows the overall results considering both applications under test, Petclinic and Shopizer. A simple conclusion of the current study, considering the three analyzed aspects (RQ1 productivity, RQ2 effectiveness, and RQ3 efficiency), could be as follows:

Assertions

- The best approach considering execution time (Efficiency)
- The worst approach considering the number of bugs found (Effectiveness)

Recheck explicit

- The best approach considering development time (Productivity)

Recheck implicit

- (Slightly) the best approach considering the number of bugs found (Effectiveness)
- (Greatly) the worst approach considering execution time (Efficiency)

Recheck implicit is the most effective in finding bugs, but it is enormously slower in running tests, and it showed a tendency to be the slowest to be developed in complex web applications therefore, the effectiveness/costs ratio of Recheck implicit is somewhat unfavorable. Regarding assertions, their main advantage is having the lowest execution time, but they significantly lose in efficacy when it comes to finding bugs, and they are not even the fastest method to implement. From our analysis, it would appear that the *best approach*, taking into account benefits and costs, is probably Recheck explicit: it has a great increment of efficacy in finding bugs (up to +31% and on average +21%) without considerably increasing the costs; it is one third slower to run tests compared to assertions, but in return, it is also the quickest regarding development time. Note that our opinion is based on the fact that increasing the bug detection capability of the 21% is much more valuable than requiring about 33% more execution time: the two metrics cannot be compared directly since bugs detection is, in general, a more important characteristic. Clearly, if the execution time increases several orders of magnitude, this could be a problem, as in the case of Recheck implicit.

5.5 Threats to Validity

The main threats to validity affecting an empirical study are: Internal, External, Construct, and Conclusion validity [18].

Internal Validity threats concern confounding factors that may affect a dependent variable. In our case, mainly the number of detected mutants for RQ2. In this context, the main threat is probably related to the choice of the tool for executing the mutations. Indeed, different tools could be potentially able to generate different mutants. This could, potentially, change the mutant-detection capability of the three considered approaches. To reduce as much as possible this threat, we selected PIT, a mature mutation tool already used in other scientific works [2,6,12]. In fact, PIT is capable of generating a variety of possible mutations in the web apps' source code mimicking realistic bugs.

External Validity threats are related to the generalization of results. In our case study, there could be two threats of this type. The limited number of web apps and the fact that only one developer was involved in the study. However, both the web apps employed in our study are examples of real systems and the involved developer is very experienced in developing Selenium WebDriver test suites. This makes the context quite realistic, even though further studies with existing, more complex applications and more developers will improve the generalizability of the results. It is, however, important to highlight that only the results for RQ1 are strongly influenced by the developer's abilities, while the results for RQ2 and RQ3 are relatively little dependent on who developed the test suites (the only factor is that, in principle, a more skilled developer could adopt more effective assertions when defining the Gherkin test cases specifications, but we believe that the professional tester already performed an accurate job in this context). So having only one developer involved in the experiment is mainly a threat only to RQ1.

Construct validity threats concern the relationship between theory and observation. Concerning RQ2, they are due to how we measured the effectiveness of the oracle mechanisms in detecting bugs/faults. To minimize this threat, we decided to measure the effectiveness objectively, thanks to mutation testing (a technique that we already adopted in previous works [8, 11]). Instead, for RQ1 and RQ3, construct validity threats are due to how we measured the times. We believe that the measure is objective since we measured times automatically and, to minimize any fluctuation (due to possible active processes during the calculation), for RQ3, we averaged the obtained values over multiple executions.

Threats to conclusion validity concern issues that may affect the ability to draw a correct conclusion, i.e., issues that may affect an adequate analysis of the data, as for example, using inadequate statistical methods. As our empirical study is a case study and based only on two web apps, we found it inappropriate to use statistical tests and therefore, this threat to validity does not apply to our case.

6   Conclusions and Future Work

To evaluate the potential benefits of differential testing applied to E2E Web test scripts, in this work, we empirically compared: (1) classical assertions and (2) two different oracle mechanisms implemented in the Recheck tool. In the study, we considered three factors: the development time (developer productivity), the number of detected bugs (effectiveness), and the execution time (efficacy).

Results show that, on average, Selenium WebDriver test scripts equipped with the Recheck oracle mechanisms (both explicit and implicit) can detect more bugs than classic assertions (up to +34% on complex apps). The development time is similar between the approaches. The execution time is slightly higher than classic assertions for Recheck Explicit (+33%), while it is by far higher when adopting Recheck Implicit (3.6 times more). Mediating the considered factors, from our study Recheck explicit seems to be the best choice: it can detect considerably more bugs without significantly increasing the overall costs.

As future work, we plan to extend our study in many directions by: (1) including more web applications, (2) implementing more complex test suites, (3) evaluating the maintenance cost of the three kinds of oracle mechanisms during the evolution of AUT, (4) replicating the experiment with less skilled developers, in order to evaluate if and how the observed results (in particular for RQ1) vary depending on the seniority of the tester, and (5) analyzing whether the considered approaches are complementary, in which phases of the development they can be used advantageously, how they can be combined, and whether they are able to discover the same error types.

References

1. Barr, E.T., Harman, M., McMinn, P., Shahbaz, M., Yoo, S.: The oracle problem in software testing: a survey. IEEE Trans. Softw. Eng. **41**(5), 507–525 (2015). https://doi.org/10.1109/TSE.2014.2372785
2. Coles, H., Laurent, T., Henard, C., Papadakis, M., Ventresque, A.: Pit: a practical mutation testing tool for java. In: Proceedings of the 25th International Symposium on Software Testing and Analysis, pp. 449–452 (2016)
3. García, B., Gallego, M., Gortázar, F., Organero, M.: A survey of the selenium ecosystem. Electronics **9**, 1067 (2020). https://doi.org/10.3390/electronics9071067
4. Gulzar, M.A., Zhu, Y., Han, X.: Perception and practices of differential testing. In: 2019 IEEE/ACM 41st International Conference on Software Engineering: Software Engineering in Practice (ICSE-SEIP), pp. 71–80 (2019). https://doi.org/10.1109/ICSE-SEIP.2019.00016
5. Howden, W.: Theoretical and empirical studies of program testing. IEEE Trans. Softw. Eng. **SE-4**(4), 293–298 (1978). https://doi.org/10.1109/TSE.1978.231514
6. Laurent, T., Papadakis, M., Kintis, M., Henard, C., Le Traon, Y., Ventresque, A.: Assessing and improving the mutation testing practice of pit. In: 2017 IEEE International Conference on Software Testing, Verification and Validation (ICST), pp. 430–435. IEEE (2017)
7. Leotta, M., Clerissi, D., Ricca, F., Tonella, P.: Approaches and tools for automated end-to-end web testing. Adv. Comput. **101**, 193–237 (2016). https://doi.org/10.1016/bs.adcom.2015.11.007
8. Leotta, M., Olianas, D., Ricca, F.: A large experimentation to analyze the effects of implementation bugs in machine learning algorithms. Future Gener. Comput. Syst. **133**, 184–200 (2022). https://doi.org/10.1016/j.future.2022.03.004
9. McKeeman, W.M.: Differential testing for software. Digit. Tech. J. **10**(1), 100–107 (1998)
10. Offutt, A.J., Untch, R.H.: Mutation 2000: uniting the orthogonal. In: Wong, W.E. (eds) Mutation Testing for the New Century. The Springer International Series on Advances in Database Systems, vol. 24. Springer, Boston (2001). https://doi.org/10.1007/978-1-4757-5939-6_7
11. Olianas, D., Leotta, M., Ricca, F.: MATTER: a tool for generating end-to-end IoT test scripts. Software Qual. J. 1–35 (2021). https://doi.org/10.1007/s11219-021-09565-y
12. Papadakis, M., Shin, D., Yoo, S., Bae, D.H.: Are mutation scores correlated with real fault detection? A large scale empirical study on the relationship between mutants and real faults. In: 2018 IEEE/ACM 40th International Conference on Software Engineering (ICSE), pp. 537–548. IEEE (2018)
13. Peters, D., Parnas, D.L.: Generating a test oracle from program documentation: work in progress. In: Proceedings of the 1994 ACM SIGSOFT International Symposium on Software Testing and Analysis, pp. 58–65. ISSTA 1994, Association for Computing Machinery, NY (1994). https://doi.org/10.1145/186258.186508
14. Project, S.: Selenium webdriver documentation (2021). https://www.selenium.dev/documentation/webdriver/
15. Runeson, P., Host, M., Rainer, A., Regnell, B.: Case Study Research in Software Engineering: Guidelines and Examples. Wiley Publishing, 1st edn. (2012)

16. Shrestha, K., Rutherford, M.J.: An empirical evaluation of assertions as oracles. In: 2011 Fourth IEEE International Conference on Software Testing, Verification and Validation, pp. 110–119 (2011). https://doi.org/10.1109/ICST.2011.50
17. Unadkat, J.: Selenium webdriver tutorial: getting started with test automation (2021). https://www.browserstack.com/guide/selenium-webdriver-tutorial
18. Wohlin, C., Runeson, P., Hst, M., Ohlsson, M.C., Regnell, B., Wessln, A.: Experimentation in Software Engineering. Springer, Heidelberg (2012). https://doi.org/10.1007/978-3-642-29044-2

Skills and Education

Roadblocks to Attracting Students to Software Testing Careers: Comparisons of Replicated Studies

Rodrigo E. C. Souza[1], Ronnie E. de Souza Santos[1,2]([✉]), Luiz Fernando Capretz[3], Marlon A. S. de Sousa[1], and Cleyton V. C. de Magalhães[1]

[1] Agile Testing Program, CESAR School, Recife, Pernambuco, Brazil
souzasantos.ronnie@gmail.com, mass@cesar.school
[2] Faculty of Computer Science, Dalhousie University, Halifax, NS, Canada
[3] Department of Electrical and Computer Engineering, Western University,
London, ON, Canada
lcapretz@uwo.ca

Abstract. Context. Recently, a family of studies highlighted the unpopularity of software testing careers among undergraduate students in software engineering and computer science courses. The original study and its replications explored the perception of students in universities in four countries (Canada, China, India, and Malaysia), and indicated that most students do not consider a career in software testing as an option after graduation. This scenario represents a problem for the software industry since the lack of skilled testing professionals might decrease the quality of software products and increase the number of unsuccessful projects. **Goal**. The present study aims to replicate, in Brazil, the studies conducted in the other four countries to establish comparisons and support the development of strategies to improve the visibility and importance of software testing among undergraduate students across the globe. **Method**. We followed the same protocol in the original study to collect data using a questionnaire and analyzed the answers using descriptive statistics and qualitative data analysis. **Results**. Our findings indicate similarities among the results obtained in Brazil in comparison to those obtained from other countries. We observed that students are not motivated to follow a testing career in the software industry based on a belief that testing activities lack challenges and opportunities for continuous learning. **Conclusions**. In summary, students seem to be interested in learning more about software testing. However, the lack of discussions about the theme in software development courses, as well as the limited offer of courses focused on software quality at the university level reduce the visibility of this area, which causes a decrease in the interest in this career.

Keywords: Software testing · Software engineering education · Replication

A. Vallecillo et al. (Eds.): QUATIC 2022, CCIS 1621, pp. 127–139, 2022.
https://doi.org/10.1007/978-3-031-14179-9_9

1 Introduction

Testing is an indispensable part of software development. It is the activity responsible for verifying that a system meets the planned requirements and validating that it satisfies its intended purpose [1]. The history of software development indicates that testing activities existed before the establishment of processes, practices, and models for software development [2, 3], which reinforces the importance of this area. The relevance of software testing has been studied and practiced since the beginning of computing as researchers and practitioners are consistently following the way this activity evolved from a simple task focused on checking the results obtained from the source code execution to a leading and interactive process essential for the development of software products [2]. As a result, especially given the agile nature of software development, testing activities are widely spread throughout the development process and the system is continuously tested [1, 2, 3].

Precisely because testing has proven to be a vital activity in software development, researchers and practitioners are frequently searching for different approaches and techniques to improve the testing process and the resulting software quality. Among other strategies, such improvement could be reached by increasing the number of joint industry-academia collaborations [4]. However, recent studies have indicated that researchers and practitioners are not collaborating enough to solve industrial problems [5, 6, 7, 8]. The reality is that the distance between industry and academia likely existed before scientific and research contexts, as careers focused on software testing appear to be underrated by undergraduate students in software and computer engineering programs [9]. The unpopularity of software testing among students is pointed to as the main finding of a family of replications recently published in two studies that investigated the perception of students in universities across four countries, namely, Canada, China, India, and Malaysia [10, 11].

These findings have direct implications for academia and industry since they demonstrate the need for improving the perception of testing careers among students to prepare highly skilled professionals to work in this area in software companies. However, since the results are dependent on cultural and social factors related to the country where the data was collected, more replications would be the appropriate next step for extending discussions and increasing generalizability. The lack of skilled testing professionals is a major issue for the software industry because of the centrality of core quality elements to a successful project. In addition, usually testing processes take up about 40–50% of a project's time [5], which produces a direct impact on costs and deliveries. Therefore, understanding the interests of students from several different regions in software testing, as well as their reasons for taking up or not testing careers is an aspect of software engineering that requires immediate attention. In this sense, the present study is a replication of the above-cited studies [10, 11] focused on answering the following general research question:

RQ: How do Brazilian undergraduate students from software and computer engineering perceive software testing careers?

In this paper, we present the initial results obtained by utilizing the same survey used in [10] and [11], and this introduction, is organized as follows. In Sect. 2, we present a brief background about [10, 11] hereafter referred to as original study and first replication, respectively. In Sect. 3, we describe how this replication was conducted and how the research method was applied. In Sect. 4, we present the main findings and discussions. Finally, in Sect. 5, we present our conclusions and directions for future investigations.

2 Background

This section discusses findings from the literature on software testing in software and computer engineering programs and presents the original study and the first replication, which were replicated in this research.

2.1 Software Testing in Academic Curricula

The way students are trained in the academy including the content they study, but also their experiences in class—impacts their development as professionals. In other words, the professional education that individuals receive before joining any organization will have a direct effect on their perception of the work, and consequently, on what profession they will opt to take up [12].

When young software professionals start to work in the industry, they will depend almost exclusively on what they have learned at the university over the previous four or five years. However, recent studies have emphasized the existence of a gap between the software engineering industry and software engineering education. Such a gap arises from a series of elements, such as a lack of activities to develop soft skills, and considerable differences between projects developed at the university and real-life industry projects (e.g., size, requirement details, management, etc.), which leads to a third element, the distance of the school from the actual industry reality [13, 14].

In this scenario, the role of software testing in software and computer engineering programs is curious. Since the early 2000's researchers have noted that this area received little treatment in most curricula, even though it can represent almost 50% of the cost of software [15]. Over the years, as quality became essential, companies started to indicate that students should develop good problem solving, debugging, and analysis skills, since many graduates begin their careers in industry with exceptional programming skills, but lack competence in testing, debugging, and analysis skills [16, 17].

To address this problem, we need to introduce and improve teaching in undergraduate software testing programs. This will have the goal of enabling students to recognize the importance of testing and quality in software development, while also solving practical problems by applying contemporary technologies and methods to verification and validation processes [16, 18]. However, a recent study reported an additional new challenge regarding this difficulty, the unpopularity of testing careers among software practitioners [19].

2.2 Replications of Empirical Studies in Software Engineering

The replication of empirical studies represents an important component in the construction of knowledge in software engineering. Through replications, studies can be repeated, results can be checked, and the validity of outcomes can be expanded to different contexts [21].

In software engineering, replications are mostly used to generalize the results of an original study to a different population [24]. According to [25] other uses for replications in software engineering include:

a) confrontation of results from a new study in contrast to previous ones.
b) improve the research design of a previous study.
c) increase the external validity of results from previous investigations.
d) improvement research skills.
e) understand costs and efforts for future studies.

According to this definition, the main goal of the present research is related to (a) and (c), since we replicated a study conducted in four different countries to check how the findings apply to a fifth one.

2.3   Original Study and First Replication

The present study is a replication of two previous research papers conducted in Canada, China, and India (original study) [10], and posteriorly in Malaysia (first replication) [11]. Both research papers aimed to investigate the perception of undergraduate students in software and computer engineering programs of a career in software testing to discuss the (un)popularity of this profession [19]. Based on the classification of replications in software engineering, we consider the present study as an external replication. This means that the replication was performed by a different group of researchers [24].

In all three studies, the research method conducted to address this problem was a survey, which was designed to collect the opinion of several undergraduate students by applying a questionnaire to answer three main questions:

a) What is the likelihood of them taking up a career in software testing?
b) What are the advantages of taking up a career in software testing?
c) What are the drawbacks of taking up a career in software testing?

For the first question, the participants selected one of the provided options, namely, *Certainly Yes, Yes, Maybe, No*, and *Certainly Not*. The following two questions were open-ended. For data analysis, the authors pointed out that a qualitative approach was applied to explore the phenomena within their real-life context.

The original study obtained answers from 254 computer and software engineering students from three different countries, 85 participants from Canada, 99 participants from China, and 70 participants from India. Following this study, the first replication surveyed 82 students from software engineering-related programs, such as information technology and computer science at two Malaysian universities. The general results demonstrated that software testing is very unpopular, especially among students from Canada, China, and India, while a career in this area would be considered by an average number of Malaysian students. Table 1 summarizes these results, which will be used to discuss the results obtained from the current replication.

Table 1. Choosing a career in testing

Responses	Canada	China	India	Malaysia
Certainly no	31%	24%	14%	1%
No	27%	0%	31%	7%
Maybe	33%	74%	47%	52%
Yes	7%	2%	7%	34%
Certainly yes	2%	0%	0%	6%

Regarding the advantages of working with software testing, the original study and the first replication demonstrated that viewing this career as a learning opportunity and as comprising easy tasks were the main benefits observed across Canada, China, India, and Malaysia, although the percentage varies considerably among the four countries. The number of positions available caught the attention of Canadian, Chinese, and Malaysian students, while Canadian, Indian, and Malaysian students consider software testing an important job, which represents an advantage. Other benefits highlighted by the participants include monetary benefits and fun during work, e.g., exploring and finding bugs.

On the other hand, the drawbacks associated with the work in software testing are the monotony, which is present across the four countries, and the complexity, which is less perceived by Canadian students. The lack of development activities is also a disadvantage pointed out by all the groups of students. Other drawbacks include a lack of interest, especially in finding others' mistakes (code mistakes), and the lack of recognition in the industry. Minor disadvantages would be related to low salary in comparison to other professionals and stressful activities.

In summary, the results obtained from the original study and the first replication demonstrate that the perception of students about a career in software testing varies significantly depending on the country, which will require specific and targeted actions to emphasize the importance of testing activities to undergraduates and to highlight the perks of working with software testing in the industry. In addition, the findings revealed the existence of myths among students, such as the belief that the testing process always lacks programming.

We expect that our replication represents a step forward in improving the knowledge acquired so far. Thus, based on the data collected from five countries and over 400 students we will be able to start designing and proposing strategies to improve the popularity of software testing in the academy, and consequently increase the number of highly skilled professionals to work in this area in the software industry.

Lastly, even though we are replicating two previous studies that are interrelated, e.g., the original study [10] and the first replication [11], it is important to mention that additional studies focused on this theme may be available in the literature, and these can be analyzed in the future to improve the results of the current research. As an example, Deak et al. [20] investigated the factors that influence Norwegian students when deciding to choose a career in the area of software testing and based on the results identified strategies that can be used to motivate students and improve course contents.

3   Method

In this study, we consider replication as a conscious and systematic repeat of an original study [22]. Therefore, we followed the same protocol used by the original study and the first replication to collect and analyze data, as described below.

3.1   Data Collection

Following the previous studies, in the present replication, we applied the same questionnaire to collect data from undergraduate students from software and computer engineering-related programs. However, the instrument was slightly modified to achieve the goal of our research. First, the questionnaire was translated into the native language of the targeted participants (i.e., Portuguese). Second, we introduced the questionnaire with a quick definition of software testing, so all respondents would have basic knowledge of the topic under study. Third, we added to the questionnaire a quick question asking about the undergrad level of the respondents, e.g., what year of the undergraduate program the students are enrolled in. Lastly, we added an extra question asking students to justify why they would consider or not consider a career in software testing. We believe that more qualitative data associated with this closed question presented in the previous studies could help in the process of proposing solutions to the main problem observed in this context, e.g., motivating young professionals to work with software quality in the industry.

The translated questionnaire was validated through a pilot round, conducted with five members of our research group, which are not involved in this study. They were asked to read and compare the original questions with the translations, answer the questionnaire, and provide feedback about it. No update was performed after the pilot round since the questions are straightforward. Table 2 presents the final version of the questionnaire applied in this study. Once the instrument was validated the research team started to announce the research and the questionnaire to student groups, professors, researchers, and professionals, asking for help to collect the data from the targeted population.

Regarding the population, our study focused on all students enrolled in software/computer engineering programs and popular related programs in this area in Brazil such as information systems, computer science, and technology, among others. Invitations were sent to all regions of the country and no restriction was defined regarding the student level, which means that we were expecting data from individuals that were starting at the university right up to those about to graduate. Data collection ran for about two months and all questionnaires received were anonymous.

3.2   Data Analysis

The nature of the questions posed to participants in this study required both quantitative and qualitative approaches to data analysis. Descriptive statistics were applied to analyze

Table 2. Questionnaire

According to the SWEBOK, software testing is defined as the dynamic process of verifying and validating a software under development to attest it works as expected and possesses all the planned features and behaviors. Based on this definition and your previous knowledge/experience with software testing before your graduation, please answer the following questions

Topic	Questions
Choosing a career in software testing	1. After you graduate, would you consider a career in software testing? () Certainly No () No () Maybe () Yes () Certainly Yes 2. Please, briefly justify our answer for the previous question
Advantages and Drawbacks	3. What are three advantages (from the most to less important) of taking up a career in software testing? 4. What are three drawbacks (from the most to the less important) of taking up a career in software testing?

the answers to closed-ended questions designed to assess the likelihood of students deciding to work in software testing. Following this, qualitative analysis was applied to consolidate, reduce, and interpret all data obtained from open-ended questions, which were focused on revealing the advantages and drawbacks of software testing from the participants' perspective, along with a descriptive answer to the close-ended question.

The guidelines for conducting qualitative research suggest that the process should be based on coding the answers provided by participants and making sense of them [23]. In qualitative analysis, open coding is the process of reducing the narratives collected in interviews or questionnaires into discrete parts which can be closely examined and compared, looking for similarities and differences, and organizing concepts into representative categories [23]. This is the main process followed in this research to synthesize the answers collected from students. Figure 1 illustrates the open coding process and the construction of categories developed in this study.

4 Findings

We obtained 92 valid questionnaires with answers from Brazilian students, distributed as follows: 29% of students were in their first year, 32% in their second year, 16% in their third year, 13% in the fourth, and 10% in the fifth year. Unlike in other countries, it is common in Brazil for students to take up to 5 years of instruction in colleges and universities. However, in computer/software engineering programs the dropout rate tends to increase after the second year. This is one of the factors that explains the larger number of participants in the first and second years of this study. Following this

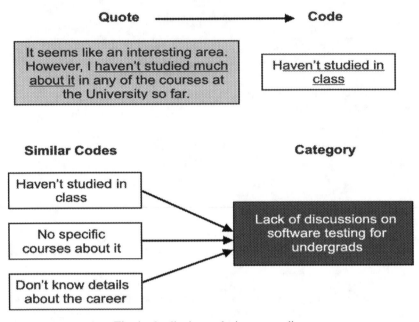

Fig. 1. Qualitative analysis: open coding.

general characterization of our sample, we answer each of the questions presented on the questionnaire.

4.1   After you Graduate, Would you Consider a Career in Software Testing?

Initial results indicate asymmetry in the perception of Brazilian students regarding the popularity of working with software testing since the likelihood of respondents choosing to work in this area is demonstrated to be well-balanced. About 27% of students expressed an interest in taking up this career. The same percentage of respondents expressed no desire to work in this area whatsoever. On the other hand, almost half of the sample (46%) indicated that they could (or could not) choose this career by answering *maybe* to this question. Figure 2 summarizes this information.

By comparing the results from the present study with the results from the original study and the first replication, we observed that considering the countries surveyed so far, work in software testing is more popular in Malaysia, followed by Brazil, then, Canada, India, and China at lowest. Table 3 summarizes these results.

However, both Malaysia and Brazil present a similar outcome regarding the percentage of students who would be inclined to work in software testing, which are those individuals who answered *maybe*. Many factors could explain this reality. However, such explanations are outside of the scope of this study at this point. We can only hypothesize, based on the literature, that cultural aspects of each country and the dynamics of university programs might be core factors influencing this reality. Further, unlike the previous studies, our study also requested participants to justify their answers to this question.

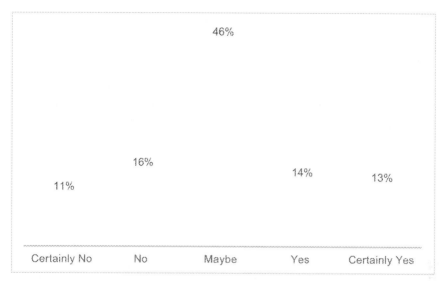

Fig. 2. Likelihood of Brazilian students choosing a career in software testing

Table 3. Choosing a career in testing - Second replication

Responses	Brazil	Canada	China	India	Malaysia
Certainly no	11%	31%	24%	14%	1%
No	16%	27%	0%	31%	7%
Maybe	46%	33%	74%	47%	52%
Yes	14%	7%	2%	7%	34%
Certainly yes	13%	2%	0%	0%	6%

Thus, by applying open coding we obtained the main broad reasons students cited for being willing or unwilling to consider a career focused on testing.

There are two main reasons associated with the fact that 27% of students would not work with software testing after graduation (Certainly No, and No responses). First, some individuals in this group have already developed interests in other areas of software development and expect to work in those areas in the future. Second, some students have an outdated perception about the job and the impact of software testing on software development, e.g., individuals relate testing with a lack of opportunity for coding and monotony at work, while in other cases they cannot even perceive the connection between testing and the rest of the software development activities.

Those who answered *Certainly Yes* and *Yes* to the possibility of working with software testing in the future seem to be oriented by the previous contact with the area. First, some students who attended courses or lectures focused on software testing, developed a positive attitude regarding this career, which turned into a willingness to experiment more in this area. Second, some students first interacted with software testing through internships and now they want to continue working in this area. Finally, some students do not have software testing as their main interest, but they are open to working with it depending on several factors, such as payment, benefits, and learning opportunities, among others.

In our analysis, the reasons for the *Maybe* response proved to be more dynamic and fluid than the *Yes/No* answers. Therefore, this analysis will be part of our future work. Table 4 presents quotations extracted from the questionnaires that elucidate the students' reasons.

Table 4. Students' reasons for choosing a career in testing

After you graduate, would you consider a career in software testing?	
Answer	Justification (quotations)
Certainly no/No	- "I am not an enthusiastic of software testing. I rather be coding new features" - "Certainly, never caught my attention" - "I want to create games in the future, not this thing." - "Testing is not really of my taste. I like challenges and working with new people, new problems…"
Certainly yes/Yes	- "Since I am working with this lately, I don't really see me working with something else [after graduation]. This is what I like" - "I liked it, since I learnt about it on a lecture." - "Testing is an area that caught my attention, it will give opportunity to learn a lot"

4.2 What are the Advantages and Drawbacks of Taking up a Career in Software Testing?

Similar to what was pointed out in the previous paragraph, in this paper, the analysis of advantages and drawbacks pointed out by students is still underway. Based on the data, it is possible to indicate the most often cited advantages and drawbacks. However, further analysis is necessary to provide a representative description for each of these elements, considering not only their meaning but also their relationship with several factors, e.g., the student's level (years), their attitude towards software testing (more positive or negative), their previous experience with testing, e.g., through internships, among others.

We identified 28 advantages of working with software testing based on participant responses. In the sample, the most prominent benefits are:

a) The number job of positions and opportunities currently available for professionals was cited by 39% of individuals.
b) Payment and financial compensation for professionals in this career were cited by 38% of individuals.

c) The sense of satisfaction in supporting the release of the software with high levels of quality was cited by 28% of individuals.
d) Constant learning and training opportunities were cited by 17% of the subjects.
e) Challenges at work were cited by 16% of individuals.

The list includes other advantages such as the possibility of supporting other areas of software development, working with programming (test automation), do not work with programming, and teamwork, among others. On the other hand, we obtained 32 different drawbacks cited by students regarding the work with software testing. The most representative disadvantages of this profession would be:

a) The fact that the work is monotonous and not interesting enough was mentioned by 30% of the participants.
b) The repetitiveness of tasks was cited by 22% of participants.
c) The work is stressful, according to 16% of participants.
d) The salary is low in comparison to other professionals, according to 15% of participants.

In addition, 15% of participants claim to have e no knowledge about the area, which would explain several drawbacks. The list of disadvantages also includes a lack of opportunity for coding activities, complexity, low number of positions available, and low relevance for software development as software testing career.

5 Conclusions

We presented the results obtained from the replication of studies that were conducted in Canada, China, India, Malaysia, and Brazil. In summary, our analysis demonstrates similarities among the results obtained in Brazil, India, and Malaysia regarding the perception of undergrad students towards working with software testing. In these countries, students tend to be more receptive and enthusiastic about testing careers. Further analysis can reveal aspects related to these places, e.g., cultural, educational, economic, or technical, that can be used to discuss strategies to improve the visibility of software testing for students in other countries.

Future works include additional analysis of the supplementary qualitative data that we collected from Brazilian students, which can be used to further explore and describe the scenario in Brazil while raising detailed comparisons among the countries researched so far. Long-term future work includes replicating this study with professionals working in the industry to draw a line between expectations (students' perception) and reality (practitioners' routine) regarding the advantages and drawbacks of a software testing career.

This study has implications for both the academy and the software engineering profession. For academia, the comparisons established among the replications might be used to create strategies for improving software/computer engineering programs by including more testing courses to provide students with the knowledge and the skills necessary to work in software testing careers in the industry. For industry, these results create awareness of the need of developing strategies to motivate and engage software QA professionals, in particular trainees and individuals at the beginning of their career. Both strategies are crucial for the development of high-quality software.

References

1. Bertolino, A.: Software testing research: achievements, challenges, dreams. In: Future of Software Engineering (FOSE 2007), pp. 85–103. IEEE, May 2007
2. Gillenson, M.L., Zhang, X., Stafford, T.F., Shi, Y.: A literature review of software test cases and future research. In: 2018 IEEE International Symposium on Software Reliability Engineering Workshops (ISSREW), pp. 252–256. IEEE, October 2018
3. Alaqail, H., Ahmed, S.: Overview of software testing standard ISO/IEC/IEEE 29119. Int. J. Comput. Sci. Netw. Secur. (IJCSNS) 18(2), 112–116 (2018)
4. Beecham, S., O'Leary, P., Baker, S., Richardson, I., Noll, J.: Making software engineering research relevant. Computer 47(4), 80–83 (2014)
5. Garousi, V., Herkiloglu, K.: Selecting the right topics for industry-academia collaborations in software testing: an experience report. In 2016 IEEE International Conference on Software Testing, Verification and Validation (ICST), pp. 213–222. IEEE, April 2016
6. Garousi, V., Felderer, M., Kuhrmann, M., Herkiloğlu, K.: What industry wants from academia in software testing? Hearing practitioners' opinions. In: Proceedings of the 21st International Conference on Evaluation and Assessment in Software Engineering, pp. 65–69, June 2017
7. Garousi, V., Petersen, K., Ozkan, B.: Challenges and best practices in industry-academia collaborations in software engineering: a systematic literature review. Inf. Softw. Technol. 79, 106–127 (2016)
8. Garousi, V., Felderer, M.: Worlds apart: industrial and academic focus areas in software testing. IEEE Softw. 34(5), 38–45 (2017)
9. Santos, R.E., Bener, A., Baldassarre, M.T., Magalhães, C.V., Correia-Neto, J.S., da Silva, F.Q.: Mind the gap: are practitioners and researchers in software testing speaking the same language?. In: 2019 IEEE/ACM Joint 7th International Workshop on Conducting Empirical Studies in Industry (CESI) and 6th International Workshop on Software Engineering Research and Industrial Practice (SER&IP), pp. 10–17. IEEE, May 2019
10. Capretz, L.F., Waychal, P., Jia, J.: Comparing the popularity of testing careers among Canadian, Chinese, and Indian students. In: 2019 IEEE/ACM 41st International Conference on Software Engineering: Companion Proceedings (ICSE-Companion), pp. 258–259. IEEE, May 2019
11. Capretz, L.F., Basri, S., Adili, M., Amin, A.: What Malaysian software students think about testing?. In: Proceedings of the IEEE/ACM 42nd International Conference on Software Engineering Workshops, pp. 195–196, June 2020
12. Tomer, G., Mishra, S.K.: Professional identity construction among software engineering students: a study in India. Inf. Technol. People (2016)
13. Oguz, D., Oguz, K.: Perspectives on the gap between the software industry and the software engineering education. IEEE Access 7, 117527–117543 (2019)
14. Karunasekera, S., Bedse, K.: Preparing software engineering graduates for an industry career. In: 20th Conference on Software Engineering Education & Training (CSEET 2007), pp. 97–106. IEEE, July 2007
15. Jones, E.L.: Software testing in the computer science curriculum--a holistic approach. In: Proceedings of the Australasian Conference on Computing education, pp. 153–157, December 2000

16. Astigarraga, T., Dow, E.M., Lara, C., Prewitt, R., Ward, M.R.: The emerging role of software testing in curricula. In: 2010 IEEE Transforming Engineering Education: Creating Interdisciplinary Skills for Complex Global Environments, pp. 1–26. IEEE, April 2010
17. Bin, Z., Shiming, Z.: Curriculum reform and practice of software testing. In: International Conference on Education Technology and Information System (ICETIS 2013), pp. 841–844 (2013)
18. Sampath, P.: The emerging role of software testing in curriculum. Poster presented at the Computing and Information Technology Research and Education New Zealand (CITRENZ), Queenstown, New Zealand. CITRENZ (2015)
19. Capretz, L.F., Waychal, P., Jia, J., Varona, D., Lizama, Y.: International comparative studies on the software testing profession. IT Prof. **23**(5), 56–61 (2021)
20. Deak, A., Stålhane, T., Cruzes, D.: Factors influencing the choice of a career in software testing among Norwegian students. Softw. Eng. **796** (2013)
21. de Magalhães, C.V., da Silva, F.Q., Santos, R.E., Suassuna, M.: Investigations about replication of empirical studies in software engineering: a systematic mapping study. Inf. Softw. Technol. **64**, 76–101 (2015)
22. La Sorte, M.A.: Replication as a verification technique in survey research: a paradigm. Sociol. Q. **13**(2), 218–227 (1972)
23. Seaman, C.B.: Qualitative methods in empirical studies of software engineering. IEEE Trans. Software Eng. **25**(4), 557–572 (1999)
24. Bezerra, R.M., da Silva, F.Q., Santana, A.M., Magalhaes, C.V., Santos, R.E.: Replication of empirical studies in software engineering: an update of a systematic mapping study. In: 2015 ACM/IEEE International Symposium on Empirical Software Engineering and Measurement (ESEM), pp. 1–4. IEEE, October 2015
25. de Magalhães, C.V., Baldassarre, T., Santos, R.E., da Silva, F.Q.: Ooops, I replicated again. Let me tell you why!. In: Proceedings of ROSE Festival 2018 - Recognizing and Rewarding Open Science in Software Engineering. ACM Joint European Software Engineering Conference and Symposium on the Foundations of Software Engineering, vol. 2018 (2018)

Analyzing Quality Issues from Software Testing Glossaries Used in Academia and Industry

Luis Olsina[1]([⊠]), Philip Lew[2], and Guido Tebes[1]

[1] GIDIS_Web, Facultad de Ingeniería, UNLPam, General Pico, LP, Argentina
{olsinal,guido_tebes}@ing.unlpam.edu.ar
[2] XBOSoft, Woodbridge, VA, USA

Abstract. This paper analyzes quality issues from three software testing glossaries used in academia and industry. The quality issues we analyzed primarily deal with a sub-characteristic of information quality such as consistency, which includes syntactic and semantic consistency. To conduct the study for the testing domain, eight terminological categories were conceived, in which, for each candidate glossary, a corresponding term is included in a category, considering the semantics intended by the authors of these standards. To count the occurrence frequency of a term in the glossaries, a tool was built that also takes into account the matching of synonyms. Then, a consistency analysis was performed for all terms ending with the word "testing". This study identifies some inconsistencies that merit further attention and efforts to promote agreement and harmonization among the authors/editors of these three glossaries in order to provide their readers with the most consistent and easiest way to learn and understand software testing concepts.

Keywords: Training · Glossary · Terms · Consistency · Software testing

1 Introduction

It is been said that the only constant is change. However, as we have discovered with the pandemic, change is not constant. In fact, it is accelerating. We encounter a new virus, we develop a vaccine; then the virus mutates. Keeping up with accelerating change is difficult. What can we do? Two primary strengths of the human race are communication and the ability to understand abstract concepts. These two primary reasons have been critical to our success as a species. Can you imagine any other animal that can collaborate on such a large scale? For instance, over 10 million Portuguese belong to a nation called Portugal due to collaboration and communication at a national level. Can other animals collaborate like this? No. Can other animals conceive of such an abstract idea as a country or money? No. And communication, especially when it comes to abstract concepts, requires a common language and understanding. Hence, our optimal use of written language is critical to creating understanding and thus helping us to deal with change. Software, as one of the primary drivers of change in our society, is crucial to understand, especially its quality.

A. Vallecillo et al. (Eds.): QUATIC 2022, CCIS 1621, pp. 140–155, 2022.
https://doi.org/10.1007/978-3-031-14179-9_10

To support the understanding of software quality and testing, several organizations have developed software testing glossaries. A glossary, regardless of whether it is for software testing or not, includes entries, that is, terms and their definitions –and occasionally synonyms, acronyms, and relevant notes– considering the most significant sources in a given domain. Glossaries certainly serve as a reference to establish a common ground for terms and definitions not only in learning and understanding but in communicating with others.

Thus, an entire profession and field have been focused on improving software engineering processes and any professional in the field of software engineering will have come across and used many glossaries, either in their formal training or in their daily work. In particular, most professionals in the field of software testing are familiar to some degree with glossaries such as ISO/IEC/IEEE 29119-1 [3], TMMi (Test Maturity Model integration) [9], and ISTQB (International Software Testing Qualifications Board) [2]. We chose these three glossaries because they are all focused on software testing. Even though their usage context, intended purpose, and audience varies, they provide a common foundation and intersection of terms related to software testing.

The ISO 29119-1 glossary is part of a series of standards designed to be used by an organization when performing software testing as a reference for the other parts of the standard. Thus, the glossary is written to assist those reading and interpreting the five parts of the standard by introducing concepts and vocabulary as a basis for understanding. TMMi is a reference model to support organizations to *"improve their software and system testing and achieve higher and sustainable levels of product quality for the systems they are developing and maintaining. With TMMi, these organizations can assess and improve their test processes and, if required, become formally certified"* [9]. Hence, the TMMi glossary is intended to support organizations in their test process improvement efforts.

ISTQB is a training and certification organization. Thus, its glossary is intended to help those taking training and certification syllabus in understanding software testing and specifically to obtain certifications.

As mentioned, each of the glossaries has a different purpose and context, hence different size, scope, and audience related to the other materials in context. Thus, ISTQB is intended to assist individuals whereas both ISO and TMMi are intended to assist larger organizational entities. While individuals studying for certifications may have different needs than organizations looking for definitions as a means for collaborative discussion, many of the terms intersect and have different usages as well as synonyms.

Certifications in the software testing field and formal training are often based on some of these glossaries, and in light of this, these glossaries should be of high quality. But what is quality when it comes to analyzing glossaries?

As a starting point, and without giving a complete answer to the previous question, the authors of this work carried out a comparison and analysis of syntactic and semantic consistency of the terms in the three cited glossaries, mainly highlighting the often inconsistent use of the word "testing". Through a systematic categorization of terms coupled with an analysis of quality issues, we have identified inconsistencies in these glossaries that we hope will benefit the profession in eliminating confusion and misunderstanding amongst their readers/users while also providing the authors of these glossaries a foundation for improvement. Ultimately, we argue that the proposed categorization, quality requirements, metrics, and analysis techniques can be utilized not only for the current candidate glossaries that we have analyzed but also for examining the quality of other glossaries from other professions in general.

The rest of the paper is organized as follows. Section 2 provides the rationale for dividing software testing glossaries into terminological categories and motivates the scope of this quality exploratory study. Section 3 shows the comparison and analysis of syntactic and semantic consistency between the three glossaries. In addition, other quality issues are outlined and discussed. Section 4 provides a summary of related work and discussion. Finally, Sect. 5 describes our conclusions and future work.

2   Terminological Categories for Testing and Study Scope

Despite attempts to standardize software testing concepts structured in glossaries by various initiatives such as ISO, TMMi, and ISTQB, in addition to many attempts to document testing terms and relationships structured in ontologies by different researchers as analyzed in a secondary study in [7], there is often a lack of broad consensus in the software testing literature and among practitioners on the explicit definition of many terms and their purpose. For instance, Arnicane *et al.* [1] found quality issues in the ISTQB glossary related to consistency, completeness, and correctness. Instead of focusing solely on a glossary as in [1], the present work mainly tries to obtain evidence of syntactic and semantic consistency among the glossaries mentioned above for a subset of categorized terms. In particular, to reduce the complexity of this exploratory study, a consistency analysis is carried out for terms ending with the word "testing".

Therefore, Subsect. 2.1 presents the terminological categories and numbers for each glossary of the software testing domain, while Subsect. 2.2 details the scope of this quality exploratory study.

2.1   Terminological Categories and Numbers

To carry out this study in a systematic way, eight terminological categories were conceived, in which, per each glossary, a corresponding term is included in a category, considering the semantics intended by the authors of the quoted glossaries. The inclusion of terms in categories was initially carried out independently by the authors of the present work followed by multiple collaborative sessions to verify the coherence in their placement. As a result of this verification via video streaming, some issues were raised and categorization discrepancies in the placement of terms according to the given semantics were resolved.

Table 1 exhibits the eight terminological categories we have designed for software testing glossaries. The terms included in categories 1 (C1) to 6 (C6) are domain-specific for software testing. In turn, C7 incorporates terms somewhat related to software testing, while C8 covers terms beyond the domain of software testing that belongs to broader fields such as software engineering or software quality requirements and evaluation. It is important to note that the terminological coverage of a glossary is often a bit broader than the specific terms of a field or domain that it conceptualizes. In this sense, [2] indicates that "*some related non-testing terms are also included if they play a major role in testing, such as terms used in software quality assurance and software lifecycle models*".

The main reason for designing categories C1 to C6 adheres to the development idea of TestTDO [8], which is a software testing top-domain ontology. In the process of defining the ontology scope using competency questions, the authors of that work found it helpful to devise conceptual blocks for them. From these conceptual blocks, we designed the categories C1 to C6 shown in Table 1. The keywords used in the label of each category name are borrowed from terms or properties in TestTDO, so the reader can refer to their definitions in [8].

Let us briefly describe, not in sequential order, categories C1 to C6, which are intended to include, in particular, terms from the field of software testing. Category 2 is called "Testing Work Process-, Activity-related Terms", which is intended to include terms with the semantics of testing process or activity. The terms testing process, activity, or task encompass the meaning of 'what to do' rather than 'how to do' a testing activity. Instead, Category 5 (labeled "Testing Method-, Technique-, Procedure-, Rule-related Terms" in Table 1) is dedicated to including testing method terms, which have the semantics of 'how to do' a testing task description. For example, the term Testing Method is defined in [8] as "*a specific and particular way to perform the specified steps for a task included in a Testing Activity*". The explicit semantic distinction between glossary terms that represent 'what to do' and 'how to do' has a clear benefit for learning and understanding. According to the authors of [8], to the same Design Testing activity, different Testing Design Methods or techniques can be assigned.

Category 4 is labeled "Test Work Product-related Terms", which is devoted to covering terms with the semantics of artifacts or results produced or consumed by processes, activities, or tasks. Category 6 (labeled "Testing Agent-, Role-, Tool-related Terms") is expected to encompass terms with both automated and human agent semantics. The term tool represents an instrument that facilitates the automation and execution of procedures and rules of methods/techniques, whereas the term role embraces skills that an agent must possess in order to perform activities or tasks.

Category 1 is called "Test Project-, Strategy-, Organizational Test-related Terms". ISO 29119-1 states that the term test strategy "*...describes the approach to testing for a specific test project or test sub-process or sub-processes.*". While in [8] is defined as "*Principles, patterns, and particular test domain concepts and framework that can be specified by a set of core testing processes, in addition to a set of appropriated testing methods and tools, as core resources, for helping to achieve the project's test goal purpose.*" Hence, a strategy for testing simultaneously encompasses at least the concepts of 'what to do' and 'how to do' testing in a test project. It is worth noting that organizational test-related terms include concepts at a higher level than at the project level.

Lastly, Category 3 is labeled "Test Goal-, Requirements-, Entity-related Terms", which is devoted to covering terms with the semantics of test goal, purposes, test requirements, systems, or entities under test including the environment or context entities.

Table 1. Labels of the eight terminological categories for terms in software testing glossaries

Category ID	Terminological category name
C1	Test Project-, Strategy-, Organizational Test-related Terms
C2	Testing Work Process-, Activity-related Terms
C3	Test Goal-, Requirements-, Entity-related Terms
C4	Test Work Product-related Terms (e.g. Artifact, Report, Result, Specification)
C5	Testing Method-, Technique-, Procedure-, Rule-related Terms
C6	Testing Agent-, Role-, Tool-related Terms
C7	Other Terms somewhat related to Test (e.g., Anomaly, Defect, etc.)
C8	Terms beyond the Test Domain related to Quality or Software Engineering

Table 2. Metrics, values, and category percentages for all three software testing glossaries

Metric name/acronym	ISO 29119	TMMi	ISTQB
Total Number of Terms with Synonyms per Glossary (#TwithSxG)	105	283	748
Total Number of Unique Terms per Glossary (#UTxG)	88	279	588
Number of Synonyms per Glossary (#Sy = #TwithSxG - #UTxG)	17	4	160
Number of Unique Terms per Glossary in Category1 (#UTxGC1)	7	19	38
Percentage of Unique Terms per Glossary in Category1 [%UTxGC1 = (#UTxGC1/#UTxG) * 100]	7.95%	6.81%	6.46%
Number of Unique Terms per Glossary in Category2 (#UTxGC2)	45	43	103
Percentage of Unique Terms per Glossary in Category2 [%UTxGC2 = (#UTxGC2/#UTxG) * 100]	51.14%	15.41%	17.52%
Number of Unique Terms per Glossary in Category3 (#UTxGC3)	5	9	10
Percentage of Unique Terms per Glossary in Category3 [%UTxGC3 = (#UTxGC3/#UTxG) * 100]	5.68%	3.23%	1.70%
Number of Unique Terms per Glossary in Category4 (#UTxGC4)	25	42	63
Percentage of Unique Terms per Glossary in Category4 [%UTxGC4 = (#UTxGC4/#UTxG) * 100]	28.41%	15.05%	10.71%
Number of Unique Terms per Glossary in Category5 (#UTxGC5)	2	27	46
Percentage of Unique Terms per Glossary in Category5 [%UTxGC5 = (#UTxGC5/#UTxG) * 100]	2.27%	9.68%	7.82%
Number of Unique Terms per Glossary in Category6 (#UTxGC6)	0	20	32
Percentage of Unique Terms per Glossary in Category6 [%UTxGC6 = (#UTxGC6/#UTxG) * 100]	0.00%	7.17%	5.44%
Number of Unique Terms per Glossary in Category7 (#UTxGC7)	3	25	57
Percentage of Unique Terms per Glossary in Category7 [%UTxGC7 = (#UTxGC7/#UTxG) * 100]	3.41%	8.96%	9.69%
Number of Unique Terms per Glossary in Category8 (#UTxGC8)	1	94	239
Percentage of Unique Terms per Glossary in Category8 [%UTxGC8 = (#UTxGC8/#UTxG) * 100]	1.14%	33.69%	40.66%

After designing the above categories, we classified each term into its appropriate category. The reader can find the ISO glossary terms categorized in Appendix II of the document at https://arxiv.org/ftp/arxiv/papers/2205/2205.10668.pdf. The TMMi glossary terms and the ISTQB glossary terms are classified and documented in Appendixes III and IV, respectively. As a result, Table 2 shows the size and scale of each of the glossaries as well as the numbers of classified terms and percentages for all categories.

2.2   Scope of the Quality Exploratory Study

Once the terms were categorized and the basic numbers obtained, comparison and analysis of syntactic and semantic similarities and discrepancies between the three glossaries can be performed. As mentioned earlier, we have scoped this exploratory study to include the term "testing" both as a single term or as part of others. Table 3 depicts the unique term "Testing" found in the three glossaries.

First, we can state as a result of this observational comparison that the term "Testing" syntactically matches and therefore has full syntactic similarity. Or, in other words, it has an occurrence frequency of 3, simultaneously considering the three glossaries as the target entity to be observed and analyzed. It should be noted that this term does not have a synonym in any glossary studied. Second, looking at the definition of the "Testing" term in the three glossaries, we can state that it has the semantics of process or activity. The three terms were then included accordingly in C2 as introduced above.

Table 3. Definitions of the "Testing" term in the three glossaries

Term	Definition	Glossary	Category
Testing	**Set of activities** conducted to facilitate discovery and/or evaluation of properties of one or more test items	ISO 29119-1	C2
Testing	**The process** consisting of all lifecycle activities, both static and dynamic, concerned with planning, preparation and evaluation of a component or system and related work products to determine that they satisfy specified requirements, to demonstrate that they are fit for purpose and to detect defects	ISTQB	C2
Testing	**The process** consisting of all lifecycle activities, both static and dynamic, concerned with planning, preparation and evaluation of software products and related work products to determine that they satisfy specified requirements, to demonstrate that they are fit for purpose and to detect defects	TMMi	C2

Additionally, the reader may notice that the "Testing" entry in TMMi and ISTQB fully match semantically, while a slightly different definition is in ISO. However, they are closely similar, which is why they fell into the same semantic category C2. In other words, we can state that the entries are syntactically and semantically consistent concerning the information suitability sub-characteristic, as we will see below.

As indicated at the beginning of this section, the scope of this study analyzes only terms ending with the word "testing". Thus, terms such as "white-box testing", "scenario testing" and "risk-based testing" are included, among many others.

Table 4 exhibits summed values for the three glossaries. For example, the Total Sum of Unique Terms is 955. Considering that the word "testing" is domain-specific, no term ending with "testing" must be categorized in C7 and C8. Therefore, the "Total Sum of Unique Terms ending with the word Testing in Categories 1 to 6" is 154, which represents

28.73% of the unique terms in categories C1 to C6. So, we consider the selected subset of terms from categories C1 to C6 to be significant for illustration purposes, due to the numbers and percentages shown.

The underlying hypothesis the reader can assume is that considering both the syntactic and semantic aspects of the terms ending with "testing" according to the definitions given by authors of these glossaries to the term "Testing" (Table 3), all these terms should fall in C2 (what to do). But this will not be the case. After filtering the terms ending with the word "testing" and calculating the syntactic frequency (similarity), we analyzed the semantic match of these categorized terms. As a result, the terms fell into three categories, namely: C1, C2, and C5. Consequently, there are syntactic and/or semantic inconsistencies between the glossary terms that could make learning and understanding somewhat difficult.

Table 4. Summed values of unique terms for the three software testing glossaries. Recall that the values per each glossary (#UTxGlossary) are in Table 2, while the others are in Appendix V

Metric name/acronym	Value
Total Sum of Unique Terms [TUT = (#UTxISO + #UTxTMMi + #UTxISTQB)]	955
Total Sum of Unique Terms in Categories 1 to 6 [TUTC1-6 = (TUTC1 + TUTC2 + TUTC3 + TUTC4 + TUTC5 + TUTC6)]	536
Percentage of Unique Terms in Categories 1 to 6 [%TUTC1-6 = (TUTC1-6/TUT) * 100]	56.13%
Total Sum of Unique Terms ending with the word "Testing" in Categories 1 to 6 [(TUTeTC1-6 = (TUTeTC1 + TUTeTC2 + TUTeTC3 + TUTeTC4 + TUTeTC5 + TUTeTC6)]	154
Percentage of Unique Terms ending with the word "Testing" in Categories 1 to 6 [%TUTeTC1-6 = (TUTeTC1-6/TUTC1-6) * 100]	28.73%

The recorded syntactic and semantic similarities and discrepancies promote the detection of quality problems not only for the three glossaries as a whole but also for the terms within each glossary. Table 5 defines some characteristics and attributes of Information Quality (adapted from [5]) that will be used in the next sections to analyze the glossaries. But the main aim of this work is to analyze the syntactic and semantic consistency (coded 2.3 in Table 5) and give some recommendations for improvement.

3   Analyzing Quality Issues Between Glossaries

This section discusses the results obtained by the analysis of syntactic and semantic consistency carried out. The analysis is documented in Subsect. 3.2 and was performed for the three glossaries terms considering terms' names endings with the word "testing". Also, it is important to note that we have developed a tool to calculate the syntactic frequency (similarity) between terms of the glossaries, which is presented in Subsect. 3.1. Finally, Subsect. 3.3 analyzes other quality issues detected in the glossaries related to missing terms and coverage.

Table 5. Characteristics and attributes of Information Quality. Extract adapted from [5]

Characteristic/*Attribute*	Definition (Note that definitions start with "Degree to which")
Information Quality	… a product or system delivers accurate and suitable information which meets stated and implied needs when used under specified conditions
1 Information Accuracy	… a product or system delivers information that is correct, credible, and current
1.1 Correctness	… the information is correct both semantically and syntactically in a given natural language
1.1.1 Semantic correctness	… the information is unambiguous in a given natural language
2 Information Suitability	… a product or system delivers information with the right coverage, added value, and consistency, considering the specified user tasks and intended goals
2.1 Added value	… the information can be novel, beneficial, and contribute to causing a reaction for a given user and task at hand
2.1.1 Beneficialness	*… the information is advantageous, meaningful, and contributes to making better decisions for an intended user goal*
2.2 Coverage	… the information is appropriate, complete, concise, and not redundant for the task at hand for an intended user
2.2.1 Completeness	*… the pieces of information regarding coverage are the sufficient amount of information for an intended user goal*
2.2.2 Conciseness	*… the piece of information is compactly represented without being overwhelming*
2.2.3 Non-redundancy	*… the pieces of information regarding coverage are not repeated unnecessarily*
2.3 Consistency	…the information is coherent both semantically and syntactically against informational things, parts, categories, or human expressions previously shown or stated and agreed
2.3.1 Syntactic consistency	*… the information has the necessary and sufficient keywords to coherently convey the message in a given natural language in front of something previously stated and agreed upon*
2.3.2 Semantic consistency	*… the information coherently conveys and harmonizes meaning with something previously stated and agreed upon*

3.1 Procedure to Get Syntactically Matching Terms Between Glossaries

When we started to collect all the terms and their corresponding synonyms from each software testing glossary, we have noticed different situations similar to the following:

- The ISTQB glossary has the main term "white-box testing" with the following synonyms: clear-box testing, code-based testing, glass-box testing, logic-coverage testing, logic-driven testing, **structural testing,** and structure-based testing.
- The ISO glossary has the main term "structure-based testing" with the following synonyms: **structural testing**, glass-box testing, and white box testing.
- The TMMi glossary has only the term "white-box testing" without synonyms.

Consequently, the term "white box testing" has a syntactic frequency of 3. One way to obtain this result is that "white box testing" is synonymous with the term "structural testing" in the ISTQB glossary, and the ISO glossary has the term "structural testing" as a synonym for the term "structure-based testing". Hence, we have a syntactic matching between the terms of these two glossaries. In addition, the TMMi glossary has the term "white-box testing" which syntactically matches with the term "white-box testing" of the ISTQB glossary and, therefore, the TMMi glossary "white-box testing" term syntactically matches with the term structure-based testing of the ISO glossary or any of its synonyms (structural testing, glass-box testing, and white box testing) by transitivity between glossary terms and synonyms.

Note that we can get the same result (frequency 3) in different ways, e.g. considering the "structure-based testing" synonym in ISTQB and the main term "structure-based testing" in ISO. Also, at this point, it is important to remark that we considered removing the hyphens in the terms for the syntactic analysis. Note that ISO has the term "white box testing" and the other glossaries have the terms "white-box testing".

Therefore, considering the above example, we have used the following rule when we calculated the syntactic frequency between glossary terms: *Let's suppose that we have the term T1 in the glossary G1, and T2 is a synonym of T1. Also, we have the term T2 in the glossary G2, and T3 is a synonym of T2. Then, if we have the term T3 in the glossary G3, the term T1 syntactically matches with the term T3 by transitivity of terms and synonyms between glossaries. Therefore, T1 (or T2 or T3) has a syntactical frequency of 3.* Note that we have developed a tool that follows this rule to automatically calculate the syntactic matching between glossary terms and their synonyms.

3.2 Analysis of Syntactic and Semantic Consistency

Once the results of the syntactic frequency of each glossary term have been obtained using the tool described above, we filtered the terms that end with the word "testing". We then only analyzed these terms and calculated the numbers and percentages shown in Table 6. Note that we used a set of metrics, which are described below.

The first metric shown in Table 6 is the Number of Terms ending with the word "testing" with Frequency 3 in Categories 1 to 6 (#TeTFq3C1-6). Note that Frequency 3 implies a Syntactic Similarity of the same term, considering the synonyms, in the 3 glossaries, e.g. the same term "dynamic testing" is in the 3 glossaries. Also, we found 9 terms more with a frequency of 3, so #TeTFq3C1-6 is 10 in total.

Then, we calculated the Percentage of Terms ending with the word "testing" with Full Syntactic Similarity in Categories 1 to 6 (%TeTFSySC1-6) and it resulted in 19.48%.

Table 6. Metrics and their values for the syntactic frequencies of the terms ending with the word "testing" in the three glossaries. Recall that TUTeTC1-6 = 154 according to Table 4

Metric name/acronym	Value
Number of Terms ending with the word "Testing" with Frequency 3 in Categories 1 to 6 (#TeTFq3C1-6)	10
Percentage of Terms ending with the word "Testing" with Full Syntactic Similarity in Categories 1 to 6 [%TeTFSySC1-6 = ((#TeTFq3C1-6*3)/TUTeTC1-6) * 100]	19.48%
Number of Terms ending with the word "Testing" with Frequency 2 in Categories 1 to 6 (#TeTFq2C1-6)	25
Percentage of Terms ending with the word "Testing" with Partial Syntactic Similarity in Categories 1 to 6 [%TeTPSySC1-6 = ((#TeTFq2C1-6*2)/TUTeTC1-6) * 100]	32.47%
Number of Terms ending with the word "Testing" with Frequency 1 in Categories 1 to 6 (#TeTFq1C1-6)	74
Percentage of Terms ending with the word "Testing" without Syntactic Similarity in Categories 1 to 6 [%TeTwSySC1-6 = (#TeTFq1C1-6/TUTeTC1-6) * 100]	48.05%

At this point, it is important to remark that the metric %TeTFSySC1-6 uses the value obtained in #TeTFq3C1-6 multiplied by 3 since we have 3 terms per each term with frequency 3. Also, the total amount of terms in the calculated percentage is 154 corresponding with TUTeTC1-6. Although we considered analyzing categories 1 to 6, we noted that the 3 selected glossaries only have terms ending with the word "testing" in categories 1, 2, and 5.

Analogously to what we made for terms with syntactic frequency 3, we did the same for terms with syntactic frequency 2 and 1. For frequency 2, the Number of Terms ending with the word "Testing" with Frequency 2 in Categories 1 to 6 (#TeTFq2C1-6) is 25. This implies that a term in a certain glossary syntactically matches with another term of only one of the other 2 remaining glossaries.

For example, the term "acceptance testing" is in ISTQB and TMMi glossaries, and the term "accessibility testing" is in ISTQB and ISO glossaries. Hence, the Percentage of Terms ending with the word "Testing" with Partial Syntactic Similarity in Categories 1 to 6 (%TeTPSySC1-6) is 32.47% ($\frac{25*2}{154} * 100$). The reader can see the other obtained values for frequency 1 in Table 6. Note that frequency 1 may imply absent terms in the other two glossaries. If we compare the obtained results shown in Table 6 for the glossaries terms ending with "testing" in categories 1 to 6, we can conclude that the 3 glossaries have few terms with full syntactic similarity (19.48%). Furthermore, most of the terms have a frequency of 1 (48.05%).

On the other hand, in Table 7, we illustrate the results of metrics related to semantic similarities. Regarding the semantic similarities and discrepancies of the 10 terms with a syntactic frequency of 3 (Table 6), only 6 terms have full semantic similarity (#TeTFSSFq3C1-6 = 6), i.e., the 3 syntactically same terms in the 3 glossaries have the same intended semantics as well. Also, 3 terms have a partial semantic similarity (#TeTPSSFq3C1-6 = 3), i.e., they have a semantic similarity of only 2 terms out of 3. Additionally, we found only 1 term ("exploratory testing") with a syntactic frequency of 3 and having 3 different intended semantics (#TeTwSSFq3C1-6 = 1).

We show in Fig. 1 a word cloud that illustrates the abovementioned 10 terms with a syntactic frequency of 3. Note that the biggest size terms (blue highlighted) have a full semantic similarity, the medium size ones (red highlighted) have a partial semantic similarity, and the single smallest one (the "exploratory testing" term highlighted in purple) has no semantic similarity.

Thus, the term "white-box testing" has a full semantic/syntactic similarity, and the term "risk-based testing" has a full syntactic similarity but partial semantic similarity.

To explain what a "semantic matching" between two terms from 2 glossaries with the same syntax means in this work, we will use Table 8. The term "white-box testing" (or structure-based testing) is a kind of "dynamic testing" in ISO. Also, the term "dynamic testing" is a kind of "testing", which in turn is a set of activities (recall Table 3). Then, we conclude that testing, dynamic testing, and structure-based testing fall in C2 since they are terms related to processes/activities according to their definitions. Something similar happens for the term "white-box testing" in the other 2 glossaries. As a result, the term "white-box testing" falls in the same category for the 3 glossaries.

Furthermore, if we take a deep look at the 3 definitions of "white-box testing", we can conclude that all 3 glossaries mention the structure of the test object (i.e. the test item, system, or component) and then the intended semantics of the term is closely similar for all 3 glossaries. Therefore, there is a semantic consistency.

Table 7. Metrics and their values for syntactic frequencies and semantic similarities/discrepancies of the terms ending with the word "testing" that are included in the three glossaries. The results were taken from the data processed and recorded in Appendix VI at http://arxiv.org/abs/2205. 10668. Recall that TUTeTC1-6 = 154 according to Table 4

Metric name/acronym	Value
Number of Terms ending with the word "Testing" with Full Semantic Similarity for Frequency 3 in Categories 1 to 6 (#TeTFSSFq3C1-6)	6
Number of Terms ending with the word "Testing" with Partial Semantic Similarity for Frequency 3 in Categories 1 to 6 (#TeTPSSFq3C1-6)	3
Number of Terms ending with the word "Testing" without Semantic Similarity for Frequency 3 in Categories 1 to 6 (#TeTwSSFq3C1-6)	1
Number of Terms ending with the word "Testing" with Full Semantic Similarity for Frequency 2 in Categories 1 to 6 (#TeTFSSFq2C1-6)	25
Number of Terms ending with the word "Testing" without Semantic Similarity for Frequency 2 in Categories 1 to 6 (#TeTwSSFq2C1-6)	0
Percentage of Total Terms ending with the word "Testing" with Full Syntactic and Semantic Similarity in Categories 1 to 6 [%TTeTFSSSC1-6 = (#TeTFSSFq3C1-6 * 3/TUTeTC1-6) * 100]	11.69%
Percentage of Total Terms ending with the word "Testing" with Partial Semantic Similarity in Categories 1 to 6 [%TTeTPSSC1-6 = ((#TeTPSSFq3C1-6 * 2 + #TeTFSSFq2C1-6 * 2)/TUTeTC1-6) * 100]	36.36%
Percentage of Total Terms ending with the word "Testing" without any Semantic Similarity in Categories 1 to 6 [%TTeTwSSC1-6 = ((#TeTPSSFq3C1-6 + #TeTwSSFq3C1-6 * 3 + #TeTwSSFq2C1-6 * 2 + #TeTFq1C1-6)/TUTeTC1-6) * 100]	51.95%

Fig. 1. Word cloud for glossary terms with a full syntactic similarity that includes 10 terms ending with "testing" belonging to categories 1 to 6 and with a syntactic frequency of 3. Among them, the largest terms (6 blue terms) have full semantic similarity, the medium size terms (3 red terms) have partial semantic similarity, and the single smaller one (the "exploratory testing" term purple highlighted) don't have any semantic similarity (Color figure online)

On the other hand, if we do the same analysis above for the term "exploratory testing", we can conclude that the intended semantics for the term in the TMMi glossary is technique and therefore falls in C5. In TMMi the term "test design technique" (in bold in Table 8) is defined as "*Procedure used to derive and/or select test cases*", which has the semantics of technique/procedure (C5) according to our judgment. In ISO, the term "exploratory testing" falls in C2, i.e., it has the semantics of process/activity. Lastly, in ISTQB, it falls in C1 since its definition mention that is an "approach", i.e., has the

Table 8. Definitions of the "white-box testing", "exploratory testing" and "risk-based testing" terms in the 3 candidate glossaries, as well as some related terms with their definitions. See the definitions of the "Testing" term in the 3 glossaries in Table 3

Term	Definition	Glossary	Category
Dynamic testing	**Testing** that requires the execution of the test item	ISO 29119-1	C2
Structure-based testing	**Dynamic testing** in which the tests are derived from an examination of the **structure** of the **test item**. *Note that "structure-based testing" is a synonym of "white-box testing" in ISO 29119-1*	ISO 29119-1	C2
White-box testing	**Testing** based on an analysis of the **internal structure** of the **component or system**	ISTQB	C2
White-box testing	**Testing** based on an analysis of the **internal structure** of the **component or system**	TMMi	C2
Exploratory testing	Experience-based **testing** in which the tester spontaneously designs and executes tests…	ISO 29119-1	C2
Exploratory testing	An **approach** to testing whereby the testers dynamically design and execute tests…	ISTQB	C1
Exploratory testing	An informal **test design technique** where the tester actively controls the design of the tests…	TMMi	C5
Risk-based testing	**Testing** in which the management, selection, prioritisation, and use of testing activities and resources are consciously based on corresponding types and levels of analyzed risk	ISO 29119-1	C2
Risk-based testing	**Testing** in which the management, selection, prioritization, and use of testing activities and resources are based on corresponding risk types and risk levels	ISTQB	C2
Risk-based testing	An **approach** to testing to reduce the level of product risks and inform stakeholders on their status, starting in the initial stages of a project. It involves the identification of product risks and…	TMMi	C1

semantics of approach/strategy. In order to be "syntactically consistent" (recall 2.3.1 attribute in Table 5), the TMMi term "exploratory testing" could be called "exploratory testing technique" or change the definition by explicitly mentioning that it is a kind of testing (i.e., activity or process). Likewise, ISTQB could name "exploratory testing" as "exploratory testing approach" or "exploratory testing strategy".

Another term to analyze is "risk-based testing". To this, ISO and ISTQB share the same semantics and are, according to our criterion, syntactically consistent since both names end with the word "testing" and fall into C2. But, in TMMi, "risk-based testing" falls in C1 since its definition mention that is an "approach". Therefore, to be syntactically consistent, we suggest disambiguation by using the term "risk-based testing approach".

Recall that, in Table 5, the attribute Semantic consistency (2.3.2) is defined as the *"degree to which the information coherently conveys and harmonizes meaning with something previously stated and agreed upon"*. Therefore, if the definition of the "Testing" term states that it is a kind of process/activity (Table 3), thus falling into category 2, we would expect any other glossary term ending with the word "testing" must fall into category 2 as well. In other words, and according to the definition of attribute 2.3.2, we would expect the semantics of glossary terms ending with the word "testing" to be consistent with the semantics of the term "Testing", which is previously stated and agreed

Table 9. Metrics and their values related to glossary terms that end with the word "testing" in categories 1, 2 and 5

Metric name/acronym	Values per Glossary		
	ISO 29119-1	TMMi	ISTQB
Total Number of Terms that end with the word "Testing" in Categories 1 to 6 per Glossary (#TeTC1-6xG)	28	33	93
Total Number of Terms that end with the word "Testing" in Category1 per Glossary (#TeTC1xG)	0	4	9
Percentage of Total Terms that end with the word "Testing" in Category1 per Glossary [%TTeTC1xG = (#TeTC1xG/#TeTC1-6xG) * 100]	0%	12.12%	9.68%
Total Number of Terms that end with the word "Testing" in Category2 per Glossary (#TeTC2xG)	28	18	63
Percentage of Total Terms that end with the word "Testing" in Category2 per Glossary [%TTeTC2xG = (#TeTC2xG/#TeTC1-6xG) * 100]	100%	54.55%	67.74%
Total Number of Terms that end with the word "Testing" in Category5 per Glossary (#TeTC5xG)	0	11	21
Percentage of Total Terms that end with the word "Testing" in Category5 per Glossary [%TTeTC5xG = (#TeTC5xG/#TeTC1-6xG) * 100]	0%	33.33%	22.58%

upon as a kind of activity/process. Therefore, we show the metrics in Table 9 to analyze this issue.

Table 9 shows in the %TTeTC2xG (Percentage of Total Terms that end with the word "Testing" in Category2 per Glossary) metric that most of the terms having the "testing" word in their names fall in C2 in the 3 glossaries. Recall that we classified the terms analyzing their semantics given by the authors of the glossaries and not by the name of the entry. However, only ISO uses the "testing" word consistently (%TTeTC2xG = 100%). ISO includes 28 terms that have the word "testing" in the term name and, considering that the "Testing" term definition has the semantics of activity/process, these 28 terms fall in the category C2 accordingly. The same does not happen in the other two glossaries, since the %TTeTC2xG metric gives 54.55% in TMMi and 67.74% in ISTQB. This can lead to semantic consistency issues in these glossaries.

Although ISO uses the "testing" word consistently in C2, we noted in the definition of the term "test design technique" that it has the given process/activity semantics when it should have the method/technique semantics (i.e., related to C5 as TMMi and ISTQB did). Besides, ISO has the terms "statement testing" and "scenarios testing", and we categorized them in C2 since their definitions mention that are a kind of "test design technique" and therefore, considering that in ISO semantically a "test design technique" falls in C2, then these 2 terms fall in C2 as well. However, if the given semantics of "test design technique" were more accurate, the terms "statement testing" and "scenario testing" would fall in C5 and ISO will not be 100% consistent with using the word "testing" in the terms' names. We might recommend updating the definition of "test design technique" in ISO to be more accurate, and then falling into C5, as well as adding the word "technique" at the end of these 2 terms to harmonize them.

3.3   Other Quality Issues

When we look at the result of the Percentage of Terms ending with the word "Testing" without Syntactic Similarity in Categories 1 to 6 (%TeTwSySC1-6 = 48.05%) in Table 6, we can note that most glossaries' terms do not have a syntactic similarity with other glossary terms, considering terms ending with "testing". This issue implies a large absence of terms in the glossaries. A cause of this is the different proportions of glossaries' terms. As shown in Fig. 2, ISTQB contributes to TUTeTC1-6 (Total Sum of Unique Terms ending with the word "Testing" in Categories 1 to 6, in Table 4) with more than half of all the glossaries terms.

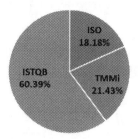

Fig. 2. The ratio of glossaries' terms ending with the word "testing" for categories C1-6. Recall that TUTeTC1-6 = 154 according to Table 4

Regarding the 2.2.1 completeness attribute (Table 5), we note that ISTQB is the glossary with more coverage in general. As shown in Fig. 2, ISTQB is the glossary with more terms ending with "testing" in categories 1-6 (60.39%). Also, according to Table 2 and comparing the metrics "Number of Unique Terms per Glossary in Categories 1-8" (i.e., #UTxGC1, #UTxGC2, #UTxGC3, ..., and #UTxGC8), ISTQB has more terms than the other 2 glossaries in all categories, i.e., ISTQB semantically covers all categories to a greater extent than the other 2 glossaries. Also, we noted that ISO does not consider including terms in C6 (testing agent/role/tool related terms) since #UTxGC6 = 0. Additionally, ISO has fewer terms in C5, C7, and C8 than the other 2 glossaries.

4   Related Work and Discussion

On the one hand, when searching for categories of glossary terms, we only found two works for software testing in the literature. One of them is the classification of the ISTQB glossary represented in a recent draft document. It has the following terminological categories: Testing, Requirements, Software Engineering, Quality, and General. Considering the terms that are specific to the software testing domain, the Testing category is the most used; although the Requirements category also includes some test-specific terms. Contrary to this, we have designed six categories as shown in Table 1, in which terms for Test Requirements are included in C3. Additionally, for the rest of the ISTQB categories, we have conceived C7 and C8.

The other somewhat related work for categorization carried out by Kuļešovs et al. [4] aims at structuring testing concepts into eight categories or classes. For example, the category called "How to test (approach, method, technique)?" corresponds mainly to C5 and a lesser extent to C1, in which the testing approach and strategy-related terms are placed. However, an explicit class for C2 (Testing Work Process-, Activity-related Terms) is missing in [4].

On the other hand, regarding measurement, comparison, and analysis, to the best of our knowledge, no directly related work in the literature considers a comparative analysis of syntactic and semantic consistency for a set of software testing glossaries. In order to look at related work in digital libraries, we primarily searched Scopus with a variety of keywords and operators, even including glossaries outside the software testing domain. The result was less than 10 papers, which we analyzed in depth. Among them, the most relevant research was done by Arnicane *et al.* [1]. Contrary to our research, they analyzed only inconsistencies in a software testing glossary, i.e., in ISTQB, without performing a comparative analysis across glossaries.

In [1] the authors detected some syntactic and semantic issues in the ISTQB glossary. For example, they detected that the terms "test process" and "testing" have the same semantics in ISTQB. So they assume that one of them is a redundant term in this glossary. Recalling the definition of non-redundancy given in Table 5, we noted that the same situation occurs in the other two glossaries.

Lastly, a seminal but preliminary work that analyzes consistency and conflict in terminology in software engineering standards is documented in [6]. But this paper, in the words of Rout, the author, is merely an attempt to identify and provide some scope for the problem of consistency of terminology in software engineering standards. It seems that the author has no more publications on this after 2000.

Looking at the results evidenced in Sect. 3 and taking into account the hypothesis stated in Subsect. 2.2 that according to the definitions given by the authors of the ISTQB, TMMi, and ISO glossaries to the term "Testing", all terms ending in "testing" should have fallen into C2, but fell into C1, C2, and C3, so we would like to stress at least one easy-to-adopt recommendation that can promote harmonization, consistency and ultimately learnability. Regarding the syntactic aspect of naming terms in C2 (what to do) and C5 (how to do), we recommend a clear distinction between them, for example, adding the word "technique" or "method" to some terms in C5. Instead, for C1, particularly for the analyzed terms, we recommend adding the word "approach" or "strategy".

5   Conclusions and Future Work

This work has analyzed the quality of the information between the terms of three software testing glossaries (ISTQB, TMMI, and ISO) used in academia and industry. Quality issues have been addressed primarily for a subcharacteristic of information quality, such as consistency, which includes syntactic and semantic consistency. Other quality attributes have been also addressed initially. The analysis has been limited to all the terms that end with the word "testing" and has been supported by the use of a set of categories and metrics that helped us semantically categorize all the terms and obtain results.

Based on the hypothesis mentioned in Subsect. 2.2, and discussed in Sect. 4, a list of recommendations was outlined that can promote consistency, harmonization, and ultimately improve the understanding and learnability capabilities of the different stakeholders. As a matter of fact, the last statement should be supported by a set of experimental studies that might be planned and carried out further.

Nevertheless, what became clear from this study is that there are opportunities to improve terminologies in order to achieve broader standardization in the area of software testing.

As future work, we will extend the analysis of this work considering other families of terms included in the categories mentioned above for the domain of software testing. In addition, we will explore the information quality characteristic for terms in other software engineering glossaries, such as for the area of project management.

Acknowledgments. This line of research is supported partially by the Engineering School at UNLPam, Argentina, in the project coded 09/F079.

References

1. Arnicane, V., Arnicans, G., Borzovs, J.: Building of concept system to improve systematic collection of terminology. Front. Artif. Intell. Appl. **291**, 313–326 (2016). https://doi.org/10.3233/978-1-61499-714-6-313
2. International Software Testing Qualifications Board (ISTQB®): Standard Glossary of Terms used in Software Testing, version 3.5 (2021). https://www.istqb.org/
3. ISO/IEC/IEEE 29119-1: Software and systems engineering – Software Testing – Part 1: Concepts and definitions (2013)
4. Kuļešovs, I., Arnicane, V., Arnicans, G., Borzovs, J.: Inventory of testing ideas and structuring of testing terms. Balt. J. Mod. Comput. **1**(3–4), 210–227 (2013)
5. Olsina, L., Lew, P., Dieser, A., Rivera, B.: Updating quality models for evaluating new generation web applications. J. Web Eng. **11**(3), 209–246 (2012). Special Issue: Abrahão, S., Cachero, C., Cappiello, C., Matera, M. (Eds.) Quality in New Generation Web Applications. Rinton Press, USA
6. Rout, T.P.: Consistency and conflict in terminology in software engineering standards. In: 4th IEEE International Software Engineering Standards Symposium and Forum (ISESS 1999), Best Software Practices for the Internet Age, pp. 67–74 (1999)
7. Tebes, G., Peppino, D., Becker, P., Matturro, G., Solari, M., Olsina, L.: Analyzing and documenting the systematic review results of software testing ontologies. Inf. Softw. Technol. **123**, 106298 (2020). https://doi.org/10.1016/j.infsof.2020.106298
8. Tebes, G., Olsina, L., Peppino, D., Becker, P.: Specifying and analyzing a software testing ontology at the top-domain ontological level. J. Comput. Sci. Technol. **21**(2), 126–145 (2021). https://doi.org/10.24215/16666038.21.e12
9. TMMi Foundation: Test Maturity Model Integration (TMMi®) - Guidelines for Test Process Improvement, Release 1.2 (2018)

Can Source Code Analysis Indicate Programming Skills? A Survey with Developers

Johnatan Oliveira[1]([✉]), Maurício Souza[2], Matheus Flauzino[2], Rafael Durelli[2], and Eduardo Figueiredo[1]

[1] Department of Computer Science, Federal University of Minas Gerais (UFMG), Belo Horizonte, Brazil
{johnatan.si,figueiredo}@dcc.ufmg.br
[2] Department of Computer Science, Federal University of Lavras (UFLA), Lavras, Brazil
{mauricio.ronny,rafael.durelli}@ufla.br,
matheus.flauzino2@estudante.ufla.br

Abstract. *Background:* Both open-source and proprietary software systems have become increasingly complex. Despite their growing complexity and increasing size, software systems must satisfy strict release requirements that impose quality, putting significant pressure on developers. Therefore, software projects' success depends on the identification and hiring of qualified developers. Several approaches aim to address this problem by automatically proposing models and tools to automatically identify programming skills through source code. However, we still lack empirical knowledge on the applicability of these models in practice. *Aims*: Our goal is to evaluate and compare two models proposed to support programming skill identification. *Method*: This paper presents a survey with 110 developers from GitHub. This survey was conducted to evaluate the applicability of two models for computing programming skills of developers based on the metrics Changed Files and Changed Lines of Code. *Results:* Based on the survey results, we conclude that both models often fail to identify the developer's programming skills. Concerning precision, the Changed Files model obtained 54% to identify programming languages, 53% for back-end & front-end profiles, and 45% for testing skills. About the Changed Lines of Code model, we obtained 36% of precision to identify programming languages, 45% for back-end & front-end profiles, and 30% for testing. *Conclusion*: Practitioners can use our survey to refine the practical evaluation of professional skills for several purposes, from hiring procedures to the evaluation of team.

Keywords: Hard skills · Programming skills · Developer expertise

1 Introduction

In large and nontrivial software systems, it is crucial to identify developers with the right skills for maintaining a piece of code—although it is a challenging and

A. Vallecillo et al. (Eds.): QUATIC 2022, CCIS 1621, pp. 156–171, 2022.
https://doi.org/10.1007/978-3-031-14179-9_11

time-consuming task [7]. This problem is even more critical since open-source and proprietary systems have become increasingly complex. Therefore, successful software projects demand the identification and hiring of qualified developers to build strong and cohesive teams with comprehensive sets of programming skills. Programming skills are the set of previous knowledge a software developer holds, such as in programming languages and libraries [1]. The current practice in industry and research for assessing programming skills is mainly based on proxy variables of skills, such as education, years of experience, and multiple-choice knowledge tests [1]. However, poor hiring decisions may hurt the success of a software system [7]. In particular, software projects have many open positions and not as many qualified candidates [1]. Identifying qualified candidates with the right combination of skills is crucial to the success of a software project.

Several approaches aim at addressing this problem by proposing models [3,5,8,15,21] and tools [7,12] to identify the programming skills via source code analysis. Many data about developers and projects are available from social coding platforms, such as GitHub. Such social and programming data about developers have a vast potential to support the effective identification of programming skills. For instance, Greene and Fischer [7] proposed a tool (CVExplorer) to identify developers with programming skills, such as expertise in programming languages, libraries, and frameworks. Although previous approaches may potentially identify the programming skills, we still lack empirical knowledge on their applicability based on an independent evaluation.

To fill this gap, this paper provides a survey with 110 developers from the GitHub platform to understand how automatically generated curricula of developers map to the perception of developers about their programming skills. We identified candidate participants by mining 1,678 public repositories. Then, we developed a tool for creating a curriculum for each candidate, based on two typical source code metrics, named Changed Files and Changed Lines of Code. Finally, we sent the curricula for the participants and invited them to answer in a survey to assess the precision of both models to calculate skills.

In general, the precision of the models evaluated in this paper are low. For programming languages skills, we obtained a precision of 54% using Changed Files versus 36% using Changed Lines of Code. Concerning back-end & front-end profiles, we obtained a precision of 53% using Changed Files versus 45% using Changed Lines of Code. Finally, about test skills, we obtained a precision of 45% using Changed Files versus 30% using Changed Lines of Code. Despite the low precision of both models, our results indicate that Changed Files seem more suitable than Changed Lines of Code to identify programming skills.

Our contribution targets both researchers and practitioners. Researchers can use our results to design studies related to skills and reflect on the complicated relationship between source code activities and skills. Practitioners can use it to refine practical evaluation of professional skills for several purposes, from hiring procedures to the evaluation of team formation. Understanding the effectiveness of the different approaches is the first and necessary step for building tools that will genuinely indicate programming skills by analyzing software repository [26].

2   Identifying Programming Skills

The goal of this study is to evaluate 2 models for the identification of skills of developers from the analysis of source code activities. Therefore, we implemented 2 models, (i) one based on Changed Files (CF) and (ii) the other based on Changed Lines of Code (CLOC) to compute programming skills. We implemented these models inspired by previous work [7,14,15,22]. For each model, we compute 3 programming skills: Programming Language, Back-end & Front-end profiles, and Testing. To illustrate how the models work, let's suppose Mary changed 8 files and 5 lines of code in the file "A.py". John changed only 5 files and changed 3 lines of code (LOC) in file "A.py".

Concerning the CF model, we compute Programming Languages by the number of files changed that share the same file extensions. Mary modified 3 Python, 2 Java, 2 CSS, and 1 HTML files. Therefore, according to the CF model, her skill in programming languages is distributed as follows: 37.5% Python, 25% Java, 25% CSS, and 12.5% HTML. In a similar fashion, the model CLOC considers the number of LOC added or removed by a specific developer. To calculate Johns' skill distribution in programming languages, we need to count the total number of changed LOC for all files that share the same file extension. John, for instance, has a skill distribution in programming languages as follows: 70% Python, 0% Java, 20% CSS, and 10% HTML.

Besides skill distribution for programming languages, we also analyzed (a) alignment between back-end & front-end profiles and (b) skills in test development. For the former, we classified a set of programming languages as front-end (e.g., CSS) and another set as back-end technologies (e.g., Java). Therefore, we also used the models previously described to calculate back-end & front-end profiles. To calculate the test skills, we to identify if a particular folder contains test files. The source code is parsed, and we search for directory structures mentioning "tests".

3   Study Settings

3.1   Goal and Research Questions

It is important to collect the perception of developers about their programming skills to get insights into the main strengths and weaknesses of the evaluated models. We performed the study following a predefined protocol and documenting the results of each step. This allows the traceability between our study goal, the research questions, the questionnaire design, and the collected data from the participants. It also supports future studies that may aim at replicating. We define the scope of our study following the Goal/Question/Metric (GQM) method [2]. Therefore, the scope of this study can be summed up as follows.

> **Analyze** two models that compute programming skills
> **for the purpose of** evaluating their applicability
> **with respect to** developers perception of their programming skills
> **from the point of view of** researchers and practitioners
> **in the context of** source code analysis of open-source software projects.

To achieve this goal, we framed our research around the following research questions (RQs).

RQ1 – *What is the precision of source code analysis to compute the programming language skills of a developer?*

RQ2 – *What is the precision of source code analysis to compute the back-end & front-end profiles of a developer?*

RQ3 – *What is the precision of source code analysis to compute the test development skills of a developer?*

RQ4 – *What feedback do developers provide about source code analysis to compute programming skills?*

3.2   Evaluation Steps

The main idea of our analysis is to collect data for different variables to investigate the feasibility of computing programming skills from source code. Therefore, our study consists of computing the skills of actual developers using the models described in Sect. 2, and asking the developers' agreement level regarding the results of these models. This way, we design this study in three steps: (1) Dataset Collection, (2) Survey Design, and (3) Data Analysis.

Step 1 – Dataset Collection: We randomly selected 1,137 developers from GitHub. The inclusion criterion was that the developer had to have at least 10 public repositories because we need vast source code data to be analyzed. As a result, we obtained a list of 2,758 repositories from these developers to be analyzed. We present this step in Sect. 3.3.

Step 2 – Survey Design: We then conducted an empirical study through a survey with the selected developers. More specifically, we sent emails asking them their agreement with the estimated programming skills computed by each model evaluated in this study. This step is presented in Sect. 3.4.

Step 3 – Data Analysis: In this last step, we conducted a qualitative and quantitative data analysis about the results. In addition, we translate the RQ into hypotheses. Section 3.5 shows this step.

3.3   Dataset

To create our dataset, we conduct a process of filtering to select the developers. Figure 1 shows the steps performed. First, we select 2,000 developers randomly according to trending GitHub[1]. Second, we made a filter by developers with the

---

[1] https://github.com/trending/developers.

160 J. Oliveira et al.

top-10 programming languages[2] investigated in this paper: JavaScript, Python, Java, Go, C++, Ruby, PHP, TypeScript, C#, and C. Besides, we selected the style sheet language CSS and HTML. Note that programming languages selected are between top-10 most used from GitHub[3]. As a result of this filtering step, we remove 300 developers. Third, from the last filter, we delete developers with less than ten projects. Therefore, we remove 271 developers and select 1,429 developers. Fourth, we select from the previous step, developers with at least 100 commits in projects. Consequently, we discard 136 developers and select 1,293. In the fifth and last step, we select developers with at least a thousand lines of code committed. That way, we eliminated 156 developers and obtained the 1,137 developers able to participate in our analysis. After, we automatically cloned 2,758 repositories from these developers through Ghcloneall[4]. We extracted from each commit: lines of code and files modified organized by the file extensions, such as, *.py*, *.java*, and *.css*.

Finally, we computed the developers' skills. These repositories provide the dataset with high variability in the size, complexity, domains, and technologies. Together, these repositories have a history of over 2.5 million commits. We obtained in total 110 responses from the survey (10% response rate).

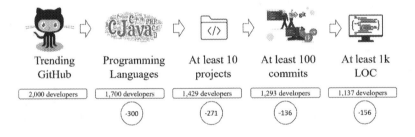

Fig. 1. Steps to select developers from GitHub

3.4 Survey Design

According to Easterbrook et al. [6], survey studies are used to identify the characteristics of a population and are usually associated with the application of questionnaires. Besides, surveys are meant to collect data to describe, compare or explain knowledge [10,18]. In this study, the survey is the main empirical strategy used to collect data to evaluate the two models for computing developers' programming skills.

Target group – The survey is composed of developers from GitHub.

Questionnaire Structure – Based on our goal and RQs, we designed a questionnaire supported with a *README* that explains the details of the study.

---
[2] https://madnight.github.io/githut/#/pull_requests/2021/4.
[3] https://githut.info/.
[4] https://pypi.org/project/ghcloneall/.

Type of questions – The questionnaire consists of a single answer. The goal of the questionnaire was to collect the participant opinion of two mini curricula generated from our scripts based on the CF (Option A) and CLOC (Option B) models. Each item of the questionnaire asked the participants to rate the agreement with the curriculum items in their skills. The items used five Likert-scale options for answers: "Strongly agree", "Agree", "Neither agree nor disagree", "Disagree", and "Strongly disagree". The questionnaire had no mandatory item. Therefore, participants are not forced to answer when they are not sure about a specific technology.

Pilot study – We performed a pilot study with eight developers to assess the understandability of the questions and to estimate the time required to answer them. We encouraged the eight developers to take notes on any problems or doubts regarding the meaning of the questions and track the time they spent filling out the questionnaire. As a result, we changed one question classified as confused by two developers. Worth emphasizing that this pilot study was applied in October 2021. The final survey execution was between November and December 2021. The survey remained open for twenty days.

Questionnaire length – The designed questionnaire includes up to five questions written in English (Google Forms)[5]. The time needed for answering the questions of the questionnaire was between three and five minutes (Table 1).

Table 1. Survey questions

ID	Questions	Option A	Option B
SQ1	Your GitHub username:		
SQ2	With respect to programmings languages:	Likert-scale	Likert-scale
	we mined some languages you are likely to know		
	How much do you agree or disagree with the level distribution presented in Option A and Option B?		
SQ3	With respect to back-end & front-end:	Likert-scale	Likert-scale
	we mined your possible profile		
	How much do you agree or disagree with the level distribution presented in Option A and Option B?		
SQ4	With respect to software test:	Likert-scale	Likert-scale
	we mined your likely knowledge		
	How much do you agree or disagree with the level distribution presented in Option A and Option B?		
SQ5	Please leave any comments that you consider relevant to our research		

---

[5] https://www.google.com/forms/.

3.5   Data Analysis

From the survey results, we performed quantitative and qualitative data analyses to address the research questions. For research questions RQ1, RQ2, and RQ3, we conducted a descriptive analysis of the data and statistical tests to identify the precision similarity of both models. For the statistical tests, each research question was translated into hypotheses, as follows.

Regarding RQ's, we defined the following hypotheses:

> **Null Hypothesis,** $H_{0\,RQ1||RQ2||RQ3}$: there is no difference in the precision of both models regarding the $<$ *programming language* $||$ *back-end & front-end* $||$ *test* $>$ skills of a developer.
>
> **Alternative Hypothesis,** $H_{1\,RQ1||RQ2||RQ3}$: there is a difference between both models regarding $<$ *programming language* $||$ *back-end & front-end* $||$ *test* $>$ skills of a developer.

Then, our hypotheses can be formally stated as:

$$\mathbf{H}_{0\,RQ1||RQ2||RQ3}:\ \overline{x}_{changeFile} = \overline{x}_{changeLOC}$$

and

$$\mathbf{H}_{1\,RQ1||RQ2||RQ3}:\ \overline{x}_{changeFile} <> \overline{x}_{changeLOC}$$

We perform statistical tests over the data in *RQ1*, *RQ2*, and *RQ3*. The independent variables for the first three research questions are the CF and CLOC models. Precision is our dependent variable. We verify if answers from every case deviate from normality using the Shapiro-Wilk test (p-value ranges from 0.7 to 0.9). Since normality was not always met, we used a Wilcoxon Signed-Rank Test with a 95% confidence interval. We conducted a Wilcoxon signed-rank test [19] to check the significance of the difference between the two paired groups. Because we are interested in the differences of the values, we report the effect size with the median and mean differences. We use R to conduct these analyses.

For *RQ4*, we used an approach inspired by the open and axial coding phases of Ground Theory [23]. Two researchers analyzed the responses of open questions individually and marked relevant segments with "code". Later, the researchers compared their codes to reach a consensus and grouped them into relevant categories. We examined the data line-by-line using the following questions as a lens to identify codes (open coding) [23]: (1) What is this saying? What does it represent? (2) What is happening here? (3) What is at issue here? (4) What is the participant trying to convey? (5) What process is being described? Consequently, it is possible to count the number of occurrences of codes and the number of items in each category to understand what recurring aspects are pointed by the participants and then discuss possible lessons learned. The developers are our oracle to evaluate the models. For this, we calculated the precision.

4   Results

4.1   Overview

This section presents an overview of results for the CF and CLOC models. Figure 2 shows the opinion of the developers of each model. In this figure, we have 3 blocks, one for each evaluated programming skill. The first block of charts represents programming language skills. The second block depicts the back-end & front-end profiles. Finally, the last block shows the test skills. Concerning the CF model agreement, we observe in the programming language perspective that 27% of the participants answered "strongly agree" and "agree" with this model. On the other hand, we observe that to the CLOC model, 14% and 22% of the participants answered respectively "strongly agree" and "agree". Concerning disagreements, we have 12% and 18% to "strongly disagree" and "disagree" to the CF model. While for CLOC, we observe 18% and 19%, respectively, to "strongly disagree" and "disagree". This way, we note that the CF models, in general, are better evaluated by developers to capture their programming language skills.

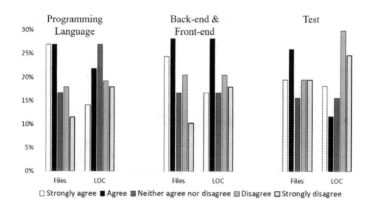

Fig. 2. Overview

4.2   Programming Language Skill

In this section, we answer the first research question (RQ1). For RQ1, we found a statistically significant difference between CF and CLOC model (p-value = 0.02423) with Wilcoxon-Signed Rank test. This result allows us to reject the null hypothesis. Therefore, the models CF and CLOC are statistically different. To analyze the precision, we sum "agree" with "strongly agree". This way, we obtained the 54% precision to CF and 36% to CLOC.

In general, the developers do not agree with the models evaluated. To understand the factors leading a developer not to agree, we create 3 categories: Hard Divergence, Soft Divergence, and Convergence. The category Hard Divergence indicates the number of developers against one of the models and favorable to the other. Soft Divergence means that a developer agrees or disagrees with a given model and is neutral about the other. Finally, Convergence indicates they share the same opinion (agree, disagree, or neutral) for both models. Our focus is on Hard Divergence because our goal is to understand how the models differ.

Figure 3 presents the opinion of the developers into these 3 categories. In this figure, we use 3 colors for convergence: light grey (negative), dark grey (neutral), and black (positive). "Hard Divergence" and "Soft Divergence" correspond to, respectively, 20% (22) and 33.64% (37) of the answers. Therefore, we can observe that 20% of the developers agree with a model and disagree with another, 33.64% agree with one and are neutral with the other. The remainder of the answers (46.37%) shows convergence, where: 17.27% agree on neither of the two models, 24.55% agree with both models, and 4.55% are neutral towards both. Our qualitative analysis (SQ5) investigates patterns of answers.

We note that the models were discrepant in some causes. That is, they presented a result different from the other. In some cases, the models present the same languages. However, a model presented a different sorting. In general, the model that prioritizes the most mainstream languages from the viewpoint of a developer is that they agree-for example, Python and JavaScript were considered mainstream languages. On the other hand, when the model ranks CSS above the other languages, overall, the developers disagree with this model.

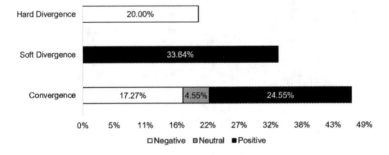

Fig. 3. Programming language skills

RQ1 summary: We obtained 54% precision to CF versus 36% to CLOC. However, it is possible to see that less than 20% strongly disagree with both evaluated models (negative convergence).

4.3   Back-end & Front-end Profiles

In this section, we answer the second research question (RQ2). To investigates RQ2, we conducted the same configuration presented in RQ1. The Wilcoxon signed-rank test indicated *p-value= 0.06896*. Since the *p-value is 0.06896*, which is greater than our *0.05* significance level, we could not reject the null hypothesis in this case. Figure 4 shows the results of this RQ. In this figure, we have the same configurations presented previously. "Hard Divergence" and "Soft Divergence" correspond to, respectively, 34.55% (38) and 25.45% (28) of the answers. On the other hand, "Convergence" corresponds to 40% of the answers, where 15.45% (17) of the developers did not agree with the either models (negative convergence). This way, to these developers, both models cannot represent their Back-end & Front-end profiles. For this RQ, we obtained a precision of 53% to CF versus 45% to CLOC. Therefore, we observe that CF from survey results obtained better precision than CLOC.

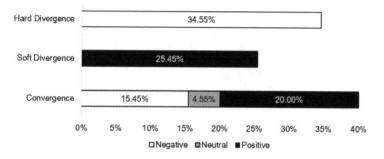

Fig. 4. Back-end & Front-end Skill

RQ2 summary: Overall, the precision of the model evaluated is low to back-end & front-end profiles. We obtained 53% precision to CF versus 45% to CLOC.

4.4 Test Development

To answer RQ3, we investigate the test skills of developers computed by the 2 models, CF and CLOC. For this, we used the same configurations presented in the last RQs. The Wilcoxon signed-rank test indicated *p-value < 0.01*. Since the p-value is smallest than the *0.05* significance level, we reject the null hypothesis. Therefore, there is a difference between the 2 models evaluated concerning test development skills.

Figure 5 presents the results in the same way as presented previously. From all skills evaluated, tests obtained the worst results. We compute 52.73% (58) of answers for Hard Divergence against 12.73% (14) to Soft Divergence. From these results, we can observe that 17.27% (19) converge negatively to both models. Therefore, to 19 developers, both models cannot compute their skills in tests. We also note that only 10.91% (12) of developers agree with models evaluated,

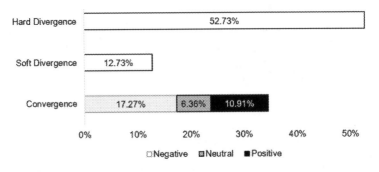

Fig. 5. Test skill

and 6.36% (7) are neutral. For this RQ, we obtained a precision of 45% to CF versus 30% to CLOC. The precision did not achieve 50% in either models.

RQ3 summary: We obtained a precision of 45% to CF versus 30% to CLOC. We argue that the models need to improve the precision to compute programming skills for test development.

4.5 Feedback from Developers

In this section, we address the results the fourth research question (RQ4). To gather and synthesize such feedback, we employed an approach inspired by the coding phrase of Ground Theory (as discusses in Sect. 3.5). We grouped the identified codes into 8 categories (shown in Table 2): *Imprecision of detecting skills, Expertise not captured, Lack data from private repositories, Problems in presentation, Positive feedback, Negative Feedback, and others.*

Table 2. Feedback categories

Category	#
Imprecision of detecting skills	17
Expertise not captured	16
Others	6
Positive feedback	6
Problems in presentation	5
Lack data from private repositories	4
Negative feedback	4
Time factor	3

The most frequent feedback is related to *Imprecision of detecting skills* and to *Expertise not captured*, mentioned by 17 and 16 participants, respectively.

The first represents the imprecise detection of programming language, back-end & front-end, and test. Seven participants expressed concerns about the lack of treatment of what was created by the developer in contrast to what was committed. Six participants did not agree with the models for calculating their front-end & back-end profiles. Four participants pointed problems in the models for calculating language skills, such as wrong recognition of languages. Two participants pointed criticism towards the results of test development.

The codes categorized as *Expertise not captured* are mostly related to the absence of specific programming languages or testing skills in the resulting curriculum. Eight participants indicated that the results did not compute any testing skills. These comments helped us understand that the models of simply considering directory path referencing to test are not enough to capture fragments of codes that implement tests. Seven participants mentioned they missed specific languages in their respective curriculum. From these cases, six participants mentioned languages that our scripts did not capture them. Finally, one participant mentioned that the model could not assess their front-end/back-end orientation since they do not post it on GitHub.

Concerning *Positive feedback*, we have a favorable opinion of the developers about the evaluated models. Between these comments, we highlight one in particular, which the developer said that the models have the potential to use in the industry if improved. Another category we created was *Problems in presentation*. This category represents the problems concerning the presentation of the curriculum. For instance, type of charts, layout, percentage, and text at curriculum. This problem typically occurred when the curriculum showed similar data for both models, for example. The codes categorized as *Lack of data from private repositories* indicate the observations of developers about data not captured at private repositories. Some developers related that their skills were not computed correctly because most of their source code is available in private repositories. *Negative Feedback* reports comments from developers that did not like the results presented by the models. For example, a developer stated: "None of these results captures the useful nuance".

5   Discussion

5.1   Accuracy of the Evaluated Heuristics

From the developers' comments, we observe that many of them cited low accuracy of the models evaluated. Given this scenario, we investigate the causes of these comments. We checked developers on GitHub that reported these problems, and we verified that both models fail to compute skills, particularly for tests. Each heuristic used the same procedure to classify the file as test through a path with the substring "test". Therefore, we observe that the evaluated models need to improve to show better results, mainly to compute test skills. Table 3 presents a summary about precision presented in RQs 1, 2 and 3. In this table, it is possible to see an overview of the models precision and observe that all models were below 60%. This value indicates low precision to both models to identify programming skills from source code.

Table 3. Summary of precision

Model	Skill	Precision
CF	Programming languages	54%
	Back-end & Front-end profile	53%
	Test	45%
CLOC	Programming languages	36%
	Back-end & Front-end profile	45%
	Test	30%

6   Threats to Validity

In this section, we detail the threats that may affect the validity of the study and how they are handled.

Construct Validity– Self-selection is a threat. However, we try to select the biggest group of developers from GitHub without evaluating the number of commits, amount of stars, programming languages, and organizations. The use of generated distribution of skills based on GitHub contributions as a proxy for general individual skill level evaluation is a limitation. Professional experiences can be much broader than individual contributions to open-source projects.

Internal and External Validity– We developed many steps to mitigate this threat: (i) Respondents were assured of their anonymity to avoid evaluation apprehension; (ii) We sent an email only to developers mined by GitHub; and (iii) All questions were not mandatory. The survey target number might not be a representative sample. However, our sample is diversified; the subjects have different programming experiences and work with freelancers or other companies. Therefore, we believe that these steps contributed to obtaining a sample that is quite heterogeneous in terms of knowledge, job role, profile, and company.

Conclusion Validity– The participants may not answer the questionnaire honestly. Participants may feel that they needed to provide positive feedback for better scores. This threat is minimized by announcing that the questionnaire is not mandatory (feedback without pressure). In this study, we only used the absolute number and percentages to compute programming skills.

7   Related Work

Studies to identify the knowledge of developers based on their contributions to online platforms have gained relevance in the field of software engineering [4, 20, 24]. The evaluation of such approaches is essential to guarantee the quality of the analysis and to ensure an effectiveness of the specialist identification model [16]. Just like us, some studies use reports through forms [20] or choose to carry out such an assessment manually [17,25]. Others compare it to previous studies [13]. Researchers performed automatic evaluations comparing data extracted from GitHub with the content of responses made in Stack Overflow [5,20].

Approaches to identify and extract technical skills, known as hard skills, have gained prominence among research, often supported by tools to perform the extractions [9,11]. Greene and Fischer [7] proposed a tool named CVExplorer, which can be used to assist non-technical users to extract, filter, and identify developers according to technical skills (programming languages, libraries, and frameworks) demonstrated across all of their open-source contributions, in order to support more accurate candidate identification. Tags are mined from the project's READMEs and from commit messages. Note that we did not evaluate the models using CVExplorer [7] because this tool relies on ReadMe file, number of commits, number of files, and file extension. However, CVExplorer did not use changed lines of code as parameter.

8   Conclusion and Future Work

In this paper we described a survey that evaluated two models based on, (i) Changed Files and (ii) Changed Lines of Code. We conducted a survey with 110 developers from GitHub. These developers received a curriculum generated automatically by the two models investigated in this study and were invited to answer 5 questions. Our study evaluates 3 perspectives of programming skills, (i) Programming Languages, (ii) Back-end & Front-end profile, and (iii) Test Development. We conclude that both models evaluated need more investigations to improve the accuracy of skills detection. However, we believe that both models may be combined for better results. We also hope that this paper paves the way for more research related to programming skills detection. As future work, we plan to extend to following directions. First, we plan to extend both models to other programming languages and explore other approaches to compute programming skills. Second, we intend to develop a tool capable of computing programming skills from the source code from findings identified in this paper.

Acknowledgments. This research was partially supported by Brazilian funding agencies: CNPq, CAPES, and FAPEMIG.

References

1. Baltes, S., Diehl, S.: Towards a theory of software development expertise, pp. 187–200 (2018)
2. Basili, V., Caldiera, G., Rombach, H.D.: The goal question metric approach. Online Technical Report (1994)
3. Bizer, C., Heath, T., Berners-Lee, T.: Linked data: the story so far. In: Semantic Services, Interoperability and Web Apps: Emerging Concepts, pp. 205–227 (2011)

4. Constantino, K., Zhou, S., Souza, M., Figueiredo, E., Kästner, C.: Understanding collaborative software development: an interview study. In: Proceedings of the 15th International Conference on Global Software Engineering, pp. 55–65 (2020)

5. Constantinou, E., Kapitsaki, G.M.: Identifying developers' expertise in social coding platforms. In: 42th Euromicro Conference on Software Engineering and Advanced Applications (SEAA) (2016)

6. Easterbrook, S., Singer, J., Storey, MA., Damian, D.: Selecting empirical methods for software engineering research. In: Shull, F., Singer, J., Sjøberg, D.I.K. (eds) Guide to Advanced Empirical Software Engineering. Springer, London (2008). https://doi.org/10.1007/978-1-84800-044-5_11

7. Greene, G.J., Fischer, B.: CVExplorer: identifying candidate developers by mining and exploring their open source contributions. In: Proceedings of the 31st IEEE/ACM International Conference on Automated Software Engineering (ASE), pp. 804–809 (2016)

8. Hauff, C., Gousios, G.: Matching GitHub developer profiles to job advertisements. In: IEEE/ACM 12th Working Conference on Mining Software Repositories (MSR), pp. 362–366 (2015)

9. Huang, W., Mo, W., Shen, B., Yang, Y., Li, N.: CPDScorer: modeling and evaluating developer programming ability across software communities. In: International Conference on Software Engineering and Knowledge Engineering (ICISDM) (2016)

10. Kitchenham, B.A., Pfleeger, S.L.: Personal opinion surveys. In: Shull, F., Singer, J., Sjøberg, D.I.K. (eds) Guide to Advanced Empirical Software Engineering. Springer, London (2008). https://doi.org/10.1007/978-1-84800-044-5_3

11. Kourtzanidis, S., Chatzigeorgiou, A., Ampatzoglou, A.: RepoSkillMiner: identifying software expertise from GitHub repositories using natural language processing. In: 35th IEEE/ACM International Conference on Automated Software Engineering (ASE), pp. 1353–1357 (2020)

12. Marlow, J., Dabbish, L.: Activity traces and signals in software developer recruitment and hiring. In: Proceedings of the 2013 Conference on Computer Supported Cooperative Work, pp. 145–156 (2013)

13. Matturro, G.: Soft skills in software engineering: a study of its demand by software companies in Uruguay. In: 6th International Workshop on Cooperative and Human Aspects of Software Engineering (CHASE), pp. 1–10 (2013)

14. Mockus, A., Herbsleb, J.D.: Expertise browser: a quantitative approach to identifying expertise. In: Proceedings of the 24th International Conference on Software Engineering (ICSE), pp. 503–512 (2002)

15. Montandon, J.E., Silva, L.L., Valente, M.T.: Identifying experts in software libraries and frameworks among GitHub users. In: IEEE/ACM 16th International Conference on Mining Software Repositories (MSR), pp. 276–287 (2019)

16. Mori, A., et al.: Evaluating domain-specific metric thresholds: an empirical study. In: Proceedings of the 2018 International Conference on Technical Debt, pp. 41–50. TechDebt 2018, Association for Computing Machinery, NY (2018)

17. Oliveira, J., Viggiato, M., Figueiredo, E.: How well do you know this library? Mining experts from source code analysis. In: Proceedings of the XVIII Brazilian Symposium on Software Quality, pp. 49–58. SBQS 2019, Association for Computing Machinery, NY (2019)

18. Pfleeger, S.L., Kitchenham, B.A.: Principles of survey research: part 1: turning lemons into lemonade. SIGSOFT Softw. Eng. Notes **26**, 16–18 (2001)

19. Rosner, B., Glynn, R.J., Lee, M.L.: The Wilcoxon signed rank test for paired comparisons of clustered data. Biometrics **62**, 185–192 (2006)

20. Saxena, R., Pedanekar, N.: I know what you coded last summer: mining candidate expertise from GitHub repositories. In: 17th Conference on Computer Supported Cooperative Work and Social Computing (CSCW), pp. 299–302 (2017)
21. da Silva, J.R., Clua, E., Murta, L., Sarma, A.: Niche vs. breadth: calculating expertise over time through a fine-grained analysis. In: 2015 IEEE 22nd International Conference on Software Analysis, Evolution, and Reengineering (SANER) (2015)
22. Singer, L., Filho, F.F., Cleary, B., Treude, C., Storey, M.A., Schneider, K.: Mutual assessment in the social programmer ecosystem: an empirical investigation of developer profile aggregators. In: 13th Conference on Computer Supported Cooperative Work (CSCW), pp. 103–116 (2013)
23. Stol, K.J., Ralph, P., Fitzgerald, B.: Grounded theory in software engineering research: a critical review and guidelines. In: 38th International Conference on Software Engineering (ICSE), pp. 120–131 (2016)
24. Tantisuwankul, J., et al.: A topological analysis of communication channels for knowledge sharing in contemporary GitHub projects. J. Syst. Softw. **158**, 110416 (2019)
25. Teyton, C., Palyart, M., Falleri, J.R., Morandat, F., Blanc, X.: Automatic extraction of developer expertise. In: 18th International Conference on Evaluation and Assessment in Software Engineering (EASE), pp. 1–10 (2014)
26. Vadlamani, S.L., Baysal, O.: Studying software developer expertise and contributions in stack overflow and GitHub. In: 36th International Conference on Software Maintenance and Evolution (ICSME), pp. 312–323 (2020)

Industrial Experiences and Applications

Improving the Quality of ICT and Forestry Service Processes with Digital Service Management Approach: A Case Study on Forestry Liquids

Marko Jäntti[1]([✉]) and Markus Aho[2]

[1] CEMIS, Kajaani University of Applied Sciences,
P.O. Box 52, Ketunpolku 1, 87101 Kajaani, Finland
marko.jantti@cemis.fi
[2] Funlus Oy, Sepontie 15, 73300 Nilsia, Finland
markus.aho@funlus.fi

Abstract. Harvesting forests requires consumption of various types of liquids: fuels, lubricating oil for harvester saw chains, marking colours in liquid form, and urea-based fungicide. Forest machines consume large amounts of these liquids that are ordered from several sources. Forest machine operators have challenges in measuring the consumption of liquids and receiving up-to-date information on liquid levels, especially in remote storage areas. In this action research study, we focus on improving the quality of ICT and forestry service processes and monitoring consumption of liquids through Internet of Things (IoT) sensors and a mobile application. The research problem of this study is: how to improve quality of ICT and forestry service processes with digital technologies? The main contribution of this paper is to describe the development of an IoT-based order system with an action research method and present challenges, activities and benefits of using IoT technology in quality improvement of service processes.

Keywords: Service request management · ICT quality · Internet of Things · Forest machine operator

1 Introduction

Companies that ignore the value of digital service management shall likely struggle with keeping customers satisfied in the long run, suffer from poor productivity in dealing with service requests and incidents from users, deliver products and

Supported by Development of AIKA Ecosystem in Kainuu project (Regional Council of Kainuu, A78688) and DIH-World (co-funded by the Horizon 2020 Framework Programme of the EU under grant agreement No 952176).

services tool later than their competitors losing competitive advantage little by little, and may lose their key employees to other companies due to old fashioned tools.

Although typical companies starting adopting digital service management are ICT or technology companies, organizations from other business domains such as forestry could also benefit from combining digital transformation and service management approaches together.

Previous studies on service management improvement have mainly focused on improving service management based on IT Infrastructure Library [5], exploring challenges related to service desk operations [11], utilizing knowledge-centric approaches in improving help desk processes [6], and impact of IT service management implementations [14]. There are only few studies that have focused directly on service request management [12] and to our knowledge none of these studies have dealt with a merger of digital service management and service request management. Modern service request management should be data-based and should utilize opportunities of data analytics [15].

Digital service management as a research field has evolved from various service-related research areas such as services computing [22], service science, service operation management and service process improvement. Service science focuses on studying service systems, aiming to create a basis for systematic service innovation [13].

Basically, service science aims at using scientifical knowledge and understanding to design, improve, and scale service systems. It is important to understand the varying scope of a service system, it is definitely not a single application, tool or technology used by the organization. Rather, it is a model representing how all the components and activities of an organization work together to facilitate value creation [1]. Spohrer et al. emphasize that a service system is the basic abstraction of service Science [20]. In order to fully understand the concept of service systems and its underlying behavioral elements, a service researcher should exposure him/herself to different types and scopes of service systems from different domains. The following examples of service systems have different scopes, objectives, roles and operative models:

- A digital technology-enabled business service system (IoT-based order system for a forest machine operator, IoT-enabled plantation monitoring system [21])
- A service organization (a company providing services to its customers, such as IT services)
- A Service Management System based on a service management standard (ISO/IEC 20000:1 [9] and ISO/IEC 20000:2 [10])
- An Enterprise Service Management system (set of tools, technologies and data the organization is using to run daily service management and manage records)
- A Service Management Office (organizational function, typically involved in service management governance and making decisions on broader process improvement such as Continual Service Improvement (CSI) [2] or maturity improvement of service processes based on CMMI for services [19])

However, all of the above mentioned service systems could be found within a single organization. This demonstrates the versatility, complexity and granularity of service systems. In our study, we focus on the first service system on the list: the digital technology-enabled business service system. Modern service systems are increasingly digital service systems that merge various digital technologies and tools, methodology frameworks, and process management approaches together. In IT service management, IT Infrastructure Library (ITIL) has been the most widely used service management process framework providing guidance for implementing service operation processes including service request management [3].

Latest editions of ITIL [1] highlight the role of digital services in service management, but clear definition of digital service management is still missing. Thus, we extend the service management definition of IT Infrastructure Library to cover a clear digital dimension of service management. Thus, digital service management can be defined as a set of specialized organizational capabilities for enabling value for customers in form of services and operating with digital mindset and modern digital technologies, tools, processes and practices. In this paper, we focus on applying IoT technologies for monitoring tank levels. There are only few academic studies that have dealt with the topic but in the different context than forestry [17,23].

What does the digital dimension of service management mean in practice in the context of order management? The traditional way of providing service support is that a helpdesk answers phone calls and email messages from users to solve their worries. In order to get rid off the unstructural data due to phone calls and emails, companies started deploying ticket systems. When organizations evolved further, they started to change their business orientation from delivering products and projects towards service delivery model. Service delivery model resulted a need for introducing entirely new processes for managing service provision such as service request management, service level management and service catalogue management. Shrestha et al. discuss in their paper [18] how to select service management processes for improvement by using a systematic model. However, in many cases, the improvement of service management starts from an identified business challenge that in our case was how to monitor the consumption of forestry liquids.

The remainder of the paper is organized as follows. Section 2 describes the research methods. Section 3 presents the results of the action research study Sect. 4 provides an analysis, and conclusions are given in Sect. 5.

2   Research Methods

This study aimed at answering the following research problem: how to improve quality of ICT and forestry business processes with digital technologies? In this study, we used an action research method to answer the research problem with a single case organization, Motoajo Oy, a forest machine operator from Finland. The research problem was divided into following three research questions:

- What types of challenges exist in applying IoT technology to service request management?
- What activities are specific to IoT-based digital transformation and ICT quality improvement?
- How new digital technologies and digital transformation help in creating business value for a forest machine operator's service management?

In our study, we focused on exploring a digital transformation initiative (digital experiment) in the context of forest machine operator company. In order to guide digital transformation and information system development, we utilized digital service management approach as well as information system research framework (see Fig. 1).

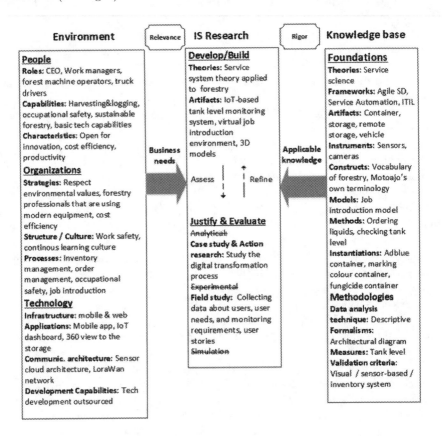

Fig. 1. The context of the study.

The information system research framework was used to increase understanding of the research target including high level description of people, organization, technology applied during the digital experiment as well as theory foundations such as theories, frameworks, artifacts, instruments, constructs models, method and instantiations.

2.1 Target Organization

Our target organization Motoajo Oy (SME) is a family-owned professional forestry contractor company with 70 employees. The company's office is located in Nurmes, Eastern Finland, where the company also mainly operates. While logging and transporting roundwood and coppice, Motoajo always pays attention to the nature and operates by all means to protect it. The company's vehicles (45 forest machines) are modern and made according to current emission standards. With harvesters the company follows the Measuring Instruments Act with random sampling of tree trunks. All the vehicles are equipped with loader scales. Motoajo's aim is to work cost-effective and on schedule with professional staff and modern vehicles also in challenging environments, not forgetting safety at work. The company has several quality certificates (ISO9001 quality management system, ISO14001 environmental management systems and OHSAS 18001 occupational health and safety management system) that guide managers and employees in managing operations and the quality. The case organization was selected because it was a representative case of an SME that aims at improve its operations through digital transformation. This study was an exploratory case study [16] documenting the first steps of a digital experiment funded by Horizon 2020 programme.

Receiving forestry liquids (fungicide, diesel exhaust fluid, fuel) in time to right destinations is critical to the company's harvesting business. Digital transformation is needed to automate the process of monitoring inventory of liquids, especially in remote storage areas. There are growing sustainability requirements towards forestry actors due to EU forest policies.

2.2 Data Collection Methods

Data for this study was collected by using multiple sources of evidence from the case organization during a 8-month data collection period: August 2021–March 2022. The data was captured by both authors that participated in implementing the digital experiment and documenting the case study findings.

- Documentation: Experiment handbook, safety instruction document, quality manual.
- Archival records: Internet of Things data records in the IoT dashboard.
- Interviews/discussions: discussions and interviews with CEO of Motoajo, CEO of IoT provider, technical specialist of IoT provider, 2 work managers of Motoajo, discussions with IoT sensor providers (Teams, phone calls).
- Participative observation: Experiment Handbook meetings, field visits to case organization's storage and remain mote storage areas.
- Physical artifacts: Fuel containers (metal), Fungicide containers (metal), AdBlue and marking colour containers (plastic), IoT sensor modules, IBC container cap, waste collection containers, printed QR codes. These artifacts were studied while scoping the experiment and choosing the relevant monitoring target.
- Direct observations: Observations during the field visit to Motoajo's logging destination in the forest.

2.3 Data Analysis Methods

Data analysis of this study focused on analyzing the action research cycle from the perspective of four research questions. The first research question focused on the challenges and was analyzed by categorizing challenges by four viewpoints of service management [1]: people and organizations, information technology and data, processes and value streams, suppliers and partners.

3 Results

The results of this study are presented in this paper according to five steps of the action research cycle: problem diagnosis, action planning, action taking, evaluating action and specifying learning.

3.1 Diagnose Problem

Diagnosing the problem started by initiating discussions between researchers and Motoajo's employees. The first site visits were conducted to Motoajo's main storage area and one of the remote storage areas. The remote storage area was unmanned with two large metal containers and several plastic IBC containers filled with blue liquids. In the container, there was a QR code that we scanned and received a link to a MS Forms form designed for entering information on refilling liquid containers (container truck drivers) and information on retrieving liquids (forest machine drivers) from a container. We observed that instructions for both truck drivers and forest machine drivers could have been more clearer and one could have provided an URL to the form next to the QR code in case the employee who wants to enter information on refilling/retrieval of liquids does not have a QR code scanner in his/her mobile phone.

As part of Problem Diagnosis stage an experiment kick off event (November 11th, 2021) was organized. Both researchers and representatives of Motoajo participated in the event. The foreman and CEO explained the benefits of more accurate monitoring capabilities for forestry liquids: "Information on liquid levels helps in predicting when orders for more liquids need to be placed. For example, regarding fungicide we can estimate when forest machine drivers retrieve liquids from remote storages and we can also monitor total amount of consumption, how much liquids were consumed this year versus last year. There may also be liquids from three different organizations in the container".

The following challenges were identified in service request management related to forestry liquids:

- No sensors were used to monitor liquid levels. Monitoring consumption is based on manual check through the surface glass where one can see the liquid level of the container.
- The company does not have any digital means to receive information on the contents of containers (especially in a situation where the consumption rate is rapid).

- Major fuel companies in Finland have refused to transport fuel to remote harvesting destinations without an official street address.
- Location data related to forest machines is changing and inaccurate in many cases (due to different types of GPS systems) causing challenges for automating orders.
- Truck drivers do not enter systematically information on refilling of containers or retrieval of liquids from containers. This might be due to poor user experience (inconsistency of questions) of MS Forms form that is currently used for collecting data. Thus, the company does not have accurate information on the liquid levels of containers and there may occur situations that important forestry liquids are unavailable.
- The coverage of IoT data network in Nurmes was a question mark during the experiment. Lack of 4G and 5G, even 3G coverage in some areas might cause challenges for monitoring containers.
- There is lack of job introduction material for operating liquids safely.
- The company does not have a digital channel (such as mobile app) for ordering and monitoring liquids.

Based on our site visits and discussions with Motoajo we observed that the service process regarding refilling containers as well as retrieving liquids from containers was in large extent manual, except the Forms form that was not used in a systematic manner. The main challenge is that company does not have accurate view on inventories of forestry liquids that forest machines consume. This may result in a situation that forest machine drivers may not get mandatory liquids. This in turn may further lead to expensive interruptions in production or increased costs if liquids need to be purchased at rapid notice in small quantities through alternative channels.

We also realized that automating fuel orders is more complicated than expected. The orders cannot be fully automated in a way that a delivery truck would deliver fuel directly to the forest. One of the main fuel companies in Finland requires an official street address for deliveries and this information is not always available because logging and harvesting destinations can be located in very remote places. A phone call between a forest machine driver and a fuel delivery truck driver seems to be necessary to provide information of exact fuel delivery location. Because of high complexity of the fuel ordering process, we decided to focus on the request process of other forestry liquids: marking dyes (red and blue marking colour used to mark different types of roundwood), fungicide (a chemical needed to prevent forest diseases during the summer season from May to November, when the average temperature is over 0 Celsius) and Diesel Exhaust Fluid (DEF) that is delivered to Motoajo in 600–1000 liter cubics or as container deliveries. To the forest destinations, Diesel Exhaust Fluid, is delivered in smaller amounts.

3.2   Action Planning

The Action Planning stage started by describing improvements to the liquids ordering process. We decided that our proposed solution is an IoT-based monitoring system for liquid containers (Adblue, fungicide) located in remote storage areas. The monitoring system would contain a mobile app that machine drivers use when they pick up supplies and liquids from storage areas. The app would provide ability (a simple dashboard) to monitor containers remotely showing the level of liquids (with traffic light colour codes), how much liquid a specific driver took from a container, a history data on the container and ability to trigger alert to a work manager's email address when $3/4$ of liquids has been consumed.

Additionally, our solution would improve job introduction of new employees from the viewpoint of dealing with forestry liquids (how to position a fuel container safely in the forest, how to sort forestry waste in main storage area, where is the engine oil, and what type of protection is required while dealing with the fungicide).

Action planning stage involved many discussions with several providers of tank level sensors and through these discussions we were able to learn the limitations in IoT sensor systems as well as pricing models, issues related to data processing and different options for implementing data network for IoT sensors. In this stage, we had to finally reject the fuel monitoring scenario because of its complexity and we decided to focus on monitoring containers in remote storage areas (Diesel Exhaust Fluid, marking colour). Additionally, we had to make a build or buy decision regarding IoT dashboard and we decided to purchase a cost efficient service from a provider that was familiar to our development team. Here the main challenge was to find a service provider with reasonable pricing model. Some of the providers would have charged a basic fee 700–900 eur per sensor module, 40–50 eur for dashboard per each container, 1000–2000 eur for installation of sensors and integration fees for any integration work. There were no existing well-defined integration APIs we could have tested before purchasing IoT sensors.

3.3   Action Taking

The Action Taking stage started with writing trial handbook parts 1–2 (Nov 1–15, 2021) because it was a project deliverable that each experiment team had to deliver as part of project results. Capturing user stories (Nov 19) was carried out by using both agile methods and service blueprint approach of the service automation framework (SAF). While developing the service blueprint, we focused on an end-user perspective and analyzed how a container truck driver and a forest machine driver would act when they approach the remote storage area and how they enter the data related to refilling the container and retrieving liquids from the container. As a result of this exercise, we observed that both of these situations (refilling, retrieving liquids) are kind of service requests although they look like informational events. Notifications related to retrieving liquids can be seen requests for access to liquids and notification related to refilling containers can be seen a part of a service request fulfillment (order fulfillment). Additionally, this stage involved the following activities:

- Technical specification and purchasing IoT sensors (November 2021)
- Development of mobile app (sprints), IoT dashboard, configuring and coding
- Delivery of tank level sensors to Motoajo, 360 demo from a storage (Dec 22)
- UI design review (Jan 5, 2022)
- 360/Video shootings in arctic conditions $-23\,\mathrm{C}$ (Jan 11, 2022) (challenges due to cold weather)

In action taking, we experienced new types of challenges. When we delivered the tank level sensors to Motoajo, we immediately observed that the IoT sensor module was too large and could not be installed to the cap of the container due to a tank refilling pistol (see Fig. 2):

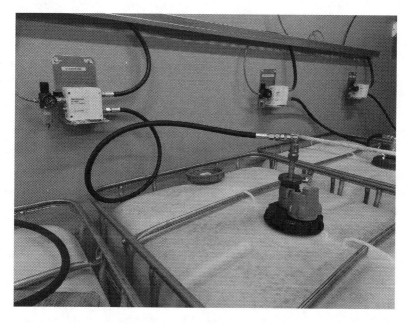

Fig. 2. The IoT sensor module installed in the cap of the marking colour container.

Thus, Motoajo staff needed to make a new adapter in order to install the tank level sensor to the marking colour container. Another challenge was to create a data conversion for the IoT data. The default data that was received from the IoT module (ultrasound sensor) showed the distance from the sensor to the surface of the liquid in centimeters. However, this data was not very illustrative for end user purposes and needed to be converted into different format, showing the container level in percentages (100% meaning a full container). Additionally, CEO of Motoajo commented that one container could involve liquids of three different organizations: "The problem with fungicide is that some customers want to pay for liquids as a service, but some companies bring their own liquids to our containers as a refill. So liquids can be stored in the same tank. This is one reason why we want remote monitoring."

In order to create an invoice for one of those organizations based on real consumption, Motoajo would have first to identify the service consumer and then record the consumption of liquids in litres. In addition to IoT based monitoring of liquids consumption, we also aimed at developing virtual job introduction environment for increasing employees' awareness of recycling such as reusable oil and marking colour canisters.

3.4   Evaluating Action

In general, our digital transformation experiment was success. Motoajo can use the knowledge (derived from data of tank level sensors) to make informed decisions when to order more liquids and to ensure availability of liquids. Data-oriented service processes help Motoajo to transition towards a learning organization [7] by converting the data and information to knowledge.

Motoajo has communicated to research team several further development ideas both for IoT-based monitoring and virtual job introduction. These have a lot of new business potential. Global component outage caused some minor delays in obtaining sensors and also affected the decision which data network solution we would apply. The estimated order time for GSM-based IoT modules was 4–6 months when we started our experiment. LoraWAN modules in turn were available in stock. However, there was a small delay caused by ordering of adapters needed for installing sensor modules to the cap of the container. Additional delay (a week) was caused by installation challenges due to large size of the tank level sensor module. During the evaluating stage, the war situation in Ukraine affected the availability of forestry liquids, especially Adblue, because Finland imports it mainly from Russia. Motoajo's employee addressed the challenges: "At the moment, we can not get Adblue ordered in containers although we shall pick up it from gas stations with smaller canisters (everything we can get because they have set restrictions for buying Adblue)".

A clear process description for ordering, monitoring, delivering and consuming liquids would have helped the research team to better get familiar with Motoajo's service operation practices. However, data collection through discussions and workshops was easy because Motoajo's staff was very helpful and they had assigned right persons to the digital transformation experiment.

From a technological perspective, LoraWAN public mode seems to be a reasonable option for implementing data network for IoT solutions in Finland. We would have needed more information and hands on experiences on implementing IoT solutions with other data network options (GSM, Zigbee, NB-IoT).

In Finland, there is only one major LoraWAN network provider that also provides IoT devices such as sensors and gateways as well as IoT consultancy services (with the help of partner network). Regarding virtual job introduction environment, one of the potential future improvement directions might be adding some type of gamification [4] to the process. This virtual job introduction environment could also include a question and answer system for knowledge sharing [8] among Motoajo's employees.

From a financial perspective, IoT based monitoring also seems profitable with the technological components, services and data transmission models we selected for the experiment. The solution shall result in cost savings in labor costs and fuel costs while traveling to remote storage areas shall be minimized.

4   Analysis

Table 1 shows the analysis of action research results related to the three research questions of the study. Data source has been described by using abbreviations: IN = Interviews of Motoajo employees DI = Discussions, DO = Documentation, PO = Partic. observation, DOB = Direct observation, PA = Physical artifactsts.

One of the most important challenges we observed during the study was that Motoajo did not get reliable and timely data on inventory of liquids. Main reasons for this seemed to be inconsistent data logging during refilling containers (truck drivers) and retrieving liquids (forest machine providers). Invoicing data showed actual ordered amounts but was not useful for proactive order management.

We also recorded activities that were specific to IoT-based digital transformation of service processes and ICT quality improvement. These included making a decision on data network solution GSM, LoraWAN, Zigbee, other) in early phase of the project, defining the data storage and data sharing points (JSON) between IoT sensor provider and other developers as well as performing data conversion for data received from IoT sensors because original data values showed distance between sensor and surface of liquids. This data needed to be transformed into user friendly format to show the liquid level of the container in percents.

Additionally we analyzed how digital technologies such as IoT and digital transformation help in creating business value for a forest machine operator's service management. Remote checking and alerting were mentioned multiple times as benefits by case organization's representatives. They also used terms 'proactive' and 'predictive' to describe the future state of order management. Identifying consumption trends was mentioned as one of the future benefits when more data has been collected.

Table 1. Key findings from the action research study

Research question	Findings (source)
RQ1 challenges	Lack of API for testing IoT DO
	Data on refilling not systematically entered IN
	Calibration of sensors data DOB
	Data conversion needed for IoT data AR, DO
	Unreliable or missing data on liquids consumption PO
	Sensor installation challenges PO
	Data on machine locations is not always accurate DI
	Lack of alerts DI, IN
	Protecting sensors from movements IN
	Identifying a cost-effective sensor provider DI, IN
	Selecting a data network solution DI, PO
	Poor availability of DEF (Adblue) due to a war DI
	A container may involve liquids of several orgs DI
	External order for liquids is not automated IN
	IoT monitoring target is changing PO
	Unclear development boundaries PO
	Awareness of recycling liquids canisters DI
	Manual checks require traveling to storage areas IN
RQ2 IoT activities	Select the IoT sensor type DI
	Make a decision on data network solution DI, DO
	Data conversion needed for IoT data AR, DO
	Define the data storage for IoT stream DI
	Install IoT module to the container AR, PO
	Calibration of sensors DOB
RQ3 value	Foremen can check liquid levels remotely IN, DI
	Enables setting alerts on critical levels DI
	Proactive way to ensure availability of liquids DI
	Provides data on consumption trends DI
	May reveal unauthorized acces DI
	Easy access to container data by QR AR, PO
	IoT data enables automated charging for liquids IN

5   Conclusions

This study aimed at answering the research problem: how to improve quality of ICT and forestry service processes with digital technologies? As main contribution of this paper, we described the development of an IoT-based order system for forestry liquids by using an action research method. The action research method suited very well to this study because it focuses on capturing the details of a change situation. In our case, the context was a digital transformation project co-implemented by a Finnish SME and Digital Innovation Hub.

Regarding the first research question, our findings showed that merging IoT and service request management is not a simple task. During our experiment, we identified several challenges such as unreliable data, lack of clear APIs for testing, unavailability of certain IoT components due to global component outage and mechanical sensor installation problems. Additionally, difficulties were caused by changing monitoring target and complex decision making on IoT data network selection. Field visits to remote storage areas revealed valuable information on the scope and limitations of IoT system boundaries. Concerning the second research question, we highlighted activities that were specific to IoT-based digital transformation such as selecting right sensor and data network solution, performing data conversion, defining data storage mechanism for IoT data as well as installing the sensor modules. All of these require work efforts. Finally, related to the third research question, we studied benefits of integrating new technologies to the service process. Using IoT helped Motoajo to achieve a better situational overview of forestry liquids inventories and to have a proactive approach on ordering liquids decreasing stress and extra efforts due to unexpected unavailability of liquids.

The following limitations are related to this study: First, our study included only one action research cycle. Documenting and analyzing multiple research cycles could have provided a richer view on the change situation of the SME. However, providing a detailed description of multiple cycles was not possible due to page limitations of conference papers. Second, the study was performed during a relatively short period of time between from August 2021 to March 2022. Broadening the time line could have provided fruitful information on the background of our experiment. However, we decided to focus solely on the time period when the digital transformation project was implemented in order to have clear scope and boundaries of the study. Third, the study included the research effort of two researchers. Involving a larger research team to participate in exploring the business operations of Motoajo could have given a deeper analysis on challenges that Motoajo is aiming at resolving by investing in digital transformation. However, we had a limited number of researchers available in this study.

Further research on digital transformation and ICT quality could focus on delivering more information on technology choices, limitations and drawbacks of Internet of Things projects especially those that focus on automating order management processes.

References

1. Axelos: ITIL Foundation - ITIL 4 Edition. Stationary Office Books, UK (2019)
2. Cabinet Office: ITIL Continual Service Improvement. The Stationary Office, UK (2011)
3. Cabinet Office: ITIL Service Operation. The Stationary Office, UK (2011)

4. da Conceicao, F.S., da Silva, A.P., de Oliveira Filho, A.Q., Silva Filho, R.C.: Toward a gamification model to improve IT service management quality on service desk. In: 2014 9th International Conference on the Quality of Information and Communications Technology, pp. 255–260 (2014)
5. Duffy, K., Denison, B.: Using ITIL to improve IT services. In: AMCIS08: Proceedings of the Fourteenth American Conference on Information Systems 2008. Association for Information Systems, Toronto (2008)
6. Halverson, C.A., Erickson, T., Ackerman, M.S.: Behind the help desk: evolution of a knowledge management system in a large organization. In: Proceedings of the 2004 ACM Conference on Computer Supported Cooperative Work, pp. 304–313. CSCW 2004, ACM, NY (2004)
7. Henninger, S.: Using software process to support learning software organizations. In: 1st International Workshop on Learning Software Organizations. Kaiserslautern (1999)
8. Iske, P., Boersma, W.: Connected brains: question and answer systems for knowledge sharing: concepts, implementation and return on investment. J. Knowl. Manag. 9(1), 126–145 (2005). https://doi.org/10.1108/13673270510583018
9. ISO/IEC 20000-1:2018: Information technology - Service management - Part 1: Service management system requirements. ISO/IEC JTC1/SC40 Secretariat (2018)
10. ISO/IEC 20000:2: Part 2: Guidance on the application of service management systems. ISO/IEC JTC 1 Secretariat (2019)
11. Jäntti, M.: Examining challenges in it service desk system and processes: a case study. In: Proceedings of the 7th International Conference on Systems 2012, pp. 105–108. CPS Publishing (2012)
12. Ludwig, H., et al.: Catalog-based service request management. IBM Syst. J. 46(3), 1–18 (2007)
13. Maglio, P., Spohrer, J.: Fundamentals of service science. J. Acad. Mark. Sci. 36, 18–20 (2007)
14. Marrone, M., Kolbe, L.: Impact of IT service management frameworks on the IT organization: an empirical study on benefits, challenges, and processes. Bus. Inf. Syst. Eng. J. 3(1), 5–18 (2011)
15. Roedder, N., Dauer, D., Laubis, K., Karaenke, P., Weinhardt, C.: The digital transformation and smart data analytics: an overview of enabling developments and application areas. In: 2016 IEEE International Conference on Big Data (Big Data), pp. 2795–2802 (2016)
16. Runeson, P., Höst, M.: Guidelines for conducting and reporting case study research in software engineering. Empir. Softw. Eng. 14, 131–164 (2009)
17. Shah, P., Patil, A., Ingleshwar, S.: IoT based smart water tank with android application. In: 2017 International Conference on I-SMAC (IoT in Social, Mobile, Analytics and Cloud) (I-SMAC), pp. 600–603 (2017)
18. Shrestha, A., Cater-Steel, A., Tan, W.G., Toleman, M.: A model to select processes for IT service management improvement. In: Proceedings of the 23rd Australasian Conference on Information Systems. Deakin University (2012)
19. Software Engineering Institute: Capability Maturity Model Integration for Services v1.3. Carnegie Mellon University (2010)
20. Spohrer, J., Vargo, S., Caswell, N., Maglio, P.: The service system is the basic abstraction of service science. In: Proceedings of the 41st Annual Hawaii International Conference on System Sciences (HICSS 2008). IEEE Press, NY (2008)
21. Wang, Y., Song, J., Liu, X., Jiang, S., Liu, Y.: Plantation monitoring system based on internet of things. In: 2013 IEEE International Conference on Green Computing

and Communications and IEEE Internet of Things and IEEE Cyber, Physical and Social Computing, pp. 366–369 (2013)

22. Zhang, L.J., Zhang, J., Cai, H.: Services Computing. Tsinghua University Press, Beijing. Springer, Heidelberg (2007). https://doi.org/10.1007/978-3-540-38284-3

23. Zhou, C., Jiang, P.: A design of high-level water tank monitoring system based on internet of things. In: 2020 7th International Forum on Electrical Engineering and Automation (IFEEA), pp. 769–774 (2020)

Towards a Process Reference Model for Clinical Coding

Ismael Caballero[1]([⊠]) [iD], Júlio Souza[2,3] [iD], Fernando Lopes[2,3] [iD],
João Vasco Santos[2,3,4] [iD], and Alberto Freitas[2,3] [iD]

[1] Institute of Technology and Information Systems (ITSI), University of Castilla-La Mancha (UCLM), Ciudad Real, Spain
Ismael.Caballero@uclm.es
[2] Center for Health Technology and Services Research (CINTESIS), Faculty of Medicine, University of Porto, Porto, Portugal
[3] Department of Community Medicine, Information and Health Decision Sciences (MEDCIDS), Faculty of Medicine, University of Porto, Porto, Portugal
[4] Public Health Unit, ACES Grande Porto VIII–Espinho/Gaia, Espinho, Portugal

Abstract. Coding of medical data is a very important previous step for many activities in Health Care management, since it is the basis for several activities ranging from hospital reimbursement to clinical research. Literature identifies some issues related to coding clinical data, which derives in inadequate levels of quality leading to some in acceptable situations in health care organizations, impacting even to their sustainability. To alleviate these undesirable effects, we posse that the standardization of some best practices around clinical coding can lead to a better performance of the clinical coding process. One of the most relevant concerns in the process is the quality of the data used at the various stages of the data life cycle from its generation by clinicians up to the usage and exploitation of the data once coded. The main contribution of this work is twofold: on a hand to identify which are the best practices related to clinical coding, and on the other hand to investigate how these best practices can be enriched with some other related to data quality management and data governance. As a result, we produced CODE.CLINIC, a framework that can be used to support institutions to better code their medical data. This framework consists of two main components: a Process Reference Model (PRM) and a Process Assessment Model (PAM). In this paper we are going to first introduce the CODE.CLINIC PRM, which gather 16 process grouped in 4 blocks.

Keywords: Coding of medical data process · Data quality management · CODE.CLINIC

1 Introduction

Most of the actions happening in health care institutions are based and largely depends on data. While data regarding patients are typically stored in their corresponding health records [1], it is also necessary to gather how the medical attendance processes have been conducted: which the diagnostics tests were driven, which diseases were diagnosed, which treatments were applied and where the patients went once treated. In this sense, relevant diagnoses and treatment procedures should be abstracted and conveniently cate- gorized for ulterior inspections about the performance of the health institution. Examples of these inspection include calculations to reimbursement to health institutions, medical research, epidemiological surveillance, or the calculation of numerous quality indicators, performance monitoring, hospital output, and benchmarking among other purposes [2]. In different countries, specific ways to gather and store all this data once categorized are proposed. For instance, in Portugal, the Hospital Morbidity Database (HMD) maintains a wide range of information on inpatient and outpatient episodes occurring in National Health System (NHS) health institutions, a type of diagnosis-related groups (DRGs) [3].

This comprehensive set of clinical data, the HMD, results from a series of routine processes in hospitals, typically embracing the clinical coding process [4]. These routines begin by documenting all clinical information and services provided to patients through data collection instruments, either in paper or digital format; after patient discharge, this set of information is then accessed by coding physicians, who must translate and classify the diagnoses and procedures according to any of the varieties of the WHO's International Classification of Disease, 10th Revision (ICD-10) codes manually or being supported for automatic classification systems [4, 5]. For instance, in Portugal – the first European country implementing a DRG-based hospital systems in 1989 – the current version used is ICD-10 Clinical Modification (ICD-10-CM/PCS) [6].

Given the importance of this information for the wide range of purposes previously pointed, it is then essential to ensure that the clinical data coded in the different hospitals are of high quality and have accurate, reliable, and fully reported procedure and diagnosis codes to support the reuse of these data at different levels.

In this sense, the literature points to the existence of several quality problems in coded clinical data [7], and many of these stems from barriers that exist in the clinical coding processes themselves in general terms [8], or more specifically in Portugal to some barriers as [9] identified. Differences in coding of diseases and procedures between coding physicians and hospitals, interpretation of guidelines and instruments used, as well as gaps in clinical documentation, delays and lack of health record standards are some of the several problems already mentioned [10].

In this investigation, the researcher team posed that to mitigate or at least to alleviate these problems, it was possible to gather, and group set of best practices (also known as process) that can be used to ensure homogeneous behavior during the clinical coding process and during the use of the resulting data either internally in every health institution or externally when this health institution needs to exchange data with third parties like national governments. This set of best practices should cover aspects of the clinical coding process as well as some other aspects of data quality management and data governance.

In this sense, the research team relied on the idea of the process-based approach set forth in international standards such as ISO/IEC 8000-61 [11] for data quality manage- ment or ISO 12207 [12] for the case of software process to develop a framework called CODE.CLINIC to better support the clinical coding. Thus, the idea of CODE.CLINIC is to serve as reference that every health institution can use to customize their own set of clinical coding practices according to their own restrictions, possibilities, and demands. CODE.CLINIC consists of two main components:

- A **Process Reference Model (PRM)**, containing four groups of processes addressing specific aspects of the clinical coding activities considering the various stages of the clinical coded data lifecycle. This PRM also meets the data governance, data management and data quality management process requirements included in the Alarcos' Model for Data Improvement (MAMDv3.0) [13], an ISO 8000-61-framework compliant. In Sect. 3, explanations about the construction of the PRM has been provided. In addition, this PRM can be also used as a body of knowledge for the various processes of the clinical coding, for instance, to identify relevant stakeholders, specific information systems to better support the processes, or even recommended key process indicators to monitor the institutionalization of the PRM processes. The current version of CODE.CLINIC PRM is the main contribution of this paper.
- A **Process Assessment Model (PAM)**, containing the elements required for organizations to assess and improve their clinical coding activities according to the provided PRM. This PAM will be built by meeting the requirements of ISO/IEC 33003 [14] along with some other parts of ISO/IEC 33000 series. One of the most important components of the PAM is a Maturity Model, in which the processes of the PRM are ordered in an increasing level of difficulty according to the capabilities of the health institution. The CODE.CLINIC Maturity Model has been developed meeting the requirements of ISO/IEC 33004 [15], and it is compliant with MAMD-Maturity Model based on ISO 8000-62 [16]. However, the description of CODE.CLINIC PAM and the corresponding Maturity Model is outside of the scope of this paper.

The paper is structured as follows. Section 2 described the state of the art of the best practices in clinical coding processes. Section 3 summarizes the research method that we have used to produce the framework. Section 4 introduce the Process Reference Model (PRM) of the CODE.CLINIC process, describing the structure of the four groups of processes along the structure of every process. Finally, Sect. 5 introduces discussion, some conclusions, and future works.

2   State of the Art and Related Works

2.1   Existing Works on Clinical Coding

Alonso et al. in [10] identified several problems during the process of the clinical coding in Portugal through the conclusion raised after a the conduction of a focus group like: (1) Variability in clinical coding – (1a) coding process-electronic vs paper, (2) Difficulties in the clinical coding process: (2a) Difficulties in assigning diagnoses code, (2b) Coding process by clinical specialty; (3) Coding delay; (4) Hospital resources made available to coding activities; (5) Clinical coding audits. They also identified two important barriers: (1) limited understanding of medical terminology by coders, and (2) coder experience or problems in health records. All these problems and barriers were grouped in four main categories: (1) the standardization of the documents used for coding an episode,

(2), the adoption of the electronic coding, (3), the development of tools to help coding and audits, and (4) the recognition of the importance of coding by the management.

As of 2014, the CHKS produced the report *"The quality of clinical coding in the UK's NHS"* [17]. In this report, the following areas are identified for a senior management to support with the aim of assuring the adequate levels of quality for the patient care data: (1) source of documentation, (2) discharge summaries, (3) deadline and completeness for the clinical coding, (4) clinical engagement, (5) audit and analysis, (6) staffing, (7) training and guidance, (8) IT systems, (9) assessment units, and (10) broader users.

The Australian CCSA produced in 2019 the *"Clinical Coding Practice Framework"* [18], whose main aim is *"to provide guidance in defining and promoting good practices for those involved in the clinical coding process (e.g. clinical coders, clinical documentation improvement specialist, clinical coding auditors, health information managers and managers (at all levels) of the coding process)"*. The framework engaged all those involved in the clinical coding process to: (1) gain access to all relevant and pertinent clinical information, (2) ensure the assignment and diagnoses and intervention codes include all the necessary information, (3) apply conveniently the classification conventions stated in the official recommendation of the Australian National Health Services, (4) actively participate in the interdisciplinary meeting for the purpose of clarification of diagnosis and intervention, and (5) improve the clinical understanding of the roles of those involved in the clinical coding process. In addition, the framework establishes that involved in the clinical coding process must not: (1) assign diagnoses or intervention codes without the adequate supporting information, (2) deliberately committing errors in code assignment to minimize financial losses, (3) deliberately manipulating the interdisciplinary engagement inappropriately to maximize financial benefits for the health institution, (4) omit information about an episode of care to prevent the accurately reporting, and (5) submit to pressure from other or to others to misrepresent the patient's episode of care or prevents adherence to the stated classification conventions.

Reid et al. in [19] and in [20] they presented some insights obtained by using four research methods (literature review, workshop, assessment of coding services, and medical record audit) from the state of clinical coding services in the Republic of Ireland as of 2017 studied during one year. The reports raised relevant results and recommended some best practices in several concerns: (1) quality of medical records, (2) coding work allocation and supervision processes, (3) data quality control measures, (4) communication with clinicians, and (5) visibility of clinical coders, their managers, and the coding services. They find that the best managed coding services had the following characteristics: (1) they did larger use of the available checking resources, (2) the medical records were more electronic, and (3) there were much higher levels of direct clinical coders contact with clinicians.

As consequence, it can be said that the coded clinical data often lacks quality enough to successfully be used in the management or research activities.

2.2 Alarcos' Model for Data Improvement (MAMDv3.0)

The Alarcos' Model for Data Improvement (MAMDv3.0) [13] is a framework to assess and improve the maturity of the organization's processes related to data management, governance and quality. MAMDv3.0, which is publicly accessible[1], is aligned to several international open standards such as ISO/IEC 8000-61 [11], ISO/IEC 8000-62 [16], ISO 38505-1 [21], ISO 38505-2 [22], and it also gather some best practices from standards like COBIT 2019 [23] or DAMA's DMBOK 2 [24].

It consists of two main components:

- A Process Reference Model (PRM) consisting of twenty processes grouped in three categories: Data Management (DM), Data Quality Management (DQM) and Data Governance (DG).
- A Process Assessment Model (PAM), with indications to assess and improve the maturity of an organization regarding the capability of the organization of their DM, DQM and DG processes. One of the most important elements of the PAM is a maturity model which can be used for the both the certification of the maturity model and to outline roadmaps for the improvements.

These components can be used within any type or organization to enrich the design and execution of the business processes with DM, DQM and DG concerns to make them more efficient and effective. In addition, it is important to state that organizations can certify with external thirds their maturity regarding to these disciplines.

3   Research Method

To produce the CODE.CLINIC framework, we are following the Action Research (AR) Method [25] because it is necessary to *"focus on social systems and put knowledge into action as soon as possible"*. AR is a collaborative research form that seeks to unite theory and practice between researchers and practitioners through a process that is cyclical in nature, producing new knowledge that is useful in practice. AR has been successfully used in Information Systems [26] and Software Engineering [27], and given the very nature of the medical domain of our research we feel it can be successfully used given the strong component about the "social" fact.

In this case, the research goal is the *"design and testing of clinical coding frame-work"*. To achieve our goal, three AR cycles has been planned. For each AR cycle we identified different critical reference groups, but we maintained as potential beneficiaries, any Portuguese health institution (mainly hospitals) that wants to customize and institutionalize their own clinical coding process.

- An Initial **AR Definition Cycle**, where the main goal is to build a first version of CODE.CLINIC PRM. In this initial cycle, we explored the corresponding literature and existing documentation to identify the common problems in the coding clinical process; once identified the problems, we proposed an initial version of the processes in the PRM grouped in four groups (see Sect. 4) with the idea of tackling the specific problems, along with common ways to address data quality problems by means of the alignment of the alignment of the proposed processes with MAMDv3.0. This

---

[1] MAMDv3.0 can be downloaded for free from https://mamd.dqteam.es.

first version was validated with the Portuguese *Associação dos Médicos Auditores e Codificadores Clínicos* (AMACC)[2], who acted as critical reference group. Through four cycles of meetings with the underlying refinements, we produce the first version of the PRM, which is introduced in this paper.

- A Second **AR Acceptance Cycle**, where the main goal is to present the whole framework to several preidentified stakeholders with different responsibilities for the clinical coding process in various Portuguese health institutions (mainly hospitals), to identify its weaknesses and strengths from various points of view. This is to be done by means of surveys and personal interviews. With the obtained feedback, we will produce a more refined PRM, and a refined version of the PAM.
- The Third **AR Validation Cycle**, where the final version of CODE.CLINIC will be applied to a reference hospital following the case study research methodology.

4   The CODE.CLINIC Process Reference Model

In this section the PRM is to be introduced. The main purpose of the PRM is to identify the processes that can be used to describe and characterize the entire lifecycle and formal pathways of coded data in health institution to identify differences and constraints to achieve higher data quality under the perspective of the various stakeholders, ranging from medical coders to clinical coding office managers. This set of processes can be used as body of knowledge to address the required specific practices during the clinical coding. In this sense, every process can be seen as a box where every stakeholder can find the required knowledge (including the common activities and work products, like communication schemas or underlying key process indicators) for the clinical coding activities. In addition, this knowledge can be reviewed over the time to enrich by including new activities and/or work products. This knowledge can be used to outline the clinical coding activities when designed from scratch or to review or enrich existing ones by identifying potential root causes for existing problems.

The structure of the organization of the sixteen processes included in the PRM is adapted from the concept of Primary, Support and Organizational process in ISO/IEC/IEEE 12207:2017 [12]. This enables a better understanding of the purpose of every process, and it can be also used to better determine the contribution of every process to the general goal of the clinical code. As a result, we identified the following groups of processes: (1) Strategic Processes (G Processes), (2) Main Processes (M Processes), (3) Support Processes (S Processes), and (4) Other Processes (O Processes). See Sects. 4.1–4.4 for a larger description of this groups of processes.

As said, the definition of the PRM has been aligned to MAMDv3.0. Due to this reason, and for the sake of interoperability with MAMD, and other process-approaches based on ISO standards, the process description of every process in the CODE.CLINIC-PRM has been done according to ISO/IEC/TR 24774 [28], and it consists of the following elements:

- Title, which is a descriptive heading for the process at task.

---

[2] https://amacc.med.up.pt.

- Purpose, which describes the main goal of the health institution when executing the corresponding process.
- Outcomes, which represent the observable results expected from the successful execution of the process.
- Activities, which is a list of actions (best practices) that can achieve the outcomes.

It is worthy to state that, due to length paper restrictions, unfortunately we will not include the full description (e.g., the full description of the four previous elements for every process). However, we will show the title and purpose of everyone, and we will offer some outcomes and activities for some relevant processes.

In the following subsections we identify the types of process, we listed the title and purpose of every process providing some examples of outcomes and activities.

4.1   The Strategic Process Group

This group of processes (see **Error! Reference source not found.**) address the concerns related to the governance of the clinical coding activities, namely, those related to the creation of internal standards, identification of best practices, norms, guidelines, and policies to rule all details –including data quality concerns from the organizational point of view– regarding the various stages of all data considered for clinical coding. It is also worthy to note the special focus on the organizational structure and human resource parts. It should be addressed not only who should oversee the various activities, but also how the communication should be established. To better support the clinical coding activities, specific competences, and hard and soft skills are required, and health institutions must provide training plan to their workers to achieve such competences and skills for the sake of the sustainability of the organization.

Just an example, we introduce the outcomes we identified for G.01:

- Updated list of best practices in clinical coding.
- Updated list of clinical coding data guidelines.
- Updated list of clinical coding data policies.
- Resources to propagate the best practices, norms, policies, and guidelines.

To achieve and manage the previous outcomes for the processes G.01, we identified the following activities:

- AG01.1. To select and define the best coding practices for different medical areas.
- AG01.2. To assign episodes to medical coders according to pre-defined rules.
- AG01.3. To list and define and develop the corresponding controls to the most important norms and regulations regarding data protection/security, quality, and access/use, to comply with the General Data Protection Regulation (EU GDPR).
- AG01.4. To define norms regarding standard reference books, supporting instruments and clinical coding guidelines.
- AG01.5. To define and harmonize patient documentation sources to be considered for clinical coding.

- AG01.6. To ensure continuous awareness, training, and preparation on clinical terminologies and DRG grouper updates.
- AG01.7. To define norms and standards regarding software and hardware resources to be used within the clinical coded data lifecycle (Table 1).

Table 1. The strategic processes.

Process title	Purpose
G.01. Creation or Selection, implementation, and maintenance of standards, best practices, norms, guidelines, and policies	The main goal of this process is to set up the management environment required to execute the coding clinical activities according to the capabilities of the health institutions and following the criteria and recommendations provided by the authorized organizations at a national level
G.02. Development and maintenance of controls to meet policies	The main aim of this process is to develop and maintain the corresponding controls to check if the proposed policies are being met during the execution of the coding clinical activities
G.03. Organizational Structure Management	This process is aimed to establish and maintain a supportive organization for the coding clinical data processes, identifying roles and responsibilities and to also define the competences and skills that are required for every responsibility. In addition, communication means, and protocols are also observed in this process
G.04. Stakeholders' skills and competences management	The process is aimed at maintaining a catalogue of the training required for assuring different stakeholders can achieve the associated competences and skills required to play their roles

4.2 The Main Process Group

This group of seven processes is aimed at covering all the concerns related to the proper clinical coding itself describing the various activities related to the coded data lifecycle, from data acquisition (e.g., health records) to the use and exploitation of the coded data for health institution management or for medical and epidemiologic research. See Table 2 for the purpose of every Main process.

Following the same structure of the previous subsection, the outcomes for two relevant processes are introduced as example. In this sense, the following outcomes for process M.01 are introduced:

- Identification and access to all required patient documentation.
- Reports on the levels of quality of the acquired patient documentation.

And the corresponding activities for this process M.01 are the following one:

- AM01.1. To list and identify all patient documentation sources to be used for clinical coding.
- AM01.2. To access patient documentation sources for clinical coding.
- AM01.3. To ensure that all medical coders have access to all patient documentation sources for clinical coding.

Table 2. The main processes group

Process title	Purpose
M.01. Data acquisition	This process is aimed at selecting and acquiring the required data from the typical data sources (e.g., health records both paper-based and electronically)
M.02. Data Integration (internal)	In this process, the integration coming from the various data sources should be achieved to create a solid basis for the clinical coding process
M.03. Data Coding	This process is aimed at properly coding the data
M.04. Submission of clinically coded data to the national repository	This process covers the exportation of the results of the codification of the data corresponding to the episodes towards the considered destinations
M.05. Incorporation of Coded Data to APR-DRG (DRG grouper software)	The purpose of this process is to incorporate the coded data into the APR-DRG
M.06. Data exploitation for hospital management, financing (billing), and public health	The objective of this process is to support all the necessary operations for hospital management, billing, and public health
M.07. Data exploitation for clinical and epidemiologic research	The main purpose of this process is to produce research reports on clinical aspects

The main intention of CODE.CLINIC is to be a generic framework valid for any country, for any health institution, and for any technology. CODE.CLINIC should be customized for any context. In this sense, as an example, the activities of process M.04 can be customized for Portugal as follows:

- AM04.1. To submit coded data to SIMH.
- AM04.2. To retrieve coded data from SIMH to perform corrections.

Being SIMH the *Sistema de Informação de para a Morbilidade Hospitalar*[3], whose main goal is to gather, edit and group in Homogeneous Diagnoses Groups the patient episodes.

4.3 The Support Process Group

In this group of four processes, the specifics of quality management of the data used as input (patient documentation) and output (coded data) of the coding clinical is covered. In addition, the concerns related to technological infrastructure management along with the maintenance of the reference data standards are also covered. See Table 3 to see the process title and purpose.

Table 3. The support processes group

Process title	Purpose
S.01. Data quality management of patient documentation	The main aim of this process is to evaluate and improve the level of the quality of the health record documents
S.02. Data quality management of coded data	Once produced the data, the main aim of this process is to evaluate and improve the quality of the resulting clinical coded data
S.03. Reference data management	This process is aimed at maintaining the various reference data involved in the codification of the clinical data (e.g., ICD-10-CM)
S.04. Technological infrastructure management	This process is aimed at establishing the required technology to support the flow of information through all the main processes, as well as to interact with some other agents (e.g., some other hospitals, some other regulatory organizations)

For illustrative purpose, and due to its importance, we proposed the following activities for the S.01 processes:

- AS01.1. Identify the most relevant data quality characteristics/dimensions for health records.
- AS01.2. Define measurement methods to assess the levels of quality of health records.
- AS01.3. Analyze the root causes of inadequate levels of quality.
- AS01.4. To perform internal auditing of health records.
- AS01.5. Analyze the root causes of inadequate levels of quality.
- AS01.6. Improve the levels of quality of health records.
- AS01.7. Generate data quality management reports for health records, with learned lessons.

---

[3] https://www.spms.min-saude.pt/2021/03/simh/.

And for S.02. Data quality management of coded data process, the following activities were proposed:

- AS02.1. To perform internal auditing of coded data according to established norms.
- AS02.2. To retrieve episodes with coding issues from SIMH.
- AS02.3. To correct (recode) and resubmit the episodes to SIMH.
- AS02.4. To define standard auditing controls.

Once again, let us recall that the framework should be customized for the specific reality of the county in which they will be applied. In this sense, the outcomes of the M.06. Data exploitation for hospital management, financing (billing), and public health would be customized for Portugal, by including the following outcome:

- ACSS benchmarking tool[4].

4.4   The Other Process Group

Finally, in the other processes group, consists of the process shown in Table 4.

Table 4. The other group processes group

Process title	Purpose
O1. Health care taking process	This process is aimed at diagnosing diseases and providing the corresponding treatment these diseases. This process should produce and store the corresponding the necessary data to describe the most relevant details

To illustrate this process, the following activities have been proposed:

- AO01.1. To report accurate and complete information in the admission note (e.g., symptoms, comorbidities), following the patient's admission.
- AO01.2. To report accurate and complete information in the discharge notes (e.g., patient's diagnoses, treatment, and disease progression), following the end of the episode.
- AO01.3. To report accurate and complete information in the anesthesia report.
- AO01.4. To report accurate and complete information in the surgical report.
- AO01.5. To report accurate and complete information in the pathology report.
- AO01.6. To report accurate and complete information in the nursing records.

4.5   Customization of the Framework for a Specific Context

We intended the PRM of CODE.CLINIC would be complete and flexible enough to be adapted and suitably customized for various context (e.g., specific countries). In this

---

[4] https://benchmarking-acss.min-saude.pt/.

sense, the outcomes and activities should be selected and reinterpreted for the specific context. This involves, for instance, to identify who are the most relevant actor and stakeholders for the various process groups in every context. In this sense, we have identified specific actors/stakeholders that are relevant for the customization of CODE.CLINIC for Portuguese health institutions, considering the various stages of the coded data lifecycle. We classify them in three large groups:

Consultive Roles and Responsibilities. General policymakers or policy-proposers for health domain, that are typically outside of the organization, mainly in the regional or national government. They provide some hints about general concerns and recommendations for the clinical coding activities. Some of these concerns consists in recommendations for technical support (e.g., like the AMACC), while others are more related to management and interoperability support (e.g., SPMS). This are not typically active roles in the specific case of Portugal we can list:

1. Administração Central do Sistema de Saúde (ACSS).
2. Serviços Partilhados do Ministério da Saúde (SPMS).
3. Ordem dos Médicos.
4. Colégio Competência de Codificação Clínica da Ordem dos Médicos.
5. Associação dos Médicos Auditores e Codificadores Clínicos (AMACC).

   Active Roles and Responsibilities for the Process. Workers that are somehow involved in clinical coding tasks at institutional level for the Strategic and Main and Support Processes.

6. Hospital managers (departments and services).
7. Health care provider.
8. IT (Information Technology) Staff.
9. Hospital manager for clinical coding.
10. Clinical coding office managers (internal auditors).
11. Medical coders.
12. Physicians.

    Benefited Roles, played by workers that will use the coded data for the various purposes.

13. Public Health authorities and health care administrators (health management users).
14. Researchers (health research users).

Customization of CODE.CLINIC for Health Institutions. The institutionalization of CODE.CLINIC involves the identification and customization of the various outcomes and activities for the reality of the health institutions, by considering the specifics for the regular flow of data (episodes and coded data) following the main processes. During the presentation of the processes in Sects. 4.1–4.4 we introduced some examples of customization. As part of the customization of the activities, the specific positions in the health institutions corresponding to the previously introduced roles must be identified and their responsibilities conveniently assigned, and the communication protocol and means adequately established. Regarding outcomes and work products, every health institution should raise consensus on how to name, store and establish guidelines by means of policies and procedures to exploit them.

Finally, it is important to note that the customization will be better supported by the CODE.CLINIC PAM along with the underlying maturity model, as it will enable the creation of roadmaps.

5   Discussion, Conclusions and Future Work

This research has been motivated by the hypothesis that having and implementing a framework for clinical coding will not only contribute to a greater homogenization of clinical coding processes not only internally in health institutions, but also to enable better interoperability between other organizations, enabling even benchmarking. In addition, the institutionalization of the framework will make the clinical coding much more efficient, interoperable, and error-free, by facing the list of problems listed in Sect. 2.1 in a unified and controlled way from an organizational point of view.

The main expected impact of this PRM is not only to identify, map and structure the various processes and activities related to clinical coding in day-to-day life at health institutions (mainly hospitals), but also to provide a working tool to promote data reuse, good clinical coding practices and to organize processes, promoting data quality improvement, and body of knowledge.

As part of our near-term future work, we will conduct the AR acceptance cycle, in which we aim to gain buy-in from the medical community involved in the clinical coding process. To this end, we will conduct a series of questionnaires and interviews with representatives of the various stakeholders described in Sect. 4.5. The feedback obtained will be used to refine both the process reference model and the evaluation model. Once the framework will be refined, we will disseminate it in different forums.

Acknowledgements. We would like to first thank to Associação dos Médicos Auditores e Codificadores Clínicos for the valuable support during the AR Definition Cycle.

This investigation is partially supported by the Grant PID2020-112540RB-C42, AETHER-UCLM (A smart data holistic approach for context-aware data analytics), funded by MCIN/AEI/10.13039/501100011033/; The project "Clikode - Automatic Processing of Clinical Coding, (3I) Innovation, Research of AI models for hospital coding of Procedures and Diagnoses", POCI-05-5762-FSE-000230, is financed by Portugal 2020, through the European Social Fund, within the scope of COMPETE 2020 (Operational Programme Competitiveness and Internationalization of Portugal 2020), and the project ADAGIO: Alarcos' DAta Governance framework and systems generation (SBPLY/21/180501/000061), funded by the Consejería de Educación, Cultura y Deportes of the Junta de Comunidades de Castilla-La Mancha (Spain).

References

1. Gesulga, J.M., Berjame, A., Moquiala, K.S., Galido, A.: Barriers to electronic health record system implementation and information systems resources: a structured review. Procedia Comput. Sci. **124**, 544–551 (2017)
2. Alonso, V., et al.: Health records as the basis of clinical coding: is the quality adequate? A qualitative study of medical coders' perceptions. Health Inf. Manag. J. **49**(1), 28–37 (2020)
3. Fetter, R.B.: Diagnosis related groups: understanding hospital performance. Interfaces **21**(1), 6–26 (1991)

4. Stanfill, M.H., Williams, M., Fenton, S.H., Jenders, R.A., Hersh, W.R.: A systematic literature review of automated clinical coding and classification systems. J. Am. Med. Inform. Assoc. **17**(6), 646–651 (2010)

5. Hazelwood, A.C.: ICD-9 CM to ICD-10 CM: implementation issues and challenges. In: ICD-9 CM ICD-10 CM: Implementation Issues and Challenges/AHIMA, American Health Information Management Association (2003). http://library.ahima.org/doc?oid=59978

6. CMS: ICD-10-CM Official Guidelines for Coding and Reporting. Centers for Medicare and Medicaid Services (2021). https://www.cms.gov/files/document/2021-coding-guidelines-upd ated-12162020.pdf

7. Carvalho, R., et al.: Analysis of root causes of problems affecting the quality of hospital administrative data: a systematic review and Ishikawa diagram. Int. J. Med. Inf. **156**, 104584 (2021). https://doi.org/10.1016/j.ijmedinf.2021.104584

8. de Lusignan, S.: The barriers to clinical coding in general practice: a literature review. Med. Inform. Internet Med. **30**(2), 89–97 (2005). https://doi.org/10.1080/14639230500298651

9. Alonso, V.: A Codificação Clínica e os problemas associados à qualidade dos dados: perspetiva dos codificadores. Maestrado em Informática Médica. Faculty of Medicine. University of Porto, Porto (2018). https://repositorio-aberto.up.pt/bitstream/10216/118231/2/306324.pdf

10. Alonso, V., et al.: Problems and barriers during the process of clinical coding: a focus group study of coders' perceptions. J. Med. Syst. **44**(3), 1–8 (2020). https://doi.org/10.1007/s10916-020-1532-x

11. ISO: ISO/IEC 8000-61:2016: Data quality – Part 61: Data quality management: Process reference model. ISO (2016). https://www.iso.org/cms/render/live/en/sites/isoorg/contents/data/standard/06/30/63086.html. Accessed 4 Aug 2021

12. ISO: ISO/IEC/IEEE 12207:2017 – Systems and software engineering – Software life cycle processes. ISO/IEC/IEEE 12207:2017 (2017). https://www.iso.org/cms/render/live/en/sites/isoorg/contents/data/standard/06/37/63712.html. Accessed 11 Apr 2022

13. DQTeam: MAMD: Modelo Alarcos Mejora Datos (2020). https://mamd.dqteam.es. Accessed 11 Apr 2022

14. ISO: ISO/IEC 33003:2015: Information technology – Process assessment – Requirements for process measurement frameworks. ISO (2015). https://www.iso.org/cms/render/live/en/sites/isoorg/contents/data/standard/05/41/54177.html. Accessed 11 Apr 2022

15. ISO: ISO/IEC 33004:2015: Information technology – Process assessment – Requirements for process reference, process assessment and maturity models. ISO (2015). https://www.iso.org/cms/render/live/en/sites/isoorg/contents/data/standard/05/41/54178.html. Accessed 11 Apr 2022

16. ISO: ISO 8000-62:2018: Information technology – Process assessment – Requirements for process reference, process assessment and maturity models. ISO (2018). https://www.iso.org/cms/render/live/en/sites/isoorg/contents/data/standard/06/53/65340.html. Accessed 11 Apr 2022

17. Capita: The quality of clinical coding in the NHS: payment by results data assurance frameworks. Capita Health and Wellbeing Limited (2014). https://www.chks.co.uk/userfiles/files/The_quality_of_clinical_coding_in_the_NHS.pdf

18. CCSA: Clinical Coding Practice Framework. Clinical Coders' Society of Australia (2019). https://www.ccsofa.org.au/wp-content/uploads/2021/05/HIMAA-CCSA-CCPF-FINAL5-Sep2019.pdf

19. Reid, B.A., Ridoutt, L., O'Connor, P., Murphy, D.: Best practice in the management of clinical coding services: insights from a project in the Republic of Ireland, Part 1. Health Inf. Manag. J. **46**(2), 69–77 (2017)

20. Reid, B.A., Ridoutt, L., O'Connor, P., Murphy, D.: Best practice in the management of clinical coding services: insights from a project in the Republic of Ireland, Part 2. Health Inf. Manag. J. **46**(3), 105–112 (2017)

21. ISO: ISO/IEC 38505-1:2017 Information technology – Governance of IT – Governance of data – Part 1: Application of ISO/IEC 38500 to the governance of data. ISO/IEC 38505-1:2017 Information technology – Governance of IT – Governance of data – Part 1: Application of ISO/IEC 38500 to the governance of data (2017). https://www.iso.org/standard/56639.html. Accessed 9 May 2021

22. ISO: ISO/IEC TR 38505-2:2018 Information technology – Governance of IT – Governance of data – Part 2: Implications of ISO/IEC 38505-1 for data management. ISO/IEC TR 38505-2:2018 Information technology – Governance of IT – Governance of data – Part 2: Implications of ISO/IEC 38505-1 for data management (2018). https://www.iso.org/standard/70911.html. Accessed 23 May 2021

23. ISACA: COBIT 2019 Framework. Introduction and methodology. Schaumburg, IL. EE.UU (2018)

24. DAMA: DAMA-DMBOK: Data Management Body of Knowledge. Technics Publications, LLC (2017)

25. Wohlin, C., Runeson, P.: Guiding the selection of research methodology in industry–academia collaboration in software engineering. Inf. Softw. Technol. **140**, 106678 (2021). https://doi.org/10.1016/j.infsof.2021.106678

26. Avison, D.E., Davison, R.M., Malaurent, J.: Information systems action research: debunking myths and overcoming barriers. Inf. Manage. **55**(2), 177–187 (2018). https://doi.org/10.1016/j.im.2017.05.004

27. Staron, M.: Action Research in Software Engineering. Springer, Cham (2020). https://doi.org/10.1007/978-3-030-32610-4

28. ISO: ISO/IEC/IEEE 24774:2021 Systems and software engineering – Life cycle management – Specification for process description. ISO (2021). https://www.iso.org/cms/render/live/en/sites/isoorg/contents/data/standard/07/89/78981.html. Accessed 11 Apr 2022

Digital Twin for IoT Environments: A Testing and Simulation Tool

Luong Nguyen[1] (ORCID), Mariana Segovia[2] (ORCID), Wissam Mallouli[1(✉)] (ORCID),
Edgardo Montes de Oca[1] (ORCID), and Ana R. Cavalli[1,2] (ORCID)

[1] Montimage, 39 rue Bobillot, 75013 Paris, France
{luong.nguyen,wissam.mallouli,edgardo.montesdeoca}@montimage.com
[2] Telecom SudParis, 9 rue Charles Fourier, 91011 Evry, France
{ana.cavalli,segovia}@telecom-sudparis.eu

Abstract. Digital Twin (DT) is one of the pillars of modern information technologies that plays an important role on industry's digitalization. A DT is composed of a real physical object, a virtual abstraction of the object and a bidirectional data flow between the physical and virtual components. This paper presents a DT-based tool, called TaS, to easily test and simulate IoT environments. The objective is to improve the testing methodologies in IoT systems to evaluate the possible impact of it on the physical world. We provide the conditions to test, predict errors and stress application depending on hardware, software and real world physical process. The tool is based on the DT concept in order to detect and predict failures in evolving IoT environments. In particular, the way to prepare the DT to support fault injection and cybersecurity threats is analyzed. The TaS tool is tested through an industrial case study, the Intelligent Transport System (ITS) provided by the INDRA company. Results of experiments are presented that show that our DT is closely linked to the real world.

Keywords: Digital Twins · IoT · Sensors · Actuators · Gateway · Simulation · Testing

1 Introduction

Testing is a crucial step of any software development process [3]. As a result, various test cases (e.g., unit tests, integration tests, regression tests, system tests) need to be designed and executed in a production-like environment that reproduces the same conditions where the software under test would run. However, having access to such an environment may be hard to achieve and it is even particularly challenging in the IoT area.

The access to IoT devices might be non-trivial or limited due to many factors. For example, networks of physically deployed devices are typically devoted to production software. Testing applications on top of those networks might involve additional testing software, which might affect the overall performance and the revenue generated by the devices (e.g., applications need to be stopped to load their new versions).

Software simulators proved to be valuable in easing the verification of the software requirements. They provide software developers a testing environment to at least

A. Vallecillo et al. (Eds.): QUATIC 2022, CCIS 1621, pp. 205–219, 2022.
https://doi.org/10.1007/978-3-031-14179-9_14

manage the execution of test cases. IoT Testbeds play a similar role in testing IoT applications. They offer a deployed network of IoT devices where developers can upload their applications and test their software in a physical environment. IoT-Lab [1] and SmartSantander [17] are good examples of IoT testbeds. Testbeds often have a predefined fixed-configuration and architecture. They are also usually shared with other users, which can be a problem for measuring application quality. Hence, this problem might make simulators more attractive since they provide a more customized and controlled environment. Furthermore, simulators avoid the need for a more expensive physical network of devices.

The main issue regarding simulators is that they are not directly linked to the real environment and any evolution of this latter (e.g., addition or deletion of a new IoT device or gateway) is not automatically taken into account in the simulation mode. Also, physical process dynamics may be hard to be reproduced in simulations. As a result, physical properties and events, such as process disturbances or devices failure, may not be quantified during the software testing process. Besides, simulation can rely on predefined scenarios that can have different behaviours in real environments since simulation is based on the abstraction of some layers. The continuous monitoring of real systems is needed to feed simulators in order to have more accurate results. In addition, recommendations from simulators can be taken into account in the real world if a bidirectional relationship between these two worlds exist. This is exactly the essence of Digital Twins.

The main contribution of our paper is the design of a tool, called TaS (stands for Test and Simulation), based on the concept of Digital Twin, to simulate, test and predict errors in real IoT systems. The tool supports functional and non-functional testing through the real-time connection of the physical system to a new software version deployed in the DT. This way, it is possible to verify that the changes made in the code do not impact the existing software functionality. Also, the DT may be used to elaborate a what-if analysis resulting in a better evaluation of attacks, error cases, scalability and performance stress situations. For example, it is possible to perturb the system to test unexpected scenarios and analyze the response. TaS has been validated through different experiments performed in the context of H2020 ENACT project[1].

The paper is organized as follows: Sect. 2 presents several solutions for the simulation of IoT environments as well as the usage of DT for this kind of technology. Section 3 presents the basics to understand the concepts of DT as well as simulation and testing. Section 4, presents the TaS tool, its architecture and different details of its implementation. In Sect. 5, we present the application of such DT-based Test and Simulation tool on an industrial experimental case study called ITS. Finally, we conclude the paper and discuss future work in Sect. 6.

2   Related Work

In recent years, both academia and the commercial market offered solutions in the design of DT. Following we present some relevant works regarding DT as well as simulation and testing for IoT systems. We also explain the existing challenges in IoT applications and how our approach can help to solve these limitations.

---

[1] https://www.enact-project.eu/.

Digital Twins—are a digital representation of a physical object or system or a system of systems (like an IoT network). The technology behind Digital Twins has expanded to include complex elements such as buildings, factories and networks, and some even consider that people and processes can have DTs.

A DT is composed of a virtual object that models a physical component. Both components exchange information and the virtual object continually adapts to operational changes based on the collected data from the physical component. The connection between the physical and virtual objects can forecast the future of the physical component using the collected data [19]. This way, DTs supply a system with information and operating status providing capabilities to create new business models and decision support systems. Also, it is possible to make more accurate predictions and information-based decisions using analytic, predictive diagnosis, and performance optimization. Other uses of DT include reducing costs and risks, improving efficiency, security and resilience.

The idea first arose at NASA, where full-scale mockups of early space capsules, used on the ground to mirror and diagnose problems in orbit, eventually gave way to fully digital simulations [14]. But the term became very popular when Gartner named DTs as one of its top 10 strategic technology trends for 2017[2] saying that within three to five years, "billions of things will be represented by Digital Twins, a dynamic software model of a physical thing or system". In essence, a Digital Twin is a computer program that takes real-world data about a physical object or system as inputs and produces as outputs predictions or simulations of how that physical object or system will be affected by those inputs.

IoT Simulation and Testing—The field of simulation and testing in IoT also has gained momentum when it comes to generating novel, cutting-edge ideas. In the recent years, academia proposed several IoT simulators each mostly focusing on a particular layer of the communication stack. For instance, Cooja[3] and OMNeT++[4] focus on simulating networking aspects of the systems. Other simulators, like SimIOT [18] or IOTsim [22], focus on data analytics rather than lower aspects of the systems. Another approach, like iFogSim [7], try to perform a complete simulation. However, having a full stack simulation from a single component or product can be challenging. Other alternatives proposed hybrid models, such as [2], which try to leverage several simulators, each for a particular layer, to reproduce the behaviour of a system from a holistic perspective.

The DTs are a development of modelling and simulation technology. Traditional simulation methods are of limited capabilities in evaluating system performance. By integrating IoT technology, DTs are the breakthrough of the existing limitations on the modelling and analysis capabilities of simulation [11]. The major difference between a simulation and a DT is the data interconnection that allows to exchange information between the physical and the virtual object, i.e., a simulation predicts future states of a physical system based on a set of initial assumptions [21]. However, a DT tracks the current and past states of the physical component that is being used in operation and

---

[2] https://www.gartner.com/smarterwithgartner/gartners-top-10-technology-trends-2017.

[3] https://github.com/contiki-os/contiki/wiki/An-Introduction-to-Cooja.

[4] https://omnetpp.org/.

is being simulated within the virtual object. Often the computational models which are used to infer the current state of the physical objects are the same models which can be used in simulation to predict future states. The simulation models can provide additional decision-making information for optimizing future operations, forecasting degradation mechanisms, and predicting future failures.

Research-based simulators often ignore problems such as the lack of standardization, which poses a challenge when it comes to creating synergies and inter-operation between different simulators. A research-based simulator can be volatile and can change its application interface rapidly. This volatility generates extra overhead since developers need to adapt their code to the new changes. In addition, simulators created by research are often not maintained or discontinued, i.e. bugs remain and new features or improvements are not made. Nevertheless, some simulators are open source, allowing contributions from the community to their development and maintenance.

Testing Challenges—The research work regarding testing point out that there is a need for a complete set of tests and simulation solutions for IoT. Systems should be tested based on different scenarios that involve the generation and use of high amounts of sensor and actuator data, which is not always practical to set up in a given IoT environment, but serves to stress the boundaries of the environment in order to detect potential problems. This is exactly what we propose in this paper by conceiving a DT-based on a simulation and testing tool. Notice that the concept of DT for IoT has been used the first time in 2016 [6] where the authors proposed first ideas to define DT for industrial IoT. Then this concept has been studied mainly from a research point of view in [15] to address, e.g., smart grids and smart factories. The proposed tool that we present in this paper is generic enough so that it can be applied to different sectors (e-health, transport, telecommunication, etc.) and tackle different test objectives such as security, scalability, energy consumption. In addition, most of the existing DT proposals are designed for optimization of the physical object, system security and resilience, real-time monitoring, prediction of future behavior or training for operator users. Less attention has been paid to DTs applications to overcome the mentioned simulation limitations and improve IoT testing methodologies. Some proposals that have addressed this problem are analyzed as follows.

The paper [13] presents a survey providing the DT original definition and addressing the relevant aspects that a DT should support. It illustrates the application of the DT concept in four application scenarios. One of them is of particular interest for us, this regarding DT for sensors. Following this paper, sensors can be represented by a logical object or several ones, which are associate to the physical entities. In this DT, it is required that logical objects should be strongly synchronized with the physical objects. The objects are continuously updated. We have the same requirements regarding the sensor DT we defined in this paper. In addition, we go beyond this approach by developing a tool that implements the proposed solution.

In [16], it is presented an IoT-based DT of a cyber-physical system that interacts with the control system to ensure its proper operation. The proposed DT is validated on a distributed control system. Security measures are also implemented based on cloud computing. This work has the advantage that the proposed DT can contribute to mitigate individual as well as coordinated attacks.

The work in [9] proposes a tool to validate models of legacy systems. Their objective is to test the models of an existing production system through simulation and then incorporate this validated model in a DT. In this case, the proposition is oriented to create the modelling of an existing system. In our proposal, we go further by proposing a tool that test the whole system considering also the physical interaction.

The authors of [8] designed an open-source toolkit composed by five open-source tools (Eclipse Hono[5], Eclipse Ditto[6], Apache Kafka[7], Influx DB[8] and Grafana[9]) for each data processing layer of IoT and DT reference architectures. The toolkit is evaluated using a benchmark dataset. The architecture of the toolkit is more complex than the proposed for our tool. Some experimentation showed that Hono and Ditto platforms have some limitation on massive packet processing [10] which may be a serious limitation to scale IoT applications.

In [4], the authors propose a DT for testing properties and characteristics of the physical object, i.e., for physical experimentation. Their work is motivated by the limited possibilities to physically experiment with convoy belts and how time-consuming this activity is. DT present a solution to create an environment to test objects using models without carrying out it physically. Our work provides also testing functionalities but with a focus in the software that controls the physical process and which are the possible impacts of it in the physical world. In this paper, we explore the creation of a DT to improve the development process of the software that controls the physical system. For that, we present a testing tool to evaluate functional and stress tests.

3 A Test and Simulation (TaS) Tool Based on Digital Twin for IoT Environment

This section contains three subsections. In the first subsection, the architecture of the tool called TaS enabler is presented. The second section presents its functionalities. The third section describes its implementation.

3.1 The Approach and Architecture of the Tool

In this subsection, we present the architecture of the TaS enabler, which is based on the concept of DTs [5]. Figure 1 illustrates the TaS enabler architecture.

On the left-hand side, we have the system in a real (production) environment. The communication between the sensors, actuators with the IoT component is typically done via a broker. The sensors capture and send the surrounding information (e.g., "temperature") to the IoT system. Based on input data, the IoT system reacts differently and sends actuation data to change the actuator settings (e.g., "change the heating level").

On the right-hand side of the figure, we have the Smart IoT System (SIS) in a test environment and the TaS enabler. The system under test is the SIS that needs to be

---

[5] http://www.eclipse.org/hono/.

[6] https://www.eclipse.org/ditto/.

[7] http://kafka.apache.org/.

[8] https://www.influxdata.com/.

[9] https://grafana.com/.

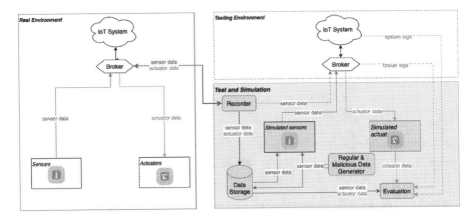

Fig. 1. Test and Simulation (TaS) enabler approach and architecture

tested. The TaS enabler simulates sensors and actuators. The topology on the left side is very similar to the topology on the right side. The only difference is the simulated sensors and actuators. The simulated actuators collect the actuation data sent from the IoT system. The simulated sensors play the same role as the physical sensors providing the data signal to the IoT components. However, they are much more valuable than a physical sensor in terms of testing in the following ways:

- Firstly, by using the dataset recorded from the physical environment, the simulated sensors can repeatedly simulate the surrounding environment at a specific time. In reality, an event may happen only once, but the simulated sensor can generate the same event as many times as needed for testing purposes.
- Secondly, the physical sensors passively capture the state of the surrounding environment. It can be challenging to obtain different data from the physical sensors. In contrast, the simulated sensors use the dataset in the Data Storage as a data source. Therefore, we can generate various testing scenarios by modifying the events in the Data Storage.
- Moreover, the TaS enabler also provides a module to manipulate the data from the sensors. The Regular and Malicious Data Generator can generate regular data to test the functionalities, operations, performance, and scalability (relying on pre-recorded data). It can also generate malicious data to test the resiliency of the system to attacks.

Besides the simulated sensors and actuators, the TaS enabler also provides some modules which support the testing process 1. The *Data Recorder* module records all the messages going through the broker in the physical environment. Each message can be considered as an event happening in the physical environment. Then, the recorded messages are forwarded to the broker in the testing environment. In this way, we have a "twin version" of the physical environment. What has happened in the physical environment is reproduced in the testing environment. Besides, the recorded messages are stored in a *Data Storage* as a dataset for later testing. The recorded dataset can be modified (muted) to create a new dataset, e.g., "change the event order", "delete an event", "add a new event". All the testing datasets are stored in the Data Storage. The *Regular and Malicious Data Generator* enables the simulation of different sensor behaviors, from normal behavior to abnormal behavior, such as a DOS attack (the sensor publishes massive data messages in a short time), node failure (the sensor stops sending data). With data mutation, the TaS enabler can help build datasets for testing many different cases hard to produce in real life. Finally, the *Evaluation* module analyses the simulation input and output and combines them with the logs collected from the IoT system to provide the final result of a testing process.

The next section presents more details on the functionalities of the tool.

3.2 Tool Implementation

Most of the testing scenarios are defined by the information about the surrounding environment captured by sensors. The following subsection goes into detail about the simulation of sensors.

The Simulation

The simulation of sensors—The sensor provides the input data of an IoT system. The simulation of a sensor corresponds to the simulation of the data stream it provides. The simulated sensor has been designed for flexibility in the following ways:

- It supports different types of data report formats:
- It supports different data sources which are used for simulation:
- It supports simulating several abnormal behaviours, such as, low energy, node failure, DOS attack, and slow DOS attack.
- It supports multiple measurements with the different data types, such as Boolean, Integer, Float and Enum. For each measurement, there are several abnormal behaviours that can be selected, such as "fixed value", "value out of range", and "invalid value".

The simulation of actuators—An actuator can be considered as a device that receives the IoT system reaction based on the input data. We simulate the actuator as a component that will receive the reaction signal (actuation data) from the IoT system.

The simulation of a IoT device—In an IoT system, the sensor and actuator are usually part of the same device. An IoT device can contain one to many sensors as well as one to many actuators

The simulation of a network topology—A list of simulated IoT devices forms the simulated network topology. Besides the list of devices, a network topology can also provide the identifier of the dataset (*datasetId*),which contains the data to simulate the SIS in a given time, the global replaying options, the configuration to connect with the database, and the definition of the new dataset where the data generated from the simulations will be stored.

The Testing Methodologies. In this section, we present the testing methodologies and techniques we have adapted in the TaS enabler.

Data Driven Testing—The Data Storage contains the datasets recorded from the IoT system or entered manually. Each dataset contains sensor data (inputs for TaS) and expected actuator outputs. The expected actuator outputs can be the value recorded from the IoT system in a normal scenario. Engineers can also enter them manually via the Graphical Interface. The Evaluation module will use the expected outputs to compare them with the simulation output to determine if they match. A test case passes if the simulation output is within the range of the expected output. The Data-Driven Testing method is suitable for functional and regression testing.

The Data-Driven Testing has been implemented as the main testing methodology of the TaS enabler.

Data Mutation Testing—The Mutant Generator generates new sensor data from existing data stored in the Data Storage by applying one or many mutated functions, such as "change the event order", "change a value", and "delete an event". The mutated data are input for the simulation. The Evaluation module generates a report about the output differences when testing the system with the mutated and the original input data. The Data Mutation Testing method is for penetration, robustness, security, and scalability testing (e.g., mutating the device identifier to obtain new devices). In the TaS enabler, we can mutate the device identity to generate many devices while testing the system scalability. There is also an interface to apply some mutation functions to a dataset manually.

Model-Based Testing [20] and Risk-Based Testing [12] are two other methodologies that we have studied but not yet implemented in the TaS enabler at the time of writing of this paper.

The Testbeds

The Data Recorder—The TaS enabler provides the possibility to simulate an IoT system using historical data. The data is used to create a model that represents the behavior of the physical controlled process. This way, the model works as a digital copy of the physical components. To this end, a Data Recorder module is needed. The Data Recorder records all the events in the real system (coming from the broker). This data (including both sensor and actuator data) is stored in the Data Storage as a dataset. The sensor data can be forwarded directly to the testing system (using the forwarding broker). The more data from sensors are recorded, the more test scenarios are tested. By synchronizing the Sensor simulator timestamps with the Data Recorder, it is possible to simulate a particular SIS (following the DT concept). By monitoring the SIS input and output, we can build an automatic testing process for a complex IoT system.

The Regular and Malicious Data Generator—When testing the IoT system, there are many testing scenarios and cases that do not frequently occur in reality. With the real IoT system, it is almost impossible to collect the datasets for many testing scenarios. The Regular and Malicious Data Generator module helps developers to create a testbed which contains sensor data for various scenarios, e.g., making the temperature too high or too low. By combining multiple data, one can create a testbed that includes many incidents or attack scenarios, such as DDoS and data poisoning. The Data Storage stores all the generated data for further use.

4   Experimentation and Validation

This section presents the application of TaS in a use case which provided by INDRA company[10].

Overview. The rail domain requires infrastructure and resources that are usually expensive and require a long-time planning and execution. Therefore, the usage of the rail systems must be highly optimized, following strict security and safety regulations. Several functionalities could be implemented within the rail systems to ensure that the system could tackle its high critical requirements as planned.

The implemented measurements to track and keep a safe behavior of the rail system are developed by the Intelligent Transport Systems (ITS) Domain Use Case. This Use Case will describe logistic and maintenance rail activities. The focus of the demonstrator is placed in the logistics activities.

A Logistics and Maintenance scenario is defined with the aim to provide information of the wagons that conform the rolling stock to assure the well-functioning of the system. These events are only possible through the confirmation of the train integrity, when the different wagons are locked and moving together. This situation ensure the proper transportation of the rolling stock, avoiding possible accidents. A representation for an architecture of this scenario is shown in the Fig. 2.

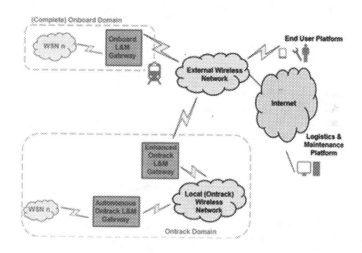

Fig. 2. Wireless sensor network architecture. Source: INDRA

In the Fig. 2, the ITS system is located in the Logistics and Maintenance Platform, it receives and handles the data provided from the train (OnBoard) and from the track (OnTrack). On each train, there is a WSN (Wireless Sensor Network) which includes several sensors, such as: accelerometer, ultra sound sensor, RSSI (Received Signal Strength Indicator) detector, GNSS (Global Navigation Satellite System) receivers,

---

[10] https://www.indracompany.com/en/.

RFID (Radio Frequency Identification), Humidity, Temperature, CO_2 concentrations, Title Detectors; actuators: LED and Display. One OnBoard gateway on each train to send sensor's data to and receive actuated data from the ITS system on the Cloud. The WSN on track contains only a single sensor: RFID. An OnTrack gateway send sensor's data to the ITS system on the Cloud.

The DevOps role in the Use Case consists in providing useful tools to manage the behavior of the different rail components through SW tools. One of them was TaS which focus on simulating and testing the ITS system on two aspects:

- To ensure the ITS handles properly all kind of input data, such as: normal input data, malformed input data, invalid input data, etc.
- To ensure the ITS is able to handle a large number of trains.

4.1 Application of TaS to ITS Use Case

Figure 3 presents the TaS-ITS integration architecture. EDI (Elektronikas un datorzinātņu institūts, Lavia) provides a testing train on which there are 13 sensors in total. The OnBoard gateway on the testing train connect with the Partners Gateway in INDRA infrastructure. The Partners Gateway receives the input data, then do some validation and pre-processing, the final data is forwarded to the Central Gateway. The TaS tool located in Montimage infrastructure, connects with the Partners Gateway and the Central Gateway to provide three main functions:

- Use a recorder model to record the Partners Gateway data, the recorded data is stored in a Data Storage.
- Use a simulation model to simulate the behaviors of a train based on historical data which was recorded and stored in the Data Storage.
- Use a recorder model to monitor the status of the Central Gateway. The metrics on the Central Gateway are the key values to evaluate the performance of the ITS system.

4.2 Results

The tests are divided in two stages. At the first stage, a recorder model has been used to record the normal behaviors of a single train. The second stage consists on re-injecting the recorded data to perform some tests:

- Scalability testing: adding some scaling factor to check if the gateway can deal with a specific number of trains.
- Penetration testing: adding some data mutation to check if the gateway can deal with some invalid data such as: malformed, invalid value.

The recording stage is shown in the following figures. The Fig. 4 shows the status of the Central Gateway before activating the train. At this phase, there is no sensors data, however there are still some messages which are the internal messages of the gateways. The Fig. 5 shows the state of the Central Gateway after activating the train. As shown on the figure, the traffic peak is recorded, the published rate is around 170 messages/s,

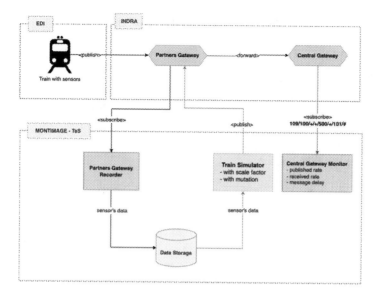

Fig. 3. The TaS-ITS integration architecture

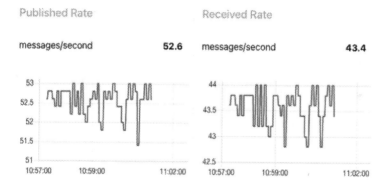

Fig. 4. Before activating the train

and the received rate is around 150 messages/s. This traffic is constant as it is required by the the safety system. The recorded data is stored in the Data Storage, then it can be used as an input of a simulation, or it can be duplicated, then mutated to generate a new testing data-set.

Functional Testing—The Table 1 has shown the result of functional testing, as it must be noted that the system can handle malformed and invalid value data without crashing.

Table 1. Functional testing result summary

Mutation operation	Partners gateway	Central gateway
Add a valid data row	Processed and forwarded	Received
Delete an existing data row	Operators as normal	Operators as normal
Modify - malformed data	Dropped the modified data row	Did not receive
Modify - invalid data	Dropped the modified data row	Did not receive

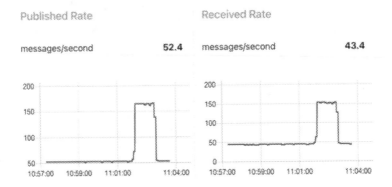

Fig. 5. After activating the train

Scalability Testing—For scalability testing, several scale factors have been tested as shown in Table 2.

Table 2. Scale factors in scalability testing

Scale factor	Number of simulated trains	Total number of sensors
1	1	13
5	5	65
10	10	130
20	20	260
50	50	650

The Fig. 6 shows that with the scale factors of 1, 5, 10 and 20, the messages are carried without any issues, the metrics of the Central Gateway are scaled up with a ratio almost the same with the scale factor. However, with the factor of 50, the Central Gateway started to show some delays and the outputs messages are not the same as the input messages, there are some failure indicators which means the ITS Gateway is starting to queue the messages.

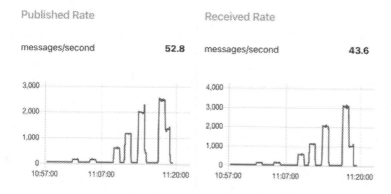

Fig. 6. Scalability testing result

5 Discussion

The proposed TaS tool helps testing new IoT applications and overcome the simulation limitations. For that it uses data from the real system to create a model of the behavior and create functional, security and stress tests. The tool allows to improve the detection capabilities by automating several steps (e.g., test execution). But still test generation can be improved to cover relevant test scenarios according to defined objectives (e.g., functional testing, regression testing, performance or security testing etc.). The automation of this task will allow to reduce the time of testing the target system as well as improving its coverage.

In the same way, an analysis of real system traces and logs can be used to automate its model building. This reverse engineering task is a complex task that can be also explored as an enhancement of TaS tool.

6 Conclusion and Future Work

In this paper we presented a Digital Twin based tool for an IoT environment, named Digital Twin Test and Simulation tool (TaS). The main objective of this Digital Twin tool is to detect and predict failures in real IoT environments. The TaS tool has been applied in different domains (e-health, transport, telecommunications, smart houses, etc.) showing that the proposed solution is generic and can be applied to achieve different test objectives: security, scalability, energy, etc. In the future, it will be adapted and used in several other collaborative projects dealing with other domains and contexts. To illustrate its application we present a case study, an Intelligent Transport System (ITS) application that provides a simulation of a rail system describing logistic and maintenance activities. Experiments show that our Digital Twin is closely linked to the real world. We can say that both worlds, the real and the digital one are synchronised. In practice, it can help the IoT application developer save time and money on setting up the testing environment and, thus, allows faster delivery of the applications.

Acknowledgements. This paper has received funding from the European Union's H2020 Programme under grant agreement no 780351 for the ENACT project as well as grant agreement no 101021668 for the PRECINCT project. Thanks are also addressed to INDRA team that contributed to the experimentation.

References

1. Adjih, C., et al.: Fit IoT-lab: a large scale open experimental IoT testbed. In: 2015 IEEE 2nd World Forum on Internet of Things (WF-IoT), pp. 459–464 (2015). https://doi.org/10.1109/WF-IoT.2015.7389098
2. D'Angelo, G., Ferretti, S., Ghini, V.: Distributed hybrid simulation of the internet of things and smart territories. CoRR abs/1710.04252 (2017). http://arxiv.org/abs/1710.04252
3. Faber, F.: Testing in DevOps. In: The Future of Software Quality Assurance, pp. 27–38. Springer, Cham (2020). https://doi.org/10.1007/978-3-030-29509-7_3
4. Fedorko, G., Molnár, V., Vasiľ, M., Salai, R.: Proposal of digital twin for testing and measuring of transport belts for pipe conveyors within the concept Industry 4.0. Measurement **174**, 108978 (2021). https://doi.org/10.1016/j.measurement.2021.108978
5. Fuller, A., Fan, Z., Day, C., Barlow, C.: Digital twin: enabling technologies, challenges and open research. IEEE Access **8**, 108952–108971 (2020). https://doi.org/10.1109/ACCESS.2020.2998358
6. Grieves, M.: Origins of the digital twin concept (2016). https://doi.org/10.13140/RG.2.2.26367.61609
7. Gupta, H., Dastjerdi, A.V., Ghosh, S.K., Buyya, R.: iFogSim: a toolkit for modeling and simulation of resource management techniques in internet of things, edge and fog computing environments. CoRR abs/1606.02007 (2016). http://arxiv.org/abs/1606.02007
8. Kamath, V., Morgan, J., Ali, M.I.: Industrial IoT and digital twins for a smart factory: an open source toolkit for application design and benchmarking. In: 2020 Global Internet of Things Summit, GIoTS 2020, Dublin, 3 June 2020, pp. 1–6. IEEE (2020). https://doi.org/10.1109/GIOTS49054.2020.9119497
9. Khan, A., Dahl, M., Falkman, P., Fabian, M.: Digital twin for legacy systems: simulation model testing and validation. In: 2018 IEEE 14th International Conference on Automation Science and Engineering (CASE), pp. 421–426 (2018). https://doi.org/10.1109/COASE.2018.8560338. ISSN 2161-8089
10. Lee, J., Kang, S., Chun, I.G.: mIoTwins: design and evaluation of mIoT framework for private edge networks. In: 2021 International Conference on Information and Communication Technology Convergence (ICTC), pp. 1882–1884. IEEE, Jeju Island (2021). https://doi.org/10.1109/ICTC52510.2021.9621144
11. Leng, J., Wang, D., Shen, W., Li, X., Liu, Q., Chen, X.: Digital twins-based smart manufacturing system design in Industry 4.0: a review. J. Manuf. Syst. **60**, 119–137 (2021). https://doi.org/10.1016/j.jmsy.2021.05.011
12. Matheu-García, S.N., Hernández-Ramos, J.L., Skarmeta, A.F., Baldini, G.: Risk-based automated assessment and testing for the cybersecurity certification and labelling of IoT devices. Comput. Stand. Interfaces **62**, 64–83 (2019). https://doi.org/10.1016/j.csi.2018.08.003
13. Minerva, R., Lee, G.M., Crespi, N.: Digital twin in the IoT context: a survey on technical features, scenarios, and architectural models. Proc. IEEE **108**(10), 1785–1824 (2020). https://doi.org/10.1109/JPROC.2020.2998530
14. Muhissen, M., Shaikh, N., Salah, Z.: Digital twin in artificial intelligence empowerment pisiq. Open Artif. Intell. J. **2** (2018)

15. Park, K.T., et al.: Design and implementation of a digital twin application for a connected micro smart factory. Int. J. Comput. Integr. Manuf. **32**, 1–19 (2019). https://doi.org/10.1080/0951192X.2019.1599439
16. Saad, A., Faddel, S., Youssef, T., Mohammed, O.A.: On the implementation of IoT-based digital twin for networked microgrids resiliency against cyber attacks. IEEE Trans. Smart Grid **11**(6), 5138–5150 (2020). https://doi.org/10.1109/TSG.2020.3000958
17. Sanchez, L., et al.: SmartSantander: IoT experimentation over a smart city testbed. Comput. Netw. **61**, 217–238 (2014). https://doi.org/10.1016/j.bjp.2013.12.020
18. Sotiriadis, S., Bessis, N., Asimakopoulou, E., Mustafee, N.: Towards simulating the internet of things. In: 2014 28th International Conference on Advanced Information Networking and Applications Workshops, pp. 444–448 (2014). https://doi.org/10.1109/WAINA.2014.74
19. Tao, F., Zhang, H., Liu, A., Nee, A.Y.C.: Digital twin in industry: state-of-the-art. IEEE Trans. Industr. Inform. **15**(4), 2405–2415 (2019). https://ieeexplore.ieee.org/document/8477101/
20. Tappler, M., Aichernig, B.K., Bloem, R.: Model-based testing IoT communication via active automata learning. In: 2017 IEEE International Conference on Software Testing, Verification and Validation (ICST), pp. 276–287 (2017). https://doi.org/10.1109/ICST.2017.32
21. VanDerHorn, E., Mahadevan, S.: Digital Twin: generalization, characterization and implementation. Decis. Support Syst. **145**, 113524 (2021). https://doi.org/10.1016/j.dss.2021.113524
22. Zeng, X., Garg, S.K., Strazdins, P., Jayaraman, P.P., Georgakopoulos, D., Ranjan, R.: IOT-Sim: a simulator for analysing IoT applications. J. Syst. Archit. **72**, 93–107 (2017). https://doi.org/10.1016/j.sysarc.2016.06.008

Safety, Security and Privacy

Simpler Is Better: On the Use of Autoencoders for Intrusion Detection

Marta Catillo⬤, Antonio Pecchia⬤, and Umberto Villano$^{(\boxtimes)}$⬤

Dipartimento di Ingegneria, Università degli Studi del Sannio, Benevento, Italy
{marta.catillo,antonio.pecchia,villano}@unisannio.it

Abstract. The ever-growing occurrence of computer security incidents calls for advanced intrusion detection techniques. A wide body of literature dealing with Intrusion Detection Systems (IDSes) is based on machine learning; many proposals rely on the use of autoencoders (AEs), due to their capability to analyze complex, high-dimensional and large-scale data. Most of the times, AEs are used as building blocks of much more complex detection architectures, possibly in combination with sophisticated feature selection techniques. This paper summarizes several years of work in this field, suggesting that "simpler is better" and that a carefully tuned and trained AE can be used in isolation, obtaining recognition results comparable with those attained by more complex designs. The best practices presented here, regarding dataset production and sanitization, AE set-up and training, threshold setting, possible use of simple feature selection techniques for performance improvement can be valuable for any practitioner willing to use autoencoders for intrusion detection purposes.

Keywords: Intrusion detection · Autoencoders · Denial of service

1 Introduction

Due to the ever-growing occurrence and complexity of computer security incidents, intrusion detection is, and will steadily remain, a hot research topic. A wide body of literature aims at proposing effective solutions to the lack of security of the computer networks and devices our lives currently rely on, by presenting new proposals of Intrusion Detection Systems (IDSes) [12]. The aim of these systems is to discover (and possibly block or divert) on-going attacks before any harm can be done. For a number of different reasons, present-day IDSes are only partially successful to avoid the occurrence of security incidents. These reasons include the high complexity and the huge bandwidth of currently used networks, the use of brand new or unknown exploits, the amplitude of the so-called attack surface. Moreover, often the security problem is blamelessly ignored, and suitable countermeasures are set up only when it is too late.

In this situation, given the growing success of machine learning (ML) techniques and the availability of processors suitably designed for this domain, a very large number of proposals in the cybersecurity field rely on ML [7]. The "pattern" followed by most papers on ML and IDSes is typically the same: an algorithm or an architecture based on neural networks (possibly deep ones) are proposed, then they are tested on reference datasets, very high performance figures (often close to 100% intrusion detection capabilities) are proven by limited-width experiments. But the continuous flow of new proposals clearly indicates the intrusion detection problem is still there, and that the experiments mentioned in the papers have only limited validity in real-world networks.

Our previous work has tackled the problem of the lack of transferability of the impressive results obtained on reference datasets (possibly outdated and not free from statistical biasing) in even slightly-different data collection settings [4]. This paper will instead focus on the unnecessary complexity of many existing IDS proposals. Among the wide corpus of the existing proposals, multiple autoencoder (AEs) networks are often used in complex configurations, possibly complemented by sophisticated feature selection methods. We develop around the intuition that this complexity is not justified because a single autoencoder –if suitably trained and correctly used– is enough to obtain similar (if not better) performance figures compared to existing proposals. This proposition is investigated in the context of the widely-used CICIDS2017 intrusion detection benchmarking dataset. The IDS solution proposed in this paper achieves 0.988 recall, 0.976 precision and 0.982 F1 with no feature selection and a single autoencoder; moreover, the results indicate that the use of feature selection yields negligible improvements over the metrics, at the cost of demanding tuning attempts. Based on the results, we discuss all our findings in several years of use of autoencoders for IDS, pointing out a number of best practices that can lead to successful performance results without unnecessary architectural complications.

The rest of this paper is organized as follows. Section 2 presents related work; Sect. 3 deals with the basics of autoencoders, their use for classification and the reference dataset. Section 4 discusses our proposal based on a single autoencoder for intrusion detection, the issues related to its design and training. Section 5 investigates the possibility to perform feature selection, and present the results obtained on the dataset. Section 6 closes with lessons, conclusions and directions of future research.

2   Related Work

Despite decades of research and development, existing intrusion detection systems still face challenges in improving the detection rate, reducing the false positives and –possibly– detecting unknown attacks. To solve the above problems, many researchers and practitioners have focused on developing intrusion detection systems that capitalize on **machine learning** and **deep learning** methods [13]. Moreover, in order to tune and test these techniques, many ready-to-use **public intrusion detection datasets** have been produced [23]. Most of these datasets are collected in synthetic environments under normative conditions and different intrusion scenarios. They emulate real network traffic and –at least in theory– they do not contain any confidential data. Almost all datasets are released as labeled network flows, organized in comma-separated values files specially crafted to apply modern machine learning techniques. In particular, each record is a flow and the label states if it is an attack or not. An example of an intrusion detection dataset, flow-based and widely used in literature is certainly CICIDS2017 [24]. Released by the Canadian Institute for Cybersecurity (CIC) in 2017, it simulates real-world network data and uses the tool `CICFlowMeter` –more on this later– to produce labeled flow records. Other known flow-based intrusion datasets are USB-IDS-1 [1], UGR'16 [17] and UNSW-NB15 [21].

Over the last few years, a boundlessness of machine learning methods for misuse detection as well as anomaly detection have been proposed [16]. In general, these approaches can be denoted as *supervised* or *unsupervised* depending on whether there is a need to train the algorithm on labeled instances. In the case of supervised learning techniques, the algorithm is trained on labeled data points and it determines a function to map points to classes. Many supervised approaches rely on a limited number of classifiers or only one classifier by achieving outstanding performance –detection close to 100% [22]. However, a large number of supervised methods also exploit artificial neural networks [25]. In the case of unsupervised techniques, instead, there is no need for labeled data points during the training phase. In this context the aim is to find the hidden structure of unlabeled data. Indeed, the vast majority of the unsupervised detection schemes proposed in the literature are based on clustering and outliers detection [11, 28].

Autoencoders are neural networks capable of learning features from unlabeled data by automatically uncovering the underlying structure of the data and by removing sources of variation in the input. They are designed to map the input data points to an internal latent representation, which is then used to reconstruct the input. Autoencoders were first developed as *nonlinear* extension of the standard linear principal component analysis (PCA) in order to make **dimensionality reduction** [14]. For example, in [15] the authors use an autoencoder to perform automatic features extraction with the aim to reduce the dimensions of the data being processed. Thereafter, they classify the attacks by means of the support vector machine algorithm. Feng et al. [9] show a graph and autoencoder-based feature selection (GAFS) method, which projects the data to a lower-dimensional space using a single-layer autoencoder. The approach proved to be effective when compared with existing state-of-the-art methods. In [26] the authors propose a model which adopts two types of autoencoder. A generic autoencoder is used to capture the generic features which are common to all intrusions, while several ad-hoc autoencoders are trained with the aim to capture patterns that are specific only to particular groups of intrusions. Combining these two feature maps the authors propose a new feature map to classify the intrusions by means of the random forest classifier.

However, autoencoders are often used also in recent studies for **anomaly detection** purposes. In this context they are mainly components of a more complex network, specially crafted with the aim to design sophisticated detectors. In [20] the authors propose Kitsune, an unsupervised learning approach to detect attacks online. Kitsune's core algorithm is KitNet, which uses a collection of auto-encoder neural networks to distinguish between normative and abnormal traffic. The approach involves the integration of multiple autoencoders into a classifier. Experimental results show that Kitsune is effective with different attacks, and its performance is as outstanding as offline detectors. In [29], instead, the authors propose an effective deep learning method, namely autoencoder-IDS (AE-IDS) based on random forest. In particular, they use the random forest algorithm to select the actual features from the original dataset. The main innovation of the approach lies in the combination of 3-layer shallow autoencoders and traditional unsupervised machine learning clustering algorithm. The experimental results show that the proposed approach, evaluated by means of the CSE-CIC-IDS 2018 dataset, is superior to traditional machine learning methods in terms of easy training, strong adaptability and high detection accuracy. A further heterogeneous ensemble method for intrusion detection is proposed by Zhong et al. [30]. In particular, the authors propose HELAD (Heterogeneous Ensemble Learning Anomaly Detection), an unsupervised approach where an autoencoder is combined with a long short-term memory (LSTM) predictor. The authors evaluate their approach by means of the MAWILab3 and CICIDS2017 datasets. The experimental results show that the HELAD algorithm has better adaptability and accuracy than other state-of-the-art algorithms. Min et al. [19] propose a network intrusion detection method using a memory-augmented deep autoencoder (MemAE), which can solve the over-generalization problem of autoencoders. MemAE solves this problem by bringing the reconstruction of the attack inputs closer to the normal sample through the memory module. Experiments are conducted on the NSL-KDD, UNSW-NB15, and CICIDS2017 datasets.

It is worth pointing out that all the aforementioned autoencoder systems adopt fairly sophisticated infrastructures. The detection of different classes of anomalies has been recently addressed by means of system log analysis and a deep autoencoder [2]: the proposed approach, called AutoLog, is based solely on a deep autoencoder network without any kind of artifice in the infrastructure.

3   Background and Datasets

3.1   Autoencoders (AE)

An autoencoder (AE) is a feedforward neural network where the *output layer* has the same dimension as the *input layer*. In fact, the purpose of an AE is to "reconstruct" the input at the output layer. The middle *hidden layer* of an autoencoder is also known as the **bottleneck layer** and its dimension is lower than the input/output layer. Figure 1 shows the representation of a basic autoencoder with three hidden layers.

It is possible to design different types of autoencoders [10]. In particular, deep learning can be applied to autoencoders: multiple hidden layers are used to provide depth. The resulting network is known as *deep* or *stacked autoencoder* [27].

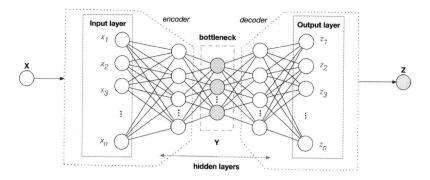

Fig. 1. Representation of an autoencoder.

An autoencoder consists of two parts: **encoder** and **decoder**. Let **x** be an input vector of n real numbers $[x_1, x_2, ..., x_n]$, the encoder maps **x** to a code vector or hidden representation **y** at the bottleneck layer. On the other hand, the decoder transforms **y** into a vector of n real numbers $\mathbf{z} = [z_1, z_2, ..., z_n]$. It tends to reconstruct the input vector **x** from **y**. Encoding-decoding formulas are given in Eq. 1 and Eq. 2. They represent the case of a "basic" autoencoder with only one hidden layer:

$$y = \sigma(Wx + b) \tag{1}$$

$$z = \sigma'(W'y + b') \tag{2}$$

where W, W', b and b' are weight matrices and bias vectors, while σ and σ' are activation functions.

Regardless of the architecture, an autoencoder has one primary objective: reconstruct its input as accurately as possible. The goodness of the reconstruction is given by the **reconstruction error** (RE), which measures the difference between the reconstructed, i.e., **z**, and the original version of the input, i.e., **x**:

$$RE = \frac{1}{n} \sum_{i=1}^{n} (z_i - x_i)^2 \tag{3}$$

where z_i and x_i (with $1 \leq i \leq$ n) denote the components of the output and input vector, and n is the dimensionality.

3.2 AE for Classification and Evaluation Metrics

The rationale underlying the use of the AE for classification is that it can be trained to reconstruct a given set of inputs. After training, the autoencoder will reconstruct accurately, i.e., obtaining low RE, future points "similar" to those used for training, while it will reconstruct badly, i.e., obtaining high RE, future points "different" from those used for training.

Threshold Setting. In order to discriminate *good* from *bad* reconstructions we rely on a cutoff threshold value. The **threshold** is the value of RE over which the flows are considered malign. In our first attempts [3], the threshold was set in a supervised manner, reserving a small part of the dataset in hand to obtain an optimal balance between false positives (benign flows falling over the threshold) and false negatives (malign flows under the threshold). In our attempt to set up an autoencoder that never sees malign flows and it is potentially fit to detect any type of attack, we resorted successively to a threshold set at a given percentile of the RE [2]. This approach was not completely satisfactory, because it may produce some false positives. In this paper, thresholds are set *in unsupervised manner* (i.e., without any cognition of the attack flows) by considering the outliers produced in the reconstruction of the benign flows used in the training step.

Evaluation Metrics. The overall performance of the classification is measured by analyzing the typical metrics of *recall* (R), *precision* (P), *false positive rate* (FPR), and *F1 score*. These metrics are computed as follows:

$$R = \frac{TP}{TP + FN} \quad P = \frac{TP}{TP + FP} \tag{4}$$

$$FPR = \frac{FP}{FP + TN} \quad F1\ score = 2 \cdot \frac{P \cdot R}{P + R} \tag{5}$$

where True Positive (TP) and True Negative (TN) represent the points that are correctly classified, while False Positives (FP) and False Negatives (FN) indicate misclassifications. For example, TP is the set of attack points whose RE is higher that the threshold; similarly, TN is the set of normal points whose RE is lower that the threshold.

3.3   Reference Dataset: CICIDS2017

CICIDS2017 is a flow-based dataset based on `CICFlowMeter`[1]. The flows synthesize the characteristics of any interaction between two systems on the net, and can be generated from network captures by many existing tools. `CICFlowMeter` derives from a tool originally conceived to recognize the type of encrypted traffic and provides detailed information on the flow of packets occurring and their timing. Table 1 shows the 83 features associated with a flow by `CICFlowMeter`. It is a fact that this information can be successfully exploited to recognize malign flows, which is the primary aim of an IDS.

Extensive research on erroneously classified flows lead us to discover that often the attack flows contained in CICIDS2017 do not really harm a correctly-configured server [5] and that the flows produced by the original release of the `CICFlowMeter` tool –commonly used in the context of IDS research– contain inexplicable flows. These are actually fragments of an incorrectly truncated flow. A patch to the latter issue was recently provided in [8], along with a new version

---

[1] https://github.com/ahlashkari/CICFlowMeter.

Table 1. The features of a network flow produced by CICFlowMeter

Feature	Short	Feature	Short	Feature	Short
Flow ID	f1	Fwd IAT Std	f29	ECE Flag Count	f57
Source IP	f2	Fwd IAT Max	f30	Down/Up Ratio	f58
Source Port	f3	Fwd IAT Min	f31	Average Packet Size	f59
Destination IP	f4	Bwd IAT Total	f32	Avg Fwd Segment Size	f60
Destination Port	f5	Bwd IAT Mean	f33	Avg Bwd Segment Size	f61
Protocol	f6	Bwd IAT Std	f34	Fwd Avg Bytes/Bulk	f62
Timestamp	f7	Bwd IAT Max	f35	Fwd Avg Packets/Bulk	f63
Flow Duration	f8	Bwd IAT Min	f36	Fwd Avg Bulk Rate	f64
Total Fwd Packets	f9	Fwd PSH Flags	f37	Bwd Avg Bytes/Bulk	f65
Total Backward Packets	f10	Bwd PSH Flags	f38	Bwd Avg Packets/Bulk	f66
Total Length of Fwd Packets	f11	Fwd URG Flags	f39	Bwd Avg Bulk Rate	f67
Total Length of Bwd Packets	f12	Bwd URG Flags	f40	Subflow Fwd Packets	f68
Fwd Packet Length Max	f13	Fwd Header Length	f41	Subflow Fwd Bytes	f69
Fwd Packet Length Min	f14	Bwd Header Length	f42	Subflow Bwd Packets	f70
Fwd Packet Length Mean	f15	Fwd Packets/s	f43	Subflow Bwd Bytes	f71
Fwd Packet Length Std	f16	Bwd Packets/s	f44	Init_Win_bytes_forward	f72
Bwd Packet Length Max	f17	Min Packet Length	f45	Init_Win_bytes_backward	f73
Bwd Packet Length Min	f18	Max Packet Length	f46	act_data_pkt_fwd	f74
Bwd Packet Length Mean	f19	Packet Length Mean	f47	min_seg_size_forward	f75
Bwd Packet Length Std	f20	Packet Length Std	f48	Active Mean	f76
Flow Bytes/s	f21	Packet Length Variance	f49	Active Std	f77
Flow Packets/s	f22	FIN Flag Count	f50	Active Max	f78
Flow IAT Mean	f23	SYN Flag Count	f51	Active Min	f79
Flow IAT Std	f24	RST Flag Count	f52	Idle Mean	f80
Flow IAT Max	f25	PSH Flag Count	f53	Idle Std	f81
Flow IAT Min	f26	ACK Flag Count	f54	Idle Max	f82
Fwd IAT Total	f27	URG Flag Count	f55	Idle Min	f83
Fwd IAT Mean	f28	CWE Flag Count	f56		

of both CICIDS2017 and `CICFlowMeter`: the experimentation presented in this paper is based on the fixed version of CICIDS2017[2].

We consider 490,968 flows related to normal traffic and Denial of Service (DoS) attacks, the CICIDS2017 capture of Wednesday, July 5, 2017. Flows are split into three disjoint subsets used for *training, validation* and *test* by a stratified sampling strategy with no replacement. This means that the ratio between benign and attack classes of the total flows is preserved in the splits. Flows are divided as follows:

- **CICIDS-TRAINING**: *70%* of the total (i.e., 343,680) divided into 223,430 BENIGN and 120,250 ATTACK flows;
- **CICIDS-VALIDATION**: *15%* of the total (i.e., 73,644), divided into 47,877 BENIGN and 25,767 ATTACK flows;
- **CICIDS-TEST**: *15%* of the total (i.e., 73,644), divided into 47,877 BENIGN and 25,767 ATTACK flows.

---

[2] https://downloads.distrinet-research.be/WTMC2021/tools_datasets.html.

4   Proposed IDS Approach with a Single AE

The idea of leveraging a relatively simple neural network and to train it with normative traffic (thus using a *semi-supervised* approach), making it possible to detect intrusions simply because of their divergence from the "normal" behavior the AE was trained on, is indeed fascinating. Our first results, obtained by setting the threshold with a supervised approach (balancing false positives and false negatives on a labeled portion of the dataset) and published in [3], were not so bad (F1 score = 0.942), but inferior to those obtained by supervised detection methods [18]. A successive attempt exploiting three AEs lead to better performance [6].

In the following, we discuss our best practices for setting up an AE for successful intrusion detection, using the above mentioned dataset as case study. It is worth noting that out of the 83 features in Table 1, six of them (f1–f5, f7) can be neglected outright for detection purposes –it is too easy to detect malign flows in a dataset by exploiting the IP of the attacker– as such, the initial experiment is conducted with the 77 features in Table 2. We will demonstrate that even a single-AE design can obtain remarkable results, avoiding unnecessary complications and undue overhead. Along with our indications for AE tuning and set-up, we will outline the research issues still open.

Table 2. Initial features used in experiments

77-features set
f6, f8, f9, f10, f11, f12, f13, f14, f15, f16, f17, f18, f19, f20, f21, f22, f23, f24, f25, f26, f27, f28, f29, f30, f31, f32, f33, f34, f35, f36, f37, f38, f39, f40, f41, f42, f43, f44, f45, f46, f47, f48, f49, f50, f51, f52, f53, f54, f55, f56, f57, f58, f59, f60, f61, f62, f63, f64, f65, f66, f67, f68, f69, f70, f71, f72, f73, f74, f75, f76, f77, f78, f79, f80, f81, f82, f83

4.1   AE Dimensions and Depth

The first step to set-up an AE for intrusion detection is to choose a suitable form factor, i.e., the number of levels and neurons at each level. Given the number of input and output units, which are necessarily equal to the number of features considered, it is necessary to choose the number of hidden levels and the number of units at each level. Unfortunately, there are no rules to guide this choice, and so the only way is to proceed by trial and error.

Almost unexpectedly, we have found that the number of levels and units is not a particularly-critical parameter. It is possible to obtain low RE with three hidden levels (encoding-bottleneck-decoding), or with five hidden levels as well. The only criticality is the number of units at the bottleneck, which have to hold the encoded flow state. In the case of network flow processing considered here we have found the best results by using a bottleneck made of 6 up to 8 units.

In the following, we will always present results relative to a 48-24-8-24-48 *relu* units *deep* AE.

It is interesting to note that there exist frameworks to automatize the search of a "good" network (e.g., *Keras optimizers*). For a simple network such as our AE, we think that the use of extensive optimization procedures is overkill.

4.2   Training and Validation

Unlike the previous step, the modality of training is critical to obtain high detection performance. The AEs we have used for IDS are always trained in *semi-supervised* mode. By semi-supervised training we mean that a subset of the dataset in hand is reserved for training, from which only the normative traffic (*benign* label) is selected: during training, the AE sees no flows related to attacks. Benign flows are presented in input to the AE, whose weights are progressively tuned trying to obtain low RE, i.e., an output as close as possible to the flow presented in input, feature by feature.

The rationale is to instruct the AE to reproduce normative flows, hoping that any divergence with respect to a "benign behavior" could lead to a high reconstruction error, making it possible to recognize attack flows. We will not discuss here if an AE could be some sort of "universal" detector. The issue is tough; however, at the state of the art there is evidence that, even if an AE can be fooled by a hand-crafted or adversarial learning-produced attack, it tends to behave better than supervised networks for unseen attack flows (see for example the experiments reported in [3,4]).

Our AEs are implemented by the ubiquitous deep learning framework *Keras*, which in its turn founds on *Tensorflow*. As for any learning framework, training is based on training-validation sets (i.e., CICIDS-TRAINING and CICIDS-VALIDATION after having filtered out the attack flows). When the training is started, the AE neurons are randomly initialized and input data are presented in batches through a given number of epochs. The system tries to minimize the *loss*, setting aside a small ratio of reserved data to validate the optimization actions performed –modifications of the weights in the network– so as to signal overfitting. A solution is to compute the loss as the mean squared error at the output units; this matches the definition of reconstruction error (RE) above.

> **Issue 1:** The training process is highly dependent on the hardware running Keras/Tensorflow.

Different CPUs (or GPUs) will lead to different schedules of the threads used for optimization in the training phase, and in the end to different weights in the network. The same is true for the *seed* of the pseudo-random generator used for units initialization. This is a physiologic characteristic of machine learning environments as Keras/Tensorflow: while we would expect only a slight variability of the results from run to run due to the seed, this is not the case for a semi-supervised autoencoder to be used for intrusion detection, as shown in the following subsection.

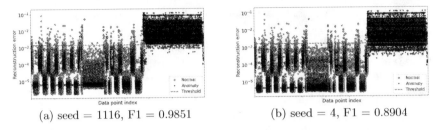

(a) seed = 1116, F1 = 0.9851   (b) seed = 4, F1 = 0.8904

Fig. 2. Reconstruction error for different seed values measured with the test set (CICIDS-TEST).

4.3   Results

It is a fact that all possible trainings on the same input data lead to fairly similar loss values. In other words, whatever the hardware used or the random seed, it works. The bad surprise is that at equal values training losses do not correspond equal abilities to detect malign flows.

Issue 2: A successful training leading to low loss values does not guarantee good classification performance.

Figure 2 shows two plots of the reconstruction error obtained on the CICIDS-TEST file (i.e., the split of benign and malicious flows *held out* from training) by the same AE in perfectly equal conditions, let aside the random seed value. Both networks are perfectly able to recognize benign flows, which are mostly under the threshold. However, in the plot on the right the dots corresponding to malign flows are in a lower position, and so the detection performance is completely unsatisfactory. Simply by changing the seed, the F1 score falls from 0.9851 (a fairly good result) to 0.8904 (an unsatisfactory detection performance). Most notably, the two networks have similar final training loss values (1.2119e−04 and 1.3234e−04, respectively), but different detection performance.

The RE (or the loss measured by *Keras*, which is the same) is a mean of squares, extended to all features. The loss being equal, the contributions of the single features may be distributed differently. Possibly, one of the non-deterministic distribution of weights might lead to high error on the features that are most fit to recognize a given type of attack. There is no possible solution, as the attempt to provide an "universal" detector makes it impossible to assign higher weights to some of the features when computing the loss, simply because we do not know which could be the most relevant features for an unknown or new type of attack.

Issue 3: The seed used to start the random sequence generation matters, in that it leads to different trained models.

This is an open research issue. For the time being, the only viable solution is to validate the training performed using a (labeled) subset of the dataset (the *validation* file reserved for this purpose), and try to change the random seed until

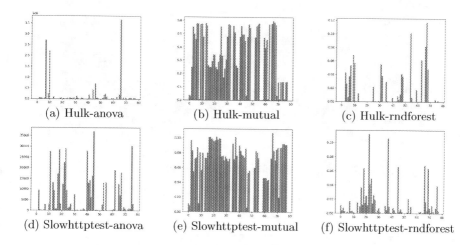

(a) Hulk-anova (b) Hulk-mutual (c) Hulk-rndforest

(d) Slowhttptest-anova (e) Slowhttptest-mutual (f) Slowhttptest-rndforest

Fig. 3. Scores of the 77 features, Hulk and Slowhttptest from USBIDS1 dataset

Table 3. Reduced sets of features used in experiments

67-features set
f6, f8, f9, f10, f11, f12, f13, f14, f15, f16, f17, f18, f19, f20, f21, f22, f23, f24, f25, f26, f27, f28, f29, f30, f31, f32, f33, f34, f35, f36, f37, f41, f42, f43, f44, f45, f46, f47, f48, f49, f50, f51, f52, f53, f54, f55, f57, f58, f59, f60, f61, f68, f69, f70, f71, f72, f73, f74, f75, f76, f77, f78, f79, f80, f81, f82, f83
57-features set
f6, f8, f9, f10, f11, f12, f13, f14, f15, f16, f17, f18, f19, f20, f21, f22, f23, f24, f25, f26, f27, f28, f29, f30, f31, f32, f33, f34, f35, f36, f37, f41, f42, f43, f44, f45, f46, f47, f48, f49, f50, f51, f52, f53, f54, f55, f57, f58, f59, f60, f61, f68, f70, f71, f72, f73, f75
47-features set
f6, f8, f9, f10, f11, f12, f13, f15, f16, f17, f19, f20, f21, f22, f23, f24, f25, f27, f28, f29, f30, f32, f33, f34, f35, f36, f37, f41, f42, f43, f44, f46, f47, f48, f49, f50, f51, f53, f54, f58, f59, f60, f61, f71, f72, f73, f75

satisfactory results are obtained. It is clear that this process leads to a detector able to manage at best the attacks present in the dataset, but that *possibly* could be less successful for different types of attack.

5   Feature Selection

Feature selection techniques are widely used in the intrusion detection context to help obtain higher detection accuracy, neglecting the features which are redundant or statistically do not contribute significantly to the classification of flows. Out of the features listed in Table 1, it is very unlikely that all of them are useful for detection purposes. Sometimes a few ones are constant through all the dataset, and so have no utility for flow classification. Given the problems linked to the mean used to compute the loss discussed in Subsect. 4.3, any reduction of the number of features actually used can help to obtain, being equal the loss, an

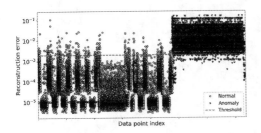 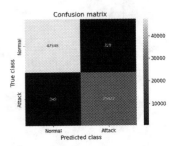

Fig. 4. Reconstruction error and confusion matrix of the 47-features AE

Table 4. Classification performance of the feature sets

	77-features set	67-features set	57-features set	47-features set
R	0.988	0.987	0.986	0.987
P	0.976	0.982	0.984	0.987
FPR	0.013	0.009	0.008	0.007
F1	0.982	0.984	0.985	0.987

AE better tuned to the "significant" features. But, once again, without knowing the characteristic of attacks is not possible to know which features can be useful for malign flow recognition and which are useless.

Figure 3 shows a sample of the results of widely used statistical tests (*ANOVA f-test, mutual information* statistic, *random forest*) performed on different type of attacks[3]. Each histogram reports the scores (y-axis) of the 77 features (x-axis). Higher score means higher contribution to the classification of the flow as a malign one. As can be seen at a glance comparing the histograms, the set of the most relevant features is not uniform across all types of attack, and also depend on the statistical test performed. In light of the above, selecting only some of the 77 features can help detection, but the detector loses "universality", as at least in principle unknown attacks could be spotted by the neglected features. However, a reasonable trade-off can be made by neglecting a small number of features which are ranked in the lowest positions according to the tests performed.

We have tried to discard the lowest-ranked 10, 20 and 30 features, obtaining "reduced" sets of 67, 57 and 47 features, respectively, as shown in Table 3. As expected, reducing the features helps a bit to obtain good classification performance. Table 4 shows the P, R, FPR and F1 values obtained; the best performance is obtained with the 47-features set. Most notably, the reduction of features makes it possible to halve the false positive rate. However, it should be noted that this might involve bad classification performance on unseen attacks (i.e., those not present in the dataset used to compute the feature rankings).

---

[3] Attacks are taken from the USB-IDS-1 dataset.

5.1   Results

As previously shown in Table 4, the best performance results have been obtained by the AE processing 47 features, with seed = 1062 and 90 training epochs. In Fig. 4 we present the graph of the RE over the testing set and corresponding the confusion matrix. Maybe further tuning could help to obtain a slightly higher performance, but at these levels of precision and recall, it is likely to would be simply a waste of time, since the flows misclassified are only 674 (329 + 345) on a total of 73,644 test flows. By the way, many of these flows are "tails" of long-duration flows (namely, those generated by slow DoS attacks) that have been truncated after the standard `CICFlowMeter` timeout of 120 s.

Our figures are comparable with the results obtained on the CICIDS2017 or similar datasets by supervised methods [22] or by AEs as components of more complex classification architectures. For example, the authors of HELAD system [30] –autoencoder combined with a long short-term memory– achieve an F1 score of 0.995. The performance is even worse –F1 score of 0.955 for DoS slowloris– for the approach using memory-augmented deep auto-encoder (MemAE) [19].

In our opinion, resorting to a single "basic" AE without any assistance from other neural networks or complex feature selection methods is a clear advantage in term of simplicity of training and tuning, use of processing power at recognition time. Another strong point of our solution is good adaptability to unknown attacks, as only feature selection –which is just an option, not a strict requirement– requires a minimum notion of the attacks to be detected. A solution as ours requires no powerful or specialized processor, and is amenable to processing large quantity of data in real-time. This is why we claim that "simpler is better" and promote the use of a single autoencoder in future IDS designs.

6   Lessons Learned and Conclusion

In this paper we have explored the use of a single autoencoder to classifly network flows for intrusion detection purposes. We have presented the results of several year of research on this topic, the lessons learned and the open research issues. It is worth summarizing the main lessons learned throughout our research on AE for network flow classification:

- if the AE is developed by *Keras/Tensorflow*, the trained models obtained with the same training data on different computing systems (alternative CPUs or GPUs) are likely to differ;
- the seed used to start the random sequence generation matters, in that leads to different trained models;
- trained models characterized by similar values of loss can be very different as far as their classification performance is concerned. Hence, multiple models should be produced and suitably tested on a validation subset of the dataset so as to make it possible to choose the one with the best performance;

– a rigorous feature selection procedure requires information on the attacks to be detected. If this information is available, discarding scarcely significant features can improve classification accuracy. However, this is obtained at the expense of possible accuracy losses on unconsidered attacks.

The results obtained show that a single AE can obtain classifications accuracy comparable to the ones published in the research literature for supervised networks and for more complex designs built around one or several AEs. Our single autoencoder detection scheme is less probe to transferability problems than supervised schemes and can be more easily tuned and managed than designs adopting AE as components.

The accuracy results obtained on the CICIDS2017 dataset leave little room for further improvements. Our future research will oriented to the study of a training procedure and to the production of normative training data able to pave the way to the set up of an autoencoder able to recognize even unseen attack flows with reasonable accuracy.

References

1. Catillo, M., Del Vecchio, A., Ocone, L., Pecchia, A., Villano, U.: USB-IDS-1: a public multilayer dataset of labeled network flows for IDS evaluation. In: Proceedings International Conference on Dependable Systems and Networks Workshops (DSN-W), pp. 1–6. IEEE (2021)
2. Catillo, M., Pecchia, A., Villano, U.: AutoLog: anomaly detection by deep autoencoding of system logs. Expert Syst. Appl. **191**, 116263 (2022)
3. Catillo, M., Rak, M., Villano, U.: Discovery of DoS attacks by the ZED-IDS anomaly detector. J. High Speed Netw. **25**(4), 349–365 (2019)
4. Catillo, M., Del Vecchio, A., Pecchia, A., Villano, U.: Transferability of machine learning models learned from public intrusion detection datasets: the CICIDS2017 case study. Softw. Qual. J. (2022). https://doi.org/10.1007/s11219-022-09587-0
5. Catillo, M., Pecchia, A., Rak, M., Villano, U.: Demystifying the role of public intrusion datasets: a replication study of DoS network traffic data. Comput. Secur. **108**, 102341 (2021)
6. Catillo, M., Rak, M., Villano, U.: 2L-ZED-IDS: a two-level anomaly detector for multiple attack classes. In: Barolli, L., Amato, F., Moscato, F., Enokido, T., Takizawa, M. (eds.) WAINA 2020. AISC, vol. 1150, pp. 687–696. Springer, Cham (2020). https://doi.org/10.1007/978-3-030-44038-1_63
7. Dina, A.S., Manivannan, D.: Intrusion detection based on machine learning techniques in computer networks. Internet Things **16**, 100462 (2021)
8. Engelen, G., Rimmer, V., Joosen, W.: Troubleshooting an intrusion detection dataset: the CICIDS2017 case study. In: 2021 IEEE Security and Privacy Workshops (SPW), pp. 7–12. IEEE (2021)
9. Feng, S., Duarte, M.F.: Graph regularized autoencoder-based unsupervised feature selection. In: Proceedings International Conference on Signals, Systems, and Computers, pp. 55–59. IEEE (2018)
10. Goodfellow, I., Bengio, Y., Courville, A.: Deep Learning. MIT Press, Cambridge (2016)

11. Jiang, J., Han, G., Liu, L., Shu, L., Guizani, M.: Outlier detection approaches based on machine learning in the Internet-of-Things. IEEE Wirel. Commun. **27**(3), 53–59 (2020)
12. Khraisat, A., Gondal, I., Vamplew, P., Kamruzzaman, J.: Survey of intrusion detection systems: techniques, datasets and challenges. Cybersecurity **2**(1), 1–22 (2019). https://doi.org/10.1186/s42400-019-0038-7
13. Kilincer, I., Ertam, F., Sengur, A.: Machine learning methods for cyber security intrusion detection: datasets and comparative study. Comput. Netw. **188**, 107840 (2021)
14. Kramer, M.A.: Nonlinear principal component analysis using autoassociative neural networks. AIChE J. **37**(2), 233–243 (1991)
15. Kunang, Y.N., Nurmaini, S., Stiawan, D., Zarkasi, A., Firdaus, Jasmir: Automatic features extraction using autoencoder in intrusion detection system. In: Proceedings International Conference on Electrical Engineering and Computer Science (ICECOS), pp. 219–224. IEEE (2018)
16. Kwon, D., Kim, H., Kim, J., Suh, S.C., Kim, I., Kim, K.J.: A survey of deep learning-based network anomaly detection. Clust. Comput. **22**(1), 949–961 (2017). https://doi.org/10.1007/s10586-017-1117-8
17. Maciá-Fernández, G., Camacho, J., Magán-Carrión, R., García-Teodoro, P., Therón, R.: UGR'16: a new dataset for the evaluation of cyclostationarity-based network IDSs. Comput. Secur. **73**, 411–424 (2017)
18. Maseer, Z.K., Yusof, R., Bahaman, N., Mostafa, S.A., Foozy, C.F.M.: Benchmarking of machine learning for anomaly based intrusion detection systems in the CICIDS2017 dataset. IEEE Access **9**, 22351–22370 (2021)
19. Min, B., Yoo, J., Kim, S., Shin, D., Shin, D.: Network anomaly detection using memory-augmented deep autoencoder. IEEE Access **9**, 104695–104706 (2021)
20. Mirsky, Y., Doitshman, T., Elovici, Y., Shabtai, A.: Kitsune: an ensemble of autoencoders for online network intrusion detection. In: Proceedings International Conference of Network and Distributed System Security Symposium (NDSS) (2018)
21. Moustafa, N., Slay, J.: UNSW-NB15: a comprehensive data set for network intrusion detection systems (UNSW-NB15 network data set). In: Proceedings International Conference Military Communications and Information Systems Conference, pp. 1–6. IEEE (2015)
22. Panigrahi, R., et al.: Performance assessment of supervised classifiers for designing intrusion detection systems: a comprehensive review and recommendations for future research. Mathematics **9**(6), 690 (2021)
23. Ring, M., Wunderlich, S., Scheuring, D., Landes, D., Hotho, A.: A survey of network-based intrusion detection data sets. Comput. Secur. **86**, 147–167 (2019)
24. Sharafaldin, I., Lashkari, A.H., Ghorbani., A.A.: Toward generating a new intrusion detection dataset and intrusion traffic characterization. In: Proceedings International Conference on Information Systems Security and Privacy, pp. 108–116. SciTePress (2018)
25. Taher, K.A., Mohammed Yasin Jisan, B., Rahman, M.M.: Network intrusion detection using supervised machine learning technique with feature selection. In: Proceedings International Conference on Robotics, Electrical and Signal Processing Techniques (ICREST). IEEE (2019)
26. Thakur, S., Chakraborty, A., De, R., Kumar, N., Sarkar, R.: Intrusion detection in cyber-physical systems using a generic and domain specific deep autoencoder model. Comput. Electr. Eng. **91**, 107044 (2021)

27. Vincent, P., Larochelle, H., Lajoie, I., Bengio, Y., Manzagol, P.A.: Stacked denoising autoencoders: learning useful representations in a deep network with a local denoising criterion. J. Mach. Learn. Res. **11**, 3371–3408 (2010)
28. Wei-Chao, L., Shih-Wen, K., Chih-Fong, T.: CANN: an intrusion detection system based on combining cluster centers and nearest neighbors. Knowl. Based Syst. **78**, 13–21 (2015)
29. XuKui, L., Wei, C., Qianru, Z., Lifa, W.: Building auto-encoder intrusion detection system based on random forest feature selection. Comput. Secur. **95**, 101851 (2020)
30. Zhong, Y., et al.: HELAD: a novel network anomaly detection model based on heterogeneous ensemble learning. Comput. Netw. **169** (2020)

A Proposal for FPGA-Accelerated Deep Learning Ensembles in MPSoC Platforms Applied to Malware Detection

Alessandro Cilardo[ID], Vincenzo Maisto[✉][ID], Nicola Mazzocca[ID],
and Franca Rocco di Torrepadula[ID]

Department of Electrical Engineering and Information Technologies (DIETI),
University of Naples Federico II, Naples, Italy
{acilardo,vincenzo.maisto2,nicola.mazzocca,
franca.roccoditorrepadula}@unina.it

Abstract. Ensembles of Deep Neural Networks can be profitably employed to improve the overall network performance in a range of applications, including for example online malware detection performed by edge computing systems. In such edge applications, which are often dominated by inference operations, FPGA-based MPSoC platforms may play a competitive role compared to GPU devices because of higher energy efficiency. Furthermore, their hardware reconfiguration capabilities offer a perfect match with the requirement of model diversity posed by Ensemble Learning. This exploratory short paper presents a research plan towards an FPGA-based MPSoC platform exploiting dynamic partial reconfiguration in edge systems for accelerating Deep Learning Ensembles. We present the background and the main rationale behind our envisioned architecture. We also present a preliminary security analysis discussing possible threats and vulnerabilities along with the mitigations enabled by the architecture we plan to develop.

Keywords: Deep learning ensemble · MPSoC · FPGA · Malware detection

1 Introduction

Deep Neural Networks (DNNs) have today become ubiquitous. Emerging approaches towards improved performance in DNNs include solutions based on combining outputs from different networks by voting or more sophisticated approaches. The combined use of different models is referred to as *Ensemble Learning* (EL) and has been explored in different domains, as model diversity featured by EL enables more accurate and robust results. Among other application domains, DNNs have been applied to security-related tasks, such as malware detection [13,17]. EL can bring significant benefits in this field, as it can help reduce false negatives and detect more complex attacks. In that respect,

© The Author(s), under exclusive license to Springer Nature Switzerland AG 2022
A. Vallecillo et al. (Eds.): QUATIC 2022, CCIS 1621, pp. 239–249, 2022.
https://doi.org/10.1007/978-3-031-14179-9_16

online malware detection is an important application area for *Edge Computing* (EC) systems, referring to systems placed at the edge of a distributed networked infrastructure. In this work, we focus on dedicated acceleration of Deep Learning computing tasks. While Graphics Processing Units (GPUs) are the leading technology for DNN acceleration in high-end general-purpose computing environments, Field-Programmable Gate Arrays (FPGAs) have proven to be competitive in terms of energy efficiency for edge applications dominated by DNN inference. Furthermore, hardware reconfiguration capabilities offered by FPGAs provide a perfect match with the requirement of model diversity posed by Ensemble Learning.

Driven by the above considerations, this exploratory short paper presents a research plan towards an FPGA-based Multi-Processor System-on-Chip (MPSoC) platform exploiting dynamic partial reconfiguration in edge systems for accelerating Deep Learning Ensembles, with possible applications to online malware detection. We analyse the state of the art and observe that current FPGA-based MPSoC platforms support fully fledged software stacks, even including virtualization. Based on that, we aim at a scenario where run-time hardware reconfigurability is exploited in a hypervisor-based hardware/software co-designed architecture to offer a pool of virtualized functionalities, which are loaded on-demand to the FPGA fabric [15,22]. Indeed, as we discuss in the paper, virtualization can provide support for isolation at the platform level, a key security property improving the attack confinement capabilities of the architecture. We anticipate the possible adoption of Virtual Machine Introspection (VMI) techniques to collect data related to the execution of user Virtual Machines (VMs) [8], then analysed through DNNs or Ensembles of DNNs to detect anomalies, e.g., malware or intrusions [3].

The rest of the paper is organised as follows. Section 2 describes the background that is relevant for our proposal, including Ensemble Learning, DNN-based solutions for malware detection, and state-of-the-art platforms for DNN acceleration in edge applications. Section 3 presents the hardware/software architecture we envision for our research plan, along with a preliminary security analysis discussing possible threats and mitigation strategies. Finally, Sect. 4 concludes the paper with a few final remarks.

2 Preliminaries and Related Works

2.1 Ensemble Learning

Although Deep Learning techniques are able to obtain considerable levels of accuracy, Neural Networks (NNs) are still prone to mistakes. *Ensemble Learning* [21] is a way to address this issue by combining the outputs of several NNs through voting or more sophisticated operations. The benefit of Ensemble Learning can be explained through the *bias-variance decomposition*, in which the error of a Machine Learning model can be calculated as the sum of three terms, namely: the *bias*, caused by erroneous assumptions in the learning algorithm; the *variance*, related to an excessive sensitivity of the model to the variations of the training set; the *irreducible error*, resulting from noise in the problem itself, which cannot be avoided. In order to increase the model performance we need to reduce the bias, by better fitting the data, and the variance, by reducing the overfitting. To achieve this objective, EL combines several models that are different in terms of structure/technique or the training set [9]. Several policies are available to combine models' outputs. The easiest way is majority voting, in which the output class is the one predicted by the majority of models. In case of numeric outputs, a simple strategy is computing the average of the outputs. On the other hand, a more complex solution is stacking Ensemble Learning, where the output aggregator is another learner, namely the metalearner.

Ensemble Learning for Malware Detection. Malwares are malicious softwares designed to exploit vulnerabilities of computer systems, with the intention of altering core functions, stealing or corrupting sensitive data, or monitoring users activities [13,17]. Several Machine Learning techniques have been applied to malware detection. They can be broadly classified into a *static* and a *dynamic* approach: the former analyses malware code without executing it, the latter executes the malware to analyse its behavior [1]. However, the use of Machine Learning requires a phase of feature engineering, preliminary to the classification step, which is time consuming and can be easily invalidated by small changes in malwares [24]. Deep Learning can mitigate this problem, as it automatically performs feature extraction [23]. Furthermore, Nataraj et al. [14] demonstrated that: 1) a malware binary file can be represented as a grey scale image; 2) through this representation, malwares of the same family have common visual pattern. Based on this result, Convolutional Neural Networks (CNNs) can be effectively exploited for malware detection, by setting the problem as an image-classification one [13]. Nevertheless, selecting the best model for a specific problem is a complex task and the variety of possible malwares may potentially degrade the effectiveness of a trained model. Therefore, EL can be effective also in this domain, as it permits combining multiple models to improve performance [21]. For instance, Sang et al. [17] use different methods to extract features from portable executable files, and then DNNs with different structural complexity to detect malwares. The DNN output, i.e. the probability values, are combined by computing their average. Saharkizan et al. [16] designed a system to detect cyber-attacks against IoT systems. They integrate a set of Long Short-Term Memory (LSTM) modules, and then merge their outputs using a decision tree. Last, Yan et al. [24] extract different malware representation (i.e., greyscale image and opcode sequence) and combine the CNN and the LSTM to detect malware. On the one hand, by using the CNN they learn from the greyscale image. On the other hand, with LSTM they analyse the opcode sequence. The DNN outputs are then combined with a *stacking* Ensemble approach.

Ensemble Learning at the Edge. The *Edge Computing* paradigm refers to technologies allowing computation to be performed at the edge of the network, on downstream data on behalf of cloud services and upstream data on behalf of

IoT services [19]. The main advantages is the reduction of network overhead and latency. For this reason, some studies propose approaches to employ Ensemble Learning at the edge, whenever the latency caused by the cloud is not acceptable for the task to be performed. For example, in [25] the authors use EL at the edge for anomaly detection in e-healthcare systems. They combine weak classifiers selected with a Classification and Regression Tree classifier (a type of decision tree algorithm) by majority voting. In [2], an Ensemble of DNNs is used for image classification on IoT devices. To deal with the limited resources of an IoT environment, the authors use pruned DNNs.

2.2   Deep Learning Hardware Solutions

GPUs have become the leading hardware technology for Deep Learning algorithms. However, GPUs are energy-hungry devices and are not viable for applications with limited energy budgets. Ensemble techniques further increase requirements in terms of computation, hence energy consumption. This poses a potential limitation to the use of Deep Learning in the embedded realm. In order to replace GPUs, matrix/tensor co-processors from industry (i.e., Google TPUs) and academia [5] have been developed and matrix extensions [12] have been added to Intel® ISA for server processors. Albeit effective in their respective fields of application, these approaches do not match the requirements of an embedded system.

Quantization. Deep Learning applications require the movement of large amounts of data, which causes increased energy consumption. Reducing the volume can thus simultaneously boost performance and energy efficiency. A common approach in this direction is network *quantization*. Such technique consists in reducing the precision of the data types for the network weights and biases, from floating-point to fixed-point, short integers, and even binary values, i.e., Binarized Neural Networks (BNNs) [6]. This approach can be adopted in the training and/or inference phase. Other techniques, like pruning, layer merging, and parameter sharing can be also used to reduce the computational needs and the energy consumption of the network.

Implementing DNNs on FPGAs. During the last years FPGA technologies have made their entrance in the Deep Learning domain. Hardware reconfiguration makes them a good candidate for synthesizing Deep Learning co-processors, although the number of logic and memory elements available for synthesis limits its parallelism and performance. In that respect, quantization can help reduce synthesis requirements of a co-processor, increasing energy efficiency and performance. Targeted at edge applications, current FPGA-based MPSoC platforms provide tight integration of general-purpose CPUs and the reconfigurable hardware fabric, enabling lower energy consumption and simplifying collaborative CPU-FPGA computation. Although FPGAs can be used for both training and inference, they are best fit for inference when the model is deployed on the field, while training is performed offline. There are two main approaches for implementing DNNs accelerators on FPGAs: 1) instruction-based programmable co-processors, or 2) model-specific hardware accelerators. The former allows us to re-use the same device for the execution of a stream of instructions, compiled from a DNN model. The latter can only execute one model. This poses a trade-off as a more specialised accelerator can deliver better performance in terms of execution time and energy consumption, while a more general co-processor offers greater programmability. Examples of frameworks from Xilinx® include Vitis-AI[1] featuring the Deep Learning Processing Unit (DPU) programmable solution, and the FINN framework [20], supporting the synthesis of specialised BNNs accelerators. Both of these approaches use quantization and only support CNNs. Above we mentioned how RNNs, and LSTMs in particular, are also relevant Deep Learning schemes for malware detection. Similarly to CNNs, FPGA accelerators for RNNs have been proposed in the literature, e.g., [10]. The hardware logic for CNNs and RNNs is inherently different and, typically, FPGA-based accelerators do not support both CNNs and RNNs at the same time. The interested reader can refer to [4] for a detailed discussion.

Dynamic Partial Reconfiguration. FPGAs can be fully reconfigured at run-time for deploying another instance of an accelerator. The downside of this approach is that the timing overhead of full configuration can be nonnegligible. Modern FPGAs support Dynamic Partial Configuration (DPR), allowing reconfiguration of a subset of the device with lower time overheads. DPR has been used in several research works to time-multiplex layers of DNNs on an FPGA [7,18]. In this exploratory paper, we propose the use of DPR to enlarge the pool of hardware functionalities, rather than fit larger models, while at the same time reducing the reconfiguration time. Such feature will enable the acceleration of CNNs and RNNs on the same integrated platform. In order to increase the portability and extensibility of our design, we plan to use the *Linux FPGA Manager driver*[2] to handle partial and full reconfiguration. This will allow us to possibly contribute to the Linux project and port our hardware/software design on FPGA architectures from different models and vendors.

Deep Learning Ensembles on FPGA. Most of the work in the literature concerning the implementation of DNN accelerators on FPGAs focuses on the execution of a single DNN per run. Supporting ensembles of DNNs, presented in Sect. 2.1, requires the capability of executing a pool of heterogeneous DNNs. In edge settings, FPGAs are a preferred solution compared to GPUs because of reduced energy requirements, while DPR can enable a pool of diverse DNNs to be integrated in the same platform by changing the hardware functionality at run-time with minimal overhead. Furthermore, FPGA-based MPSoC platforms support fully fledged software stacks, even including *virtualization*. In server settings, virtualization of accelerators has been explored [15,22], e.g. by means of Single Root I/O Virtualization (SR-IOV) technology of PCI Express®, letting physical devices expose Virtual Functions, internally mapped to Physical Functions, each assigned by the Hypervisor to a single Virtual Machine. Likewise, we

---

[1] https://www.xilinx.com/products/design-tools/vitis/vitis-ai.html.
[2] https://www.kernel.org/doc/html/v4.19/driver-api/fpga/fpga-mgr.html.

envision a scenario where a virtualization layer in the MPSoC platform will support multiple DNN acceleration Virtual Functions, which time-share the FPGA fabric, assigned by the Hypervisor to one of multiple user Virtual Machines.

3   A Proposal for an FPGA-Based MPSoC EL Platform

This exploratory short paper is aimed to define a research plan towards an FPGA-based MPSoC platform exploiting DPR for accelerating Deep Learning Ensembles. In this section, we describe the envisioned hardware/software architecture and a preliminary vulnerability analysis. We address a situation where different applications/processes run on the same system, each being a potential target of a malware. The considerable degree of diversity in this scenario encourages the use of an Ensemble of DNNs, as discussed earlier. In principle, each DNN model would require a different co-processor. Furthermore, we aim to confine a malware affecting an application, preventing it from impacting other applications. Therefore, we identify the following key requirements for our architecture (Fig. 1):

1. offer a rich pool of diverse DNN accelerators;
2. provide secure access to them;
3. securely isolate applications;
4. support monitoring of applications with Deep Learning techniques;
5. deploy the architecture on a compact and integrated hardware platform;
6. limit the complexity of the software ecosystem.

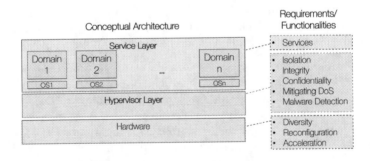

Fig. 1. Conceptual architecture and functionalities provided per layer.

3.1   System Architecture

This section provides a detailed discussion of the various components of the envisioned architecture (depicted in Fig. 2(a)) and anticipates the technical challenges for the future developments of our planned research.

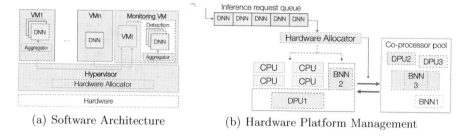

(a) Software Architecture   (b) Hardware Platform Management

Fig. 2. Details of the proposed architecture.

Hypervisor-Based Architecture. We envision a hypervisor-based architecture since virtualization technologies, like para- or full-virtualization, provide isolation among VMs, integrity, and confidentiality of data and computation. User applications will be deployed in User VMs. The latter are considered untrusted entities, as they might threat both other VMs and the hardware platform itself. By using virtualization, we plan to improve the confinement capabilities of the platform in case of a malware attack to a specific user VM. We discard container-based virtualization, like Docker or Linux Containers (LXC), since it lacks isolation between containers and introduces a nonnegligible complexity for device virtualization. Separation-based hypervisors, like Jailhouse, are also not fit for our device-sharing requirements. The hardware would be statically assigned to VMs, and once a VM is launched, in a so-called *cell*, the hypervisor loses control on the resources assigned to it. Although we plan to use FPGA-level virtualization, the complexity behind sharing physical resources by mapping statically assigned virtual devices is out of the scope of our proposal. Last, the device virtualization capabilities available in the software stack of state-of-the-art MPSoC platforms offer a perfect framework for heterogeneous accelerator virtualization. As for traditional device virtualization, we plan a split-driver architecture.

Detection Module. The detection module is in charge of performing malware detection with advanced Deep Learning techniques, used within an Ensemble learning approach, as discussed earlier. Note that if the detection module were deployed in a User VM, it could easily become the target of a malware tampering with the VM. For this reason, we envision the deployment of the detection module in a privileged VM, namely the *Monitoring VM*. In this way, thanks to the isolation enforced by the hypervisor, an attacker is precluded from targeting this module from within a User VM. One technical option enabled by the use of a Monitoring VM is the ability to detect malware by inspecting VM performance and resource utilization metrics, obtained through *Virtual Machine Introspection* [3], a technique for monitoring the activity of VMs as a black box, e.g., from a privileged VM [11]. VMI will thus be considered as a technique supporting intrusion/malware detection in our plan.

Hardware Platform Management. In Sect. 2.2 we outlined the potential of FPGA-based MPSoC platforms matching the key requirement of DNN accelerator *diversity*. We plan to leverage the support for DPR and virtualization to offer a variety of DNN accelerators on the same hardware with time-sharing access to the FPGA fabric. The envisioned architecture can be integrated in a single FPGA-based MPSoC hardware platform, avoiding the complexity of external acceleration management and hence improving energy efficiency.

Hardware Allocator. The hardware platform is managed by the *hardware allocator*, responsible for DNN accelerators. It works as a proxy in a client-proxy-server driver architecture. Client VMs submit DNN inference requests to the module, which forwards each request to the low-level driver of a compatible accelerator or, potentially, to an available CPU in case of software emulation. As soon as a request is assigned to a hardware accelerator, it is immediately served in case the accelerator is already available on the FPGA. Otherwise, exploiting DPR the FPGA fabric is reconfigured with the required hardware design, loaded from an external memory in the form a bitstream, and then the request is served. Figure 2(b) also shows how inference requests are fed to the hardware allocator through a queue, which is in charge of enforcing priorities and security policies. The key requirement is to maximise the utilization of the currently loaded co-processor, while enforcing possibly conflicting security policies. Reconfiguration operations are time-consuming and should be minimised by proper scheduling, i.e., performed in idle FPGA cycles. As part of our research plan, we will carefully evaluate the timing overheads and reliability implications of frequent reconfiguration operations.

3.2   Preliminary Security Analysis

This section discusses possible attacks, threats and vulnerabilities our system might face, along with proposed mitigations and trade-offs.

First, as mentioned in Sect. 3.1, the proposal of a hypervisor-based architecture ensures isolation among VMs, integrity, and confidentiality of data. Furthermore, the deployment of the detection module in a privileged monitoring VM precludes an attacker from targeting this module from within a User VM. The VMI mechanism is employed to inspect the performance and resource utilization metrics of VMs, from the outside, in order to perform malware detection.

Denial of Service (DoS). Exposing the same hardware and accelerators to untrusted User VMs threats the availability of the platform. Therefore, we must reserve a finite amount of bandwidth for inference requests to each VM and prioritise requests of privileged VMs over User VMs. Furthermore, user inference operations will be completely preemptable. This is in contrast with those of the Monitoring VM, which have to be prioritised and served with a larger and granted bandwidth. This conservative approach causes a quality of service degradation for User inference, as they are served with a best effort policy, but it is necessary to allow the sharing of resources and defend from malicious behaviours.

A malicious user might try to stall or slow down the system with maliciously designed data which he/she can place in memory. Therefore, a *kill switch* will be added to inference requests. Such behaviour can be easily implemented with a reset sequence. This poses a requirement on the interface of the accelerators, which must always provide an effective and efficient reset interface.

We choose to disallow the synthesis of custom designs on the FPGA fabric. If this were the case, a malicious user could corrupt the state of the underlying hardware, e.g., by indefinitely stalling its own inference requests with the help of its custom hardware design. A time bound on the inference time could not be enforced, since the reset signal could be ignored by the malicious accelerator.

Side-channel attacks are theoretically possible from several sources:

State of the Accelerators. A possible mitigation is to force a reset sequence on the accelerator at the beginning of each User inference request. Depending on the type of accelerator, the states it holds might not be a security asset. For accelerators where this is the case, the reset sequence can also be a simple stop operation for the kill switch discussed above.

Parallel Execution of Several Accelerators. Depending on the hardware requirements of each design, two or more accelerators could be accommodated in the FPGA fabric at the same time, and executed in parallel. We choose to disallow this for both performance and security-related reasons. FPGA-based MPSoC platforms usually offer a single memory interface from the FPGA to memory. Parallel execution of accelerators will cause interference and performance degradation. More importantly, this also violates the user-isolation requirement of a virtualized system.

Service Time of the Inference. An attacker could derive the reconfiguration time of the FPGA fabric by measuring the service time of its requests. Such information could expose the single accelerator and the Ensemble configuration. In case this information is sensitive, a mitigation technique is necessary: the service time of User inference requests will have to be forced to a constant value with respect to the particular data input or the DNN required. This approach is conservative and causes a significant performance degradation, as the enforced constant time must account for the longest reconfiguration-inference time among the available accelerators. Therefore, in our plan this feature will be optional.

4   Conclusion

This exploratory short paper draws a research plan towards an FPGA-based MPSoC platform exploiting dynamic partial reconfiguration in edge systems for accelerating Deep Learning Ensembles, with possible applications to online malware detection. We analysed the security and functional requirements of such a platform and discussed the opportunities and challenges posed by its implementation. We also presented a preliminary security analysis discussing possible threats and mitigation strategies. A central aspect of the envisioned architecture lies in its hypervisor-based organization, enabling malware detection and monitoring strategies such as Virtual Machine Introspection. Virtualization will also support the effective management of a rich pool of DNN accelerators to be used for Ensemble Learning, and will enable isolation at the platform level as a key security property improving attack confinement capabilities.

Acknowledgements. This work was partly founded by the PON "Ricerca e Innovazione" 2014–2020, Azione IV.5, Ministerial Decree n. 1061 of the Italian Ministry of University and Research.

References

1. Abdelsalam, M., Krishnan, R., Huang, Y., Sandhu, R.: Malware detection in cloud infrastructures using convolutional neural networks. In: 2018 IEEE 11th International Conference on Cloud Computing (CLOUD), pp. 162–169. IEEE (2018)
2. Alhalabi, B., Gaber, M.M., Basura, S.: MicroNets: a multi-phase pruning pipeline to deep ensemble learning in IoT devices. Comput. Electr. Eng. **96**, 107581 (2021)
3. Azmandian, F., Moffie, M., Alshawabkeh, M., Dy, J., Aslam, J., Kaeli, D.: Virtual machine monitor-based lightweight intrusion detection. ACM SIGOPS Oper. Syst. Rev. **45**(2), 38–53 (2011)
4. Blaiech, A.G., Khalifa, K.B., Valderrama, C., Fernandes, M.A., Bedoui, M.H.: A survey and taxonomy of FPGA-based deep learning accelerators. J. Syst. Architect. **98**, 331–345 (2019)
5. Chen, Y.H., Krishna, T., Emer, J.S., Sze, V.: Eyeriss: an energy-efficient reconfigurable accelerator for deep convolutional neural networks. IEEE J. Solid-State Circuits **52**(1), 127–138 (2017). https://doi.org/10.1109/JSSC.2016.2616357
6. Courbariaux, M., Hubara, I., Soudry, D., El-Yaniv, R., Bengio, Y.: Binarized neural networks: training deep neural networks with weights and activations constrained to +1 or −1 (2016). https://doi.org/10.48550/ARXIV.1602.02830
7. Farhadi, M., Ghasemi, M., Yang, Y.: A novel design of adaptive and hierarchical convolutional neural networks using partial reconfiguration on FPGA. In: 2019 IEEE High Performance Extreme Computing Conference (HPEC), pp. 1–7 (2019). https://doi.org/10.1109/HPEC.2019.8916237
8. Garfinkel, T., Rosenblum, M., et al.: A virtual machine introspection based architecture for intrusion detection. In: NDSS, vol. 3, pp. 191–206. Citeseer (2003)
9. Geman, S., Bienenstock, E., Doursat, R.: Neural networks and the bias/variance dilemma. Neural Comput. **4**(1), 1–58 (1992)
10. Guan, Y., Yuan, Z., Sun, G., Cong, J.: FPGA-based accelerator for long short-term memory recurrent neural networks. In: 2017 22nd Asia and South Pacific Design Automation Conference (ASP-DAC), pp. 629–634 (2017). https://doi.org/10.1109/ASPDAC.2017.7858394
11. Hebbal, Y., Laniepce, S., Menaud, J.M.: Virtual machine introspection: techniques and applications. In: 2015 10th International Conference on Availability, Reliability and Security, pp. 676–685. IEEE (2015)
12. Intel®: Intel® Architecture Instruction Set Extensions and Future Features (2021)
13. Kalash, M., Rochan, M., Mohammed, N., Bruce, N.D., Wang, Y., Iqbal, F.: Malware classification with deep convolutional neural networks. In: 2018 9th IFIP International Conference on New Technologies, Mobility and Security (NTMS), pp. 1–5. IEEE (2018)
14. Nataraj, L., Karthikeyan, S., Jacob, G., Manjunath, B.S.: Malware images: visualization and automatic classification. In: Proceedings of the 8th International Symposium on Visualization for Cyber Security, pp. 1–7 (2011)

15. Pinneterre, S., Chiotakis, S., Paolino, M., Raho, D.: vFPGAmanager: a virtualization framework for orchestrated FPGA accelerator sharing in 5G cloud environments. In: 2018 IEEE International Symposium on Broadband Multimedia Systems and Broadcasting (BMSB), pp. 1–5 (2018). https://doi.org/10.1109/BMSB.2018.8436930

16. Saharkhizan, M., Azmoodeh, A., Dehghantanha, A., Choo, K.K.R., Parizi, R.M.: An ensemble of deep recurrent neural networks for detecting IoT cyber attacks using network traffic. IEEE Internet Things J. 7(9), 8852–8859 (2020)

17. Sang, D.V., Cuong, D.M., Cuong, L.T.B.: An effective ensemble deep learning framework for malware detection. In: Proceedings of the Ninth International Symposium on Information and Communication Technology, pp. 192–199 (2018)

18. Seyoum, B., Pagani, M., Biondi, A., Balleri, S., Buttazzo, G.: Spatio-temporal optimization of deep neural networks for reconfigurable FPGA SoCs. IEEE Trans. Comput. 70(11), 1988–2000 (2021). https://doi.org/10.1109/TC.2020.3033730

19. Shi, W., Cao, J., Zhang, Q., Li, Y., Xu, L.: Edge computing: vision and challenges. IEEE Internet Things J. 3(5), 637–646 (2016)

20. Umuroglu, Y., et al.: FINN: a framework for fast, scalable binarized neural network inference. In: Proceedings of the 2017 ACM/SIGDA International Symposium on Field-Programmable Gate Arrays. ACM, February 2017. https://doi.org/10.1145/3020078.3021744

21. Vanerio, J., Casas, P.: Ensemble-learning approaches for network security and anomaly detection. In: Proceedings of the Workshop on Big Data Analytics and Machine Learning for Data Communication Networks, pp. 1–6 (2017)

22. Vu, D.V., Sander, O., Sandmann, T., Baehr, S., Heidelberger, J., Becker, J.: Enabling partial reconfiguration for coprocessors in mixed criticality multicore systems using PCI express single-root I/O virtualization. In: 2014 International Conference on ReConFigurable Computing and FPGAs (ReConFig14), pp. 1–6 (2014). https://doi.org/10.1109/ReConFig.2014.7032516

23. Xiao, Y., Xing, C., Zhang, T., Zhao, Z.: An intrusion detection model based on feature reduction and convolutional neural networks. IEEE Access 7, 42210–42219 (2019)

24. Yan, J., Qi, Y., Rao, Q.: Detecting malware with an ensemble method based on deep neural network. Secur. Commun. Netw. 2018, 1–16 (2018)

25. Yao, W., Zhang, K., Yu, C., Zhao, H.: Exploiting ensemble learning for edge-assisted anomaly detection scheme in e-healthcare system. In: 2021 IEEE Global Communications Conference (GLOBECOM), pp. 1–7. IEEE (2021)

Automated Threat Modeling Approaches: Comparison of Open Source Tools

Daniele Granata[✉][iD], Massimiliano Rak[iD], and Giovanni Salzillo[iD]

Department of Engineering, University of Campania Luigi Vanvitelli, via Roma 29,
81031 Aversa, CE, Italy
{daniele.granata,massimiliano.rak,giovanni.salzillo}@unicampania.it

Abstract. The software systems of modern architectures are characterized by high heterogeneity and by the use of a model that delegates the control of individual components to third parties, making these systems more vulnerable to cyber-attacks. As a consequence, best practices, such as the Security-by-Design development methodologies, suggest taking into account security all over the systems life cycle, starting from the very early stages (e.g. from initial requirement analysis). Thus, one of the most relevant practices is Threat Modeling (TM), i.e. the activity devoted to identifying the possible threats that may affect the system. According to most security-related best practices, TM should be done as early as possible, in order to help in the requirement elicitation. Threat Modeling is a complex activity, that requires security experts with consolidated skills, able to predict and anticipate the possible issues: as a consequence, it is a costly activity, both in terms of time and money. Due to the continuous need of enforcing security, the effect of new regulation and the wide diffusion of ICT systems, there is a recent growth of tools and techniques that support and aims at automatizing Threat modelling activities. This work illustrates the approach adopted by our research team and compares the results of our technique with two other existing tools, in order to offer a brief overview of the state of the art of threat modelling automation techniques and of state of art limits and open research topics. It is worth noting that our comparison does not aims at being complete and focuses only on open tools (or on their free/community version), but offers a basis for understanding the progress of security automation processes in terms of threat modelling.

Keywords: Security · Threat modelling · Security assessment

1 Introduction

Nowadays, Software systems are more and more complex and heterogeneous. Due to the widespread use of such IT solutions, the process of ensuring their security has become a strong requirement, as evidenced by the new regulations (e.g. GDPR, Cybersecurity Act) that impose hard privacy and security requirements. However, it is not easy to take into account security in application development and the problem grows up in emerging paradigms, like the Cloud, that

A. Vallecillo et al. (Eds.): QUATIC 2022, CCIS 1621, pp. 250–265, 2022.
https://doi.org/10.1007/978-3-031-14179-9_17

delegate resources and services to third parties. Cloud-native applications, as an example, often rely on micro-services architectures and/or on the integration of Commercial-Off-The-Shelf (COTS) components, an approach that has great advantages in terms of costs and time-to-market, but heavily affects the security. In order to address the security, best practices suggest the adoption of threat modeling and risk analysis methodologies that allow the security administrator to obtain (in a preliminary way) information on the security problems from the early stages of the software life cycle. The adoption of these procedures increases awareness of cybersecurity issues in all the involved personnel and allows the security administrator to evaluate and accordingly manage the risk, applying mitigation strategies. However, at the state of the art, there is a lack of standards and consolidated practices devoted to helping security administrators systematically apply security checks and mitigate threats [22]. As a consequence, there are many tools that offer support to threat modeling, but each relies on (i) different modeling approaches and (ii) describing threats and threat models in different ways. This paper aims at offering a simple description of the main open source tools, describing the threat modeling approaches on which the tools rely and the results they are able to produce. In particular, this paper focuses on three different tools, that adopt different modeling techniques: Threat Modeling tool by Microsoft [1], Threat Dragon by OWASP [11] and Sla-Generator [12] which implements the methodology proposed in MUSA H2020 European research project. The comparison was carried out on a simple, but significant case study, involving a well-known Content Management System (CMS) platform: Wordpress. The remainder of the paper is organized as follows: Section 2 briefly summarizes the threat modeling techniques proposed in literature, while Sect. 3 describes the three tools that we addressed in our analysis. Section 4 compares the tools, using the Wordpress application as a basis for the comparison. Finally, Sect. 5 summarizes our conclusions and future work.

2   Threat Modeling Practices

Threat modelling processes give an organized representation of all the information that influences the security of an application and it can be related to a wide run of things, as stated by OWASP [9], *threat modeling works to identify, communicate, and understand threats and mitigations within the context of protecting something of value.* As highlighted by the OWASP threat modelling manifesto [17], threat modeling aims at achieving thoroughness and reproducibility by applying security and privacy knowledge in a structured manner. It is also supported by some tools that allow you to enable repeatability and provide measurability. The use of threat modelling provides a structured representation of all the information that affects the security of an application and it can be applied to a wide range of things, including software, applications, systems, networks, distributed systems, Internet of Things (IoT) devices, and business processes.

At the state of the art, there are various methodologies that aim at modelling the threats applicable to a system, one of the related problems is that these practices are (often) carried out by a human and require a lot of execution time [21]. In order to reduce the time of these practices, there are, at the state of the art, some automated (or semi-automated) approaches: Schaad et al. [19] proposed a STRIDE-based threat modelling technique for software architecture diagrams. They introduced their own conceptual data model, consisting of assets, asset shapes and components. These concepts can be used to describe software systems and perform security evaluations. Additionally, they implemented a supporting tool, TAM, that performs an automated threat analysis, based on the described assets. Casola et al. [6–8] proposed a Security-by-Design methodology to evaluate the security of IoT systems by the means of an almost automated process for threat modeling and risk assessment. Their approach also helps at identifying the security controls to implement in order to mitigate the existing security risks. We invite the interested reader to deepen the existing automated [10,14,15] and semi-automated [4,20] threat modeling approaches. As a summary, the state of the art highlights, as can be seen especially from the literature review in [22], that there is a wide need for automating the full process, leaving to humans only the role of final control result and evaluation.

3   Threat Modeling Tools

As outlined in the previous section, even if threat modeling is a well accepted practice, it commonly relies on security expert skills and experience. As a consequence, there are no standards that aim at listing possible threats. As an example, the standard ISO 15408, Common Criteria, imposes a structured section for security threats and security objectives (the countermeasures to address the threats), but, while security requirements are catalogued in long documents, threats should be defined case-by-case in the standard documents (security profiles and/or security target) by the expert for the specific product or class of products. However, Security experts are costly and the human-driven threat modeling is costly both in terms of money and time. Accordingly, there are now a few tools that aim at offering support to experts in threat modeling, simplifying the work, requiring less experienced experts (most of the threats are catalogued) and offering solution that produce the models in limited time. According to our studies, three of this tools are the most interesting ones: *Microsoft Threat Modeling Tool*, which is probably the most largely adopted one, the *OWASP Threat Dragon*, supported by the OWASP consortium, and the *SLAgenerator* tool, developed in the H2020 MUSA European project. In the following we briefly outline the threat modeling approaches they support.

3.1   Microsoft Threat Modeling Tool

Microsoft Threat Modeling Tool we tested was released in September 2018 [1]. It aims at reducing threat modelling times, generating the threats to which a system is subjected automatically, relying on a model of the system. The system under analysis (SuA) is modeled by the user through a graph-based model. The user has the possibility to choose various stencils to be included in the application. Each node of the graph represents an application service, while each edge indicates a Generic Data Flow (i.e. Request or Response). The Microsoft Modeling technique requires that each node is characterized by two labels: Component type and Component Value. The first one describes the type of the component while the second provides further functional information. Most of the pairs (*componenttype, componentvalue*) are shown in Table 1. For instance, a node can represent a generic database, so it can be modelled as a *Generic Data Store* type and *Database* value. The table does not represent all possible values for brevity's sake.

Table 1. Example values related to each Component Type.

Component type	Component value
Generic Data Store	Azure Cosmos DB
	Azure Key Vault
	Azure Redis Cache
	Database
	Cache
Generic External Interactor	Browser
	Dynamics CRM Mobile Client
	IoT Device
Generic Process	Azure AD
	Azure ML
	Host
	Web Application
	IoT Cloud Gatewat

Once the application is modeled, the tool generates a threat report automatically. Threats are associated with each interaction between components. Each threat is selected from a proprietary catalog taking into account the type of components involved in the interaction and the type of interaction. For example, *requests* made by a *web application* toward a *storage service* can generate the *SQL Injection* threat. In addition to providing threats associated with system assets, the tool suggests possible mitigations selected from a proprietary Microsoft database.

3.2 OWASP Threat Dragon

Threat Dragon is a free, open-source, cross platform threat modelling application based on diagram models and rule engine to auto-generate threats and mitigations [5]. It supports STRIDE [3] classification and CIA. The tool was presented during the OWASP Open Security Summit in June 2020 by OWASP Lab Project and it is available as open-source code in [11]. The tool requires the application to be modelled through a graph-based model in which the nodes represent the components, while the edges define the transfer of data between them. Each node can be: (i) A generic running process, (ii) An actor or (iii) A component that stores the data. Each element (node or edge) is characterized by a set of attributes that can be used to identify its security problems. All the parameters related to each element of the graph are described in the Table 2.

Table 2. Parameters related to each Component Type.

Component type	Parameters
Actor	Provide authentication
Process	Handle card payment
	Is a web application
	Handles goods and services
Store	Is a log
	Stores credentials
	Stores inventory
	Is encrypted
	Is signed
Data Flow	Protocol
	Is encrypted
	Is over a public network

The pair $(componentType, associatedParameters)$ is used to obtain the threats associated with the component/flow (i.e. asset) of the diagram. For example, a store that has *is encrypted* as a parameter may be subject to the *Vulnerable encryption algorithm* threat that could lead a malicious user to obtain data out of the application. The threats are obtained from the related catalog [16] in a fully automatic way. The user can also define some custom threats and associate them with each element of the application. For each pair $(asset, threat)$, the tool asks the user for the *Threat status* (Open or Mitigated) field and a priority level (Low, Medium, high) and then suggest a list of possible Mitigations.

3.3 SLAGenerator

The SLAGenerator threat modelling technique [12,18] relies on MACM (Multipurpose Application Composition Model) an expressive model that describes *WHAT* to assess and test. The MACM is a graph-based modelling technique in which each graph node represents a component of the system, and each edge characterizes the existing connection between two different components. MACM offers a simple way to synthesize an application architecture, focusing on its main components and relationships, enabling the security evaluation automation of the assessed systems. Nodes have a primary label, which identifies the asset class and may have a secondary label, which further specifies the primary class. Moreover, each node has a set of properties that better describe more specific aspects. A mandatory property is the *Asset Type*, which specifies the functional behaviour of the asset represented by the node. The allowed *Asset Types* for a node depends on the labels. *Labels* and supported *Asset Types* are listed and described in Table 3.

Table 3. MACM node labels and assets.

Primary label	Secondary label	Asset type(s)	Description
CSC		CSC.Human	A customer that uses services
CSP		CSP	A service Provider like Amazon, Google, or a telecom provider
Service	*IaaS*	VM, Container	Virtual Machine or Containers
Service	*PaaS*	VM, Container	Virtual Machine or Containers
Service	*SaaS*	Service.Web, Service.DB, Service.IOTGW, Service.MQTTBroker	Software (typically COTS) offered as a service
Network	WAN	Internet	A wide area Network, typically the Internet
Network	LAN	Network.WiFi, Network.Wired	Network, the assets differs depending on the involved technologies
Network	PAN	Network.BLE, Network.ZigBee	Personal Area Network, the assets differs depending on the involved technologies
HW		HW.server, HW.PC, HW.UE HW.micro, HW.IOTDevice	A physical hosting hardware

The possible relationships between the nodes are *uses, hosts, provides, connects*, described extensively in some works, cited above. In order to manage the MACM model the tool represent them in a graph database, namely Neo4j. The MACM is preliminary produced by the user in Neo4j and then requested by the tool (available at link[1]) for the threat modeling phase. The tool communicates with the graph database, obtaining the correctly modeled applications. The technique selects all the threats applicable to the SuA by evaluating the *asset-type* field of each component (i.e. MACM node). The technique relies on a Threat Catalogue, which organizes the threats according to their asset type. The catalogue describes the threats with 8 parameters, as shown in Table 4.

---

[1] https://github.com/DanieleGranata94/SlaGenerator.

Table 4. Threat catalogue template

Threat catalogue field	Description
Threat	A synthetic high-level label of the behaviour
Asset type	The asset typology to which the threat is subject
Relationship	Relation Type
Protocol	Protocol used in the communication
Role in relationship	Role in communication
Behaviour	Detailed description of the threat
STRIDE	Stride classification [3]
Compromised	Which assets the malicious behaviour compromises

A threat can be linked to an asset (asset type) or a communication protocol. For this reason, some fields may be left blank. For example, if a threat affects a specific asset typology, i.e. the *Read DB Configuration* threat for a *service.DB* asset type, both the relationship and role fields are left unspecified.

The *Compromised* field indicates the asset that is compromised by the malicious behaviour and it can assume the following values:

- *self*, if the threat compromises only the node specified by the asset type;
- *source(relation)*, when it compromises the node pointing from the arch;
- *target(relation)*, when it compromises the node pointed by the arch;

It is worth noting that when the *Compromised* field is source or target, the argument *relation* can be *uses*, *connects* or *hosts*. The threats are then obtained by the tool by considering both the asset-type field of the component and the related communication protocols used by the component. The tool also suggests, for each selected threat, one (or more) NIST SP-800-53 [13] controls.

4   Tool Comparison

In this chapter we want to compare the different threat modeling tools and the approaches they adopt. In order to show the differences, we will use a very common application, typically executed on a cloud infrastructure: an e-commerce site developed on top of WordPress. Considering this application, we modeled the system with the three different tools and documented the threat modelling results each tool offered.

4.1   The WordPress Case Study

WordPress is an open source content management system, which allows the creation and distribution of an Internet site made up of textual or multimedia contents, which can be managed and updated dynamically. The web application WP is hosted on a cloud virtual machine on top of an Apache web server and interfaced with a mySQL database. In order to enable scalability, the WordPress component can be deployed multiple times, reusing always the same Database (that can scale only vertically, i.e. adding memory and/or CPU to the hosting VM). A Load Balancer distributes the Client requests to the connected WP instances. The developer simply customizes the WP instances, through custom plugins and customizing the application behaviour.

Even if the development of such systems is simple and commonly relies on very limited skills from the developer/system administrators, the application manages money and personal data, so it has strict security requirements. It must be considered that an incredible amount of WordPress instances on the web are vulnerable (see [2]), due to incorrect security planning and management.

4.2 Microsoft Tool Analysis

The Microsoft tool allowed us to describe the Wordpress application in complete way, as it supports a large number of stencils. As described above, the Microsoft tool considers the interactions between components (arcs of the graph) as assets and obtains security information by evaluating the type of the two components involved in the communication (Fig. 1).

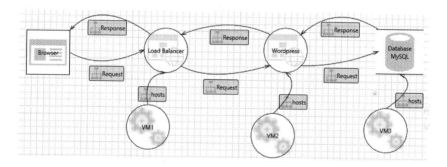

Fig. 1. Microsoft tool model Wordpress

In order to model the application, the client was modeled as a *Browser*, while Wordpress and Load Balancer as a *Web Application*. MySQL Database instead was modelled as a *Database* component value. Each service is running on a *Host* node. Once the used has modelled the application, the tool automatically generates the threats for each asset (i.e. threat model) by producing a report in HTML format. Part of the threat model is described in the Table 5.

It is important to note that the threat model shows, in this case, three values as asset field: *sourcenode, typeofrelationship, destinationnode*. From the results it can be noted that, for example, each service exposes some threats in the relation to the *Generic process* it hosts. As an example, a malicious user can get sensitive data from the service configuration files. A possible countermeasure that the tool suggests is to encrypt only the configuration files that contain sensitive

Table 5. Part of the Threat Model Wordpress using Microsoft tool.

Asset	Threat	STRIDE	Mitigation
VM-hosts-Service	An adversary can gain access to sensitive data stored in Web App's config files	Tampering	Encrypt sections of Web App's configuration files that contain sensitive data
Client-request-LoadBalancer	An adversary can steal sensitive data like user credentials	Spoofing	Explicitly disable the autocomplete HTML attribute in sensitive forms and inputs, ...
LoadBalancer-request-Wordpress	An adversary can reverse weakly encrypted or hashed content	Information Disclosure	Do not expose security details in error messages, Implement Default error handling page
Wordpress-request-MySQL	An adversary can gain access to sensitive data by sniffing traffic to database	Information Disclosure	Ensure SQL server connection encryption and certificate validation

data. The sending of the access credentials by the user to the service can also be compromised. In fact, a malicious user can steal these data in different ways. In order to reduce the risk that this threat happens, Microsoft tool suggests some countermeasures. Ad an example, the user can disable the auto-complete HTML attribute in sensitive forms and inputs. The analysis also shows problems related to the use of weak encryption algorithms in the communication between the Load Balancer and Wordpress. In fact, a malicious user can intercept the packets containing the encrypted data and apply an encryption reversing algorithm to recover the plain-text data.

4.3 Dragon Analysis

We modeled the system using Threat Dragon diagram tool. The number of stencils available is limited, so, as shown in Fig. 2, The Wordpress application was modeled using only the Process, Store and Actor.

Fig. 2. Threat Dragon model Wordpress

Load Balancer and Wordpress were modeled as two processes, while for the Client and Mysql Database we have chosen the stencil of Actor and Store respectively. Each node of the graph communicate through a DataFlow relationship. As highlighted in the previous section, the tool considers both the nodes and the arcs of the graph as assets (i.e. resource to be protected). Each asset has a set of properties aimed at selecting the related threats, as shown in the Table 6. We modeled the Load Balancer service and Wordpress application as a *Web Application*. In particular, we assumed that the Wordpress-based website is an e-commerce (manages payment cards) that stores data and encrypted credentials in a MySQL database. Each communication is made on a public network with http protocol. Considering the selected parameters, the tool automatically collects threats (i.e. threat name, description and STRIDE classification) for each component of the application and suggests the related mitigations. A partial list of threats for each component is shown in the Table 7. As the user can access from a public network, a malicious user can exploit a *fingerprinting* threat against the data exchange between the client and the load balancer, sending specific requests to obtain information in order to profile the application. The Wordpress-based web application on the other hand it can be subject to Card Cracking threat since it manages payment cards. In this case, the malicious user can carry out a brute force attack on the payment process in order to identify the missing values of the card (i.e. expiry date, security code etc.) A brute force attack prevention system can (partially) mitigate the threat.

Table 6. Parameters related to each Component Type.

Component	Selected parameters
Client	Provide authentication
Load Balancer	Web application
	Handles goods and services
Wordpress	Web application
	Handles goods and services
	Handles card payment
MySQL Database	Stores credentials
	Is a stores inventory
	Is encrypted
Each Data Flow	protocol: http
	Is over a public network

Table 7. Part of the Threat Model Wordpress using Dragon TM.

Asset	Threat	Description	STRIDE	Mitigation
Client → Load Balancer	Fingerprinting	Specific requests are sent to the application eliciting information in order to profile the application	Information Disclosure	Defence includes restricting what information is provided, for example version numbers and package details
	Use encryption	Unencrypted data sent over a public network may be intercepted and read by an attacker	Information Disclosure	Data should be encrypted either at the message or transport level
Load Balancer	Sniping	Automated exploitation of system latencies in the form of timing attacks	Elevation of privileges	Anti-automation and prevention of abuse of functionality
Wordpress	Denial of Service	Usage may resemble legitimate application usage but leads to exhaustion of resources	Elevation of privileges	Providing backoff, resource management and avoiding forced deadlock
	Card Cracking	Brute force attack against application payment card process to identify the missing values	Information Disclosure	Interaction frequency, preventing brute force attacks and anti-automation
MySQL Database	Account Creation	Bulk account creation, and sometimes profile population, by using the application's account signup processes	Elevation of privileges	Interaction frequency, enforcement of a single unique a action and enforcement of behavioral workflow

4.4   SLAgenerator Analysis

Figure 3 shows the MACM model of our case study. Each label affect the color of the nodes, while attributes are not visible in the picture. As anticipated, the system is composed of a Cloud Service Provider (e.g. Azure or a private Cloud) that *provides* three virtual machines. Which are labeled as *IaaS*, and their Asset Type is *VM*, e.g. virtual machine. One VM *hosts* a Load Balancer service while the other two VMs *host* respectively a WordPress instance and a MySQL a database instance. We modeled the Load Balancer (LB) and WordPress (WP) as *SaaS* nodes and we set their Asset Type as *Web Application*. The MySQL instance, instead, was labeled as a *SaaS*, but with *Database* (DB) value as Asset Type. The LB *uses* the WP that, in turn, uses the DB. The Client (modeled as a *CSC* node) uses the Load Balancer service, that acts as application interface. Each SaaS service is connected to the public Network. Applying our threat modelling technique we produce a list of threats but, for simplicity' sake we report in Table 8 just one for each asset type. The full list of Threats is not compatible with the length of the paper. The results show how nodes labelled as *SERVICE.Web* can be subject to *Injection* threat in which an attacker legitimately sends commands to the exposed service without proper authorization. In order to mitigate this threat, we suggest the usage of NIST Control SI-10, *Invalid input validation*. The tool also models the threats associated with the Network, such as *Message Reply* threat for which an attacker can re-transmit some packets (previously intercepted) in order to obtain data.

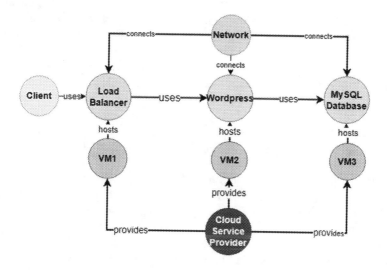

Fig. 3. Wordpress MACM

Table 8. Part of the Threat Model Wordpress using SlaGenerator.

Asset	Asset type	Threat	Description	STRIDE	NIST Control
Wordpress	SERVICE.Web	Injection	The attacker's hostile data can trick the interpreter into executing unintended commands	Tampering	SI-10 Invalid input validation
MySQL Database	SERVICE.DB	Remote DoS	Made the DBMS unaccessible to remote clients	Denial Of Service	SC-5, DoS Protection
VMs	SERVICE.VM	Authorization Abuse	An adversary is able to circumvent the authorization controls	Elevation of privileges	CA-6 Authorization
Network	Network	Message Reply	An adversary can re-transmit the content of the packets coming from the asset at a later time	Spoofing	AC-12, Session Termination

4.5 Comparison

It is worth noting that, as highlighted above, all the tool rely on a graph-based model to describe the target system, where the node represent the asset and the edge their connections. However, the tools differ on the interpretation and meta-data associated to both nodes and edges of the graph. According to Microsoft's approach, there is a large variety of possible nodes, but the key role in the threat modeling is associated to the connection among them: in fact the threat are listed *per-connection*, taking into account the connected nodes and the connection attributes. According to OWASP, on the other hand, the Threat Dragon tool evaluates both the nodes and the arcs of the graph as assets, associating the threats to each element. However the type of nodes and edges are very limited and the threats are selected according to few attributes associated to both nodes and relationship. The SLAGenerator, on the other hand, focuses on system assets (the graph nodes) and identifies the possible threats relying on the *asset type* attribute, which offer a large variety of different values, similarly to the Microsoft Threat Modeling tool. Moreover, relationships affect the possible threats to which each node, but the threats are always listed as associated to nodes. It is out of the scope of this work to say which approach is better (we aim at comparing the ideas not at making a rank of the tools), but it is worth noting that in the graph they made completely different choice: one focuses on edge, one on nodes and the last on both of them. However, the final result, in all the cases, is a list of threats that contains an explicit description of the malicious behaviour (in natural language) and the classification of the threat according to STRIDE or respect to the threat impact on Confidentiality, Integrity and Availability. The three tools, even in the case of the Wordpress application, which is pretty simple, produce a pretty long list of threats (88 for the MS threat Modeling tool, 84 for SLAgenerator and 31 for the Dragon tool). We, acting as experts, consider that the choice of listing threats only respect to assets or only respect to relationships (the choices done by SLAGenerator and by MS Threat Modeling Tool) helps the expert work in the analysis of the results, but this is and remain a subjective choice. However, the number of threat outlined by the OWASP tool looks, at state of art, limited respect to the other tools. This is due to the limited set of parameters available for the selection and, probably, to the underlying threat catalogue dimension.

Table 9. Comparison table.

Asset	SLAGenerator threat	Microsoft threat	OWASP threat
Wordpress	Data Leakage	Read web app's config files	Fingerprinting
		Steal sensitive data like user credentials	Carding
			Card cracking
Wordpress	Injection	SQL injection through Web App	–
Database	Read Injection	SQL injection	–
Database	Insert Injection		Account Creation
VM	Data Breach	Access to sensitive data from log files	–
VM	Denial of Service	–	

Another interesting aspect is that the three techniques present threats at different levels of granularity, as shown in the Table 9. As an example, the Sla-Generator tool underlines how Wordpress can be subject to *data leakage*. The same threat is (partially) expressed by the Microsoft tool with *read configuration files* and *steal user credentials* threats. According to OWASP, instead, data loss can be caused both by an application profiling technique (e.g. fingerprinting) and by techniques that aim at obtaining information on users' virtual cards. In general, the threats affecting Wordpress were 10 for both OWASP and SlaGenerator and 25 according to Microsoft. It is important to note, however, that threats are expressed with different levels of detail. The analysis also shows how a *Injection* threat can affect both Wordpress and the database. Considering Database as an asset, a Microsoft SQL injection can be as *SlaGenerator Read/Insert injection* that takes into account that a malicious user wants to get information from the database or write to it (e.g. create an account). In this case, the threats according to SlaGenerator tool are 15, while OWASP and Microsoft consider only 8. Virtual machines, on the other hand, are not considered in the OWASP model, the table shows the comparison only between SLAGenerator and Microsoft tool. One of the 13 threats described by the SLAGenerator is that of Data Breach, partially mapped with *Access to sensitive data from log files* by Microsoft (which instead considers 6 threats). Network assets were modeled only by the SLAGenerator and threat modeling reported 12 threats[2].

5 Conclusion

In this paper we have analyzed three threat modeling techniques that make use of different models in order to select the threats applicable to the system. The tools analyzed were SlaGenerator, Microsoft tool and Threat Dragon by OWASP. The analysed tools require a very simplified graph-based model of the application in which the nodes represent the components of the system and the arcs represent the interactions between the various components. The simplicity of modeling allows the user in all three approaches to obtain security information in a fully automatic way. The approaches were applied to a case study involving Wordpress, a Content Management System that allows you to manage a website. The results show that the threats are described at different levels of detail, but still compatible. In particular, OWASP threat dragon has proved to be the tool that produces a less complete threat model than the others. The number of threats related to the Wordpress component was greater (25) with the Microsoft tool, while the threat model related to the database and virtual machines was more complete with SlaGenerator. Furthermore, the tool also considered the network as an asset, highlighting 12 threats.

References

1. Microsoft threat modeling tool (2018). https://docs.microsoft.com/it-it/azure/security/develop/threat-modeling-tool
2. Abela, R.: Statistics show why WordPress is a popular hacker target (2020)
3. Ansari, M.T., Pandey, D., Alenezi, M.: STORE: security threat oriented requirements engineering methodology (2019)
4. Arsac, W., Bella, G., Chantry, X., Compagna, L.: Multi-attacker protocol validation. J. Autom. Reason. 46(3–4), 353–388 (2011)
5. Bhattacharya, D.: OWASP threat dragon review (2020)
6. Casola, V., Benedictis, A.D., Rak, M., Villano, U.: Preliminary design of a platform-as-a-service to provide security in cloud. In: Proceedings of the 4th International Conference on Cloud Computing and Services Science - CLOSER, pp. 752–757 (2014)
7. Casola, V., De Benedictis, A., Rak, M., Rios, E.: Security-by-design in clouds: a security-SLA driven methodology to build secure cloud applications. Procedia Comput. Sci. 97, 53–62 (2016). 2nd International Conference on Cloud Forward: From Distributed to Complete Computing
8. Casola, V., De Benedictis, A., Rak, M., Villano, U.: Toward the automation of threat modeling and risk assessment in IoT systems. Internet Things 7, 100056 (2019)
9. Drake: Threat Modeling. https://owasp.org/www-community/Threat_Modeling

---

[2] Full threat modelling comparison is available on request.

10. Frydman, M., Ruiz, G., Heymann, E., César, E., Miller, B.P.: Automating risk analysis of software design models. Sci. World J. **2014**, 805856 (2014)
11. Goodwin, M.: OWASP Threat Dragon. https://github.com/owasp/threat-dragon/releases
12. Granata, D., Rak, M.: Design and development of a technique for the automation of the risk analysis process in IT Security, p. 14 (2021)
13. Joint Task Force Interagency Working Group: Security and privacy controls for information systems and organizations. NIST (2020)
14. Kornecki, A.J., Janusz, Z.: Threat modeling for aviation computer security. CrossTalk **28**, 21–27 (2015)
15. Musman, S., Turner, A.J.: A game oriented approach to minimizing cybersecurity risk. Saf. Secur. Stud. **8**, 212–222 (2018)
16. OWASP: OWASP Automated Threats to Web Applications (2018)
17. OWASP: Threat Modeling Manifesto. https://www.threatmodelingmanifesto.org/
18. Rak, M., Salzillo, G., Granata, D.: EssecA: an automated expert system for threat modelling and penetration testing for IoT ecosystems. Comput. Electr. Eng. **99**, 107721 (2022)
19. Schaad, A., Borozdin, M.: TAM: automated threat analysis. In: Proceedings of the 27th Annual ACM Symposium on Applied Computing, SAC 2012, pp. 1103–1108. Association for Computing Machinery, New York (2012)
20. Singh, S., Tu, H., Allanach, J., Areta, J., Willett, P., Pattipati, K.: Modeling threats. IEEE Potentials **23**(3), 18–21 (2004)
21. Tatam, M., Shanmugam, B., Azam, S., Kannoorpatti, K.: A review of threat modelling approaches for apt-style attacks. Heliyon **7**(1), e05969 (2021)
22. Xiong, W., Lagerström, R.: Threat modeling - a systematic literature review. Comput. Secur. **84**, 53–69 (2019)

Understanding Black-Box Attacks Against Object Detectors from a User's Perspective

Kim André Midtlid, Johannes Åsheim, and Jingyue Li$^{(\boxtimes)}$ (iD)

Norwegian University of Science and Technology, Trondheim, Norway
`kamidtli@stud.ntnu.no`, {`johannes.asheim,jingyue.li`}`@ntnu.no`

Abstract. Due to recent developments in object detection systems, and the realistic threat of black-box adversarial attacks on object detector models, we argue the need for a contextual understanding of the attacks from the users' perspective. Existing literature reviews either do not provide complete and up-to-date summaries of such attacks or focus on the knowledge from the researchers' perspective. In this research, we conducted a systematic literature review to identify state-of-the-art black-box attacks and extract the information to help users evaluate and mitigate the risks. The literature review resulted in 29 black-box attack methods. We analyzed each attack from the following main aspects: attackers' knowledge needed to perform the attack, attack consequences, attack generalizability, and strategies to mitigate the attacks. Our results demonstrate an emerging increase in highly generalizable attacks, which now make up more than 50% of the landscape. We also reveal that more than 50% of recent attacks remain untested against mitigation strategies.

Keywords: Artificial intelligence · Object detection · Image classification · Adversarial attacks

1 Introduction

As Deep Neural Networks (DNNs) becomes more and more pertinent in image recognition and object detection tasks, their robustness also becomes more of a concern. Goodfellow et al. [14] have shown that the robustness of these models is susceptible to adversarial attacks. Such vulnerabilities have motivated researchers to develop adversarial attacks to exploit the object detection systems and contribute to improving their robustness. White-box attacks that assume knowledge about the target model continue to dominate the adversarial attack landscape, but there is an increase in black-box attacks. Black-box attacks assume no or very limited knowledge about the target model and are, therefore, more realistic approaches to adversarial attacks [34]. We argue that the increase in black-box attacks should be followed by a contextual understanding of the attacks from a user perspective. We define a user as a person who wants

A. Vallecillo et al. (Eds.): QUATIC 2022, CCIS 1621, pp. 266–280, 2022.
https://doi.org/10.1007/978-3-031-14179-9_18

to know the risk and impact of adversarial attacks and how to defend against these attacks without knowing specific attack implementation details. Therefore, this paper omits the technical properties of the attacks for the traditional researcher perspective. Existing surveys and reviews of adversarial attacks on image classification and object detection, e.g., [6,20], focus mostly on the information needed by researchers and do not cover sufficient up-to-date black-box attacks. Our research motivation is to summarize the state-of-the-art black-box attacks targeting object detection models to help users evaluate and mitigate the risks. We focus on answering the following research questions.

- **RQ1:** What does the attacker need to know about the target model?
- **RQ2:** How generalizable is the attack?
- **RQ3:** What are the consequences of the attack?
- **RQ4:** Which mitigation strategies have been tested against the attack?

We performed a systematic literature review on articles published between 2017 and 2021 to collect state-of-the-art black-box attacks. Through the systematic literature review and snowballing, we uncovered 29 state-of-the-art attack methods, which we analyze and present in this paper. Our study benefits industrial practitioners and scientists. The contributions of the study are twofold.

- We provide comprehensive and up-to-date consolidated knowledge about black-box attacks targeting object detection models to help users to evaluate the risks and choose effective mitigation solutions.
- We identify the trends and weaknesses of existing studies in this field, which may inspire researchers' future work.

The rest of the paper is organized as follows: Section 2 introduces the background. Section 3 presents the related work. Section 4 explains our research methods, and Sect. 5 presents the results. We then discuss our results in Sect. 6. Conclusions and future work are in Sect. 7.

2   Background

Object detection is the field of Artificial Intelligence (AI) that uses deep learning to extract high-dimensional information from images and videos. An autonomous car with camera sensors uses image processing to navigate the road and detect obstacles.

2.1   Object Detection and Image Classification

Image classification is the task of classifying an input image by assigning it to a specific label [42], while object detection is the task of localizing and classifying distinct objects in an image or video. Current object detectors can be split into two main categories: two-stage and one-stage detectors. Two-stage detectors consist of two main parts. First, the detector uses a Region Proposal Network

(RPN) to calculate proposed regions for objects. The RPN uses a set of predefined *anchor boxes* uniformly placed over the image to calculate proposed regions before outputting a predefined number of proposed bounding boxes with a corresponding objectiveness score. The objectiveness score indicates whether the proposed region belongs to an object class or the background. These proposed regions significantly reduce the computational complexity needed to localize and classify an object. In the second stage, the proposed regions from the RPN are passed to a high-quality image classifier to recognize objects. One-stage detectors aim to improve the inference speed while still achieving acceptable accuracy. One-stage detectors achieve this goal by removing the region proposal stage required by the two-stage detectors. Instead, they run detection on a dense sampling of predefined default boxes. The ability to skip the region proposal step significantly decreases inference time and has led to the development of many one-stage detectors, e.g., [30,38].

2.2   Threat Models

The threat model of an attack is based on what the adversary knows about the target model, thus we can categorize the attacks into three threat models. *White-box attacks*, e.g., FGSM [14], assume the adversary has complete knowledge of the target model, which include the model's internal structure, such as weights and parameters of the target model, and knowledge of the output given an input. In some cases, the adversary knows the training data distribution. This allows the adversary to construct attack methods specific to the given model. *Black-box attacks*, assume no internal information of the target model, but the ability to observe the output for a given input. Usually, black-box attack methods are constructed based on querying the target model [5,8,9]. Han Xu et al. [46] introduce *grey-box attacks* as a hybrid of white-box attacks and black-box attacks, where the attacker trains a generative model to create adversarial examples in white-box setting. Then the target model is attacked in the black-box setting with adversarial examples from the trained generative model.

3   Related Work

Bhambri et al. [6] performed a survey focusing on adversarial black-box attacks. The paper aims to conduct a comparative study of both adversarial attacks and defenses. Nineteen black-box attacks were compared on the number of queries, success rate, and perturbation norm. The survey categorizes the attacks based on gradient estimation, transferability, local search and combinatorics. Shilin Qiu et al. [37] presents a comprehensive study of the research of adversarial attack and defenses. The paper details white-box and black-box attack methods but mainly focuses on defense strategies. Kong et al. [25] reviewed adversarial attack literature in the different application fields of AI security. The fields include images, texts and malicious code. The paper presents attack algorithms for the different application domains and includes 13 attacks for the image domain, five of which are black-box attacks. The survey further elaborates on defense methods and how they affect the presented attacks. In order to help new researchers in the field, the paper introduces and discusses the different datasets and tools available. There are other surveys and articles, i.e., [1,27,46,48], which discuss adversarial attacks and defenses. The common limitation of these studies are the low number of included black-box attacks. In addition, the studies focus on consolidating information from the researchers' perspective.

4   Research Design and Implementation

We performed a Systematic Literature Review (SLR) and followed the SLR guidelines proposed by Kitchenham and Charters [24]. After analyzing the terms related to our research questions and their synonyms, we chose to use the search query: *Adversarial* AND *Attack* AND (*"Object detection"* OR *"Object detector"*).

We chose `oria.no`, a search engine that covers many scientific databases, including IEEE Xplore, Springer, ACM Digital library, and Scopus. To include only recent literature and to reduce the scope, we used the advanced search functionality in `oria.no`, and included only peer-reviewed and published scientific papers from the last 5 years back from 2021. The identified articles were filtered mainly based on their relevance to the research questions by reading their abstract, introduction, and, in some cases, methodology. After filtering, we identified 11 relevant primary studies. Then, we performed a snowballing search following the process proposed by [45], with the exception that forward and backward snowballing searches were limited to a single iteration each. The forward snowballing was performed using Google Scholar. The snowballing identified 16 more papers, resulting in 27 primary studies.

5   Research Results

In this section, we present our answers to each research question. Attack names preceded by asterisks (*) were not presented with a name in their corresponding paper. Therefore, a descriptive name is given based on the attack method.

5.1   RQ1—Attacker's Knowledge

How much information the attacker requires from the output labels varies across the identified papers but can be split into three categories: **Soft-labels** refer to the threat model where an attacker accesses the output probabilities $P(y|x)$ for y in the top k classes. Soft-labels also might include the label for each of the output probabilities. For object detectors, information about the bounding boxes indicates soft-labels. **Hard-labels** refer to a more restricted threat model where an attacker only has access to a list of $k \in \mathbb{Z}^+$ output labels. Different attacks make different assumptions about k. For $k = 1$, the attacker only has access to the single predicted class. In the case of $k > 1$, the list of classes is often ordered by decreasing probabilities but does not include the probabilities. For object detectors, the hard-label category signifies no information about the bounding boxes. Some attacks assume the target model outputs $k = 1$ or $k > 1$ labels. **No-labels** refer to the most restricted threat model, where an attacker requires no access to the output of the target model.

Table 1. Attacks grouped by attacker knowledge

Attack name	Year	Knowledge
NRDM [33]	2018	No-labels
DaST [51]	2020	Hard-labels and Soft-labels
HopSkipJumpAttack [9]	2020	Hard-labels
*Partial-retraining [36]	2020	Hard-labels
*Evolutionary Attack [13]	2019	Hard-labels
Label-Only Attack [20]	2018	Hard-labels
Opt-Attack [11]	2018	Hard-labels
Boundary Attack [8]	2017	Hard-labels
CMA-ES [19]	2021	Soft-labels
Simple Transparent Adversarial Examples [7]	2021	Soft-labels
*Discrete Cosine Transform Attack [26]	2021	Soft-labels
*Differential Evolution Attack [44]	2021	Soft-labels
BMI-FGSM [29]	2020	Soft-labels
*Transferable Universal Perturbation Attack [49]	2020	Soft-labels
Adv-watermark [23]	2020	Soft-labels
Evaporate Attack [43]	2020	Soft-labels
Daedalus [41]	2019	Soft-labels
One-Pixel-Attack [39]	2019	Soft-labels
Single Scratch attack [22]	2019	Soft-labels
GenAttack [2]	2019	Soft-labels
Universal perturbation attack [50]	2019	Soft-labels
Query-Limited Attack [20]	2018	Soft-labels
Partial-Info Attack [20]	2018	Soft-labels
Bandits [21]	2018	Soft-labels
Gradient Estimation Attacks [5]	2018	Soft-labels
R-AP [28]	2018	Soft-labels
ZOO [10]	2017	Soft-labels
LocSearchAdv [32]	2016	Soft-labels
*Substitute Attack [34]	2016	Soft-labels

Table 1 presents the attacks grouped by the required attacker knowledge. We notice that more than 75% of the discussed attacks use the soft-labels approach. Table 1 also illustrates that about 25% of the discussed attacks use hard-labels as part of their method. We can also see that the number of hard-label attacks has tripled from 2017 to 2020, which might indicate that hard-label attacks are becoming more popular. The new trend might suggest that hard-label attacks have room for improvement in the coming years and should be investigated further. It is also worth noting **DaST** [51], which can be used in both a soft- and hard-label scenario because the attack is customizable. This might be an indication of a new type of attack that can be modified based on the target model. **NRDM** [33] requires no labels at all. These two attacks illustrate a possibility in the landscape, as attacks can become more applicable to any target model and more independent of the attacker's knowledge.

5.2 RQ2—Attack Generalizability

The generalization of adversarial black-box attacks examines the number of different types of object detection models which are claimed to have been successfully attacked. We have defined four categories of generalization and present the results in Table 2. The categories are *None, Low, High* and *Very High*. The presented attack is tested on and successful against either one, two, three to five or six or more target models respectively. The term generalizability is only determined based on the number of attacked target models, and do not include datasets, model accuracy, attack hyperparameters and model hyperparameters. It is important to note that the generalizability is derived from the number of models claimed by the authors of the primary studies. Therefore an attack with *None* may be generalizable, but the authors only includes experiments against one target model.

Most of the attacks only target image classifiers, but the focus could be on one-stage models, two-stage models, or a combination of both for object detectors. An attack targeting both types of object detectors poses a significant threat, as it generalizes to most model architectures. This aspect is captured in the *target architecture* column in Table 2. Attacks targeting object detectors are labeled with one-stage, two-stage, or both, while attacks targeting image classifiers are labeled correspondingly.

From Table 2, we observe a balanced distribution between high and low generalizability. Both attack types show promising results, but the ones with high generalizability might be more interesting to be studied further, as they are successful across a broader range of object detectors. The number of highly generalizable attacks has increased from 2019, as shown in Fig. 1. From Table 2, we also notice that **R-AP** [28] and **NRDM** [33] stand out. They are both classified as very high, meaning they have been tested and exhibited promising performance on six or more different models. Additionally, **NRDM** has been tested against both image classifiers and object detectors, demonstrating notable generalizability. It is also worth noting that [9,28] mention the possibility of combining **R-AP** and **HopSkipJumpAttack**, respectively, with other adversarial attacks as areas for future work. This combination demonstrates a potential to improve attacks through amalgamation, which is worth considering in future research. Many of the discussed attacks have also been tested on real-world APIs, which

Table 2. Attacks grouped by their level of generalizability

Attack name	Year	Generalization	Target architecture
NRDM [33]	2018	Very High	Image classifiers
R-AP [28]	2018	Very High	Two-stage
CMA-ES [19]	2021	High	One-stage and two-stage
*Differential Evolution Attack [44]	2021	High	Image classifiers
Adv-watermark [23]	2020	High	Image classifiers
Evaporate Attack [43]	2020	High	One-stage and two-stage
HopSkipJumpAttack [9]	2020	High	Image classifiers
*Partial-retraining [36]	2020	High	Image classifiers
*Transferable Universal Perturbation Attack [49]	2020	High	One-stage and two-stage
Daedalus [41]	2019	High	One-stage
One-Pixel-Attack [39]	2019	High	Image classifiers
Universal perturbation attack [50]	2019	High	Image classifiers
Single Scratch attack [22]	2019	High	Image classifiers
Bandits [21]	2018	High	Image classifiers
Gradient Estimation Attacks [5]	2018	High	Image classifiers
Boundary Attack [8]	2017	High	Image classifiers
*Substitute Attack [34]	2016	High	Image classifiers
*Discrete Cosine Transform Attack [26]	2021	Low	Image classifiers
BMI-FGSM [29]	2020	Low	Image classifiers
DaST [51]	2020	Low	Image classifiers
*Evolutionary Attack [13]	2019	Low	Image classifiers
GenAttack [2]	2019	Low	Image classifiers
Opt-Attack [11]	2018	Low	Image classifiers
Query-Limited Attack [20]	2018	Low	Image classifiers
Partial-Info Attack [20]	2018	Low	Image classifiers
Label-Only Attack [20]	2018	Low	Image classifiers
LocSearchAdv [32]	2016	Low	Image classifiers
Simple Transparent Adversarial Examples [7]	2021	None	Image classifiers
ZOO [10]	2017	None	Image classifiers

are listed in Table 3. From a user perspective, this illustrates a potential area of focus and risks to consider in the future.

Table 3. Attacks against real-world APIs

Attack name	Year	Real-world API
*Discrete Cosine Transform Attack [26]	2021	AWS Rekognition [4]
*Partial retraining [36]	2020	Google AutoML Vision [15]
Partial-Info Attack [20]	2018	Google Cloud Vision [16]
Gradient Estimation Attacks [5]	2018	Clarifai [12]
Boundary Attack [8]	2017	Clarifai [12]
*Substitute Attack [34]	2016	Amazon and Google Oracles [3, 16]

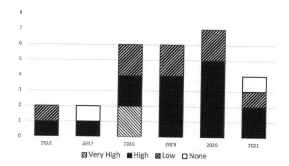

Fig. 1. The ratio of generalization levels for each year

5.3   RQ3—Attack Consequences

Classification attack is divided into targeted and untargeted attacks. Targeted attacks aim to misclassify a adversarial input image i' of class c', where the target model would have classified input image i in to class c. In other words, the attacker wants to force the target model to predict a chosen class. Untargeted attacks aim to misclassify an adversarial input image i' in to any class c', where $c' \neq c$. Object detection attack can lead to object vanishing and object population. An object vanishing attack aims to suppress all object detection in a input image, while an object population attack aims to fabricate false objects in a predicted image.

Table 4 shows the consequences of each attack. Untargeted attacks are the most common, making up more than 75% of the discussed attacks. Even though these attacks make up the majority and pose a significant threat, targeted attacks might be more dangerous from a defender's perspective. Targeted attacks still make up about 65% of discussed attacks, and it is worth noting that most image classification attacks provide both targeted and untargeted versions. This trend suggests that attacks are not limited to a single purpose but can achieve multiple goals. In the realm of object detection attacks, we have looked at five attacks. Four of them exploit the object vanishing vulnerability, while only one focuses on object population. **CMA-ES** [19] stands out because it combines object detection and image classification attacks. **CMA-ES** is a very recently

Table 4. Attacks grouped by their consequences

Attack name	Year	Target architecture	Consequences
CMA-ES [19]	2021	One-stage and two-stage	Vanishing, Targeted, and Untargeted
Evaporate Attack [43]	2020	One-stage and two-stage	Vanishing
*Transferable Universal Perturbation Attack [49]	2020	One-stage and two-stage	Vanishing
R-AP [28]	2018	Two-stage	Vanishing
Daedalus [41]	2019	One-stage	Population
*Differential Evolution Attack [44]	2021	Image classifiers	Targeted and Untargeted
BMI-FGSM [29]	2020	Image classifiers	Targeted and Untargeted
DaST [51]	2020	Image classifiers	Targeted and Untargeted
HopSkipJumpAttack [9]	2020	Image classifiers	Targeted and Untargeted
One-Pixel-Attack [39]	2019	Image classifiers	Targeted and Untargeted
Single Scratch attack [22]	2019	Image classifiers	Targeted and Untargeted
Gradient Estimation Attacks [5]	2018	Image classifiers	Targeted and Untargeted
Query-Limited Attack [20]	2018	Image classifiers	Targeted and Untargeted
Partial-Info Attack [20]	2018	Image classifiers	Targeted and Untargeted
Label-Only Attack [20]	2018	Image classifiers	Targeted and Untargeted
Bandits [21]	2018	Image classifiers	Targeted and Untargeted
Opt-Attack [11]	2018	Image classifiers	Targeted and Untargeted
Boundary Attack [8]	2017	Image classifiers	Targeted and Untargeted
ZOO [10]	2017	Image classifiers	Targeted and Untargeted
LocSearchAdv [32]	2016	Image classifiers	Targeted and Untargeted
*Discrete Cosine Transform Attack [26]	2021	Image classifiers	Targeted
*Partial-retraining [36]	2020	Image classifiers	Targeted
GenAttack [2]	2019	Image classifiers	Targeted
Simple Transparent Adversarial Examples [7]	2021	Image classifiers	Untargeted
Adv-watermark [23]	2020	Image classifiers	Untargeted
*Evolutionary Attack [13]	2019	Image classifiers	Untargeted
Universal perturbation attack [50]	2019	Image classifiers	Untargeted
NRDM [33]	2018	Image classifiers	Untargeted
*Substitute Attack [34]	2016	Image classifiers	Untargeted

developed attack that could hint at a change of focus in the landscape. Additionally, **Daedalus** [41] is the only attack that can execute object population. Results in Table 4 also show the emerging focus on attacks against object detectors from 2018.

5.4   RQ4—Mitigation Strategies

Table 5 contains a summary of all the mitigation strategies an attack is claimed to have been tested against. The *Vulnerable Mitigations* column lists all tested mitigation strategies where the attack is still able to reduce the overall accuracy of the system significantly. The definition of a significant drop in accuracy is claimed by each paper. The *Robust Mitigations* column lists all mitigation strategies where the attack cannot reduce the overall accuracy of the system significantly. It is worth noting that *None tested* in the *Robust Mitigations* column only means that the attack has not been tested on any mitigation strategy. It does not mean that the attack is able to bypass all defense strategies. This also applies to the *Vulnerable Mitigations* column. A cell with "-" means that none of the tested mitigation strategies applies to that column. A list of defenses in the *Vulnerable Mitigations* column and "-" in the *Robust Mitigations* column means that none of the tested defenses successfully defended against the attack. From Table 5, we notice that more than half of the discussed attacks have not been tested against any mitigation strategies. This illustrates that mitigation strategies have not been given enough attention. We also notice that Adversarial Training and Input Transformations repeat across different attacks in the *Vulnerable Mitigations* column. The repetition indicates that no single mitigation strategy works for all attacks, and that most modern mitigation strategies struggle to defend against the discussed attacks. It is worth noting that many of the mitigation strategies listed are umbrella terms, covering multiple defense implementations. For example, input transformations [18] cover multiple defense mechanisms such as JPEG-compression, clipping and median filtering. Although Fig. 2 shows an increase in the number of mitigation strategies evaluated, we can also see a large emerging ratio of untested attacks from 2018.

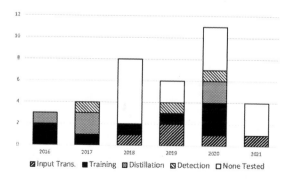

Fig. 2. The ratio of mitigation strategies each year

Table 5. Attacks grouped by mitigation strategies they have been tested against

Attack	Year	Vulnerable Mitigations	Robust Mitigations
*Differential Evolution Attack [44]	2021	Feature squeezing [47] Input Transformations [18]	-
Adv-watermark [23]	2020	Adversarial Training [40] Input Transformations [18]	-
HopSkipJumpAttack [9]	2020	Adversarial Distillation [35], Region-based classification	Adversarial Training [40]
*Partial-retraining [36]	2020	Adversarial Detection [17] Adversarial Distillation [35] Adversarial Training [40] Feature squeezing [47]	-
GenAttack [2]	2019	Adversarial Training [40], Input Transformations [18]	-
One-Pixel-Attack [39]	2019	-	Adversarial Detection [17]
Daedalus [41]	2019	MagNet [31] Minimize bounding box size	-
Single Scratch attack [22]	2019	Input Transformations (JPEG-compression) [18] Input Transformations (Clipping) [18]	Input Transformations (Median Filtering) [18]
Gradient Estimation Attacks [5]	2018	Adversarial Training [40]	Rounded output probabilities
NRDM [33]	2018	Input Transformations [18]	-
Boundary Attack [8]	2017	Adversarial Distillation [35]	-
ZOO [10]	2017	Adversarial Detection [17] Adversarial Distillation [35]	Adversarial Training [40]
LocSearchAdv [32]	2016	Adversarial Training [40]	Query-access prevention
*Substitute Attack [34]	2016	Adversarial Distillation [35] Adversarial Training [40]	-
CMA-ES [19]	2021	None tested	None tested
*Discrete Cosine Transform Attack [26]	2021	None tested	None tested
Simple Transparent Adversarial Examples [7]	2021	None tested	None tested
DaST [51]	2020	None tested	None tested
Evaporate Attack [43]	2020	None tested	None tested
BMI-FGSM [29]	2020	None tested	None tested
*Transferable Universal Perturbation Attack [49]	2020	None tested	None tested
*Evolutionary Attack [13]	2019	None tested	None tested
Universal perturbation attack [50]	2019	None tested	None tested
Bandits [21]	2018	None tested	None tested
Label-Only Attack [20]	2018	None tested	None tested
Opt-Attack [11]	2018	None tested	None tested
R-AP [28]	2018	None tested	None tested
Query-Limited Attack [20]	2018	None tested	None tested
Partial-Info Attack [20]	2018	None tested	None tested

6   Discussion

The aim of our work is to summarize the state-of-the-art black-box attacks targeting object detectors to help users evaluate and mitigate the risks. No related work outlined in Sect. 3 takes the user's perspective but rather explains black-box attacks from a researcher's perspective and focuses on explaining the attack methods. For example, Kong et al. [25] and Bhambri et al. [6] provide categories of black-box attacks, but the categorization is based on the attack method. Understanding a black-box attack method requires a high level of competence in a user. Our study does not focus on the attack methods because they are not the most relevant information for a user. The main focuses from a user perspective are covered in our research questions. Results of RQ1 (Knowledge) can inform a user of the attacks which can and cannot be executed on a system. Results of RQ2 (Generalization) warns the user of which attacks have a large impact area and could affect the system. Results of RQ3 (Consequences) give the user insight into the attacks' results. Results of RQ4 (Mitigation strategies) are highly important to the user because they contain information that can help the user implement relevant defenses to the system.

The results of the survey show that many modern adversarial attack studies have not focused on testing mitigation strategies, as shown in Table 5. Eighty percent of the discussed attacks against object detectors have not been tested against any mitigation strategies. Our study shows that the generalizability of recent attacks is increasing, which poses a more significant threat to the industry. No longer do the attacks focus on a single objective or target model, but rather, they combine all these goals into broader attacks. This means that modern attacks can bypass more defenses and achieve multiple attack objectives.

7 Conclusion and Future Work

We conducted a systematic literature review in order to summarize state-of-the-art black-box attacks targeting object detection models to help users evaluate and mitigate the risks. The literature review resulted in 29 unique black-box attack methods from 27 papers. Our analyses summarized the status and trends regarding attackers' knowledge needed to perform the attack, consequences, generalizability, and current mitigation strategies for each attack. We acknowledge that the SLR may have left out some papers due to missing search queries and limited database coverage. One finding from our study is that mitigation strategies should be comprehensively tested on the identified black-box attacks to find out which defenses are robust and which could be improved. We plan to focus on evaluating and improving different mitigation strategies as our future work.

References

1. Akhtar, N., Mian, A.: Threat of adversarial attacks on deep learning in computer vision: a survey. IEEE Access **6**, 14410–14430 (2018). https://doi.org/10.1109/ACCESS.2018.2807385
2. Alzantot, M., Sharma, Y., Chakraborty, S., Zhang, H., Hsieh, C.J., Srivastava, M.: GenAttack: practical black-box attacks with gradient-free optimization (2018). https://doi.org/10.48550/ARXIV.1805.11090. https://arxiv.org/abs/1805.11090
3. Amazon: AWS machine learning (2021). https://aws.amazon.com/machine-learning

4. Amazon: AWS Rekognition (2021). https://aws.amazon.com/rekognition/
5. Bhagoji, A.N., He, W., Li, B., Song, D.: Practical black-box attacks on deep neural networks using efficient query mechanisms. In: Ferrari, V., Hebert, M., Sminchisescu, C., Weiss, Y. (eds.) ECCV 2018. LNCS, vol. 11216, pp. 158–174. Springer, Cham (2018). https://doi.org/10.1007/978-3-030-01258-8_10
6. Bhambri, S., Muku, S., Tulasi, A., Buduru, A.B.: A survey of black-box adversarial attacks on computer vision models (2019). https://doi.org/10.48550/ARXIV.1912. 01667. https://arxiv.org/abs/1912.01667
7. Borkar, J., Chen, P.Y.: Simple transparent adversarial examples (2021). https:// doi.org/10.48550/ARXIV.2105.09685. https://arxiv.org/abs/2105.09685
8. Brendel, W., Rauber, J., Bethge, M.: Decision-based adversarial attacks: reliable attacks against black-box machine learning models (2017). https://doi.org/ 10.48550/ARXIV.1712.04248. https://arxiv.org/abs/1712.04248
9. Chen, J., Jordan, M.I., Wainwright, M.J.: HopSkipJumpAttack: a query-efficient decision-based attack. In: 2020 IEEE Symposium on Security and Privacy (SP), pp. 1277–1294 (2020). https://doi.org/10.1109/SP40000.2020.00045
10. Chen, P.Y., Zhang, H., Sharma, Y., Yi, J., Hsieh, C.J.: ZOO: zeroth order optimization based black-box attacks to deep neural networks without training substitute models. In: Proceedings of the 10th ACM Workshop on Artificial Intelligence and Security. ACM, November 2017. https://doi.org/10.1145/3128572.3140448
11. Cheng, M., Le, T., Chen, P.Y., Yi, J., Zhang, H., Hsieh, C.J.: Query-efficient hardlabel black-box attack: an optimization-based approach (2018). https://doi.org/ 10.48550/ARXIV.1807.04457. https://arxiv.org/abs/1807.04457
12. Clarifai: The world's AI (2021). https://www.clarifai.com/
13. Dong, Y., et al.: Efficient decision-based black-box adversarial attacks on face recognition (2019). https://doi.org/10.48550/ARXIV.1904.04433. https://arxiv. org/abs/1904.04433
14. Goodfellow, I.J., Shlens, J., Szegedy, C.: Explaining and harnessing adversarial examples (2014). https://doi.org/10.48550/ARXIV.1412.6572. https://arxiv.org/ abs/1412.6572
15. Google: AutoML (2021). https://cloud.google.com/automl
16. Google: Vision AI (2021). https://cloud.google.com/vision
17. Grosse, K., Manoharan, P., Papernot, N., Backes, M., McDaniel, P.: On the (statistical) detection of adversarial examples (2017). https://doi.org/10.48550/ARXIV. 1702.06280. https://arxiv.org/abs/1702.06280
18. Guo, C., Rana, M., Cisse, M., van der Maaten, L.: Countering adversarial images using input transformations (2017). https://doi.org/10.48550/ARXIV.1711.00117. https://arxiv.org/abs/1711.00117
19. Haoran, L., Yu'an, T., Yuan, X., Yajie, W., Jingfeng, X.: A CMA-ES-Based adversarial attack against black-box object detectors. Chin. J. Electron. **30**(3), 406–412 (2021). https://doi.org/10.1049/cje.2021.03.003. https://ietresearch.onlinelibrary. wiley.com/doi/abs/10.1049/cje.2021.03.003
20. Ilyas, A., Engstrom, L., Athalye, A., Lin, J.: Black-box adversarial attacks with limited queries and information (2018). https://doi.org/10.48550/ARXIV.1804.08598. https://arxiv.org/abs/1804.08598
21. Ilyas, A., Engstrom, L., Madry, A.: Prior convictions: black-box adversarial attacks with bandits and priors (2018). https://doi.org/10.48550/ARXIV.1807. 07978. https://arxiv.org/abs/1807.07978
22. Jere, M., Rossi, L., Hitaj, B., Ciocarlie, G., Boracchi, G., Koushanfar, F.: Scratch that! An evolution-based adversarial attack against neural networks (2019). https://doi.org/10.48550/ARXIV.1912.02316. https://arxiv.org/abs/1912.02316

23. Jia, X., Wei, X., Cao, X., Han, X.: Adv-watermark: a novel watermark perturbation for adversarial examples (2020). https://doi.org/10.48550/ARXIV.2008.01919. https://arxiv.org/abs/2008.01919

24. Kitchenham, B., Charters, S.: Guidelines for performing systematic literature reviews in software engineering 2 (2007)

25. Kong, Z., et al.: A survey on adversarial attack in the age of artificial intelligence. Wirel. Commun. Mob. Comput. **2021** (2021). https://doi.org/10.1155/2021/4907754

26. Kuang, X., Gao, X., Wang, L., Zhao, G., Ke, L., Zhang, Q.: A discrete cosine transform-based query efficient attack on black-box object detectors. Inf. Sci. **546**, 596–607 (2021). https://doi.org/10.1016/j.ins.2020.05.089. https://www.sciencedirect.com/science/article/pii/S0020025520305077

27. Li, G., Zhu, P., Li, J., Yang, Z., Cao, N., Chen, Z.: Security matters: a survey on adversarial machine learning (2018). https://doi.org/10.48550/ARXIV.1810.07339. https://arxiv.org/abs/1810.07339

28. Li, Y., Tian, D., Chang, M.C., Bian, X., Lyu, S.: Robust adversarial perturbation on deep proposal-based models (2018). https://doi.org/10.48550/ARXIV.1809.05962. https://arxiv.org/abs/1809.05962

29. Lin, J., Xu, L., Liu, Y., Zhang, X.: Black-box adversarial sample generation based on differential evolution (2020). https://doi.org/10.48550/ARXIV.2007.15310. https://arxiv.org/abs/2007.15310

30. Liu, W., et al.: SSD: single shot MultiBox detector. In: Leibe, B., Matas, J., Sebe, N., Welling, M. (eds.) ECCV 2016. LNCS, vol. 9905, pp. 21–37. Springer, Cham (2016). https://doi.org/10.1007/978-3-319-46448-0_2

31. Meng, D., Chen, H.: MagNet: a two-pronged defense against adversarial examples (2017). https://doi.org/10.48550/ARXIV.1705.09064. https://arxiv.org/abs/1705.09064

32. Narodytska, N., Kasiviswanathan, S.: Simple black-box adversarial attacks on deep neural networks. In: 2017 IEEE Conference on Computer Vision and Pattern Recognition Workshops (CVPRW), pp. 1310–1318 (2017). https://doi.org/10.1109/CVPRW.2017.172

33. Naseer, M., Khan, S.H., Rahman, S., Porikli, F.: Task-generalizable adversarial attack based on perceptual metric (2018). https://doi.org/10.48550/ARXIV.1811.09020. https://arxiv.org/abs/1811.09020

34. Papernot, N., McDaniel, P., Goodfellow, I., Jha, S., Celik, Z.B., Swami, A.: Practical black-box attacks against machine learning (2016). https://doi.org/10.48550/ARXIV.1602.02697. https://arxiv.org/abs/1602.02697

35. Papernot, N., McDaniel, P., Wu, X., Jha, S., Swami, A.: Distillation as a defense to adversarial perturbations against deep neural networks (2015). https://doi.org/10.48550/ARXIV.1511.04508. https://arxiv.org/abs/1511.04508

36. Park, H., Ryu, G., Choi, D.: Partial retraining substitute model for query-limited black-box attacks. Appl. Sci. **10**(20), 1–19 (2020). https://doi.org/10.3390/app10207168

37. Qiu, S., Liu, Q., Zhou, S., Wu, C.: Review of artificial intelligence adversarial attack and defense technologies. Appl. Sci. **9**(5), 909 (2019). https://doi.org/10.3390/app9050909

38. Redmon, J., Farhadi, A.: YOLOv3: an incremental improvement (2018). https://doi.org/10.48550/ARXIV.1804.02767. https://arxiv.org/abs/1804.02767

39. Su, J., Vargas, D.V., Sakurai, K.: One pixel attack for fooling deep neural networks. IEEE Trans. Evol. Comput. **23**(5), 828–841 (2019). https://doi.org/10.1109/TEVC.2019.2890858

40. Tramèr, F., Kurakin, A., Papernot, N., Goodfellow, I., Boneh, D., McDaniel, P.: Ensemble adversarial training: attacks and defenses (2017). https://doi.org/10.48550/ARXIV.1705.07204. https://arxiv.org/abs/1705.07204

41. Wang, D., et al.: Daedalus: breaking nonmaximum suppression in object detection via adversarial examples. IEEE Trans. Cybern., 1–14 (2021). https://doi.org/10.1109/TCYB.2020.3041481

42. Wang, S., Su, Z.: Metamorphic testing for object detection systems (2019). https://doi.org/10.48550/ARXIV.1912.12162. https://arxiv.org/abs/1912.12162

43. Wang, Y., Tan, Y.A., Zhang, W., Zhao, Y., Kuang, X.: An adversarial attack on DNN-based black-box object detectors. J. Netw. Comput. Appl. **161**, 102634 (2020). https://doi.org/10.1016/j.jnca.2020.102634

44. Wei, X., Guo, Y., Li, B.: Black-box adversarial attacks by manipulating image attributes. Inf. Sci. **550**, 285–296 (2021). https://doi.org/10.1016/j.ins.2020.10.028

45. Wohlin, C.: Guidelines for snowballing in systematic literature studies and a replication in software engineering. In: Proceedings of the 18th International Conference on Evaluation and Assessment in Software Engineering - EASE 2014. ACM Press (2014). https://doi.org/10.1145/2601248.2601268

46. Xu, H., et al.: Adversarial attacks and defenses in images, graphs and text: a review. Int. J. Autom. Comput. **17**(2), 151–178 (2020). https://doi.org/10.1007/s11633-019-1211-x

47. Xu, W., Evans, D., Qi, Y.: Feature squeezing: Detecting adversarial examples in deep neural networks. In: Proceedings 2018 Network and Distributed System Security Symposium (2018). https://doi.org/10.14722/ndss.2018.23198

48. Zhang, J., Li, C.: Adversarial examples: opportunities and challenges. IEEE Trans. Neural Netw. Learn. Syst. **31**(7), 2578–2593 (2020). https://doi.org/10.1109/TNNLS.2019.2933524

49. Zhang, Q., Zhao, Y., Wang, Y., Baker, T., Zhang, J., Hu, J.: Towards cross-task universal perturbation against black-box object detectors in autonomous driving. Comput. Netw. **180**, 107388 (2020). https://doi.org/10.1016/j.comnet.2020.107388. https://www.sciencedirect.com/science/article/pii/S138912862030606X

50. Zhao, Y., Wang, K., Xue, Y., Zhang, Q., Zhang, X.: An universal perturbation generator for black-box attacks against object detectors. In: Qiu, M. (ed.) Smart-Com 2019. LNCS, vol. 11910, pp. 63–72. Springer, Cham (2019). https://doi.org/10.1007/978-3-030-34139-8_7

51. Zhou, M., Wu, J., Liu, Y., Liu, S., Zhu, C.: DaST: data-free substitute training for adversarial attacks (2020). https://doi.org/10.48550/ARXIV.2003.12703. https://arxiv.org/abs/2003.12703

Alice in (Software Supply) Chains: Risk Identification and Evaluation

Giacomo Benedetti$^{(\boxtimes)}$ ⓘ, Luca Verderame ⓘ, and Alessio Merlo ⓘ

DIBRIS - University of Genoa, Genoa, Italy
{giacomo.benedetti,luca.verderame,alessio.merlo}@dibris.unige.it

Abstract. The fast pace of modern development paradigms like DevOps boosted the complexity of development pipelines. In particular, developers rely on many external assets and third-party software to build the final product and match the demanding requirements in terms of release cycles and functionalities. However, such a choice impacts all the elements of the development pipeline composing the so-called *Software Supply Chain* (SSC), degrading its maintainability and security. From a security standpoint, successful attacks can go unnoticed and impact many targets that use the affected software before being resolved. Unfortunately, traditional security assessment methodologies might detect the symptoms (e.g., the piece of vulnerable code) but not the cause, i.e., the attack vector and the affected asset of the SSC, failing to mitigate the risk of new attack campaigns.

In this paper, we propose *Sunset*, a methodology with a two-fold objective. First, it allows the automatic reconnaissance of the SSC assets and dependencies to alleviate the burden of monitoring the composition of the SSC. Then, it computes a risk profile, identifying the SSC risk sources and how they can impact the final software to support the identification of the weakest points of the SSC and activate the necessary organizational and technical countermeasures to prevent future SSC attack campaigns.

Keywords: Software supply chain · Software supply chain security · Risk identification · Software security

1 Introduction

The DevOps paradigm has tightly integrated development, delivery, and operations, into the development process, facilitating and speeding up the continuous release of software components [10]. Such a paradigm drove the tight integration of heterogeneous components such as software artifacts (e.g., third-party libraries and binaries), assets (e.g., software repositories and package managers), and personnel that contribute to a software product or that have the opportunity to modify its content (e.g., developers and maintainers). Those elements compose the so-called Software Supply Chain (SSC) [1].

© The Author(s), under exclusive license to Springer Nature Switzerland AG 2022
A. Vallecillo et al. (Eds.): QUATIC 2022, CCIS 1621, pp. 281–295, 2022.
https://doi.org/10.1007/978-3-031-14179-9_19

In the last years, however, SSC has become hard to maintain and understand, as it needs to be adapted to cope with the evolution of the underlying software and systems, including technological changes (e.g., changes in architectures, operating systems, or library upgrades) [44]. For instance, some parts of the SSC become unnecessary during the evolution of the software and can be removed, or some others (e.g., testing environments) become obsolete and should be upgraded/replaced.

In addition, from a security standpoint, the SSC offers an appealing entry point for attackers that aim to target the final software and its consumers, as witnessed by recent security reports [2,27]. In particular, a successful attack in the software supply chain might go unnoticed for a long period, impacting a large number of companies that use the affected supplier's software. The CodeCov attack [20], for example, exploited a configuration vulnerability in the Docker files of the CodeCov code coverage tool that allowed external attackers to access the source code stored in the repositories of 23000 customers. The difficulty of maintaining and evaluating the security posture of a SSC drove the attention of both the industrial and research community. For this reason, different approaches emerged in recent years. These approaches can be mainly divided into two groups. The first set of methodologies and tools focuses on detecting vulnerabilities in the software code directly in the DevOps pipelines. Notable examples include snyk [31] and slscan [29]. Other solutions, instead, focus on the integrity of software and its dependencies, such as Google SLSA [32], MITRE D3FEND [18], and ReproducibleBuilds [26]. However, we argue that the proposed solutions allow the mitigation of security vulnerabilities but fail to identify their root causes and, thus, to prevent future attack campaigns. Supporting that, the ENISA reports that 66% of attacks targeting the Software Supply Chain come from unknown sources [11]. In order to fill such a gap, this paper presents *Sunset* (Software Supply Chain Risk Identification), a methodology that supports the maintenance and the risk evaluation of Software Supply Chains. First, the methodology allows for the automatic reconnaissance of all the elements of a Software Supply Chain and their dependencies. Then, it supports the identification of all the security risks of the SSC and its components by generating a risk profile that details where threats originate, which path they follow to reach the final software, and their severity.

Structure of the Paper. The rest of the paper is organized as follows: Section 2 introduces the software supply chain along with its vulnerabilities and attacks. Section 3 details the *Sunset* methodology and its architecture. Section 4 discusses the current state-of-the-art for software supply chain security, while Sect. 5 concludes the paper and points out some future extensions of this work.

2   Software Supply Chain

The Software Supply Chain (SSC) contains all the elements, called *assets*, that contribute to the development of a software artifact, namely the final product. SSC assets include structural elements (e.g., code repositories and development servers), software components (e.g., libraries and executables), and organizational entities (e.g., developers and software maintainers). Inside the SSC, we can distinguish between *supplier assets* and *customer assets*. The former contains all assets not explicitly created or defined for the final product, e.g., an external library or a package manager. The latter comprises assets the final software will interface with once deployed in the production environment.

In a typical DevOps scenario, depicted in Fig. 1, the SSC contributes to the pre-release phase, where the organization selects (plan), implements (code), packs (build), and tests (test) all the elements composing the final software.

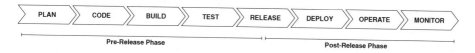

Fig. 1. The DevOps workflow.

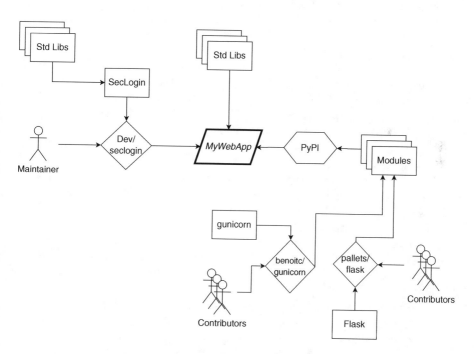

Fig. 2. *MyWebApp* software supply chain.

Figure 2 depicts an example of supplier assets composing the SSC of a Python web app called *MyWebApp*. *MyWebApp* uses a set of standard python libraries (e.g., os and glob) and two external modules (i.e., Flask and Gunicorn) imported using the PyPI package manager. Both modules are hosted on public GitHub repositories, where maintainers and contributors provide regular updates and new functionalities. Also, *MyWebApp* manually imports another library, called SecLogin. SecLogin is developed and hosted on a GitLab repository by a single maintainer and relies on standard python libraries as well.

2.1   Software Supply Chain Vulnerabilities and Attacks

An *SSC vulnerability* is defined as a security vulnerability affecting an asset that could evolve into an attack once exploited. Such vulnerability may happen during the different stages of software development. In particular, Common Weakness Enumeration [40], i.e., CWE, highlights that 91% of security weaknesses are introduced during design (462 CWEs) and implementation (724 CWEs).

One of the most significant advantages of attack campaigns targeting software supply chains is that their impacts are not limited to the final software. They can also harm assets belonging to more than one SSC and the affected software customers. As a result, this form of attack is more likely to go unnoticed and deliver a higher payout to the attacker [43].

Supporting the importance of the security evaluation of software supply chains, the MITRE ATT&CK framework [39], identified the *supply chain compromise* as an initial access tactic.

Let's consider the SSC example in Fig. 2. If the maintainer introduces a Static Application Security Testing (SAST) tool, during the build phase of the final software, to evaluate *MyWebApp*, the analysis may identify some security vulnerabilities and map them to known CWEs. In our example, the code analyzer detects CWE-20 (Improper Input Validation) [34], CWE-89 (Improper Neutralization of Special Elements used in an SQL Command) [37], and CWE-798 (Use of Hard-coded Credentials) [36].

Thanks to the SAST security report, the developers of *MyWebApp* can patch the source code. However, the developers do not have information regarding the SSC asset that caused the vulnerability or the used attack vectors.

This lack of information is caused by the closed range analysis provided by vulnerability assessment techniques, which aim to just alert developers of vulnerability. Then developers cannot effectively patch the vulnerability by taking actions considering the smallest possible piece of asset which originates the threat.

For instance, the vulnerability assessment tools cannot detect that the credential of one of the contributors of the GitLab repository of the SecLogin module has been compromised using a social engineering attack. Indeed, thanks to this attack vector, attackers can inject malicious code into the module and, thus, the SSC, reaching the final software. This lack of information prevents developers from identifying the compromised repository and adopting a mitigation action (e.g., disconnecting the SecLogin repository) to cope with the risk to the final software.

3   *Sunset*

This section introduces the basics of *Sunset* (Software Supply Chain Risk Identification), a methodology to automatically model the SSC and to identify the risk that assets pose to the final software.

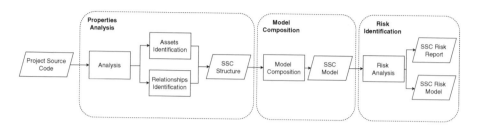

Fig. 3. *Sunset* architecture.

Sunset automatically extracts a model of the Software Supply Chain in terms of assets and dependencies, given only the source code of the final software. Then, it extracts the cybersecurity risk of each asset and computes how it can impact the security of the final software product.

The workflow of the methodology, depicted in Fig. 3, consists of three phases: *(I) The identification* of assets and the *extraction* of their functional properties. *(II) The modeling* of the assets as well as the relationships linking them. *(III) The identification of the risk* of specific assets and the computation of the risk propagation to the final software.

3.1   Property Analysis

Asset Identification. *Sunset* identifies assets based on four distinct categories, namely *software artifacts*, code *holders*, *distribution networks*, and *actors*.

– **Software Artifact.** It represents any kind of software included or developed in the SSC. *Sunset* further discerns between *(i)* compiled software (e.g., binaries and pre-compiled libraries) and *(ii)* source code artifacts.
– **Holder.** This type of asset is responsible for storing and maintaining software artifacts. A Holder can be further categorized in:
  • Local Storage. It represents storage solutions that are not connected with any management system. This category includes, for instance, a local folder containing software artifacts.
  • Version Control System (VCS). A VCS allows managing software artifacts using a management system that supports code control features like versioning and tracking. The VCS kind of holder can be classified in *remote* and *local* depending on its location.

– **Distribution Network.** Also known as package managers, it includes services and systems that allow the categorization, search, and distribution of software artifacts. Typical distribution networks include Maven and PyPI, which support the distribution of Java and Python libraries, respectively. The majority of open and closed source projects take advantage of distribution networks to import software dependencies [13].
– **Actor.** Actors represent humans involved in the software supply chain. An actor can be classified based on its privileges on the asset it is connected to, i.e.:
   • Maintainer. It has full access to the asset who is connected to. Moreover, it is able to set privileges for other actors connected to the same asset.
   • Contributor. It has restricted access to the asset who is connected to.

The identification of assets happens in the first stage of the workflow depicted in Fig. 4. In particular, the methodology analyses the project files and their content to detect the assets composing the software supply chain.

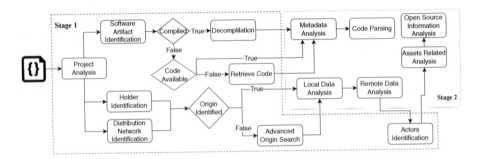

Fig. 4. Property extraction workflow.

Assets belonging to the software artifact category are identified starting from the entry file of the project. The methodology recursively identifies software artifacts via parsing the code files in the project. When *Sunset* is not able to match a software artifact with the parsed source code, it tries to find a corresponding artifact online (e.g., by searching for publicly available implementation of the software artifact). If the methodology identifies multiple artifacts, it selects the most exhaustive implementation (considering lines of code and last update time, if available). Nevertheless, when this event happens, *Sunset* collects the differences between artifact versions as evidence of possible attack vectors (e.g., typosquatting [42], i.e., trick users into downloading a malicious package by squatting the name of a popular package).

The methodology identifies holders through the analysis of project files. VCSs use the local file system to deal with code versioning (e.g., indexing files and configuration files), then *Sunset* detects this class of holder through these fingerprint files. In the case there is no local fingerprint, the methodology takes advantage of software artifacts source code to explore available public repositories in order to couple software artifacts to a VCS. When the methodology fails to associate software artifacts to a VCS, it creates a local storage holder to contain the software artifacts.

Programming languages of software artifacts defines the distribution networks involved in the SSC, i.e., a Python software artifact rely on PyPI, while a rust program on Cargo. *Sunset* identifies also private distribution networks searching for specific configurations in software artifact source code or configuration files.

The methodology identifies the actors during the analysis of holders and distribution networks. Indeed, actors interact with both of these categories of assets. An actor interfaces with an asset through a virtual identity that differs from its physical person. The methodology refers to this virtual identity to model the actor asset.

Properties Extraction. The methodology extracts a different set of properties for each category of assets. The properties of interest are divided in two categories, namely:

- *Structural properties*, which are oriented to the understanding of the structural composition of the asset. These properties provide information about the structure and the quality of the asset in terms of usage and involvement in the software supply chain.
- *Security properties*, which concern the security posture of the asset. They provide information regarding possible flaws and entry points.

Each category contains different groups of properties, as detailed in Table 1.

Sunset extracts properties from assets during their identification. Depending on the asset category, the methodology extracts the proper groups of properties. The single properties of each group receive a quantitative evaluation, depending on their characteristics and the availability of plugins to support the extraction, e.g., a static code analyzer for security properties of software artifacts.

Similarly to the identification process, Sunset adopts a strategy to extract properties based on the asset category. Stage 2 of the workflow (Fig. 4) depicts the corresponding extraction workflow.

For software artifact assets, properties extraction consists of analyzing the metadata, the source code (if available), and the result of SAST tools. In the case of a compiled software artifact, instead, *Sunset* analyses the decompiled code relying on state-of-the-art decompilation tools [17,23,25].

Assets belonging to the Holder and Distribution Network categories are analyzed by considering *(i)* the metadata located in the project (e.g., indexing files, mirror files), *(ii)* the remote information (e.g., remote branches, pull requests, versioning information), and *(iii)* the existence of known security issues on publicly available vulnerability databases.

For the actor assets, the methodology takes advantage of the information provided by the assets from which the actor has been obtained (e.g., contribution to the repository). The information gathered through the asset where the

Table 1. Properties categories and groups divided per asset category.

	Structural	Security
Software artifact	Conditional statements	Buffers validation
	Functions	Input sanitization
	Required user interactions	Insecure patterns
	Read and write operations	
Holder	Commits	Security policies
	Pull requests	Community standards
	Issues	Known security issues
	Workflows	
Distribution network	Mirrors	Known security issues
	Packages required	
Actor	Homepage	OSINT results
	Overall contributions	Known malicious actions
	Public repositories	
	Forks	

actor contributes is integrated with the analysis of open-source information [7]. Different actors can be connected to a single physical person. Analyzing the links bounding them to a physical person allows for a better understanding of their involvement in the software supply chain. Thanks to this understanding, it would be possible to capture information on potential threat actors. The identification of these links involves the use of state-of-the-art tools for the analysis of personas [21, 30].

3.2 Model Composition

The model composition phase (Fig. 3) allows for the building of a structured representation of the software supply chain.

The generation of the model organizes the assets and their inter-dependencies using a direct graph structure, where nodes represent assets and edges detail their relations.

The final software is the central node of the model. This particular node has only entering edges. The edges entering the node connect the final software to the subgraphs containing the assets identified during the Asset Identification phase. Figure 5 depicts the set of possible relationships between two assets.

Figure 6 depicts the model generated by the analysis and modeling phase of the SSC of *MyWebApp* of Fig. 2.

The SSC model also supports the graphical plotting and manipulation using state-of-the-art tools, e.g., [16]. The visual representation allows a high-level overview of the SSC that can support maintenance tasks and preliminary security

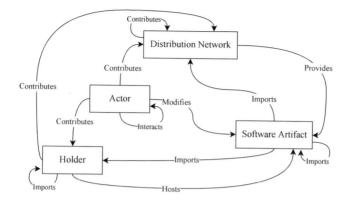

Fig. 5. Possible relationships among SSC asset categories.

assessments. For instance, the centrality of nodes [4] can be used to understand which nodes have more influence w.r.t. the final software.

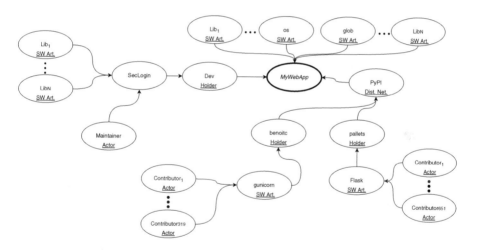

Fig. 6. Example of model representation.

3.3   Risk Identification

The *Sunset* methodology takes advantage of SSC model obtained in the model composition phase to carry on risk identification. Risk identification concerns searching and analyzing risk sources in the software supply chain. This phase considers the risk generated on the single assets and its propagation through the software supply chain. Figure 7 depicts the workflow for the risk identification phase.

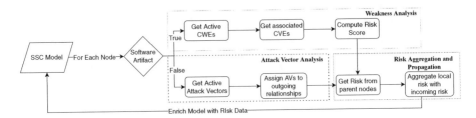

Fig. 7. Risk analysis module workflow.

Sunset explores the model graph with a breadth-first search algorithm [6]. The exploration starts from the border of the graph to represent how the outer assets' risk impacts inner nodes and reaches the final software.

The methodology defines two types of analysis depending on the category of the asset:

– Weakness analysis, for software artifacts.
– Attack Vector analysis, for holders, distribution networks, and actors.

Sunset relies on a Knowledge Base for the evaluation of weaknesses and attack vectors. The knowledge base maps assets' structural and security properties with either a CWE or an attack vector (AV). *Sunset* considers all CWEs linked to the pre-release phase, grouped in the CWE View 699 [38] and the set of attack vectors listed by ENISA [11].

In detail, the knowledge base contains a list of first-order logic statements evaluating structural properties (P), security properties (S), and the presence of specific attack vectors (AV). Each property can be compared with a threshold value (T), joint or disjoint with other properties or predicates, and evaluated in its presence or absence ($\neg$ operator).

For example, the first expression in Listing 1.1 states that attack vector AV_x is enabled when both properties P_1 and P_2 are greater than their respective critical values C_1 and C_2 and when the attack vector AV_y is active. The second statement in Listing 1.1 details how CWE_z is enabled either when properties P_1 and P_2 are greater than critical values C_1 and C_2 or when the attack vector AV_x is active. More detailed examples are presented in Listings 1.2 and 1.4.

1. $AV_x \implies (P_1 > C_1) \wedge (P_2 > C_2) \wedge AV_y$

2. $CWE_z \implies (P_1 > C_1) \wedge (P_2 > C_2) \vee AV_x$

Listing 1.1. Mapping rules of *Sunset* knowledge base.

Weakness Analysis. The weakness analysis leverages the CWE database, the CVSS scoring system [12], and the properties extracted for the software artifacts. *Sunset* considers all CWEs linked to the pre-release phase, grouped in the CWE View 699 [38].

During the analysis of a software artifact asset, the methodology identifies active CWEs. A CWE is active on an asset if it is included (or can be derived) from a security property of the asset or from an attack vector. By verifying asset properties and the attack vectors inherited from the connected edges, *Sunset* provides the list of active CWEs of the asset.

For example, the presence of conditional statements (P_{cond}) but the lack of variable sanitization (S_{san}) triggers the rule on CWE-478 [35] (lack of default condition in switch statements) detailed in Listing 1.2.

$$\text{CWE-478} \implies P_{\text{cond}} \wedge \neg S_{\text{san}}$$

Listing 1.2. KB rule for CWE-478.

After the evaluation of active CWEs, *Sunset* proceeds with the definition of the overall risk associated with the asset. For the computation, the methodology retrieves all the Common Vulnerabilities Exposures (CVE) [33] grouped w.r.t. a given CWE, i.e., the vulnerabilities linked to each CWE that are available on public databases. For each CVE, *Sunset* extracts the corresponding CVSS score [12] and uses it to compute the CVSS risk value of the asset.

In detail, we define G_x as the group of active CWEs on an asset X **(1)**; for each CWE in G_x, the methodology gathers the corresponding list of CVSS vectors (S_i), one for each CVE. Each S_i contains L different metrics M **(2)**. The risk score of the CWE j (R_{CWE_j}) is a new vector where each metric K_i is the mean value of all the same metrics of each CVSS score contained in CWE j **(3)**. The overall score R_x of the asset is the max value among the set of R_{CWE} **(4)**.

(1) $G_x = \{\text{CWE}_1, ..., \text{CWE}_T\}$
(2) $\text{CWE}_j = \{S_1, ..., S_N\}$ where $S_i = \{M_{i1}, ..., M_{iL}\}$
(3) $R_{\text{CWE}_j} = \{K_1, ..., K_L\}$ where $K_i = \frac{M_{1i}+...+M_{Ni}}{N}$
(4) $R_x = \max\{R_{\text{CWE}_1}, ..., R_{\text{CWE}_T}\}$

Listing 1.3. Equations for computing the risk score of an asset.

Attack Vector Analysis. Attack vector analysis follows the same concept as weaknesses analysis. In detail, *Sunset* identifies a set of active AVs insisting on an asset X if and only if the functional and security properties allow their presence. For the evaluation, the methodology exploits the rules defined in the knowledge base.

For example, the asset X is susceptible to manipulation attacks (AV_{man}) if the asset X inherits the attack vector social engineering (AV_{se}) from a linked asset and the security property weak password (S_{wp}) is below the threshold T_l, according to the rule in Listing 1.4.

$$AV_{\mathrm{man}} \implies AV_{\mathrm{se}} \wedge (S_{\mathrm{wp}} < T_l)$$

Listing 1.4. KB rule for the manipulation attack vector.

Risk Aggregation and Propagation. Attack vectors and risk evaluations propagate in the SSC model according to the interconnections among the different assets. Weaknesses and attack vectors flow from the boundary of the SSC model toward the final software. In this sense, a relationship between two assets has two goals:

I. Carry attack vectors useful for the weakness analysis.
II. Transport the risk value obtained on connected assets.

Hence, the total risk on an asset consists of aggregating the risk value generated on the asset with the risk values inherited from inbound relationships.

In detail, *Sunset* starts the exploration of the SSC model from the border of the final software SSC using a breadth-first search algorithm.

For each inbound connection, the methodology adds the risk score and the attack vectors inherited from the parent node. Then it iterates the process for each node until it finds the final software. On each step, *Sunset* updates the weakness analysis and the AV analysis to match the new conditions.

Looking back at example in Fig. 2, the sources of risk of the *MyWebApp* are the relationships incoming from the *Dev/seclogin* holder, the *Std Libs* software artifacts, and the *PyPI* distribution network. Suppose that the methodology reports a social engineering attack vector on the maintainer of *Dev/seclogin*. In that case, such AV will be propagated on the holder and, consequently, in the software artifact of the module and the final software.

4   Related Work

Both the industrial and scientific communities proposed several solutions to increase the security of software [9]. Most of the activities focused mainly on vulnerability analysis and software integrity.

Tools like the OWASP Dependency-Check [24], snyk [31], slscan [29], and shhgit [8] provide the developer with detailed vulnerability reports of vulnerability patterns and insecure dependencies. Also, the scientific community provided several solutions to detect and mitigate software vulnerabilities, such as [14,19].

Another field of activities was devoted to ensuring the integrity assurance of open-source software. Such works aim to prevent unauthorized modifications/-tampering of the software during the development pipeline.

Two of the most recent industry proposal are SLSA [32] and Reproducible builds [26]. Supply chain Levels for Software Artifacts (SLSA) is an end-to-end framework to guarantee the integrity of dependencies all along the development process. Through SLSA certifications, developers obtain information on the integrity assurance a given artifact can offer. However, the certification process requires an extended interaction with the developers and hardly copes with the level of automation needed for the DevOps paradigm.

Reproducible builds [26], instead, is a collection of software development processes that aims to standardize the build and compilation process in terms of configurations and requisites. This approach enables maintainers to detect if an attacker has compromised the building process by comparing the assets generated during the compilation process.

Hence, Reproducible Builds focuses on the integrity compromise happening in the build step. Weaknesses inserted in the software by mistake or intentionally are then considered a trusted part of the build. On the same approach, the authors of LastPyMile [41] proposed a methodology to detect the differences between build artifacts of software packages and the respective source code repository.

The aforementioned approaches might detect vulnerable dependencies and insecure code and contribute to software packages' integrity. Still, they hardly cope with the root cause of the problem, the attack vector, and the affected asset of the SSC, failing to mitigate the risk of new attack campaigns. Such lack of control is particularly disruptive in complex software supply chains containing thousands of assets, thereby limiting the benefits of adopting VA and integrity solutions. *Sunset* is one of the first attempts to mitigate such pain for developers and SSC maintainers.

5   Conclusion and Future Work

In this paper, we introduced *Sunset*, a new methodology to model software supply chains and evaluate their security risk and the detail of the single asset. *Sunset* is not intended to substitute traditional VA and PT procedures or risk management activities. The methodology, instead, aims to alleviate the burden of maintaining a secure and updated SSC by providing a means to *(i)* evaluate the risk of each asset and how it will influence the security posture of the final software and *(ii)* identifies the sources of risk to prioritize mitigation activities. Also, the evaluation of *Sunset* can be performed offline without impacting the performance of the development process.

In future works, we plan to extend the methodology to cope with the current limitations. First, we will enrich the type of assets and properties that can be modeled with *Sunset* to support complex scenarios. Then, we will provide an open-source prototype implementation of the methodology to test its applicability and efficacy in tracing security vulnerabilities, and sources of risk in real-world scenarios like mobile [3, 22], CPS [15] and IoT [5], whose development pipeline and threat model are well-known to our research group. The implementation will exploit both state-of-the-art tools (e.g., slscan [29] and COSMO [28] to extract security properties) and ad-hoc heuristics (e.g., a module for detecting GitHub software artifacts).

References

1. Alberts, C.J., Dorofee, A.J., Creel, R., Ellison, R.J., Woody, C.: A systemic approach for assessing software supply-chain risk. In: 2011 44th Hawaii International Conference on System Sciences, Kauai, HI, pp. 1–8, January 2011. https://doi.org/10.1109/HICSS.2011.36
2. Argon: 2021 software supply chain security report (2021). https://info.aquasec.com/argon-supply-chain-attacks-study
3. Armando, A., Costa, G., Merlo, A., Verderame, L.: Enabling BYOD through secure meta-market. In: Proceedings of the 2014 ACM Conference on Security and Privacy in Wireless & Mobile Networks, WiSec 2014, pp. 219–230. Association for Computing Machinery, New York (2014). https://doi.org/10.1145/2627393.2627410
4. Barabási, A.L.: Network Science. Cambridge University Press (2016). http://networksciencebook.com/
5. Caputo, D., Verderame, L., Ranieri, A., Merlo, A., Caviglione, L.: Fine-hearing google home: why silence will not protect your privacy. J. Wireless Mob. Netw. Ubiquit. Comput. Dependable Appl., 35–53 (2020). https://doi.org/10.22667/JOWUA.2020.03.31.035
6. Cormen, T.H., Leiserson, C.E., Rivest, R.L., Stein, C.: Introduction to Algorithms. MIT Press, Cambridge (2017)
7. Cumming, A.: Open Source Intelligence (OSINT): Issues for Congress (2007)
8. Darkport Technologies Limited: shhgit. https://github.com/eth0izzle/shhgit
9. Dowd, M., McDonald, J., Schuh, J.: The Art of Software Security Assessment: Identifying and Preventing Software Vulnerabilities. Pearson Education (2006)
10. Ebert, C., Gallardo, G., Hernantes, J., Serrano, N.: DevOps. IEEE Softw. (3), 94–100 (2016). https://doi.org/10.1109/MS.2016.68
11. European Union Agency for Cybersecurity: ENISA Threat Landscape for Supply Chain Attacks. Publications Office, LU (2021). https://data.europa.eu/doi/10.2824/168593
12. FIRST.ORG Inc.: CVSS. https://www.first.org/cvss/
13. Flynn, C.: PyPI Stats. https://pypistats.org/packages/__all__
14. Ghaffarian, S.M., Shahriari, H.R.: Software vulnerability analysis and discovery using machine-learning and data-mining techniques: a survey. ACM Comput. Surv. (4) (2017). https://doi.org/10.1145/3092566
15. Gobbo, N., Merlo, A., Migliardi, M.: A denial of service attack to GSM networks via attach procedure. In: Cuzzocrea, A., Kittl, C., Simos, D.E., Weippl, E., Xu, L. (eds.) CD-ARES 2013. LNCS, vol. 8128, pp. 361–376. Springer, Heidelberg (2013). https://doi.org/10.1007/978-3-642-40588-4_25
16. Graphviz Authors: Graphviz. https://graphviz.org/
17. Hex-Rays: Ida Decompiler. https://hex-rays.com/decompiler/
18. Kaloroumakis, P.E., Smith, M.J.: Toward a knowledge graph of cybersecurity countermeasures (2021)
19. Liu, B., Shi, L., Cai, Z., Li, M.: Software vulnerability discovery techniques: a survey. In: 2012 Fourth International Conference on Multimedia Information Networking and Security, pp. 152–156 (2012). https://doi.org/10.1109/MINES.2012.202
20. Jackson, M.: Codecov supply chain breach - explained step by step. https://blog.gitguardian.com/codecov-supply-chain-breach/
21. Maltego Technologies: Maltego. https://www.maltego.com/

22. Migliardi, M., Merlo, A.: Improving energy efficiency in distributed intrusion detection systems. J. High Speed Netw. **3**, 251–264 (2013). https://doi.org/10.3233/JHS-130476
23. National Security Agency: Ghidra. https://ghidra-sre.org/
24. OWASP Foundation Inc.: OWASP dependency-check. https://owasp.org/www-project-dependency-check/
25. radareorg: Radare2. https://rada.re/
26. ReproducibleBuilds: Reproduciblebuilds. https://reproducible-builds.org/
27. Revenera: The 2022 state of the software supply chain report (2022). https://info.revenera.com/SCA-RPT-OSS-License-Compliance-2022/
28. Romdhana, A., Ceccato, M., Georgiu, G.C., Merlo, A., Tonella, P.: COSMO: code coverage made easier for android. In: 2021 14th IEEE Conference on Software Testing, Verification and Validation (ICST), pp. 417–423 (2021). https://doi.org/10.1109/ICST49551.2021.00053
29. ShiftLeftSecurity: SLScan. https://slscan.io/
30. Shodan: Shodan. https://www.shodan.io/
31. Snyk Limited: Snyk open source. https://snyk.io/
32. The Linux Foundation: SLSA. https://slsa.dev/
33. The MITRE Corporation: CVE. https://cve.mitre.org/
34. The MITRE Corporation: CWE-20: improper input validation. https://cwe.mitre.org/data/definitions/20.html
35. The MITRE Corporation: CWE-478: missing default case in switch statement. https://cwe.mitre.org/data/definitions/478.html
36. The MITRE Corporation: CWE-798: use of hard-coded credentials. https://cwe.mitre.org/data/definitions/798.html
37. The MITRE Corporation: CWE-89: improper neutralization of special elements used in an SQL command ('SQL Injection'). https://cwe.mitre.org/data/definitions/89.html
38. The MITRE Corporation: CWE VIEW 699: software development. https://cwe.mitre.org/data/definitions/699.html
39. The MITRE Corporation: MITRE ATT&CK. https://attack.mitre.org/
40. The MITRE Corporation: MITRE Common Weakness Enumeration. https://cwe.mitre.org/
41. Vu, D.L., Massacci, F., Pashchenko, I., Plate, H., Sabetta, A.: LastPyMile: identifying the discrepancy between sources and packages. In: Proceedings of the 29th ACM Joint Meeting on European Software Engineering Conference and Symposium on the Foundations of Software Engineering, Athens Greece, pp. 780–792, August 2021. https://doi.org/10.1145/3468264.3468592
42. Vu, D.L., Pashchenko, I., Massacci, F., Plate, H., Sabetta, A.: Typosquatting and combosquatting attacks on the python ecosystem. In: 2020 IEEE European Symposium on Security and Privacy Workshops (EuroS PW), pp. 509–514 (2020). https://doi.org/10.1109/EuroSPW51379.2020.00074
43. Yan, D., Niu, Y., Liu, K., Liu, Z., Liu, Z., Bissyandé, T.F.: Estimating the attack surface from residual vulnerabilities in open source software supply chain. In: 2021 IEEE 21st International Conference on Software Quality, Reliability and Security (QRS), pp. 493–502 (2021). https://doi.org/10.1109/QRS54544.2021.00060
44. Zampetti, F., Geremia, S., Bavota, G., Di Penta, M.: CI/CD pipelines evolution and restructuring: a qualitative and quantitative study. In: 2021 IEEE International Conference on Software Maintenance and Evolution (ICSME), pp. 471–482 (2021). https://doi.org/10.1109/ICSME52107.2021.00048

Evaluating Tangle Distributed Ledger for Access Control Policy Distribution in Multi-region Cloud Environments

Carlo Mazzocca[✉][iD], Andrea Sabbioni[iD], Rebecca Montanari[iD], and Michele Colajanni[iD]

University of Bologna, Bologna, Italy
{carlo.mazzocca,andrea.sabbioni5,rebecca.montanari,
michele.colajanni}@unibo.it

Abstract. Nowadays, an increasing number of applications, services, and devices are shifting towards a less centralized cloud computing model. Cloud providers allow customers to deploy applications across multiple regions of their infrastructures to achieve high availability, be compliant with data privacy laws and regulations, and provide more robustness. Although an application can be deployed in different areas, it still has to behave as a single service that undergoes the same access control policies. However, verifying access control is a challenging task since the desired requirements are often in conflict (i.e., high availability and strict consistency) according to the use-case scenario taken into account. Different solutions have been proposed to distribute access control policies that are used to grant or deny user requests to access data or services. In this direction, Distributed Ledger Technologies (DLTs) seem to be a promising solution to distribute policies across different regions while still enabling their integrity, authenticity, and confidentiality. In this work, we propose an access control framework that uses IOTA, a novel DLT implemented through a directed acyclic graph named Tangle, to distribute policies. We implemented a prototype of our solution and compared it with its corresponding where the Tangle was replaced by a globally distributed NoSQL database.

Keywords: Access control · Multi-region · Distributed ledger · Tangle · IOTA

1 Introduction

Cloud computing is a widespread computing paradigm aiming at improving the use of distributed resources to solve large-scale computation problems [14]. Cloud providers allow customers to deploy applications across multiple regions to satisfy their needs. Multi-region applications reduce network latency and improve user experience by storing data close to end-users. Such applications provide significant robustness since the failure of a region will not cause the unavailability

A. Vallecillo et al. (Eds.): QUATIC 2022, CCIS 1621, pp. 296–306, 2022.
https://doi.org/10.1007/978-3-031-14179-9_20

of the entire service. Moreover, this kind of deployment enables customers to be compliant with data privacy laws and regulations by storing user-related data in specific areas [7].

Although this approach brings several advantages, it also introduces many security and management issues that have to be properly handled [1]. A multi-region application has to behave as a single service that undergoes the same access control policies with a unified vision of involved data. Managing data is one of the major challenges: centralizing them in a single area would impact the robustness of the system and degrade performance due to continuous data transfers; while replicating them across multiple regions would lead to synchronization issues. To offer high availability, multi-region cloud platforms replicate data at multiple locations, even across countries. Therefore, they have to guarantee that all data replicas, used by different instances of applications and services, are protected under the same access control policies. However, keeping a unified view of access control policies across different regions is a challenging task since when a policy has been updated in a certain area such modifications have to be quickly propagated to all the other instances of applications and services, thus, choosing the technology to adopt is a key point to carefully consider [9].

In this direction, Distributed Ledger Technologies (DLTs) are considered promising solutions to share access control policies in multi-region applications where involved services may be spread across different countries. In this paper, we evaluate the feasibility to employ a Tangle-based distributed ledger to store access control policies by implementing a prototype version of an access control architecture and comparing it with a corresponding implementation that uses a document-oriented NoSQL database. To the best of our knowledge, we are the first to compare a Tangle-based distributed ledger and a globally distributed NoSQL database to store and manage access control policies.

The remainder of this paper is structured as follows: Sect. 2 introduces the background and related work. Section 3 presents the proposed architecture and gives some implementation details, while Sect. 4 evaluates the performance of our proposal. Finally, Sect. 5 draws our conclusions and outlook for future work.

2 Background and Related Work

In this section, we report brief insights about DLTs and relevant technologies with a special focus on IOTA [12]. Furthermore, we discuss some of the existing research efforts that employ such technologies to distribute access control policies.

2.1 Distributed Ledger Technologies

A distributed ledger is a type of distributed database, replicated across multiple nodes where data can only be appended or read. A malicious node cannot corrupt a ledger due to the *consensus mechanism*, an algorithm that ensures to achieve an agreement on a value or a state of the network among distributed entities under consideration of network failures. Indeed, one of the main innovations of DLTs is their capability of dynamically changing a set of nodes when Byzantine failures occur without impacting the service availability [17].

DTLs owe their fame to *Blockchain*, a distributed, cryptographically secure, immutable, traceable, and transparent technology presented by Nakamoto in 2008 [10]. Such technology has been mainly employed to transfer digital assets, in particular cryptocurrencies, due to the lack of a central authority to verify the trustworthiness of transactions. However, it suffers from scalability issues, this is one of the main reasons that lead us to consider alternative DLTs. Moreover, the high automation, transparency, and security of blockchain make it the ideal enabling technology for *Smart Contracts*.

Smart contracts are executable codes that execute the terms of a contract on DLTs. The main purpose of this paradigm is to address contractual conditions while minimizing exceptions and the need for third parties. The capability of smart contracts depends entirely on the programming language adopted to express the contract and the features of the DLT employed [2]. At the state of the art, many blockchains provide support to run smart contracts.

2.2   IOTA

IOTA is a novel DLT designed and developed to address scalability issues of blockchains while still providing security, immutability, traceability, and transparency. For these reasons, it is particularly suitable for the Internet of Things (IoT) world due to its capability of handling large volumes of data coming from several IoT devices. The main novelty introduced by such cryptocurrency is the *Tangle* (sketched in Fig. 1), a distributed ledger implemented through a Directed Acyclic Graph (DAG). A DAG is a collection of interconnected nodes used to store transactions. A node represents a transaction, while an edge that connects two nodes represents its validation. In the Tangle, the are no block producers, so every user is allowed to issue new transactions and attach them to different Tangle parts. When a transaction is attached, it has to verify the two transactions to whom it is directly connected. Therefore, the progress of transactions is significantly speeded up compared to blockchain solutions. Moreover, the lack of a middleman enables zero-cost transactions.

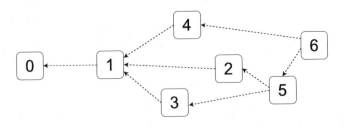

Fig. 1. The tangle.

An IOTA network is a network of nodes, either private or permissionless, where all nodes are aware of the history of transactions. Private networks can be accessed only after the network owner has granted the access, on the contrary, in permissionless networks, anyone can join and every transaction will be visible to anyone.

In IOTA there is a distinction between client and node. A client is any entity that sends to a node a transaction to attach to the Tangle, while a node is responsible for verifying the correctness of collected transactions, as well as, adding them to the Tangle. In such an environment, there are other two types of nodes named *Coordinator* and *Permanode*. Each IOTA network has only a Coordinator that regularly generates *milestones*, signed transactions that nodes trust to confirm transactions. If you randomly pick a transaction, the node you are connected could be malicious, however, nodes can not fake the signatures on milestones, hence milestones can be always considered legit. A transaction in the Tangle is confirmed only when directly or indirectly referenced by a milestone that nodes have validated. On the other hand, Permanodes are deemed to maintain the history of all the transactions that have ever happened. Since IOTA has been engineered for IoT, nodes may also be constrained devices that cannot memorize the entire Tangle, and therefore they periodically delete recorded transactions using a pruning operation. Permanodes address this need by permanently memorizing all data stored on the Tangle.

2.3   Storing Policies on DLTs

The growing interest from both academia and the industrial world for DLTs, along with their features of sharing data securely, has led to many studies to propose these technologies as an innovative solution for access control mechanisms [8]. However, most of these work focuses on blockchains, while very few consider other DLTs.

In [6], the authors addressed the problem of consistently and securely sharing data replicas within a distributed system by using blockchain technology. Similarly to this work, the blockchain is leveraged to hold a global view of security policies within the system. Maesa et al. [3] proposed an access control approach where policies, related to the right to access resources, are published on a blockchain. Due to the public nature of blockchain, every user is allowed to verify which policy has been bound to a resource and who has the right to access it. Since the right of access is stored as a transaction, it can be easily transferred from one user to another through a new transaction created by the last right owner. Moreover, blockchain is also exploited to provide trust to the owner of the resource and who is attempting to access it while policies are evaluated. To minimize the amount of data stored, the authors decided to store policies coded in a custom-built efficient format. However, policy evaluation through smart contracts was introduced only successively in [4]. Another blockchain-based framework for fine-grained access control is introduced by Wang et al. [18]. In their proposal, the data owner encrypts the system master key, stores it on the blockchain, and deploys a smart contract. Then, the user submits a

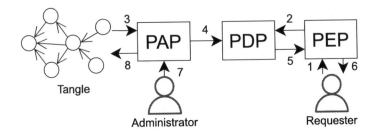

Fig. 2. Proposed access control architecture.

registration request to the owner who generates a user secret key and encrypts it with the shared key. Finally, the transaction ID and smart contract address are sent to the user through a secure channel. Such data will be used for future connections.

In [15], the authors presented a decentralized access control system for IoT based on IOTA, which is used to store policies and access rights. The owner of a resource defines and publishes the security policies on the Tangle. A request to access a resource will be granted only if it will meet the conditions specified in the access control policy. Another access control framework for IoT was proposed by [11], the authors employ the Tangle to store encrypted tokens, issued by object owners, that involve policy and access rights.

3   Proposed Architecture

In this section, we propose an access control architecture that can be employed in multi-region applications. Our proposal foresees components that typically belong to the XACML architecture [16]:

– *Policy Enforcement Point* (PEP): intercepts access requests and, for each request, builds a query in a language that can be interpreted by the PDP. Then, based on the result of the policy evaluation, performed by the PDP, it grants or denies access to a resource or a service;
– *Policy Decision Point* (PDP): evaluates the access request according to the corresponding access control policy;
– *Policy Administration Point* (PAP): is used by administrators for loading, updating, and revoking policies. This component provides policies to the PDP;
– *Tangle*: a distributed ledger that guarantees a unified view of access control policies across multiple regions.

We suppose that a requester has already been authenticated by an identity provider. In Fig. 2, we report our proposal from a high-level perspective also highlighting the information flow for the proposed framework. The steps are detailed in the following:

1. The requester sends an access request to the PEP;
2. The PEP extracts information (i.e., user attributes, resource to access, etc.) from the incoming request and builds a query that can be interpreted by the PDP;
3. The PAP retrieves policies from the Tangle;
4. collected policies are provided to the PDP that evaluates the request through the related policy queries;
5. The PDP provides the policy decision to the PEP;
6. The PEP grants or deny the access request according to the result provided by the PDP;
7. An administrator, through the PAP, can load new policies, or update and/or delete those existing;
8. The PAP interacts with the Tangle to satisfy administrator requests.

Since we are referring to multi-region applications, such components, except the Tangle, are replicated on different instances. Due to the nature of the Tangle, we are able to guarantee that an application, although it might be deployed in a different area, is subject to the same access control policies since all the instances of the PAP will access policies from a unique source.

3.1 Policies Properties

In this section, we discuss the main properties that must be addressed when policies are stored and how these requirements are met through the Tangle.

Integrity. A policy must be stored without alteration. An altered policy may cause data violation and/or grant unauthorized access. DLTs have been engineered to provide data immutability, indeed, every information memorized on the Tangle cannot be modified.

Authenticity. Using policies that have been created or modified by malicious users may lead to undesired situations. To address this worry, we decided to use a private Tangle. Therefore, only legitimate users are allowed to access the Tangle to manage policies. This choice may still present some limitations related to the difficulties of controlling how the Tangle is accessed. A solution could be accepting only the policies submitted by a set of addresses. However, since we decided to use zero-cost transactions, IOTA would not consider the address of the sender and receiver. To overcome this issue, we should distribute IOTA tokens to entities allowed to interact with the Tangle. Another solution is to resort to external mechanisms such as digital signature or HMAC. In this work, we consider a private Tangle that can be accessed only by authorized users leaving as future work the adoption of alternative techniques.

Confidentiality. In some cases, policy confidentiality can be extremely relevant. For example, a patient may not want to reveal that a doctor with a certain specialization is accessing her/his medical record because it exposes patient privacy to potential leakage. In this paper, we assume that a private Tangle can not be accessed by curios or malicious users. However, confidentiality can be easily addressed by adopting encryption mechanisms such as once implemented in IOTA through the Masked Authenticated Messaging (MAM) library that allows transmitting encrypted data to the Tangle.

3.2   Implementation

We implemented a first prototype of the architecture sketched in Fig. 2. The PEP was realized through Envoy[1], an L7 proxy and communication bus designed for large-scale modern services. As our PDP, we employed Open Policy Agent (OPA)[2], a lightweight general-purpose policy engine service that decouples the evaluation of policies from their enforcement. Policies are defined through Rego[3], the declarative policy language used by OPA, and stored on the Tangle that, as mentioned above, is realized through IOTA. In our implementation, we opted for a private IOTA network that comprises a Coordinator, a Spammer, and a node, this latter replicated for each instance. The Spammer is a node that periodically sends messages to the Tangle, thus enabling a minimal message load to support transaction approval as per the IOTA protocol. The PAP is involved in all the interactions with the Tangle. Hence, it is an abstraction of both the mechanism that implements zero-cost transactions for loading, updating, and revoking policies and the *Bundle Service*, a software application that groups Rego policies from the Tangle and provide them to OPA. To memorize policies on IOTA, we use zero-cost transactions embedding the policy as text. However, if a policy has to be modified or revoked, due to the immutability of the distributed ledger, we have to send new transactions on the Tangle. Policy modification and revocation can be achieved by adding in the message of transactions a reference to which operation it represents. In order to update policies in OPA without restarting it, OPA can periodically download a bundle of policies that will be immediately enforced. The bundle is assembled by the Bundle Service keeping into account the order of transactions. Moreover, this service has to split out policies in the corresponding Rego package, only examining rules belonging to the requested bundle. All the aforementioned information: *package name, type of action*, and *policy text* are embedded in the message of transactions as shown in Listing 1.

On the other hand, the information related to the bundle to whom a policy belongs is retrieved by the transaction tag. IOTA allows users to look up transactions based on their tag, hence policies of a bundle can be easily collected. Although the proposed mechanisms could be replicated also on other

---

[1] https://www.envoyproxy.io/docs/envoy/latest.

[2] https://www.openpolicyagent.org.

[3] https://www.openpolicyagent.org/docs/latest/policy-language.

```
{
    "package": <rules_package>,
    "action": <add | delete>,
    "policy": <policy>
}
```

Listing 1: Message structure.

DLTs, IOTA offers many features that make it more adequate to manage access control policies. Our choice is mainly motivated by the following points:

1. IOTA gives the possibility to associate a tag to a transaction, simplifying how policies are looked for from the Tangle. Not every DLTs offer this feature, so an alternative consists in adding a tag within the text of a transaction worsening the time needed to find requested policies;
2. Thanks to zero-cost transactions, we can neglect the cryptocurrency of IOTA. Such transactions significantly reduce the complexity of the mechanisms to add or revoke policies. Otherwise, we should establish a cost-value corresponding to each transaction, providing administrators and bundle services with enough founds to perform their tasks;
3. Finally, the Tangle structure enables reducing the time to memorize a new transaction. Transactions just created are memorized on the Tangle, while in blockchain-based solutions a transaction will not be memorized until it is stored into a block.

It is worthy to outline that since we are referring to multi-region applications, the components of our architecture, except the Coordinator and the Spammer, will be replicated across different areas.

4   Evaluation

In order to evaluate the feasibility of using a Tangle to distribute access control policies, we have conducted some preliminary experiments aiming to evaluate the performance of the Tangle under different circumstances. In this regard, we compared our proposal with the same architecture replacing the Tangle with CouchDB[4], a document-oriented NoSQL database that exploits a Multi-Version Concurrency Control (MVCC) protocol to enable the synchronization and replication of documents over one or more instances. All experiments were conducted on two nodes equipped with an Intel(R) Core(TM) i7-7700HQ CPU running at 2.80 GHz and 16 GB of RAM. For the first configuration, on one node, we deployed Envoy, OPA, Bundle Service, and an IOTA node, while the other node was used to reproduce the rest of an IOTA network, composed of a Coordinator, a Spammer, and an IOTA node. For the second configuration, we replaced the IOTA node with a CouchDB slave-replica and the IOTA network with a CouchDB master-replica.

---

[4] https://couchdb.apache.org.

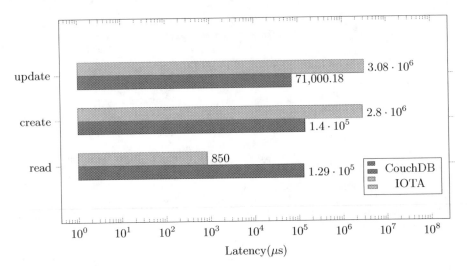

Fig. 3. Comparison of operation performance on a logarithmic scale.

4.1   Operation Performance

We evaluated the latency between the Bundle Service and data source (IOTA and CouchDB) while creating, reading, and updating policies under different load conditions. Both configurations were tested by generating a linearly growing number of requests in 60 s. In particular, we emulated 10 virtual users, each started with a delay of 5 s. The constant throughput of each user was set to 1000 requests/min for evaluating all the operations on CouchDB and the reading from IOTA, while we decreased it to 100 requests/min for creating and updating operations on IOTA. Figure 3 shows the average latency, expressed in microseconds, of the aforementioned operations.

By observing the graph, we can state that IOTA outperforms CouchDB during reading policies. On the other hand, CouchDB grants a more constant latency since all the operations take about 100 ms. Although IOTA is about one order of magnitude slower than CouchDB for creating and updating policies, this time can be still considered acceptable since creating and updating operations are not that frequent. We expected a higher time in updating policies, due to the immutability of the ledger, it consists of two create transactions: one to revoke the policy and the other one to create a new version. Moreover, we also evaluated the latency between the creation of a new policy and its availability. In this regard, the average latency of IOTA is about 600 ms, while a new policy is available after approximately 150 ms when using CouchDB. In this case, the time required by IOTA is much slower than that needed for creating and updating policies reported in Fig. 3. This is because, while evaluating availability latency, we did not stress the IOTA network as in the previous experiments. As far as CouchDB is concerned, it does not show significant variations compared to the previous experiments.

5   Conclusions and Future Work

Although many applications are currently deployed across different regions, they still have to behave as single services: each instance of an application has to undergo the same access control policies. Therefore, how these policies are distributed in different areas is a primary interest concern. In recent years, some research efforts have proposed DLTs as enabling technology for access control mechanisms, however, just a few of them consider solutions alternative to blockchain.

In this work, we proposed and implemented an access control framework that uses the Tangle to distribute access control policies. The Tangle allows achieving integrity, authenticity, and confidentiality while providing higher scalability than blockchains. We evaluated our solution by comparing it with a corresponding implementation that employs a globally distributed NoSQL database. The experimental results showed that IOTA outperforms CouchDB in reading operations, while CouchDB is one order of magnitude faster in creating and updating policies.

In future research, to satisfy different requirements of highly distributed scenarios, we aim to extend our proposal by integrating different technologies for managing policies. Moreover, we seek to lay the foundations for establishing adequate security mechanisms to enable the use of permissionless networks to further simplify network management. Finally, we plan to deploy and test the proposed architecture in a real-world scenario to evaluate how to better support popular use cases of smart cities such as smart tourism, smart agriculture, and smart transportation [5,13,19].

References

1. Casola, V., De Benedictis, A., Rak, M., Villano, U.: Security-by-design in multi-cloud applications: an optimization approach. Inf. Sci. **454–455**, 344–362 (2018). https://doi.org/10.1016/j.ins.2018.04.081
2. Alharby, M., van Moorsel, A.: Blockchain based smart contracts: a systematic mapping study. In: Computer Science & Information Technology (CS & IT). Academy & Industry Research Collaboration Center (AIRCC) (2017). https://doi.org/10.5121/csit.2017.71011
3. Di Francesco Maesa, D., Mori, P., Ricci, L.: Blockchain based access control. In: Chen, L.Y., Reiser, H.P. (eds.) DAIS 2017. LNCS, vol. 10320, pp. 206–220. Springer, Cham (2017). https://doi.org/10.1007/978-3-319-59665-5_15
4. Di Francesco Maesa, D., Mori, P., Ricci, L.: Blockchain based access control services. In: 2018 IEEE International Conference on Internet of Things (iThings) and IEEE Green Computing and Communications (GreenCom) and IEEE Cyber, Physical and Social Computing (CPSCom) and IEEE Smart Data (SmartData), pp. 1379–1386 (2018). https://doi.org/10.1109/Cybermatics_2018.2018.00237
5. Dsouza, C., Ahn, G.J., Taguinod, M.: Policy-driven security management for fog computing: preliminary framework and a case study. In: Proceedings of the 2014 IEEE 15th International Conference on Information Reuse and Integration (IEEE IRI 2014), pp. 16–23 (2014). https://doi.org/10.1109/IRI.2014.7051866

6. Esposito, C., Ficco, M., Gupta, B.B.: Blockchain-based authentication and authorization for smart city applications. Inf. Process. Manage. **58**(2), 102468 (2021). https://doi.org/10.1016/j.ipm.2020.102468
7. Ferry, N., Rossini, A., Chauvel, F., Morin, B., Solberg, A.: Towards model-driven provisioning, deployment, monitoring, and adaptation of multi-cloud systems. In: 2013 IEEE Sixth International Conference on Cloud Computing, pp. 887–894 (2013). https://doi.org/10.1109/CLOUD.2013.133
8. Ghaffari, F., Bertin, E., Hatin, J., Crespi, N.: Authentication and access control based on distributed ledger technology: a survey. In: 2020 2nd Conference on Blockchain Research & Applications for Innovative Networks and Services (BRAINS), pp. 79–86 (2020). https://doi.org/10.1109/BRAINS49436.2020.9223297
9. Hu, V.C., et al.: General access control guidance for cloud systems. NIST Spec. Publ. **800**(210), 50-2ex (2020)
10. Nakamoto, S.: Bitcoin: a peer-to-peer electronic cash system. Decentralized Bus. Rev. 21260 (2008)
11. Nakanishi, R., Zhang, Y., Sasabe, M., Kasahara, S.: IOTA-based access control framework for the Internet of Things. In: 2020 2nd Conference on Blockchain Research & Applications for Innovative Networks and Services (BRAINS), pp. 87–95 (2020). https://doi.org/10.1109/BRAINS49436.2020.9223293
12. Popov, S.: The tangle. White paper (2018)
13. Sabbioni, A., Villano, T., Corradi, A.: An architecture for service integration to fully support novel personalized smart tourism offerings. Sensors **22**(4), 1619 (2022). https://doi.org/10.3390/s22041619
14. Sadiku, M.N., Musa, S.M., Momoh, O.D.: Cloud computing: opportunities and challenges. IEEE Potentials **33**(1), 34–36 (2014). https://doi.org/10.1109/MPOT.2013.2279684
15. Shafeeq, S., Alam, M., Khan, A.: Privacy aware decentralized access control system. Futur. Gener. Comput. Syst. **101**, 420–433 (2019). https://doi.org/10.1016/j.future.2019.06.025
16. Standard OASIS: extensible access control markup language (xacml) version 3.0 (2013)
17. Sunyaev, A.: Distributed ledger technology. In: Internet Computing, pp. 265–299. Springer, Cham (2020). https://doi.org/10.1007/978-3-030-34957-8_9
18. Wang, S., Zhang, Y., Zhang, Y.: A blockchain-based framework for data sharing with fine-grained access control in decentralized storage systems. IEEE Access **6**, 38437–38450 (2018). https://doi.org/10.1109/ACCESS.2018.2851611
19. Yang, X., et al.: A survey on smart agriculture: development modes, technologies, and security and privacy challenges. IEEE/CAA J. Autom. Sin. **8**(2), 273–302 (2021). https://doi.org/10.1109/JAS.2020.1003536

Toward the Adoption of Secure Cyber Digital Twins to Enhance Cyber-Physical Systems Security

Alessandra De Benedictis[1]([⊠]) [iD], Christiancarmine Esposito[2] [iD],
and Alessandra Somma[1] [iD]

[1] University of Napoli "Federico II", Napoli, Italy
{alessandra.debenedictis,alessandra.somma}@unina.it
[2] University of Salerno, Fisciano, SA, Italy
esposito@unisa.it

Abstract. Cyber-Physical Systems (CPSs) and Digital Twins (DTs) currently represent the two most notable examples of cyber-physical integration enabled by modern ICT technologies, and their adoption is becoming predominant to implement and analyse complex systems in several application domains. So-called cyber DTs are increasingly being used to carry out security analysis, monitoring and testing on the virtual replicas of complex systems rather than on the physical counterparts, especially when these may not be directly feasible due to cost and other constraints. However, since physical and virtual replicas live side by side in complex ecosystems, the need for secure and trustworthy DTs arises. In this paper, we introduce a preliminary conceptual framework aimed to increase the level of security of a complex CPS by leveraging a cyber DT providing advanced anomaly detection capabilities, achieved by means of state-of-art machine learning solutions (i.e., federated learning). The framework will also address the security and trustworthiness of the cyber DT itself, by leveraging both HW and SW solutions to support a secure communication and storage of the critical data exchanged among the physical and virtual worlds. To this aim, the integration of the blockchain technology into the DT architecture will be investigated.

Keywords: Cyber Digital Twin · Secure Digital Twin ·
Cyber-Physical Systems · Blockchain · Federated learning

1 Introduction

State-of-the-art ICT technologies such as Internet of Things (IoT), edge computing, cloud computing, Artificial Intelligence and data analytics have greatly stimulated the development of modern applications and systems based on deep cyber-physical integration, of which Cyber-Physical Systems (CPSs) and Digital Twins (DTs) currently represent the two most notable examples. CPSs integrate sensing, control, computation and communication capabilities to achieve a tight

A. Vallecillo et al. (Eds.): QUATIC 2022, CCIS 1621, pp. 307–321, 2022.
https://doi.org/10.1007/978-3-031-14179-9_21

connection and interdependence among the physical and cyber worlds in order to enable smart decision-making, complex monitoring and control in several domains (e.g., smart manufacturing, smart grids, autonomous driving systems, smart health). DTs, on the other hand, create dynamic and self-evolving virtual replicas of physical objects or processes, characterized by a bi-directional seamless communication that allows real-time data sharing between the physical and digital worlds. DT are typically used to predict and detect possible issues in a system sooner, more accurately or at a lower cost, and/or to optimize products and processes. Noticeably, cyber-security is a major concern in CPSs, as the high levels of digitization and connectivity enable to exploit both cyber and physical vulnerabilities to negatively affect system operation and possibly endanger human life. Unfortunately, the high complexity and component heterogeneity of CPSs make it very challenging to identify and eliminate all possible vulnerabilities. Moreover, in several critical contexts, it may be very hard or not economically viable to deploy and integrate security monitoring and assessment tools into a CPS to verify the level of security and privacy achieved (which is needed, for example, for compliance verification). In this context, the DT technology may be very useful to conduct security analyses and tests on the digital replica of a CPS rather than on the original system, in order to limit/avoid interference with the system functionalities. In fact, several approaches have been recently proposed that adopt DTs to improve system security by providing intrusion detection and security testing capabilities, HW/SW misconfiguration detection, patch management and compliance verification. However, since DTs communicate and share data with the physical twins in real time and live together with them in a complex ecosystem, the need for secure and trustworthy DTs arises.

In this paper, we provide an overview of the literature related to the adoption of Digital Twins as a cybersecurity tool, and also investigate the inherent cybersecurity issues arising from the adoption of Digital Twins. Moreover, we introduce a preliminary conceptual framework, named S4DT-DT4S, providing a high-level architectural view of the HW and SW components and modules needed to realize a *secure* digital replica of a CPS able to provide anomaly detection capabilities. The framework, in particular, will leverage federated learning to detect anomalies and identify possible cyber-security issues based on the data collected in real-time from the system. The Digital Twin itself will be secured by adopting state of art HW and SW solutions, such as Trusted Execution Environment platforms, Physically Unclonable Functions (PUFs) for device authentication and secure communication, and blockchains for DT data sharing.

The manuscript is organized as follows: Section 2 will provide some background on Digital Twins, outlining their main components and applications. Section 3 will provide an overview of the uses of the DT technology for security purposes, while Sect. 4 will discuss the main security issues arising in a DT architecture and some existing blockchain-based security solutions in DTs. Finally, Sect. 5 will provide a high-level view of the conceptual S4DT-DT4S framework and Sect. 6 will present a roadmap for future work.

2 Digital Twins

Firstly presented in 2002, the Digital Twin is a virtual representation of a physical system or process characterized by the seamless two-way communication between the virtual and the real system enabling real-time data exchange. Tao *et al.* [23] proposed a five-dimensional (5D) model (Fig. 1):

$$M_{DT} = (PS, VS, Ss, DD, CN) \tag{1}$$

where i) the **physical space** (PS) consists of objects, systems and/or processes and their internal and external interactions. *Sensors* capture essential events or environmental changes are transferred to the virtual counterpart. Through the *actuators*, the physical entities reply to the inputs; furthermore, they can also accept commands that control their behavior or change parameter configurations across suitable *controllers*. ii) The **virtual space** (VS) contains the faithful digital replicas feed with real-time data obtained from the physical world combined with historical data. iii) Twin **data** (DD) are Digital Twin fuel: DT deals with multi-temporal scale, multi-dimension, multi-source, and heterogeneous data, some are obtained from the physical world and some are generated through virtual models, but there are also data coming from the service layer and knowledge gained by domain experts [23,25]. iv) The Digital Twin technology can be used for two main purposes, i.e. *interrogative* when the DT is questioned about the current or past state of its physical twin and *predictive* when the DT is used for predicting the future behavior and performance of its physical counterpart [5,25]. According to its purpose, the **Services** (Ss) offered through the DT technology are simulation, real-time monitoring, control, optimization of new or existing assets, prediction of future states [23]. v) Finally, as depicted in Fig. 1, there are 6 **connections** (CN) that enable the cooperation between the four parties.

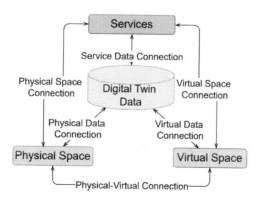

Fig. 1. Five-dimensional Digital Twin Model based on [23].

3   Digital Twin for Security

The Digital Twin technology can be profitably used to analyze and mitigate cyber-security risks affecting a system [8,17]. More specifically, with the term **Cyber Digital Twin** it is identified the application of DT technology for security analysis and monitoring, which may not be directly feasible on the physical counterpart without causing disruption [17]. According to the scientific literature, Digital Twin applications that aim to improve systems' security can be classified as follows:

1. **Secure design.** Using the Digital Twin in the planning and design stage of the physical system/process enables the so-called **security-by-design** paradigm [8,12,14,28]. In fact, it can help detect vulnerabilities and thus create a secure-aware asset, integrate security and safety rules into the system [8], and reduce the attack surface [12]. For example, a DT may help identify, at the design stage, unnecessary or unused components [14] as well as unnecessary functionalities or even unprotected services, which would allow an attacker to gain a foothold in the system [11,12]. For instance, Bécue *et al.* [6] in 2018 and Vilberth *et al.* in 2021 [28] proposed to use the Digital Twin to create cyber-ranges, namely test-beds that allow on the one hand to test the security of Cyber-Physical Systems [6] and on the other to train analysts of Security Operations Centers (SOCs) [28].

2. **Intrusion detection.** Intrusion Detection Systems (IDSs) are typically used to protect a network from malicious external attacks; therefore, they can be adopted to increase the reliability and resilience of a system by detecting and reacting to those behaviors that can damage a CPS [14]. Detection techniques belong to two types: i) detection based on anomalies or profiles uses heuristic and behavior models to identify activities that differ from normal use; ii) signature-based detection identifies threats within a system by mapping known attack scenarios [12,14]. When a Digital Twin is available that is able to faithfully replicate the behavior of a physical system [8], then it possible to **build an IDS in the Digital Twin rather than in the real system**, so that the digital counterpart can be tested without interfering with the functionalities of the real replica [9,11,12,14].

   For example, Eckhart *et al.* [11] proposed a framework for the creation of a knowledge-based IDS which automatically generates a virtual environment from the CPSs specifications; during the CPS operational stage, the Digital Twin is continuously monitored for security and safety rules breaches. However, this first solution implements an IDS into a Digital Twin that operates in simulation mode, i.e., without integrating real-time data collected by the sensors within the physical system. In their later work, Eckhart *et al.* [10] realized a behavior-specification-based IDS integrated in the DT working in replication mode, so the Digital Twin is able to detect abnormal behaviors that the real CPS exhibits.

3. **Hardware/software misconfiguration detection.** Assuming that hardware and software components of the physical system are simulated or emulated within the Digital Twin, virtual replicas of a real system must represent

the behavior of the system with a certain level of detail; therefore, if hardware and/or software configurations of physical devices were manipulated, the Digital Twin would manifest a different behavior that would be indicative of malicious activity [12,14]. For instance, manipulated software configurations could be detected by comparing the configurations data of physical devices with those of their virtual replicas [11]. The implementation of this use case assumes that the Digital Twin runs in an isolated environment protected from malicious attacks. Otherwise, an attacker may first alter the Digital Twin configurations to ensure that no manipulation of the physical configurations of the device is noted.

4. **Security testing.** Conducting security testing in Operational Technology - OT environments is a critical activity, especially when testing must be conducted during the operational phase of a CPS. The adoption of a DT would ensure the possibility to **run security tests virtually**, i.e., on the virtual replicas rather than on the real systems: this application can be used not only for **security assessments** and **security weaknesses reporting** [9,14], but also for **penetration testing**, which aims to exploit vulnerabilities to verify the feasibility of malicious activities [11,12]. In this case, the challenge is to balance the degree of fidelity of the Digital Twins and the costs of creating them. A very recent example of this application is the "SecurityTwin" project (https://www.sba-research.org/research/projects/securitytwins/) of the SBA Research Group in collaboration with the University of Vienna, in which they presented a high-level architectural proposal for the implementation of a Digital Twin whose objective is to inspect the CPS for security testing without the risk of interfering with it.

5. **Improved patch management.** Due to a lack of proper asset management and inadequate system design, many OT owners have several difficulties in patch management that typically allows a regular OT systems update. The Digital Twins can be used not only to address these issues, but also to understand the impact on the whole system when applying a security patch or changing a configuration [17]. In fact, without the DT technology, these analyses would require testing of individual devices in isolation, while DTs usage for simulating the OT systems allows to **explore possible solutions** without the need to maintain an expensive secondary system only for testing purposes. This advantage is particularly useful in the case of safety-critical applications [17].

6. **Privacy and Legal Compliance enforcement and verification.** Authors of [7] proposed a design and implementation method for privacy-enhancement mechanisms based on Digital Twins: the real-time data received by the embedded sensors are integrated into the Digital Twin with machine learning methods; before using and eventually transferring these data, they are anonymized in order to preserve privacy. The Digital Twin can also be used to ensure legal compliance. In particular, by realizing an accurate replication of the CPSs, it is possible to monitor and document safety and security aspects during the entire life cycle of the physical system. Monitoring activity can provide evidence to meet safety standards such as IEC 62443 [12,14].

7. **Digital Forensics.** When attacks occur during a real-world asset's operation phase, digital forensics can play a decisive role. The DTs can be used for both live and post-mortem digital forensics, supporting the identification and replication of malicious activities and the conservation of evidence that may contribute to investigations.

4   Security for Digital Twin

The Cyber Digital Twin benefits are not obtained for free, as Digital Twins are inherently exposed to **security threats** that significantly undermine their *availability, accessibility, integrity and confidentiality* requirements [15,17,19]. For this reason, we can classify the security threats of the Digital Twin both from the perspective of security requirements and from the perspective of DT's attack surfaces, i.e., the physical layer, the digital layer and the connectivity level that enables the closed-loop connection according to Tao *et al.* 5D model [23].

4.1   Security Requirements Perspective

1. **Availability and accessibility:** the Digital Twin technology aims to enhance the maintainability and longevity of its real replica and thus supports availability over its lifetime, even if it can be financially demanding. However, the Digital Twin results can lead to undesirable interactions which can affect the availability of the overall system; moreover, a Digital Twin can create an additional failure point in the system that can be exploited by cyber-attack [17,19]. Losing access to the Digital Twin or the Digital Twin being unreachable for any reason can lead to disruptions in the production life cycle or huge financial losses [19].

2. **Integrity:** unauthorised modification or destruction of data/operations while being processed, in transit or in storage must be prevented [15,17,19]. The integrity of the system itself must be maintained to ensure that the system is reliable and safe to operate [17] and to avoid bias estimation and decision making that could cause high risk [19]. Ensuring system integrity is also essential to ensure non-repudiation and authenticity of system commands/actions that are fundamental to its secure operation and also support incident response capabilities [17].

3. **Confidentiality:** threats to confidentiality are leak of customer data, intellectual property issues, revealing trade secrets and so on [17]. Ensuring authorised access constraints to facilities and system data are crucial for the confidence of business and personal information [19]. For example, a company with a digital twin of their industrial control system (ICS) may use real-system code in their digital twin in order to offer a more accurate virtual replica. However, this solution can increase business risk further, because any theft of damage to the Digital Twin would impact both the digital replica as well as the existing ICS components themselves.

4.2 Attack Surfaces Perspective

1. **Physical Layer:** the physical security of the IoT devices is important as they can be damaged, destroyed, or even stolen by the attacker [19]. Physical products can use many technologies to protect their data from modification such as using tamper-proof and tamper-resistant hardware, but data exfiltration and modification by attacker is still possible, as it can be implemented with data poisoning attacks or by exploiting the system, software, and data communication vulnerabilities. Side-channel attacks, for example, attempt to extract secrets from a physical device by measuring or analyzing various physical parameters such as supply current, execution time, and electromagnetic emission. Moreover, threats to the digital layer, in which lives the virtual replica, can also have effects on the physical system [15,19]. If the Digital Twin is obtained by a hacker, it can serve as a blueprint of the real system, of its components, their behaviors and their interfaces. In this way, the attacker has a complete view of the system that would allow him to compromise it [15].

2. **Connectivity Layer:** common communication technologies have well-known security issues [19], threats on data communication may be divided into five main types. In *Man-in-the-middle* (MITM) attack the attacker can inject malicious code or can disclose the conversion between two communicating nodes; *Denial of Service* (DoS) and *Distributed Denial of Service* (DDOS) affect the availability and accessibility; in *eavesdropping* attack, the network traffic between sensors to the controllers can be captured; in a *spoofing* attack the attacker changes and conceals his identity to carry out malicious and deceptive operations, e.g., spoofing-attackers could corrupt the signals or messages sent from sensors to the controller. Lastly, the *replay* attack requires that the attackers monitors, reads and saves a set of data to be used in retransmission.

3. **Digital Layer:** in this level there is a set of many components that make up the Digital Twin itself, i.e., models, codes and software environments, data and machine learning algorithms. If the attackers gain access to the early version of the digital twin software or the software source code, this can result in a threat to intellectual property and trade secrets, denial of service or heavy losses [15,19].

   Moreover, as Digital Twin data can be stored in local or cloud-based repositories, there are many trust concerns and privacy issues. Finally, Digital Twin decision systems are based on machine learning algorithms that are vulnerable to security and privacy attacks [19]. These attacks can be classified as *poisoning* attack, *evasion* attack, *impersonate* attack, *inversion* attack that will result in a decrease in the performance and reliability of the system [19].

As suggested by [1], adaptive techniques may be used to dynamically change the attack surface of a system at different architectural layers in order to introduce uncertainty for the attacker and increase overall resiliency to attacks.

4.3   Blockchain for Digital Twins

Firstly implemented in 2008 to develop the well-known Bitcoin cryptocurrency, the blockchain technology is a ***distributed, incorruptible and tamper resistant*** ledger in which verified transactions are recorded as append-only time-stamped logs by a multi-parties system.

Each party, referred to as a *node*, initiates a transaction, the basic unit in a blockchain network, by employing a digital signature using private key cryptography [20,29]; the resultant signature is attached to the transaction. All the transactions are stored in an "unconfirmed transaction pool" and flooded in the network so that peers can choose and validate these transactions according to some criteria depending on the specific blockchain protocol (mining). Verified and validated by the *miners*, i.e., network peers who use their computational power to mine blocks, the transaction is included in a block whose header contains the *previous (parent) block header hash*. The miner who can solve the computational puzzle first will become a winner and obtain the right to create a new block. Every block in the chain is divided into header and body parts. The **block header** contains not only the hash of the parent block, but also the current *timestamp* as seconds, the current hashing target in a compact format (*nBits*), block *version, nonce* field that usually starts with 0 and increases for every hash calculation and the *Merkle tree root*, i.e., the hash value of all the transactions in the block. The **block body** is composed of a transaction counter and transactions [20,29]. After successfully creating a new block, the miner receives a small amount of incentive (**reward**) and all the peers in the network verify the new block using a *consensus protocol* (e.g. the Proof-of-Work in Bitcoin blockchain). Finally, the new block will be added to the existing chain and to the local copy of each peer's immutable ledger [29].

Basically, blockchains enable a group of selected participants to share data that is suitably broken up into shared blocks, chained together with unique identifiers in the form of cryptographic hashes. There are two main types of blockchains: in a public (or **permission-less**) blockchain, anyone can participate without restrictions; **Permissioned** or private blockchains are those that allow only authorized users (i.e., users that have been granted specific permissions and that must identify themselves with certificates or other means) to access blockchain data. The blockchain technology can be employed in DTs to ensure data and data-generating sources trustworthiness, supporting secure distribution and storage of critical data. In fact, according to blockchain-based Digital Twin literature [16,27,31], the key benefits of using blockchain for Digital Twins are the followings:

Digital Twins data protection. The tamper-proof and immutable nature of the blockchain can be used to securely deliver data to multiple participating entities. On the one hand, thanks to the possession of multiple pseudonames, the nodes of the blockchain can remain anonymous (privacy). On the other hand, the data of the Digital Twin can be shared between multiple untrusted (or partially trusted) parties ensuring confidentiality, integrity and availability [16,27]. Moreover, the immutability property of the blockchain makes it possible to make the Digital Twin history transactions unalterable.

Data traceability. Creating heterogeneous data archives distributed through the blockchain allows to ensure reliability [26]. Moreover, using data provenance (metadata that records the link between data, source and set of actions performed on that data [26]) it is possible to know the current state in terms of *why, where, how* through blockchain [31]. Therefore, record keeping, provenance tracking and auditability can be easily achieved in solutions based on blockchain [31].

Access privileges of DTs. Blockchain eliminates the risks of unauthorized access that can often cause data tampering. Through blockchain-based access control, all Digital Twins information and policies can be managed in a distributed manner, so that each DT can act independently [27]. For example, smart contracts can be used to automate different scenarios depending on the application requirements [27].

Enforcing transparency and accountability. Transparency and accountability properties are guaranteed by the fact that each blockchain user has a public address, visible to everyone [26].

Counterfeits. The combination of DTs with blockchain can ensure the identification of counterfeit products through the authenticity of the product [27]. Creating a digital certificate on the blockchain provides transparency and helps build both proof-of-legitimacy and an anti-theft mechanism (for example, unverified Digital Twins cannot be used anywhere) [26].

5   S4DT-DT4S Conceptual Framework

As anticipated in the Introduction, in this work we propose a conceptual framework having two main objectives, i.e., to solve the security issues manifested in the different levels of the Digital Twin and to use the *secure* Digital Twin in order to enhance the security of a CPS by providing anomaly detection features. As depicted in Fig. 2, the framework includes a **Secure Digital Twin** architecture and a Digital Twin-based Service layer enabled by advanced machine learning algorithms fed by the DT data.

The Secure Digital Twin architecture comprises three main layers, namely the *physical layer*, represented by the CPS under study, the *digital layer*, providing the intelligence to create and maintain the CPS virtual replica, and the *storage layer*, devoted to managing the persistence and distribution of data exchanged among the two previous layers.

The *physical layer* includes the physical and digital objects belonging to the CPS, which consists of multiple `sensors` and `actuators` integrated with complex computational processes providing `intelligent decision-making` [2]. CPSs are characterized by many interconnected entities that exchange and elaborate a massive amount of data for operational and monitoring purposes. Part of these data, together with additional data obtained by suitably instrumenting the CPS, will feed the digital layer of the Secure DT and enable the dynamic evolution

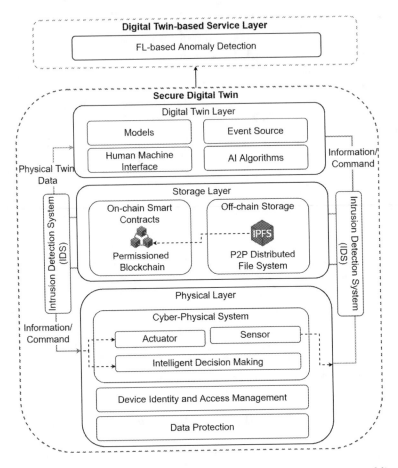

Fig. 2. The proposed framework S4DT-DT4S for securing Digital Twin enabling DT-based anomaly detection service.

of the CPS virtual replica. Ensuring trustworthiness, security and privacy of exchanged data is fundamental, not only for the inherent CPS operation, but also and even more when Digital Twins are involved, as discussed in Sect. 4. Physical devices are the most critical entities from the security point of view, due to deployment conditions and to their high heterogeneity in terms of technology and resource constraints. For example, devices may be subject to physical damage, replacement, or even theft, and generated and transmitted data must be properly secured.

Consequently, `identity and access management` capabilities in addition to `data protection` features must be enforced at the physical layer, for both devices and information systems involved. While plenty of effective security solutions are available in the IT world, devices may have specific resource constraints that would make traditional security primitives and protocols not feasible. Recently, *Physical Unclonable Functions* (PUFs) [22] have been investigated for the implementation of HW-based security primitives at the device level. Basically, PUFs are electronic circuits whose unique behavior (in terms of the response provided by the circuit to given inputs - the challenges) depends on the inherent stochastic nanoscale imperfections imprinted by the manufacturing process. PUFs can be used for identification, authentication and secure communication purposes, and have been found useful to secure IoT devices [3]. PUF-based protocols and mechanisms, together with other technologies such as Trusted Platform Modules (TPM), may be successfully leveraged in the physical layer to enhance the security of the involved devices. In particular, in our framework we envision the adoption of a decentralized solution for identity management according to which unique cryptographic PUF-based keys represent the identities of each IoT device, and mutual authentication is achieved via suitable PUF-based protocols such as [4].

The *digital layer* hosts the actual replica of the CPS under study. According to Schroeder *et al.* [25], the following main Digital Twin components can be identified: i) the Models, that digitally represent the physical asset; ii) an Event Source, that generates information and/or commands to the physical system; iii) a Human Machine Interface, that enables the interfacing between humans and the digital replica; iv) a set of AI algorithms, that aims to extract, from the storage level, useful information to feed Digital Twin models and the event generation block.

Digital Twin data, including modeling information, AI algorithms' tuning parameters and event data, as well as data conveyed by the physical layer (Physical Twin data), represent the Digital Twin fuel. For this reason, the framework presents an ad-hoc layer, i.e. the *storage layer*, devoted to storing and managing all relevant data and information. Addressing security and privacy issues in the data layer becomes imperative. Due to its decentralized and secure nature, as discussed in Sect. 4.3, the blockchain technology can be used to store information on-chain and impose a weak consistency model through distributed consensus algorithms. However, the blockchain has the block-size limitation problem. For this reason, our framework devises the combination of blockchains with a distributed file system empowered with cryptography, such as InterPlanetary File System (IPFS). IPFS-based storage ensures reliability, accessibility and integrity of the stored data and lower costs than on-chain data storage [16]: each file is stored in the IPFS and has a unique Content Identifier (CID), subsequently each file is sliced into many small chunks, each of which is hashed. This identifier can be stored within the blockchain, jointly with additional data such as DTs models which can be retrieved if authorized.

The combination of a blockchain and distributed file system solution to store information into the Data Layer and PUF-based keys to identify IoT devices of Physical Layer allows us to establish the source of data (i.e., *data provenance*) and to enforce *data integrity* [18,24]. In fact, the association of a unique ID to each IoT device through PUFs provides immunity from impersonation attacks and establish data provenance, while the blockchain provides data integrity, traceability and transparent auditing capabilities.

To conclude the discussion on the Secure Digital Twin architecture, the *bidirectional communication* between the physical and digital layer can be affected by attacks such as disrupting service delivery (denial of service attacks) or altering exchanged data (via packet injection, hijacking and spoofing). Therefore, the exchange of information between layers should be secured by means of *encryption measures* and suitable `intrusion detection system` to protect the system against external and internal sources.

As said, we plan to adopt the Secure Digital Twin to build up an `anomaly detection service`. In fact, DTs can generate the needed dataset for anomaly detection thanks to their monitoring, optimization and planning capabilities; these data will then be used as the training dataset of decentralized and collaborative machine learning (ML) algorithms. According to literature [32], *collaborative machine learning* is a type of training framework that enables several participants to construct a common model with their training data set. It can be divided into two distinct groups: centralized training approach and federated learning. Traditional machine learning approaches are realized in a centralized manner, where a central node uses all the data collected as training set of a global model and then shares the model to all participants [13,32]. However, ML-based solutions present several disadvantages such as i) all training data must be available on a central server, ii) there are security risks related to the transfer of raw data from final devices to a central server, iii) training large volumes of data on a single server can be computationally expensive [21,32]. This approach, in summary, is unsustainable for large data sets or sensitive information that participants are not interested in sharing with others.

One of the promising and well-scalable approaches that can address these drawbacks is *Federated Learning* [13,21], in which the global model is trained in a distributed manner among n participants. In FL, each participant trains the ML model locally and only the ML model weights learned are transferred to a central server. This strategy has proven its worth in securing user data privacy, making it the preferred approach over non-FL solutions [21]. However, FL still suffers from shortcomings: i) single point of failure because FL paradigm employs a central server (i.e., *aggregator*) to perform the integration of local training results and to update the global model; ii) malicious clients and false data because of the large number of participants that can not be assumed to be honest and so there can be malicious clients submitting false data about their local training results; iii) lack of incentives as traditional FL clients do not receive any payments for contributing their computing powers [30]. As our framework already requires blockchain technology for the reasons aforementioned, FL can be integrated with blockchain, implementing the so-called paradigm *FLchain* [30] that does not require any central server and mitigates the previously mentioned risks replacing the central aggregator with the peer-to-peer blockchain system.

FL technology provides not only data privacy but also seamless, flexible, scalable and high-performance communication to support highly dynamic time-critical applications, e.g., *anomaly detection*. An anomaly detection model has to capture all benign patterns of behaviour so that they can be distinguished from malicious actions. The adoption of FL for anomaly detection allows to recognize anomalies - patterns in data that do not conform to a well defined normal behavior - using decentralized on-device data ensuring security and privacy. For instance, Mothukuri *et al.* [21] proposed a decentralized federated learning approach that enables on-device training of anomaly detection ML model on IoT networks without transferring data to a centralized server. In conclusion, `FL-based anomaly detection service` detects anomalies in a decentralized manner and it is constructed upon the DTs ecosystem taking advantages from the Digital Twin capabilities, i.e., it faithfully replicates a representative use case that can be experimented under nominal operative conditions by injecting various kinds of faults and attacks.

6 Conclusion

In this paper, we have investigated the adoption of the prominent Digital Twin technology to enhance the security of Cyber-Physical systems. DTs and CPSs are both characterized by a strong integration between the physical and cyber worlds, but DTs can be used to provide CPSs with advanced security monitoring capabilities by reducing the interference with normal operations while conducting analyses on its replica. Since a system and its virtual representation typically live together in a complex ecosystem, we also addressed the inherent security of DTs, by introducing a conceptual framework that integrates state of art technologies and solutions (e.g., federated learning, blockchains, distributed file systems, PUFs) to obtain a Secure DT on top of which it is possible to build anomaly detection capabilities.

The proposed framework is currently in the concept design phase. Several open issues must be addressed, including the definition of a generalized DT architecture (that can be applied to different case studies), the identification of the measurements to take on the CPS in order to feed the models and the anomaly detection algorithms, and the blockchain architecture. Nevertheless, we believe that the framework is worth an in-depth analysis and study.

References

1. Albanese, M., Battista, E., Jajodia, S., Casola, V.: Manipulating the attacker's view of a system's attack surface. In: 2014 IEEE Conference on Communications and Network Security, pp. 472–480 (2014). https://doi.org/10.1109/CNS.2014.6997517
2. Alguliyev, R., Imamverdiyev, Y., Sukhostat, L.: Cyber-physical systems and their security issues. Comput. Ind. **100**, 212–223 (2018). https://doi.org/10.1016/j.compind.2018.04.017
3. Barbareschi, M., Casola, V., De Benedictis, A., Montagna, E.L., Mazzocca, N.: On the adoption of physically unclonable functions to secure IIoT devices. IEEE Trans. Industr. Inf. **17**(11), 7781–7790 (2021). https://doi.org/10.1109/TII.2021.3059656

4. Barbareschi, M., De Benedictis, A., La Montagna, E., Mazzeo, A., Mazzocca, N.: A PUF-based mutual authentication scheme for Cloud-Edges IoT systems. Future Gener. Comput. Syst. **101**, 246–261 (2019). https://doi.org/10.1016/j.future.2019.06.012

5. Barricelli, B.R., Casiraghi, E., Fogli, D.: A survey on Digital Twin: definitions, characteristics, applications, and design implications. IEEE Access **7**, 167653–167671 (2019). https://doi.org/10.1109/ACCESS.2019.2953499

6. Bécue, A., et al.: CyberFactory1 securing the industry 4.0 with cyber-ranges and digital twins. In: 2018 14th IEEE International Workshop on Factory Communication Systems (WFCS), pp. 1–4 (2018). https://doi.org/10.1109/WFCS.2018.8402377

7. Damjanovic-Behrendt, V.: A Digital Twin-based privacy enhancement mechanism for the automotive industry. In: 2018 International Conference on Intelligent Systems (IS), pp. 272–279 (2018). https://doi.org/10.1109/IS.2018.8710526

8. Dietz, M., Pernul, G.: Unleashing the Digital Twin's potential for ICS security. IEEE Secur. Priv. **18**(4), 20–27 (2020). https://doi.org/10.1109/MSEC.2019.2961650

9. Dietz, M., Vielberth, M., Pernul, G.: Integrating Digital Twin security simulations in the security operations center. In: Proceedings of the 15th International Conference on Availability, Reliability and Security, ARES 2020. Association for Computing Machinery, New York (2020). https://doi.org/10.1145/3407023.3407039

10. Eckhart, M., Ekelhart, A.: A specification-based state replication approach for Digital Twins. In: Proceedings of the 2018 Workshop on Cyber-Physical Systems Security and PrivaCy, CPS-SPC 2018, pp. 36–47. Association for Computing Machinery, New York (2018). https://doi.org/10.1145/3264888.3264892

11. Eckhart, M., Ekelhart, A.: Towards security-aware virtual environments for Digital Twins. In: Proceedings of the 4th ACM Workshop on Cyber-Physical System Security, CPSS 2018, pp. 61–72. Association for Computing Machinery, New York (2018). https://doi.org/10.1145/3198458.3198464

12. Eckhart, M., Ekelhart, A.: Digital Twins for cyber-physical systems security: state of the art and outlook. In: Security and Quality in Cyber-Physical Systems Engineering, pp. 383–412. Springer, Cham (2019). https://doi.org/10.1007/978-3-030-25312-7_14

13. Esposito, C., Sperlì, G., Moscato, V., Zhao, Z.: On attacks to federated learning and a blockchain-empowered protection. In: 2022 IEEE 19th Annual Consumer Communications & Networking Conference (CCNC), pp. 1–6 (2022). https://doi.org/10.1109/CCNC49033.2022.9700723

14. Faleiro, R., Pan, L., Pokhrel, S.R., Doss, R.: Digital Twin for cybersecurity: towards enhancing cyber resilience. In: Xiang, W., Han, F., Phan, T.K. (eds.) BROADNETS 2021. LNICST, vol. 413, pp. 57–76. Springer, Cham (2022). https://doi.org/10.1007/978-3-030-93479-8_4

15. Hearn, M., Simon, R.: Cybersecurity considerations for digital twin implementations. Ind. Internet Consortium (IIC) J. Innov. (Nov 2019), 107–113 (2019)

16. Hemdan, E.E.-D., Mahmoud, A.S.A.: BlockTwins: a blockchain-based Digital Twins framework. In: Choudhury, T., Khanna, A., Toe, T.T., Khurana, M., Gia Nhu, N. (eds.) Blockchain Applications in IoT Ecosystem. EICC, pp. 177–186. Springer, Cham (2021). https://doi.org/10.1007/978-3-030-65691-1_12

17. Holmes, D., Papathanasaki, M., Maglaras, L., Ferrag, M.A., Nepal, S., Janicke, H.: Digital Twins and cyber security - solution or challenge? In: 2021 6th South-East Europe Design Automation, Computer Engineering, Computer Networks and

Social Media Conference (SEEDA-CECNSM), pp. 1–8 (2021). https://doi.org/10.1109/SEEDA-CECNSM53056.2021.9566277

18. Javaid, U., Aman, M.N., Sikdar, B.: BlockPro: blockchain based data provenance and integrity for secure IoT environments, BlockSys 2018, pp. 13–18. Association for Computing Machinery, New York (2018)

19. Karaarslan, E., Babiker, M.: Digital Twin security threats and countermeasures: an introduction. In: 2021 International Conference on Information Security and Cryptology (ISCTURKEY), pp. 7–11 (2021). https://doi.org/10.1109/ISCTURKEY53027.2021.9654360

20. Monrat, A.A., Schelén, O., Andersson, K.: A survey of blockchain from the perspectives of applications, challenges, and opportunities. IEEE Access 7, 117134–117151 (2019). https://doi.org/10.1109/ACCESS.2019.2936094

21. Mothukuri, V., Khare, P., Parizi, R.M., Pouriyeh, S., Dehghantanha, A., Srivastava, G.: Federated-learning-based anomaly detection for IoT security attacks. IEEE Internet Things J. 9(4), 2545–2554 (2022). https://doi.org/10.1109/JIOT.2021.3077803

22. Pappu, R., Recht, B., Taylor, J., Gershenfeld, N.: Physical one-way functions. Science 297(5589), 2026–2030 (2002). https://doi.org/10.1126/science.1074376

23. Qi, Q., et al.: Enabling technologies and tools for digital twin. J. Manuf. Syst. 58, 3–21 (2021). https://doi.org/10.1016/j.jmsy.2019.10.001

24. Rahim, K., Tahir, H., Ikram, N.: Sensor based PUF IoT authentication model for a smart home with private blockchain. In: 2018 International Conference on Applied and Engineering Mathematics (ICAEM), pp. 102–108 (2018). https://doi.org/10.1109/ICAEM.2018.8536295

25. Schroeder, G.N., et al.: A methodology for digital twin modeling and deployment for industry 4.0. Proc. IEEE 109(4), 556–567 (2021). https://doi.org/10.1109/JPROC.2020.3032444

26. Suhail, S., Hussain, R., Jurdak, R., Hong, C.S.: Trustworthy digital twins in the industrial internet of things with blockchain. IEEE Internet Comput., 1 (2021). https://doi.org/10.1109/MIC.2021.3059320

27. Suhail, S., Hussain, R., Jurdak, R., Oracevic, A., Salah, K., Hong, C.S.: Blockchain-based digital twins: research trends, issues, and future challenges. CoRR abs/2103.11585 (2021). https://arxiv.org/abs/2103.11585

28. Vielberth, M., Glas, M., Dietz, M., Karagiannis, S., Magkos, E., Pernul, G.: A digital twin-based cyber range for SOC analysts. In: Barker, K., Ghazinour, K. (eds.) DBSec 2021. LNCS, vol. 12840, pp. 293–311. Springer, Cham (2021). https://doi.org/10.1007/978-3-030-81242-3_17

29. Wang, X., et al.: Survey on blockchain for Internet of Things. Comput. Commun. 136, 10–29 (2019). https://doi.org/10.1016/j.comcom.2019.01.006

30. Wang, Z., Hu, Q.: Blockchain-based federated learning: a comprehensive survey. CoRR abs/2110.02182 (2021). https://arxiv.org/abs/2110.02182

31. Yaqoob, I., Salah, K., Uddin, M., Jayaraman, R., Omar, M., Imran, M.: Blockchain for digital twins: recent advances and future research challenges. IEEE Netw. 34(5), 290–298 (2020). https://doi.org/10.1109/MNET.001.1900661

32. Zhao, Y., Chen, J., Wu, D., Teng, J., Yu, S.: Multi-task network anomaly detection using federated learning. In: Proceedings of the Tenth International Symposium on Information and Communication Technology, SoICT 2019, pp. 273–279. ACM, New York (2019). https://doi.org/10.1145/3368926.3369705

Author Index

Printed in the United States
by Baker & Taylor Publisher Services